BIG
HAPPINESS

Percy Kipapa of Waikāne

BIG
HAPPINESS

The Life and Death of a
Modern Hawaiian Warrior

MARK PANEK

A Latitude 20 Book
University of Hawai'i Press
Honolulu

Printed in the United States of America

16 15 14 13 12 11   6 5 4 3 2 1

Library of Congress Cataloging-in-Publication Data
Panek, Mark.
   Big Happiness : the life and death of a modern Hawaiian warrior / Mark Panek.
      p.   cm.
   "A latitude 20 book."
   Includes bibliographical references and index.
   ISBN 978-0-8248-3468-5 (pbk. : alk. paper)
   1. Kipapa, Percy, 1973–2005.   2. Wrestlers—Hawaii—Biography.   3. Sumo.
4. Oahu (Hawaii)—Social conditions.   I. Title.
GV1196.K63P36 2011
796.812092—dc22
[B]

                                                                    2010035180

University of Hawai'i Press books are printed on acid-free paper and meet the
guidelines for permanence and durability of the Council on Library Resources.

Designed by Publishers' Design and Production Services, Inc.

Printed by Sheridan Books, Inc.

For Priscilla and George Kipapa

CONTENTS

Author's Note ix

Prologue 1

CHAPTER 1 Homesick 12

CHAPTER 2 Respect 20

CHAPTER 3 Honor 40

CHAPTER 4 Invasion 49

CHAPTER 5 The Minute Man 68

CHAPTER 6 No Weapons 79

CHAPTER 7 Zapped 99

CHAPTER 8 *Gaman* 110

CHAPTER 9 Foreign Territory 124

CHAPTER 10 The Ice Is Broken 147

CHAPTER 11 The Users 169

Contents

CHAPTER 12   The Trial   193

CHAPTER 13   Honeyboy   237

CHAPTER 14   The Fall   257

              Epilogue   289

              Glossary   295

              Sources   299

              Index   315

AUTHOR'S NOTE

This is a work of nonfiction—a term that has come to require some explanation. It is a true account of the places, people, and events impacting the way that Percy Kipapa's life turned out, an account that is drawn from interviews, newspaper archives, history texts, court records and other primary source material, and my own friendship with Percy. Since I am exploring things that ultimately cannot be fully known, at times I speculate and imagine what *might* have happened. When I do move from the historical record into speculation and analysis, it will be clear that I am doing so. This narrative strategy is modeled on the work of the journalist Sebastian Junger, whose *Perfect Storm* successfully chronicles the final journey of a fishing boat right down to the moment it goes under, leaving no survivors to recount what really did happen.

Quotation marks are sacred. None of the dialogue set in quotes has been "made up" or "invented." Quoted speech that was not recorded appears in the book's autobiographical sections, such as my brief conversation with Percy at Bumbo's wedding, when I depict myself first interacting with an interview subject before we sit down for our recorded interview, and the accounts in chapters 2 and 10 of my visit to look at Percy's car—a story I told so often that it was fixed in my memory long before I wrote it down. Similarly, chapter 6 was written entirely from memory two days after the events it depicts happened. I did not digitally record the murder trial—I transcribed it as it happened. I did not record my brief spontaneous interview with Saga Maiaba in chapter 13, my brief discussion with Sergeant John Lambert in the same chapter, or my brief interview with Chiyotaikai in the epilogue, but I did transcribe them all immediately afterwards. Apart from these exceptions, every word that appears between quotation marks was either spoken into a tape recorder or quoted directly from one of my printed sources.

A book that touches on such a range of subjects as this one does requires a tremendous amount of help. First, my patient wife Noriko stuck with me through more than four years of my obsession with the story I tell in this book. Masako Ikeda, acquiring editor at University of Hawai'i Press, has done a tremendous job in moving the project from draft to finished product with the help of Cheri Dunn, Jean Brady, and the Press production staff. The many interview subjects whose voices tell this story were all invaluable. Sara Collins furnished important primary source material on the history of Waikāne. Several conversations with Bob Nakata enabled me to see Percy's experience in a much wider context. A single meeting with Ian Lind steered my research in a direction I had not anticipated. Harold Meheula deepened my understanding of his son with a poignant off-the-record conversation that does not appear in these pages. The three anonymous peer reviewers to whom Masako sent the manuscript helped me cut pages and pages of minutia and repetition. Often after a day of chasing interview subjects up and down the Windward Coast, I would stop for beers with the novelist Robert Barclay and listen to him expound upon what our writing mentor, Ian MacMillan, would have made of it all. Stan Schab, widely referred to as the living embodiment of the University of Hawai'i at Mānoa's Center for Biographical Research, offered his usual pointed insight in discussions of the murder trial. Craig Howes, the center's director, steered me through my complicated land use research at the Bureau of Conveyances and the State Archives, and he provided his usual brilliant advice on two separate drafts. The following people also provided important feedback on the manuscript at various stages: Andy Anderson, Kevin Chang, Selisa Cockett, Nicholas Conway, Emil DeAndreis, Kevin A. Dineen, Matt Haslam, Priscilla Kipapa, Anthony Locricchio, Thomas McGann, Chris McKinney, Bob Nakata, Maria O'Rourke, Patty Panahi, Jane Panek, John Panek, and Keith Ryder.

Most important has been the involvement and interest of Percy's parents, George and Priscilla Kipapa. I have tried to make it obvious within these pages that their contributions extend far beyond our multiple interviews. Quite simply, the book could not have been written without their help.

PROLOGUE

Here is how it happened: Percy Kipapa of Waikāne lay face down on the ground desperately sucking for air, his mouth opened wide, dry all the way to the back of his throat. His huge upper body heaved up and down. His mind raced as he prayed that whatever it was they were hitting him with would stop sending its stinging jolts of pain across the bare skin of his back. He tried to open his eyes, but with his already blurred vision now clouded by a well of tears, he could make out nothing, only the feeling that they were all surrounding him. When the burn of the sand and salt they had shoved into his face became too much, he shut his eyes tight, feeling their presence—more than twenty of them—shouting and taunting as the stick came down yet again with a *whack!* The sting that arose was so sharp that it must have drawn blood, but he couldn't tell for sure, the rest of his body burning with muscle fatigue so deep that even his feeble gasps for air hurt. His back, the backs of his big legs, his massive shoulders were on fire, his arms now rubbery with exhaustion. The voices kept shouting from all directions, coming closer. All he knew for sure was that he had to get up off the ground somehow, if only he could suck in enough air, if only his arms would move.

And then the kicking started. As if it wasn't already struggle enough to get some oxygen into his lungs, the biggest guy there was now kicking him in the ribs. He'd wanted it to end long before they'd even thrown him down, but no: it had gone from pushing and slaps to the head, to getting thrown to the rock-hard ground, to the beatings with the stick. And now, with each thud to his side, he'd begun to give up on the chance of it ever ending. Percy tried opening his eyes again and through the blur he could make out the shape of a man, bigger even than his brother Kurt, stepping forward like a massive five-hundred-pound field goal kicker with one leg pulled back. Then Percy's side exploded in pain, the kick pushing all the

1

air from his greedy lungs again, and for a moment he wondered if this might be what it felt like to drown. Twenty guys mobbing him, and he was going to die from lack of oxygen.

Another *whack* and this time the pain went deeper—not a sting, but a body punch that lit up every muscle in his back. The shouts around him grew louder, and when he opened his eyes, even through the blur, even on the edge of passing out, he could see that what they were now hitting him with was an aluminum baseball bat. The big Hawaiian held it high over his head with both hands for one still moment before bringing it down again hard, and it occurred to Percy that he might actually die, that all of them had gotten so caught up in the moment that they could no longer see how far they were taking this, that he would never see his mother's face again, that they would send his body home to her in a box, and what in the world would they tell her? That he couldn't get up off the ground?

And suddenly Percy began to feel the slightest drips of energy seep into his exhausted arms. If not for the fact that every ounce of his own four-hundred-pound body was now focused on the task of lifting himself to his hands and knees, he would have seen that what was now energizing him was the purest form of fear he had ever felt. Heaving loudly now, pushing the air out and then sucking in with all he had, he pushed on the floor with his big hands and rose, this first little surprising show of progress energizing him further, until he managed to bring one leg under himself, and then the other, opening his eyes to the sting of tears in search of something to hang onto. Finding nothing but the round shapes of the men standing over him, he stood at last and reached out for a shoulder to steady himself.

The shouts rang out again, now with more urgency, and Percy's thoughts exploded from someone's roundhouse open-hand to the side of his head. A voice was telling him, *The water, brah! Go get the water!* For a moment he stood in confusion—the water?—until another open-hand shook him. He followed his instincts through the surrounding bodies and over to the corner of the area, wiping his eyes so that he could just make out the tiny faucet and the long bamboo ladle leaning next to it. He managed to fill the ladle, and then fought against his heaving body to steady it and carry it over to the big Hawaiian holding the baseball bat, with enough water spilling from its sides so that when he reached the man it was only half full. Bowing his head, he offered the water and said through heavy breaths, *Mashita!*

When the Hawaiian sipped from the ladle and then spat out onto the ground, Percy found it hard to believe that he was free, that it was over. Still a bit unsure if it had really all happened, he stood against the wall and waited. The sound of his greedy gulps for air filled the room, even over the slap and swish of the next boy charging the big Hawaiian who then slid him back across the sand-covered ring, even above the grunts and shouts of encouragement from the other boys who, only moments earlier, seemed about to converge for the kill. As Percy waited for his labored breathing to show some sign of slowing down, he wondered what on earth it was they had just put him through. And suddenly, as if to answer his thoughts, a voice cut through the loud huffing sound, a knowing voice that had once been through the same thing, a *local* voice telling him this: *That's whatchoo call "kawaigari."*

Kawaigari? Still gulping for air, Percy turned to see the massive figure of Troy Talaimatai, his *senpai*, his senior, whose hair was tied into a samurai topknot that bent over his forehead into a black point. A Samoan from Hawai'i, Troy looked nearly twice the size of the biggest lineman on a Hawai'i high school football field. But even standing there almost naked—dressed in nothing but a length of canvas that covered his balls and the crack of his ass and then wound around his waist into a thick black belt—if he were to jump up and down not an ounce of his rock-hard body would jiggle.

Kawaigari means "tender loving care," Troy told him, a can-you-believe-this grin spreading out over his square jaw. Tender loving care, brah!

IF THE SLIPPERS THEY GAVE HIM were stiff-as-a-board versions of the rubber ones he wore back in Hawai'i, it was because they were made out of wood. Sumo, as it turned out, worked according to rank, and the newcomers ranked at the bottom had to wear what they called *geta*—two foot-sized rectangular boards with wooden slats running widthwise at the ball of the foot and just in front of the heel. Although the slats may have been affixed to the soles for traction, they made it hard for Percy, who stood six feet three inches tall, to balance. The idea was to roll them forward as you walked heel to toe, a motion that created a loud *clack-clack* sound that seemed to come from ancient times. Once he got the hang of it, the *geta*, along with his *yukata*—a kind of kimono tied with a long length of cloth wound around the waist and tied on the side—filled him with pride. Eighteen-year-old Percy Kipapa had come more than seven thousand miles from his home in the rural Hawaiian valley of Waikāne all the way to an official professional Japanese sumo training facility—a *sumo beya*, filled with some twenty other hungry young men—and the wooden clack of his slippers announced that he was well on his way to becoming a professional *sumōtori*.

Percy's first tender-loving-care *kawaigari* beating had been enough to show him that the path would be a long one—that sumo was not as simple as just standing up and pushing the other guy out of the ring. Every morning someone would kick him awake well before dawn. He would follow the other bottom-division boys down to the basement locker room, where they would strip down to nothing and wrap the long lengths of black canvas around each other into thick belts called *mawashi* before filing up to the ground-floor training area. They shook off the sleep by lifting first one leg and then the other high in the air to alternately pound their feet into the practice area's rock-hard clay, steam beginning to rise from their sweating bodies in the November air. Only after they warmed up the room with a couple of hours of practice bouts would the rest of the boys begin to enter, according to rank, and start their own limbering up. Percy could see that even so many steps down from the sumo he had seen on TV back in Hawai'i, guys ranked near Troy were far out of his league: quicker charges, smooth and graceful footwork, and throws so calculated they looked almost relaxed. For a long time he stood and watched, trying to pick up on how a real *sumōtori* fought off a throw or positioned his feet. Percy looked forward to watching Akebono train—Akebono was only the third *sumōtori* from Hawai'i to reach one of sumo's top two salaried divisions—but by the time he finally entered the ring, dressed in a white *mawashi* to indicate his exalted rank, Percy was in the kitchen covered in sweat, his stomach growling as he helped prepare a meal he would not be able to touch until everyone else had eaten and bathed.

No, the paid ranks could not have seemed further away—a fact brought home even harder once morning practice finally ended. The real reason they made the new guys wear the wooden slippers, Percy soon figured out, was less for tradition than it was so his *senpai* could hear them coming. Percy had grown up on Oʻahu's tough Windward side, where there had always been some punky kid singling him out just to prove to everyone how tough he was. He knew all about the anonymous elbows and fists on the packed city bus from Kāneʻohe home to the country, about getting kicked off the bus because the driver looked in his mirror just in time to see him hitting back. He also knew about charming the little punks into becoming his friends. But here there was no way to charm them, to put his tree-trunk arm around a guy's head in that affectionate way of his, because Percy couldn't understand a word they were saying, let alone speak their language. Everyone was his *senpai*, all the way from Azumazeki Oyakata—the *beya*'s boss, who had come from Maui long before Percy was born—down to the fifteen-year-old Japanese kids who'd joined only a couple of months before Percy did. And when they heard the *clack-clack* of his wooden slippers, they took advantage.

One day one of them reached up and smacked him, right in the face, right there in front of everyone, yelling on about his frickin' futon: *fix my futon, put away my futon,* is what Percy thought he must be saying. Shocked, Percy stood for a long moment—the guy wasn't even old enough to drive yet; one *week* at Castle High and his pants would be flying from the flagpole. *"Fuckin' young punk, you tell me what for do! You know, when I was brought up, you always show your elders respect. You see one grandma crossing the street, a car coming, you go and stop the cars. You see her getting hard time carrying a bag, you go grab 'um for her."* He looked around the room to see everybody watching him, waiting to see what he would do. The constant ordering around, that was one thing—this was Japan, this was sumo, of course things were different here. But back in Hawaiʻi his friend Shane, he knew, would have caught one of these punks in the alley by now. In that one long moment, Percy would have recalled walking up the concrete ramp onto the King Zoo football field to face an army of boys from the Red Rags gang, Shane and Charles at his side, *working him up fo' scrap.* In the *face.* You don't hit a local boy in the *face.* So Percy let fly not with a slap, but with a solid punch right at the kid's head.

Immediately they all converged on him, almost twenty professional sumo wrestlers battle scarred from years of fighting and tender-loving-care beatings. Shouts of *Nani! Baka yarō!* rang out all around. Incredibly, Troy managed to step in and settle the whole thing down, pulling Percy aside and telling him that when your *senpai* says anything to you—*anything*—you suck it up and *do* it. It was only because Boss was far out of sight, because Akebono was in his back room, and mainly because Azumazeki Beya's self-appointed hazing expert wasn't around—a frustrated mid-ranker named Tsuji—that things went no further.

At night when Percy was left alone in his corner of the big second-floor roomful of Japanese sumo wrestlers, the cold hardness of the tatami floor inevitably sent his thoughts towards the question that had recently started hitting him from as far out of nowhere as had that slap to the head: *Why am I here?* The first time he had walked into his crowded new home he had concluded that, if nothing else, he would never be lonely. While everyone may have fought alone in what appeared to be a sport as individual as boxing, Percy could see that sumo was a brotherhood in every other way—from the topknot on everyone's head all the way down to the rule prohibiting stable mates from meeting in the ring unless in a rare play-off match. Even the Japanese terms for the stable mates who sparred together day after day translated into the words for older brother or younger brother. When they'd surrounded Percy for hitting the young loudmouth, that's what it had looked like: a group of topknotted brothers protecting their own from some kind of invader. And now he could only listen as they talked away those last moments before drifting off to sleep. Trading stories of their hometowns, joking away the pain of their various bruises or recent losses, anticipating the upcoming tournament—whatever it was, the bond these battle-scarred boys had formed was already as strong as what he'd had at home with Shane and Charles. From time to time, Percy had made his best effort to join in, maybe trying to teach someone a "shaka" or a couple of words of English, but those exchanges could only go so far. More often than not, their happy banter and the occasional laughter that passed between them all made Percy feel like he was feeling now: more isolated than if he were sitting in the big room by himself.

When they'd recruited him back in Hawai'i, Percy had thought that sumo was supposed to be easy. Everyone knew about Takamiyama, who had competed for more than twenty years before retiring into the elder name Azumazeki Oyakata and becoming the first non-Japanese to open a sumo stable, Azumazeki Beya. Hawai'i's Konishiki was already threatening to become the first foreigner to reach sumo's top rank, *yokozuna*. Akebono, the big Hawaiian who had grown up just down the road from where Percy's brother Kurt lived in Waimānalo, was also on his way up. But Percy soon learned that for every foreign sumo star there were three or four other Hawai'i boys who had found their career options back home limited enough to give this strange, ancient sport a try—and not just Troy, and his other local *senpai*, John Feleunga. More than ten other Hawai'i *sumōtori* were spread out across Tokyo in four different *sumo beya*. At first Percy figured that the presence of the other local boys would ease his transition to Japan—he would be joining three of them at Azumazeki Beya, after all. But the recruiter—a retired Honolulu firefighter and longtime friend of Azumazeki Oyakata named Larry Aweau—must have left out the part about rank and seniority when he told him about the other local boys. Even after practice—sometimes especially after practice—the issue of rank hung over the *beya* like some kind of relationship-defining cloud that indicated who could talk to whom and how familiar they were allowed to be. Troy and John weren't as bad as Akebono, who was ranked so far out of reach that they couldn't even refer to him by name—they had to call him "*sekitori*," the honorary title for *sumōtori* ranked in the top two divisions. But this thing about rank kept them from talking with Percy much, leaving him lonelier still for the fact that it was an isolation he couldn't blame on the language.

Inevitably, the sound of the boys all talking story would get Percy thinking of Shane and Charles, friends since that first day at Waiāhole School what, thirteen years ago now? And not just friends, but blood brothers—the three of them having cut their hands and promised that "no matta what, we all going die togedda." They were right up on Grandpa's Hill when they did it, Percy recalled, that rise deep in the valley that looks out towards the steep wall of the Ko'olau Range and the mist-shrouded peak of Pu'u 'Ōhulehule—the *mountain*, their playground. The boys had grown up together on Grandpa's Hill, exploring the valley's thick jungle trails every day after school, swimming in Waikāne Stream. He could close his eyes and picture it, how that land had brought them together. And that was really what he missed, wasn't it? It wasn't just his *boys*. His visions of that vast green valley yawning out to catch the trade winds just north of Kāneʻohe, right where town suddenly becomes country, got Percy thinking that there was something more about *home* that pulled at him so strongly. It wasn't just that the valley was his playground. It was that it was *their land*, the *ʻāina*—that which provides. It had *mana* so strong you could almost hear the spirits talking to you as you walked up the trail—that's how Charles always put it. And now it was gone.

Though there would be no re-creating Waikāne's *mana* among Tokyo's narrow crowded streets, or replacing his view of Puʻu ʻŌhulehule with this endless gray skyline, Percy could at least work to find some alternative to Shane and Charles—something he was quickly able to do once he got beyond the rank-dictated confines of Azumazeki Beya and boarded a train bound for Kyūshū, Japan's southern island. The whole contingent of the Japan Sumo Association was headed there for one of sumo's six annual major tournaments: all active *sumōtori*, rotund former *sumōtori* coaches and bosses, slight and skinny referees and ring announcers, and the master artists who oiled and sculpted each competitor's hair into the kind of traditional samurai topknot that Percy's hair was still too short to form. In Kyūshū, Percy would be competing in qualifying matches in an effort to have his name added to those of the more than eight hundred *sumōtori* listed on sumo's ranking sheet. For the long ride, Azumazeki Beya's manager had the sense to seat him across from George and Bumbo Kalima, brothers from the neighborhood where Percy's brother Kurt now lived. Larry Aweau had recruited the Kalimas a couple of years earlier for Magaki Beya, which was a few blocks away from Azumazeki Beya.

What Percy saw across from him on the train were two local boys dressed in kimonos, their hair tied like samurai, and their faces beaming with bright, welcoming smiles. They laughed good-naturedly at his *geta* slippers, pointing out the incongruity of such a big guy having to balance on such footwear, since most of the low-rankers were just scrawny fifteen-year-old kids. With a smile of his own, Percy boasted that he would climb the ranks in no time. The Kalima brothers, both of whom were around a year into the sumo grind and hovering about midway up the ranking sheet, just gave each other knowing looks and shook their heads. And it became clear right away to Percy, even from this first brief exchange, that they would be friends. Though rank and seniority were still supposed to guide their conversation, with the Kalimas belonging to a different *beya* it mattered far less. So the stories poured out over the long train ride, where Percy saw Bumbo's face smirk from time to time into a look of resignation at sumo's baffling behavioral demands. Bumbo's distinct bullets of laughter came out as he told a story of trying to throw his opponent out of the ring and into the lap of his own boss whenever the man was assigned as a ring judge for one of his matches. George's warm face morphed into a look of anger that seemed to cause his prominent forehead to protrude as he recounted the story of how although his hair was long enough, they hadn't tied it into a topknot until the hair of two of his Japanese stable mates at Magaki Beya had grown long enough to tie first.

Percy told them where he was from, immediately evoking the Bruddah Waltah anthem from the 1980s, "Sweet Lady of Waiāhole," a song about an old woman from the valley adjoining Waikāne who spent her days "sitting by the highway, selling her papayas, and green and ripe bananas." The song took the homesick Kalima boys straight back to the romanticized version of what every local boy considered "paradise." They may have known better, but several months in gray and crowded Tokyo had turned home into an ideal place, its every imperfection melting into the postcard image of the parts they missed most. George and Bumbo knew that the Waimānalo they'd left, with its houses popping up on former farmland and its long line of traffic bending all the way up the hill past the golf course, wasn't the same as the one they missed. What they missed was *country*, and by creating the Sweet Lady character, Bruddah Waltah had given them a lasting piece of it. Then Percy let them know that he and his two good friends used to help the Sweet Lady as they walked to Waiāhole School, way up in the valley surrounded by papaya fields.

Right! came their reaction. *He's talking like the Sweet Lady of Waiāhole is a real person.*

No, I telling you! She's real. *Miss Matayoshi.* Every morning, Percy told them, he and Shane and Charles would take turns pushing her wheelbarrow down to the highway where she'd set up her little fruit stand, and then run back up Waiāhole Valley Road to get to school on time. Straight through their years in Kāne'ohe's King Intermediate School—"King Zoo"—they would help her. That's where the bus stop was, right in front of where she sat. They'd even found out that she'd been robbed once, and they chased the guy down and made him pay. She was *real*. That's what it was *like* in Waiāhole-Waikāne. That's what it was *still* like.

Sitting talking story with the Kalimas, Percy was, above all, relieved. Simply talking about home with someone who could relate was a vacation from the relative cold of Azumazeki Beya. So for the first time since getting his passport stamped, Percy was able to relax enough to begin thinking about beating all of these little Japanese kids, some of whom looked half the size, at best, of the three Hawaiians. It wouldn't be long, he reasoned, until they all would be called *sekitori*, just like Akebono. All George and Bumbo could do was shake their heads again and smile, as if Percy had no idea how hard the whole thing would really be. But Percy would hear none of it. Boss had come all the way up to his house in Waikāne Valley to recruit him, he reasoned. Even promised him a new car.

PERCY DID MANAGE TO QUALIFY IN KYŪSHŪ, but in the context of living in a house where everyone else was his *senpai*, nothing had changed. Still struggling simply to make himself understood, let alone figure out the complicated levels of formality and the in-group versus out-of-group Japanese verb forms and so on, Percy found himself on the phone to his mother one afternoon when an order to wash the dishes came from the kitchen. Though he thought they might understand that the rare connection to home—to his *mother*, of all people—would be enough to put the dishes on hold for a couple of minutes, he also recognized the voice of the *senpai* delivering the order: it belonged to Tsuji.

George had warned Percy about Tsuji. "The Japanese *senpai* in Azumazeki Beya," George had told him, shaking his head, "that guy is a *prick*." George's own cultural struggles at Magaki Beya were certainly not limited to the one incident about having to wait to have his topknot tied. But from time to time he would walk across the neighborhood to practice at Azumazeki Beya, and there he saw Troy and John take more abuse than he ever would have been able to tolerate himself. As Troy had explained it to George, Tsuji would "make you eat every damn grain of rice in your bowl, and if you didn't, he'd knock you on your head." And if being a prick wasn't enough, the guy was also that lowest form of creature that local guys like Troy and George and Percy learn to despise from the moment they walk through the doors of elementary school: Tsuji was a *rat*. "You broke curfew?" George said, "Five minutes late? He'd go and tell Boss." And what did that mean? It meant *kawaigari*: tender loving care, which wasn't just how you toughened someone for battle. It wasn't just how you got someone to dig deep. It was also how you managed to get a testosterone-soaked roomful of fifteen- to twenty-two-year-old fighters to stay in line. "He'd go and tell Boss." The words were enough to send many former *sumōtori* into flashbacks whose soundtracks are nothing but the primal, blood-curdling screams of grown men.

Percy was expected to hang up on his mother immediately or, barring that, offer a humbly delivered fourteen-syllable honorific form of the request, "wait." He was proud to simply know the word for "wait," which he delivered humbly enough in his usual friendly tone, but which contained only the three syllables of its most familiar form—the form everyone else used when addressing the low-ranking Percy, and thus, the one that had stuck in his brain.

Tsuji's response came in the form of a frying pan to the head that sent Percy's thick glasses flying.

Stunned, Percy again felt the moment stretch. Percy and the Red Rags—nobody ever found out about that. Whenever he'd gotten kicked off the bus, it hadn't been because anyone had ratted him out—it had been because no one, including himself, had ratted out the guy who'd thrown the first elbow when the driver wasn't looking. He could hear Troy's words: *You suck it up and do it.* Percy could have pounded Tsuji right there if he'd wanted to, but then what? He knew exactly what, and the thought frightened him into silence. It wasn't Tsuji. It wasn't Troy. It wasn't any of his *senpai* in the big tatami room. It wasn't even the *sekitori*, however loudly he might roar from his back room. It was this: *He'll go and tell Boss.*

Percy quietly said goodbye to his mother and hung up the phone. He retrieved his glasses, swallowed hard, and stood up to go and wash the dishes.

CHAPTER 1

HOMESICK

You gotta feel 'um, too, when you writing 'um, 'cause without you feeling 'um, nobody else going feel 'um. You can talk about how he made it, and how good his childhood was and what a good guy he was and alladis, and yet you can still show how this community—not how corrupt this community was, but how this community slipped and fell short, and how that yet until today, this place still has a chance because it's still untouched, and still get mana. So you gotta word 'um to the point where everything's still beautiful, it's just . . . that we missed it somehow. But we going bring 'um back, because you going make us feel 'um, and make a success, and not a success for "Whooo! 'Cause of me!" ah? A success because of the good story that it was, that this story has a meaning and it has a purpose, and it was real life. Because t'ings can still grow up there. The watah still flowing.

—Charles Kekahu of Waikāne, June 16, 2007

"WHEN PERCY FIRST STARTED," George Kalima told me, "he used to mouth off: 'Yeah, I can do that!' Us, we already seen it all, and we weren't veterans yet, but we were a year or two ahead of him. He was thinking he was going dominate already and fly up the ranks. You look on the TV, it seems easy to you, until you go there and you think, 'Whoa, what are all these odda ranks on the bottom?' So we all just kind of snicker at him: 'Okay bradda, you neva see everything yet. Going come your time. When you realize you starting at the bottom and you working your way up, it's tough.'" George, who competed for eight years and eventually reached sumo's coveted top division, was telling me that "tough" meant having to acquire the famously complex language with the help of nothing but a dictionary and the threat of an eye-tearing smack to the head. He was talking about the maddening cultural adjustments that the Hawai'i boys all had to make to compete in a sport that many Japanese viewed as a guardian of sacred national traditions. Then there was the brutal training. The hazing. The food. But above all, he was talking about simply being away from Hawai'i. Percy's *senpai* Akebono once told me how surprised he'd been early in his career to suddenly find himself missing the sweeping view of Waimānalo Bay from Makapu'u Point, realizing that for years he hadn't even known that the emerald ocean was supposed to be beautiful. George and Bumbo may have had each other at Magaki Beya, but that cold place quickly reminded them how far away they were from those Waimānalo backyard *kanikapila* jams where their sister would sing into the night, with Dad on the spoons and cousins taking turns on the washtub bass. Being away from that and more—calling it merely "tough" is the height of local boy understatement. Looking back, it's a wonder that, thousands of miles from Hawai'i, any of the boys were able to make it past the first year, let alone make a career of a sport that has no off season.

In 1998 the call of home, of that beautiful green valley and his own *'ohana* images, finally became too strong for Percy and he moved back to Hawai'i. A few months later I met him for the first time. The moment of our meeting sticks in my own memory like a photograph. Back then I rode a motorcycle, and I was driving through pouring rain to interview him for a book I was writing about Akebono—Chad Rowan. The big raindrops stung my arms, my legs, my face, pelting me as though the car ahead were spitting up a steady stream of pebbles and sand. I never thought to pull over and wait it out, or even turn back and reschedule the interview, obsessed as I was with tracking down sources for my book. Percy had just returned from nearly seven years living in the same sumo stable as Akebono, training with him, attending to his every need, watching him figure out how to deal with all of the pressure of a foreigner competing in Japan's national sport. So I squinted through the pellets of water for a fix on the red taillights ahead, and somehow made it to Percy's new Waimānalo homestead house in one piece.

The door opened and a mountain of a man looked down through thick glasses at me—a drenched, skinny haole boy, puddles beginning to form at my wrinkled feet. He immediately turned into the house and returned with a thick bath towel and an offer for something hot to drink, inviting me right inside—never mind the brand-new living room carpet. When I complimented him on the house, Percy explained that while he was away his parents had been awarded Hawaiian homestead land, and they had been able to finance construction with money he'd been sending home over the years. Of course he would rather be living in Waikāne, he said, but it was nice to have his own place so close to where his big brother Kurt lived at his house on the stretch of Waimānalo Beach everyone calls "Sherwood's," only a few blocks away.

As we sat down at the dining room table, I noticed he'd done the place up as his own, too. There were the two framed certificates commemorating his two championships in the *makushita* division—sumo's fourth division and the one that formed the proving ground for those who reach the two salaried divisions above. Two cubical glass boxes sat alone on a shelf lining one wall, each containing what looked like a piece of shiny-black molded plastic, but what turned out to be the oiled sumo topknot that was cut off with gold-plated scissors in a tearful public retirement ceremony. ("I was one of the only sumo wrestlers to have mine cut twice," he proudly told me.) The walls were lined with big framed photos: Percy in the middle of a grappling match; Percy squatting down just before a bout, his arms spread out wide to indicate that he honorably carried no weapons; Percy and Akebono dressed in formal silk kimonos and shaking hands, stern looks on their faces; a group shot taken after practice, everyone covered in sweat and sand, the big guy in the glasses waving a shaka at the camera.

And there hung the *keshō mawashi*. Just back from three months of following Akebono on two Japan-wide exhibition tours and through a major tournament, I'd seen the sumo locker room go silent as low-rankers jumped about with a military-like seriousness unfolding these beautiful gold-threaded apronlike garments, and then dressing the *sekitori* in them for sumo's sacred ring-entering ceremony. The men would line up according to rank, file out into the arena, and mount the raised ring as their names and hometowns were announced. The ritual was deeply connected to sumo's ancient past by what each man wore: stitched woodblock prints of curling waves, of brocades and chrysanthemums, of snow-capped mountains set off from bright-blue or crisp-black or maroon or forest-green backgrounds, the aprons all tasseled in bright gold that shone under the ring's lights. I'd seen *keshō mawashi* in pictures, but up close the colors jumped out. Among the many ceremonies that, in my eyes, helped turn sumo from a mere sport into a cultural institution, the ring-entering ceremony, marked by these incredibly beautiful living museum pieces, was the most powerful. These men weren't just athletes, they also were guardians of ancient traditions and codes of stoic, precise, Zenlike samurai behavior. And now right here in Hawai'i as the rain pounded down outside, the Pegasus jumping out of the royal blue sky of Percy's *keshō mawashi* seemed to glow in its brilliant whiteness, as did the two kanji characters for Percy's sumo name: "Daiki." Big Happiness.

We started off trading stories about getting lost in the maze of To-kyo's narrow streets, the crushing crowds wherever you went no matter what time of day, everyone stopping to point and stare at the *gaijin*—the foreigner—and the fear overcoming you on the train that if you missed your stop, which looked just like every single other stop, you'd fall off the edge into oblivion, hopelessly lost. I'd come from suburban Long Island and considered it a shock. But Percy had been raised on a small family farm where his mother had grown up milking cows, where his grandfather had made a living growing produce to sell in Honolulu, and he'd gone on to navigate the same constantly jostling elbows, the same quizzical—if not frightened—looks. I'd gone on to become a McTeacher at a cushy English-language "conversation" school in Tokyo, and a year later I brought back a few good bar stories and almost no ability, at the time, to speak Japanese. But Percy had returned fluent, with the *keshō mawashi*, the *makushita* championships, the two topknots.

And the stories he'd brought back, many of them punctuated with a deep laugh that came out like a shout, put anything I had to say about Japan to shame. What poured out across the dining room table was some of the most detailed and specific information I had ever heard about what life is like inside one of the world's most secretive subcultures—even after months of shadowing Akebono from one side of Japan to the other. Here, alone in this big house towards the back of Waimānalo Valley, sitting by himself day after day with little to do, I had found a twenty-five-year-old man with more insight into Japan than that held by many of the Ph.D.s whose scholarship I was then reading. Percy hadn't just studied it—he'd lived it, figuring out how to act appropriately as he learned the intricate techniques of the ancient sport, and finally reaching what everyone who ever puts on a *mawashi* dreams of reaching: the paid ranks. Though no one knew his name, he had done very nearly what Akebono had done.

"They hit me because they say they seen potential in me and stuff li'dat," he told me by way of explaining the meaning of "tender loving care." "They were trying to get me stronger. 'Cause when I went up there, every time when I do one move on somebody and hurt 'em, I was like, 'Ho, you all right?'—trying to help the guy out. And they neva like that. My boss was telling me I got too much aloha for the guy: 'You gotta break his arm! Let him suffer on the ground!'" He went on to explain that *kawaigari* beatings weren't restricted to sumo. He tied them to one of the two Japanese cultural values the beatings had helped instill in him: the *senpai-kōhai* seniority system, and *gaman*—a nontranslatable word that describes the way a salaryman endures two-hour commutes in Japan's famously overstuffed trains every single day of a near-vacationless forty-year career, or the way a *sumōtori* competes and practices when injured for fear of dropping down in the ranks because absences count as losses.

"We so afraid to tell Boss, like, our back hurt," he said. "Cause we know his reaction already: '*Gaman!* Go to the doctor *after* practice finish.' So why cry to him now? Sometimes he used to give pity: 'Oh, your back sore? Dasarrite. No practice.' But most of the time, no. That's why to me, if we could talk English to Boss—'cause the Japanee culture, and in the Japanee language, it's so hard to explain that, 'I'm in pain right now. I just need a couple days' rest, and I think my body going come betta.' But in sumo, you can be fucking bleeding out your nose: 'Here's one tissue.' I swear, sometimes my body used to be in so much pain, the more I hit somebody the more mad I get, and I forget about the pain. And sometimes I had pain, Chad or my boss whacks me on my back or my ass, I'd forget about the pain in my back because next the pain is over *here*. Look: there went the pain in my knee 'cause they just whacked me on my head.

"I was scared of my boss," Percy went on, "'cause he was more than one father figure." The first thing I had noticed upon walking into Azumazeki Beya for the first time earlier that year was the gold-framed floor-to-ceiling portrait that had hung from the sumo arena's rafters following Boss's 1972 championship, the larger-than-life Hawaiian looking down from a background of blue sky. As an eighteen-year-old then named Jesse Kuhaulua, Boss had been recruited from rural Maui and moved to Tokyo in 1964 to join one of the Japan Sumo Association's fifty-odd *sumo beya*. Competing as "Takamiyama," he struggled for years in the lower ranks, endearing himself to a historically xenophobic Japanese audience. He then made his way along a gradual march to the paid ranks, the first ever major tournament win for a foreigner, Japanese citizenship, and the unprecedented opening of his own *sumo beya* under the name Azumazeki Oyakata. He'd been gracious enough to sit for the interview that led to my meeting Akebono, and to the book that Percy was now helping me with. "How he talked to you, what he do," Percy went on, "I don't know *how* he did it, but when he talked to you he put fear in your mind. And surrounding around him, the energy is so strong when he walks into some place: '*Osssh!*'" Percy imitated sumo's military-like greeting. "I mean, people *react* to him when they see him. It's like the Godfather. You look at him, you tell yourself, 'Oh, you cannot mess with this guy. He got power behind him.'" The image didn't square with that of the man who'd invited me to his *beya* only a few months earlier—I still remember him as one of the sweetest men I've ever met. Though Azumazeki Oyakata spoke freely for most of the interview, he became almost shy when I tried to get him to talk about how he had competed—incredibly, given sumo's brutal practice requirements—to the age of forty, setting the record of 1,231 consecutive top-division bouts that may never be broken. "I guess when he went up Japan, he was the only local guy up there," Percy explained. "From what we heard from him, he had one way harder life from what we had up there. So when we went up there, he tried to treat us like how he was treated, 'cause that's how he came strong. But how I look at it, he used to hit me with the bamboo stick. Constantly. Every day. Every day for two and a half years. So one day I said, 'You're doing this to me to get me angry at the guy I'm wrestling. But the more you hit me, the more I like hit *you*, but I cannot hit you. I wouldn't *think* about hitting you, but the anger is not going towards the person in front of me; it's the guy who's hitting me.' But that's the way I guess he was trained, ah?"

Though the rain continued to pour outside, Percy's mood lightened as the afternoon wore on. By the end of the first hour, he'd become much more comfortable with me, and the stories turned to nights of partying in

Roppongi, his adventures with the groupies attracted by his sumo topknot, the thickness of his wallet once he'd reached the paid ranks. Percy was one of those guys for whom talking is like breathing, and it was difficult to imagine him confined to silence in his first lonely months as a sumo low-ranker who couldn't yet speak Japanese. Now he seemed to miss Japan so much, I asked him why he'd ever come back. This led him into a long and detailed story about how a string of injuries had sent him down the ranking sheet, how Waikāne Valley had been calling him, how he'd missed his family, and how all of it had led him finally to decide to retire. "I was sick," he said, aiming for the word's slang meaning. "I wanted for stay, but I neva like stay. That's what we always used to talk about—me, Chad, Troy, John. 'Fuck, I like quit, but I no like quit.'"

The long days home alone now had him thinking of going back to Japan to teach at one of the English-language "conversation" schools that surround every Tokyo train station. One of Boss's sponsors could get him the degree he needed for the working visa, he explained, and all he needed was a place to stay. While he was clearly envious of my recent trip there, even back then I could tell that it wasn't so much Japan that he missed but the identity the topknot had given him—the honor, the respect. Even our long interview—Percy and I had just about become braddas after one afternoon talking story. Sure, he was a friendly and generous guy to begin with. But a bigger reason why he had gone on so long, and spoken so candidly with someone he'd only just met, was that my recent research for the Akebono book had made me one of the few who could understand and respect exactly what Percy had done. Up in Japan, all he'd needed was the topknot, and people had understood. But now that he was home, no one really seemed to know the depth of what he'd accomplished in becoming a *sekitori*.

I transcribed the tape of our interview over the next couple of days and then put it in a drawer somewhere where it sat for the next ten years. Listening to it again wasn't at the top of my list when I set out to write the pages that follow, so busy was I with all of the other research involved. But when Percy's story wound up becoming so much deeper than the local-guy-in-Japan adventure I'd thought I was going to write, I knew I had to listen to the tape again. I'm not exactly sure why I'd put it off—it was something more than the fact that I already had the whole thing transcribed. Maybe I wasn't ready to hear Percy's decade-old voice and the distinct shout of his laugh coming out at me from a black box. I didn't want to hear the pauses or the shifts in tone I'd missed the first time through, or the moments where, now that I know him so much better, I can tell that he's trying to joke away a memory that stings him bitterly.

Different things do stand out as I listen now, and not only because back then I was focused more on Akebono's story than on Percy's. You can hear the radio in the background tuned to Hawaiian 105.1 the whole time, which layers the conversation with irony when an Iz song comes on, or when "All Hawai'i" is told to "Stand Together," or when Jerry Santos sings his poignant farewell to the kind of country life Percy grew up with in the Windward valleys. Percy talks about people I didn't know then but now know well, like his sumo brother Tyler Hopkins from Kailua, whose life paralleled his own in every significant way, and who now talks about Percy in the tones a war veteran would use to describe the army buddy who saved his life. I see Percy trying to laugh off the fact that he hadn't been invited to Akebono's wedding, but I can also now hear the pain in his voice.

The first real pause in his otherwise nonstop monologue doesn't appear until some thirty minutes into the tape. It comes when Percy begins talking about the dilemma he'd faced a few months earlier—the "I like quit, but I no like quit" retirement question faced by so many *sumōtori* at such young ages, their bodies battered, their spirits drained by constant homesickness. The pause comes in the middle of a story about Akebono, who had once told Percy how much he'd wanted to move back to Hawai'i after retiring. "To me," Percy said, "the way I look at it now, if I was him I would stay." Pause. In the long silent moment that follows I can hear Percy looking back over the eight months that have passed since he himself returned to Hawai'i, and now I know that he is looking into the eyes of a monster. "You can still come home and visit any time you like," he finally goes on. "This your home ground ova here. You come home when you like visit. But don't come back over here for live."

CHAPTER 2

RESPECT

I used to think, "That poor guy is getting dirty lickings, *over there." 'Cause he was big, but he was soft-hearted and he wasn't really like, one* fighta. *We used to wrestle and I could put him down, and I was way smaller than him. So I used to think, "Ho, those guys* must be busting him up." *And guarantee he was homesick something bad, because he was always stuck to his mom, ah? And he would be thinking about Waiāhole and Waikāne and just cry.*

—Shane Picanco of Waiāhole, November 28, 2007

The deep roar from the back room was so loud, angry, and sudden that it caused Percy to jump straight to his feet to see what it was that the *sekitori* wanted this time. Akebono may have been from Waimānalo, but you wouldn't know it. He acted more Japanese than local: practice, eat, sleep. And if he did go out, he would take Troy and John, who spent most of his free time in front of the TV laughing along at some comedy in perfect understanding. Mean moods, the *sekitori* had. You would think he would have remembered what it was like to come straight from Hawai'i, and offer a little help, but no. I guess, Percy thought, that's how he was treated, and he came strong, so that's how he going treat me.

The *sekitori.* That was the difference right there, the sumo ranking sheet in real life. The *banzuke*—the ranking sheet—they all talked about it like Percy's father talked about the Bible. It looked like some kind of ancient Japanese eye chart. The names of all eight-hundred-odd *sumōtori* were painted on it in thick black brushstrokes at the top, down to hair-width squiggles at the bottom. Troy had had a far-off look in his eyes when he'd pointed to the top two divisions, painted headline bold. Those ranked in the top *makunouchi* division and those ranked just below in *jūryō* were called *sekitori*, which translates into "takers of the barrier"—a term that Troy had Percy take to mean that they had, in all senses of the word, made it. The *sekitori* were the princes; those below them were the slaves. *Sekitori* took home between eight and twenty grand a *month*, and they had fan clubs showering them with gifts that could easily triple that amount. If a *sekitori* shouted, a lower-ranker jumped. Percy would learn that less than 5 percent of all the men ever to put on a *mawashi* ever became *sekitori*. In the tournaments, they fought for fifteen days instead of seven. With rooms of their own or apartments outside the *beya*, sex came as easily as all the other gifts. As Percy had already seen, they were the last to wake up every morning, the first to bathe after practice, the first to eat every meal. When they walked into a room, everyone fell all over themselves bowing and greeting them with a shout: *Osssh!* That was it: above all else, they got respect.

Percy followed the roar to the back room, where he slid the shoji door open as gently as he could and found the *sekitori*, all six-eight of him, lying on his stomach, resting on his elbows, his face locked on the TV. Percy had to wonder: would this be the humble, soft-spoken, and extremely generous giant, eager to talk story? Or would it be the brooding, moody monster?

Percy entered the room quietly, saying, "*Osssh!*"

The *sekitori* ignored him, so he waited. He wondered how anyone could be so interested in the yelling voices coming from the TV, where he could see a panel of Japanese celebrities laughing at some joke Percy had no hope of understanding. Though the guy's bulk took up much of the room, Percy, who shared a big tatami-mat room with fifteen other guys, envied him his privacy. His thoughts drifted again to the idea that Akebono had also started down at the bottom only four years earlier, and now here he was. Percy had watched the *sekitori* toy with John or Troy, both of whom could easily toy with Percy in the same way, approaching every bout like it was a foregone conclusion. Of course, he'd seen the *sekitori* on TV, the best in what to Percy was already proving to be a much more difficult sport than it appeared. This guy had *made it*—a fact that filled Percy with a deeper respect than he had for even his brother Kurt. And as Percy was wondering how Akebono had made it, the reason for his having been summoned was made clear with the *sekitori*'s soft request to take some money from his wallet, and go around the corner to McDonald's.

By now, Percy had felt the pain of having this 494-pound pure fighting machine charging into him with a blur of furious, blenderlike hand-thrusts to the head. He had felt his own giant body thrown into the training area's paneled wall. But above all, Percy had felt the purposeful pounding blows of the *kawaigari* beatings. And if it wasn't Boss standing over him with a bamboo stick or the aluminum bat, it was the *sekitori* beating him hard, shouting out in his deep baritone, "*Hayaku! Saigo, saigo!*" No doubt Percy could hear the voice in his sleep.

So he took the money and headed outside and down the street as quickly as he could, making sure to first ask Troy what the *sekitori* usually ordered, and how many of this or that he would have wanted. He'd seen Akebono crack one of the Japanese guys *just because*, and he was eager to get it right. Percy would have made sure to get more than Troy suggested, just in case, and maybe a few apple pies in case Akebono happened to have a sweet tooth. Whatever it was, it worked, because the next time the roar came, it was specifically for Percy.

EVEN BACK THEN PERCY WOULD HAVE BEEN able to boil down the interaction with the *sekitori* to a single word: respect. And though he may not have been able to say so in so many words beyond some abstraction of "local values," on some level he was beginning to see an important overlap between this ancient and ritual-defined subculture and the place where he had been raised. Back home you had aloha. You had respect. You had *mālama* for the *'aina*. If you were a farmer like Percy, your sense of respect was, ultimately, rooted in the land that fed you and the work it required from you at the direction of your strict mother and father. How far off was that, really, from this hierarchical world of sumo, where everyone was striving for the paid ranks, and for tournament victories where they actually paid you, in part, with rice? It was simpler than it looked, this adjustment thing, and once he was able to figure it out, Percy called home to thank his parents for having enforced his curfew straight up through high school, and before that, for not allowing him out at night without his sister. "Used to have one TV commercial," his father liked to say. "'Do you know where your kids are?' I thought, 'Oh me, my kids going stay *home.'"* The rules, the daily chores on the Kipapa family farm—Percy had to tell them how it was already helping him fit right in to sumo's strict daily routine.

It was only a couple of years after meeting Percy that I began to see the connection between Waikāne Valley—the land itself—and Percy's country values, and how those values came to help him so much on his Japanese adventure. Perce being Perce, that first long rainy afternoon we spent talking story had been enough to make us friends. When I met him in Tokyo a year and a half later he greeted me like we'd known each other for years, with a local-boy handshake and a big hug. We went out a couple of times when he wasn't busy filming the TV commercial he'd been flown up for, and my wife Noriko got to meet him when George Kalima had us all over for a barbecue. Noriko was about to quit her job as an ICU nurse, leave the apartment downstairs from the one where her parents lived, and move to Honolulu with me to learn to speak English and, eventually, work in an American hospital. George and Percy spent the afternoon drawing out her head-thrown-back, mouth-wide-open laugh, one moment trading funny local-guy-in-Japan anecdotes, the next comparing tales from their early days in sumo of we-can-laugh-about-it-now isolation and tear-filled daily calls home to their mothers.

Two months into our big move to Hawai'i, the only laughter I'd heard from Noriko—as much as I'd tried to reassure her and cheer her up along the way—had been that nervous and polite laugh she used around other people to mask the fact that she couldn't follow the conversation. And her calls home were nothing but tearful. She'd been trying to make the best of it—swimming at the beach every day, enrolling in courses in English as a second language at Kapi'olani Community College, volunteering at the Humane Society. But more and more I'd come home to find her climbing the walls with loneliness, her usual confidence gone. We'd go out to dinner and the tears would begin to roll down her face, brought on by the happy banter and laughter from the people at the tables all around us, babbling on in what to her may as well have been Swedish.

Then one day we ran into Percy, right in the parking lot at Waimānalo Shopping Center, his body jammed behind the wheel of an Oldsmobile Cutlass, a warm smile spread out below his thick glasses. We clasped hands, and Noriko reached down to hug him like a long-lost brother.

"It's been a while," he said to her in Japanese.

"It has, it has," she said, beaming.

"How's Hawai'i?" he asked. "I bet it's been tough adjusting." He was still smiling.

"Terrible!" she said. "I miss everybody, I'm alone all the time, and then I feel bad because I'm in such a beautiful place, but I still feel depressed."

"I bet you still cry every day," he said.

"Well, not every day," she said. "Maybe every other day."

"You're stronger than me!" he said, the eyes behind his glasses widening. "I used to cry every day, the whole first year I went to Japan." He shouted out a loud laugh.

And for the first time in two months I saw Noriko throw her head back, open her mouth wide, and let out her own joyful laughter. Though her exchange with Percy didn't seem like much, for weeks she'd been trying to draw on the experiences of Hawai'i's sumo brothers, knowing that they'd gone through far worse than what she was trying to deal with now. With his look of calm reassurance, his that's-just-how-it-is-when-you-move-away tone, Percy had done in an instant what I hadn't been able to do in two months: make Noriko believe she would eventually be fine. She wrote down Percy's number, and asked how to spell his sumo name.

"*Dai*, like in 'big,' and *ki*, like in 'happiness,'" he said, explaining the kanji characters for his sumo name, "Daiki."

Half a year later we were all heading over the mountains in that same Cutlass, a fully-adjusted Noriko in the back seat with Percy's girlfriend, and Percy and me in the front of what, given Percy's size, felt more like a Volkswagen Beetle. Percy had been the star of our wedding, going way out of his way to translate funny stories for both of our families, and sticking around deep into both of the after-parties. He'd often visited our apartment outside of Waikīkī whenever he was in the neighborhood. And after a while he became concerned that we'd been getting around Honolulu on our bikes since moving back from Japan. So one day he'd dropped by and told us to jump in with him—he had a decent running car at his parents' place in Waikāne Valley.

The thirty or so minutes it took to get over the Ko'olau mountains flew by, thanks to an unending flow of stories of growing up out in the country, each one punctuated by Percy's deep, infectious laugh: how he and his friends Charles and Shane had been allowed to drive a beat-up station wagon through the vast valley's deserted trails as thirteen-year-olds, or how they used to raise chickens and fight them against each other. Then he went on about his dream of buying a lunch wagon, going into great detail about what kinds of plate lunches he would make, and where he would park the wagon on which days. But when we turned up Kahekili Highway, he stopped in the middle of the story and pointed to the big green mountain way off in the distance outlined against the hazy afternoon sky, and took his stories almost reverently into the past, taking pride in how his mother's family had lived near the mountain since all the way back to the Great Mahele land division of the mid-nineteenth century. And for a while as we drove, the car we were coming to look at became an afterthought. What seemed more important to Percy all of a sudden was that he share his beautiful valley with us.

"Get this long trail all the way up the valley," he told us. "Up there is so quiet, so peaceful, no more concrete jungle, you can leave alladis world behind. Get one freshwata shtream, ice pond for swimming. You can eat alla the guava, lilikoi you like." Though I'd known Percy for over two years, only now did I begin to understand how rooted he was to "country." You could hear it in the way his voice changed when he started talking about Waikāne Valley. The valley was closer to downtown Honolulu than was the suburban area of Hawai'i Kai, but the Ko'olau mountains walled in Waikāne so completely that I was reminded more of the extreme isolation I'd felt when I was student teaching in Mākaha, way out at the end of the Wai'anae Coast, rather than of Hawai'i Kai's suburbia. "You can stay up there for days," he went on as we turned onto the dirt road at the mouth of the valley. "Anytime you like go up there, you let me know: the trail get one gate, and my family has the key."

He turned into a dusty driveway and parked in front of exactly what anyone would have expected to find up in Waikāne, or Waiāhole, or Kahana, or any number of valleys yet to be gentrified with McMansions and fake farms: a flock of clucking chickens and strutting roosters wandering around a post-and-pillar one-story house with a tin roof, well kept if rough around the edges. The carport was filled with the requisite washer and dryer, extra refrigerator, laundry hanging on a line strung from wall to wall just below the ceiling, centered by a folding table and folding metal chairs, all guarded by three poi dogs that came to check us out as we got out of the car.

"Lemme get my madda," was the first thing Percy said. "Ma!"

Tall palm hedges walled in the small yard, which had just been mown, and off in the far corner under a big fruit tree and blanketed with fallen leaves sat the maroon Chevy Corsica we'd come to look at.

A silver-haired Hawaiian woman stepped out of the house, a blue-print *muʻumuʻu* draped over her big body, and her face opened into one of the most welcoming expressions I'd ever seen. She looked like what Bruddah Waltah would have been picturing had he written a song called "Sweet Lady of Waikāne."

"Ma, these are my friends from Japan," Percy said.

She handed us two giant grapefruits from the tree, and leaned down to kiss each of us on the cheek. And there was no doubt that this was Percy's mother: behind her own thick glasses was an older, softer female version of his smiling face.

"Dis the guy writing that book I was telling you about," he told her, "the one about Akebono."

"I think Percy should have written it, though," I said. "He's a lot better than I am at telling stories, at putting in all the right details. He was the best source for the book—even better than Akebono."

She told us how proud she was of what Percy had done in Japan, and then she headed back into the house, inviting us to stop by any time we were in Waikāne. For a moment I felt like I'd gone back in time. Who, after all, paid attention to these little country rituals anymore? It was as though the world had passed this valley by, and as the roosters crowed and the sun began to sink behind the mountain, the image of Percy Ki-papa bantering away on national TV in fluent Japanese, his hair styled in a traditional samurai topknot, became all the more amazing. From *here* all the way to *there*? But then when I thought about it some more, I could see that except for the language part, thanks to his Waikāne farm Percy had brought along sumo's most prized set of values. Who paid attention to such rituals anymore? A lot of people in Japan did. Everyone in the Japan Sumo Association did. And perhaps more than anyone else, Akebono did.

The car story is a good one, but you'll come to see why it belongs in a later chapter. What matters here is that it brought me to a place I had no idea still existed. Even as vast tracts of former Leeward sugar plantations were being plowed into subdivisions packed full of buildings with the concrete sameness of military housing, here was a fertile country valley where people still grew their own food, twenty minutes from town. And when Percy pulled into the yard, that was the first thing he'd said—I can still hear him—"Lemme get my madda."

DURING HIS FIRST YEAR IN JAPAN, Percy drew on every ounce of his country-Hawaiian respect as he dealt not just with the *sekitori* but also with his *oyakata*, a word whose two kanji characters translate into a version of "father." This is appropriate enough in light of how a *sumo beya* is run, but even more so in the case of Azumazeki Oyakata, who quickly became one of those impossible-to-please father figures after gauging Percy's potential. Oyakata himself had gotten into sumo back on Maui as a way to rehabilitate his weak, long legs for football after a car accident. But Percy's body was almost perfect from the start, with most of the weight at the core and in the tops of the legs, meaning that from the beginning he'd have a tremendous amount of power for pushing forward. It was just that he was tall for sumo—a condition that Oyakata, who'd spent his own career chasing down smaller men and trying to keep them off his belt, understood well. Though a *sumōtori* can choose from over seventy winning techniques, and even more types of throws and pushes, there are basically only two types of sumo: one where you aim for a strong grip on the opponent's *mawashi* to either throw him down or steer him out, the other a violent open-handed pushing attack. Oyakata had groomed the top-heavy Akebono into perhaps the most fearsome pusher of all time. So along with pounding the aloha out of Percy, Boss was intent on eliminating the disadvantage of his height and grooming him into a pusher.

There was only one problem with this strategy: without his thick glasses, the world was a blur to Percy. When a *sumōtori* has a particularly good match that goes his way, invariably he'll say that he was able to do his "own sumo"—meaning he was the first out of the blocks, attained his favorite grip or hit with his first hand-thrust, had his feet moving well the whole time, and so on. The initial charge in sumo is one of the higher-stakes moments in sports, like the start of a fifty-meter dash, because whoever gets out best will more likely be able to do his own sumo, and whoever does not will usually find himself thrown into the crowd. Such moments require, above all, confidence, which is a big part of the reason behind sumo's relentless daily training regimen. Executing an open-hand-thrust to the throat of a slippery moving target is hard enough, but to do it in the moment of the initial charge, knowing how a loss will impact your place on the *banzuke* and thus your life, robbed by your poor eyesight of the confidence that the shot will land, is close to impossible. Still, Percy managed a 5–2 record in the March 1992 Ōsaka tournament. The rules were pretty simple: you fight seven times across fifteen days, and if you win more matches than you lose, you get promoted. If not, you go down. If you're hurt and can't compete, you go down. Only a handful of guys, it turned out, were realistically gunning for the overall tournament championship—the main thing was that you finished with a winning record. And when Percy did so again in Tokyo's summer tournament, he dutifully marched up to the *oyakata*'s apartment on the *beya*'s third floor, was led in to where he was watching television, and bowed, saying, *Okagesamade. Kachi-koshi shimashita*, or, with humble thanks to you I was able to finish with a winning record.

Percy's words of thanks were met with a remote control thrown at his head from across the room, and the raspy shout, "What kine sumo is that!" To reach his fourth win, Percy had resorted to using his weight and his power, wrapping up his opponent and calmly letting the guy tire before throwing him out. What he had not done was jump out at the charge with the pushing attack Boss had been trying to drill into him.

"When he first went up he had hard time," Percy's mother later said. "I told him, 'Come home already. Don't let them beat you up.' He said, 'No, I'm going try.' When he first went up I think Boss had his doubts. And some days, Percy really wanted to quit already."

"I could neva get the push down," Percy told me. "'Cause, see, I get bad eyes."

Another foreigner—perhaps one not raised in Hawai'i, and certainly not one raised by Priscilla and George Kipapa—would have tried to explain himself to Boss, or make some excuse about his poor vision, in effect telling a man with nearly thirty years experience how to do his job. But Percy reasoned that Oyakata knew what he was doing, and in any case, to open his mouth and say or even imply otherwise, as his father could have told him, would have been the height of disrespect. So he kept at it, doing as Boss said, trying to get the push down. "I don't think it's a good thing in a person's life to remember the bad things," Percy's father told me once. "It's good to be proud of the good things. Like her and I," he went on, referring to his wife, "we go to a party, guys come around, they always compliment about Kurt, Percy, Selisa. They tell you, 'You know, you get *good kids*.'"

Kurt and Selisa have a story that helps explain why this is so. "I was just a teenager, just getting into those young punk years," Kurt told me. "We were all sitting around the dinner table and I started grumbling about the food." They were eating spaghetti. Again. And Mr. Young Football Star had had enough of eating the same meal again and again.

"He had one big bush," Selisa recalled with a laugh, of her brother's seventies-style afro. Percy would have been about four or five, looking across the table at his brother, whose hair could just barely be stuffed into a football helmet. As Kurt went on complaining, Percy may even have looked down at his own plate of food and wondered why they always ate the same thing. He may have thought to follow his brother's example, and to join in with his own complaint.

But out of nowhere, another full plate of spaghetti came flying across the table, hitting Kurt squarely on the head before falling to the ground with a *crash*, leaving strings of noodles in that big black bush of an afro, red sauce dripping down Kurt's shocked face. Without a word, Percy's father had picked up his own plate of spaghetti and nailed Kurt in the face with it.

Kurt wiped his face, lifted his fork, looked down, and began to eat, a plate's worth of stringy spaghetti clinging to his hair. In his own state of shock, Percy quietly followed suit.

"Kurt ate all the spaghetti that was on his plate," Mr. Kipapa recalled.

"He look up at my fadda," Selisa said, "he figga he betta finish his plate, ah? 'He just gave up his spaghetti, I ain't givin' up mine. That was *your* share.'"

"My share is *gone* already!" Mr. Kipapa said with a laugh. And then he thought for a moment and explained it to me, a lesson in the part that violence sometimes plays in local Hawai'i culture: "Mark, I'm very sorry that happened, but he just catch me on a bad day. I got tired listening to that kine. And I think to myself, 'Eh, if I could afford it, yeah, I would ask you what you would like to eat, like you were in a restaurant.' But I'm not over there cooking 'um—*she* ova there cooking 'um. And I don't think she like go out of her way, cook four-five different stuff. She like make one simple dish and that's it. And the rule is, you just eat whateva you got in the front of your face. You don't like eat, yeah, stand up and walk away."

Though the discipline wasn't always handed out so suddenly, Percy's parents were legendary in their efforts to raise *good kids*, and most of those efforts were rooted to the land Percy had been so eager to show me. Charles, who now runs his own one-man masonry company on the Big Island, looks back with a smile on the way that farm work always seemed to be mixed into the fun he'd had with Percy as a child. "They had to feed the ducks—they used to have choke ducks—from the fifty-five-gallon drums," he recalled. "They always had animals they had to feed or clean. From my house in Waikāne, you cross the riva, you go ova this patch—it's called no-man's-land—you go up this hill, and when you come across the field, his house was up there. So I would go through my backyard to meet him up there, or he would come down. And we loved chickens," he said with a smile. "We always gathering roosters. The other thing strict was that his madda wouldn't let him sleep ova your house."

"We had to teach them responsibility," Mrs. Kipapa said. When she and her husband came home from work, "when we had only Kurt, he betta be in the property or he's in trouble. Then we had the odda two," Percy and his sister, Selisa. "We had goats, we had pigs—that was their chores every day. They had to come home from school, do their homework, do their chores. Their friends would tell them come over. 'No, you come ova!' They used to come here, just to keep them busy so they wouldn't get into mischief. On the weekends Shane and Charles would sleep ova, pup tent, and they would have good fun." She then added that once Kurt got older, he "would pull a whole row of weeds before he go to Pounders, go swimming, catch surf. His friends would help him so they could go. As long as he does his chores first, he can go."

Kurt, now a huge man with a diamond stud in each ear, a gold chain necklace shining out from skin darkened by his work for the City and County Parks Department, will follow his stories of fresh vegetables and fruits, clear mountain streams where he used to catch fresh *o'opu*, with this:

"I had to clean taro patch, brah, and I'm not talkin' about wetlands—I'm talking dry land taro. It's different. Dry land is straight from the ground. You gotta dig every weed—you cannot just break the top of the green, or that thing would grow up again. And when I was young, you act up, you get cracks. Work was work—you *work*."

Shane, who now supervises Big Island concrete pours, grew up working just as hard on a nearby twenty-acre farm about half owned by his family and half leased. "We had corn, watermelons, zucchini, string beans, alladat," he told me. The family even harvested prawns from two acres of man-made ponds on a low-lying edge of the property. "At that time we made a lot of money with vegetables," he went on. "We could live, even if my dad didn't work. We sold the produce at Ala Moana. And the corn—we'd sell 'um by the side of the road with Charles and Percy, right by Sweet Lady of Waiāhole. All the corn, all the watermelon, that was our money—we had our own acre. You put up sweet corn, was gone in like two hours. Back then you neva need go supermarket—you just go by the vegetable stands."

You respected the land because the land provided for you—that lesson was drilled home even further when they started going to Waiāhole School. "Even Percy sick," Mrs. Kipapa recalled, "he don't stay home—he *wanna go to school*." (Her husband has a stack of Percy's perfect attendance awards from Waiāhole Elementary School stretching from kindergarten to sixth grade to prove it.) "That school used to win every year for most beautiful school in the islands," Shane said. When the subject came up in our interview he dug up the one-hundred-year history of the school, written when he and Percy were in fourth grade, and flipped through its pages of black-and-white photos, interviews with former teachers and students, student-written poetry, and snippets of school history that paint the place as a distant outpost far out in the country. "Corn," he went on, pointing to a photo of some smiling kids among the towering stalks. "Waiāhole School was a farming school, 'cause it was a farming community. Our science class was real farming. We could grow all kinds of vegetables. 'Cause we had the land, ah?"

Sometimes the boys found the land providing for them in ways their teachers or parents never would have expected. "It was just typical boys growing up in the country," Shane said. "We used to camp, hunt. We used to come across rations," he said with a smile, left by the U.S. Marines who used the valley for jungle training. "They used to leave on the weekends," Shane went on, "and they would hide their rations in certain areas. But you could see the dirt all dug up, so whereva get fresh dirt, me and Percy and Charles would take out the rations, eat 'um, go swimming. Our parents would wonder how we get lunch, ah? In those days it was the good rations, too."

"Country," Charles said. "Was paradise. Because the trees was overgrown through the roads more, and had a lot less houses. And we was tight in this community 'cause we all went to this one school, Waiāhole, and we neva wear slippa, nothing. When we came home, we always had the riva, so we would meet and travel through the mountains and up to the flats, and you know, just walk through the mountain and play and throw rocks and swim. We almost had this whole mountain to ourselves." *Paradise* is the word that Charles now uses, the time and distance now having given him the perspective to really see the value of the nearly three-thousand acres stretching out from behind the little house where he used to help his friend Percy feed his ducks and goats. At first they'd just thought of it as their "playground." But it had only taken Percy a few nights on that cold, hard tatami-mat floor in cramped and gray Tokyo—a city roughly the size of Oʻahu but housing some forty times as many people—to begin to see that the valley hadn't just entertained him or provided for him. It wasn't just that it was such a beautiful place. It was more that Waikāne had shaped him into a man steeped in the local values of his ancestors.

Percy quickly came to fight as hard against the pull of such a place as he did against the hazing, the cold, and the loneliness brought on by his inability to communicate with nearly everyone. Of course his dreams of "making it" kept him from going home, as did his wish to make his family proud. But more important, Percy had been ingrained with something that would not allow him to give up easily. In Japanese they had a word for it, this put-your-head-down-and-deal-with-it way of enduring some kid's slaps to your head, or of picking your aching body up off the futon in the morning for another four-hour beating in the ring. The word was *gaman*. As he lay alone at night in that roomful of big Japanese boys babbling away with one another in those moments before going off to sleep, Percy would have thought about the word *gaman*. It would not have taken him long to try to relate it to something he could understand, and among the first images to come into his mind would have been that of his grandfather, Manuel Roberts, a man he had never met.

Stories from Percy's Grandma Roberts, from his mother and father, from his Uncle Henry Roberts, painted the man as a family legend. Percy's own towering build could be traced to the powerful bull of a man known for literally working from sunup to sundown every day of his life. Sumo may have been harder work than Percy had ever thought possible, but how could it compare to cultivating nearly sixty acres of Waikāne Valley almost single-handedly, as his grandfather had done? How could learning a few words in Japanese compare to fighting nearly thirty years to keep teams of lawyers from grabbing that land? What was some sumo *senpai-kōhai* struggle when compared to standing up to the U.S. Marines?

"The marines used to come up here," was the way his mother always told it—"up here" meaning Grandpa's Hill, where the man's farm used to sit back in the valley, not far from where the military had begun to practice jungle training just after Pearl Harbor. "When we were kids, we used to go up there and swim and stuff and we used to find the torpedoes," she would say. "One day my brothers came home, they looked *so* scared. My brother Jerry, he found two torpedoes, and he was bangin' 'em like this. My oldest brother, he knew about this kine stuff, 'cause one of his friends got killed in the Japanee war with one of the bombs. So my brother threw the torpedo and one *big* tree split in half. They could have all died that day. God was with them."

"We had cucumbas," Percy's mother's story went. "We go in the morning, we harvest only a few cucumbas, but we find a mayonnaise jar! But you know, in the meantime my father used to go up there and give them bananas that we harvest. And then they steal from us! So my dad told the C.O., 'You know, your men been eating my harvest. That's my livelihood.' They gather everybody: nobody ate." Percy's grandpa then looked down dejectedly, as Percy's mother told it, and said, "Whoever ate 'um, I'm *so* sorry." He paused dramatically and then said, "We sprayed something on the vegetables. If you eat 'um before twenty-four hours, you might die. It's insecticide." Percy's mother always finished the story with this: "Two trucks went down to the marine base to pump their stomachs! 'Whoever ate 'um, I'm *so* sorry.'"

"We used to work up there and they used to shoot over our heads," Uncle Henry would tell Percy. "*Right over us.* My dad used to jump on the tractor, drive up there, and tell them guys, 'You know what: *bullshit*. Stop this shit.' He would call the base: 'I'm farming up here.' 'Oh, but we're firing.' He said, 'I don't give a damn about your firing. I get crops that I gotta harvest.' So then they'd fire when we're not up there. It's crazy. You could feel the thing: boom! You know one night I was sleeping and the thing started to bother me and I thought, 'How can McCandless give the government permission to use the land for bombing when it's *kuleana* land?'"

Uncle Henry was talking about a haole land-grabber named Lincoln McCandless, the man who had sued in State Land Court to claim hundreds of acres of small Waikāne farms so that he could divert most of the precious Waiāhole-Waikāne water to Oʻahu's Leeward sugar plantations just after the turn of the century. Percy's mother had explained that the Roberts family had acquired what was called a *kuleana* land claim of nearly sixty acres way back in the nineteenth century, after the Great Mahele brought the concept of private landownership to Hawaiʻi. (Uncle Henry could trace the family's valley roots back further, claiming that King's Grant Map of Kamehameha III proved that his great-great grandmother—an herbal healer for the king's guards—had been awarded an even larger claim.) But the *mahele* had turned Hawaiʻi's sweeping green valleys from places that were used communally into places that were owned, and thus could be acquired. McCandless took advantage, piling up more than thirty-five thousand acres between his arrival in Hawaiʻi just after the *mahele* and his death in 1940. Just over a year later, his daughter Elizabeth McCandless Marks began leasing the valley to the U.S. military as part of the Waikāne Training Facility. The lease money—even along with the untold wealth that the Waiāhole Water Ditch had already poured into her pockets—would not satisfy Marks. Her husband, Lester Marks, rode up to Grandpa's Hill on a horse one day just to tell the Roberts family he was going to have the court evict them from their own *kuleana* land.

Grandpa's response became legendary: "You go right ahead," he said from high up on the seat of his tractor. "I'll slit you from ear to ear, you greedy man. You like take Hawaiian land? You're gonna have a miserable life."

Had Percy known how thoroughly the deck had been stacked against his grandfather in the ensuing fight for the family's land, *gaman*ing through some *senpai-kōhai* incident with Tsuji would have seemed easy by compar-

ison. According to the former University of Hawai'i ethnic studies professor Pete Thompson, McCandless himself had gotten the Land Court
system passed through the Territorial Senate in 1903, ensuring that the
process was just expensive enough to freeze out the area's native Hawaiian
families, and loading it with procedures posted in city newspapers that
only reached the rural Windward side once a month, long after important
deadlines had passed. "The exact details of how McCandless got his land
will probably never be fully known," Thompson wrote in 1973, the year
Percy was born, "but there are people still living who distinctly remember
that at one time large portions of the McCandless Estate properties belonged to them and their 'ohana." Percy didn't know exactly how these land
grabs happened, but he knew that they did happen, and that his grandpa
had spent a lifetime fighting against them to keep the farm intact. And
when Percy struggled to tell his new Japanese sumo brothers that he was
from Waikāne, he said it with pride, knowing that he was rooted to the
land, all the way back to the *mahele*, all thanks to Manuel Roberts.

"My fadda-in-law, he'd just sit down, somehow he'd kind of say things
that make *sense*," Percy's father would say. "Eh, he wasn't a guy that graduated from high school, but that guy had a mind—he was like a genius. He
was smarter than some of the lawyers. He went toe-to-toe not with one
lawyer, not with two, but with seven."

"He fought with the McCandless Estate for twenty-eight years, and
he won," Percy's mother would say. "Now Roberts and Ewelika are the
only *kuleana* claims left."

"My dad," Uncle Henry would say, "in Hawaiian history, he was the
first one that eva fought one haole under *their* law, and *won*."

☾   ☾   ☾

IF *GAMAN* WAS INGRAINED IN PERCY, it wasn't just because of the memory of his grandfather. He had in fact been born into an ongoing narrative
of people who refused to give up. Even if his "I like quit, I no like quit"
dilemma had already begun to pick its way into his thoughts, the dilemma
itself would have been forcing him to *gaman*, since "I like quit" means "I
want to go home," but "I no like quit" means that the narrative of where
I come from won't let me. Uncle Henry would pick up that narrative not

long after Percy's grandfather passed away when the suburban development spreading from the south in Kāneʻohe all at once descended upon the Windward valleys in the year Percy was born.

"I was up there making my farm," Uncle Henry said. "I raise prawns. And this guy came up there seven o'clock in the morning, and he said, 'Henry, we need your help.' I said, 'What happened?' He said, 'Windward Partners is gonna develop Waikāne. We gotta put one stop to this.' So I jumped in his truck, we came down, we went to Waiāhole School, we met in the cafeteria, we found out what they was gonna do. And then couple days later we saw that they had a big tent over there on the side of the road—they was already selling the property. So from 1973 we fought them, until today we *still* fighting them."

Windward Partners was the culmination of a marriage of convenience between the McCandless Estate and a developer named Joe Pao, whose connections extended from Oʻahu's largest landholders (Amfac, Bishop Estate, etc.) to the State Land Use Commission, deep into the office of prodevelopment governor John Burns. Pao had already achieved some notoriety for such poststatehood residential subdivisions as Kailua Heights, Pearl Harbor Heights, and Enchanted Lakes—the neighborhood he built on reclaimed Kailua wetlands that housed, among others, the City and County's planning director, its managing director, the chairman of its planning commission, and Pao's close friend Neal Blaisdell, mayor of Honolulu. Pao—whom the *Hawaiʻi Observer* quoted as envisioning not merely one new freeway, the H-3, but also an H-4 freeway to run from Kailua through Mānoa Valley—sought to subdivide the entire island. "Agriculture should be on the Neighbor Islands," he told the *Observer*. "Industry is taking over on Oʻahu. It should be all residential."

"I neva forget that morning," Uncle Henry told me many years later. "I was busy up there, finishing my prawn farm, when Thompson and Nakata came. They said, 'Mr. Roberts, we need your help—you're a landowner.' I said 'Okay, I'll talk to my brother.' And my brother Arnold, he was a kind of hard nut to talk to, so I said, 'Eh, brah, we gotta go help them *guys*. You don't want them to just put one big damn house in this property right here, and all this kind of people over here—you going get ripped off when you're not home. We gotta *stop* 'em.' And I told alla them guys in the beginning, I said, 'Instead of going down the beach, *picnic*, and *bowling*, and alladis kine *bullshit*, go clean up the land, go plant banana tree, go plant fruit tree, so when the people come, they say, ho these people get their lifestyle.' And that was how this thing got started. Bob Nakata was the guy."

Henry Roberts was talking about a soft-spoken Kahaluʻu Methodist minister named Bob Nakata, who, the second time I spoke to him, told me, "You're telling the story of the community." I'd come across his name while researching a community event that impacts Percy's story much later, and I asked to meet with him about it. Then I began seeing his name connected to every significant happening in Percy's valley, either in his capacity as a state senator, or on the State Water Board, or at the Kahaluʻu KEY Project Community Center where Percy took kung-fu lessons as a boy, or simply as the wizened community leader he has since become. Whenever some momentous history-altering event would be happening in the foreground, there would be Bob Nakata somewhere in the background helping to orchestrate the opposition. It was a style of leadership that resonated completely with the humble country values that Percy had grown up with. So when Percy's internal conflict about whether to stay in Japan emerged as the story most in need of telling, I knew I had to talk with Bob again. "You're telling the story of the community," was his assessment of my progress.

"Have you read the book *The Tattoo*?" he asked me, referring to local novelist Chris McKinney's troubling look at the Windward side. Bob, in his early sixties but looking a good ten years younger in a graying goatee and frameless glasses, was busy working on Oʻahu's growing homeless problem, the fight against the planned construction of five new North Shore hotel towers, and several other community projects that filled the boxes of overflowing files piled around his office floor. "That book actually is a backdrop to Percy and what happened to him. What struck me about the book was that sense of extreme isolation: you know, the Koʻolaus on one side and the ocean on the other, just such a *small* area, and anything outside of that felt like foreign territory. That's the tone I got from the book, and I think it's highly accurate." Set mostly in the small towns book-ending Percy's valley, *The Tattoo* looks hard at local-boy loyalties, and paints the stereotypical scrap-for-what-you-like, fuckin'-haole attitude as a direct effect of colonization—of constant pressure from the "outside."

Bob then went on to discuss the relentless encroachment of that "foreign territory" into the traditional country life he had grown up living on his father's Kahaluʻu taro farm, the kind of life that Manuel Roberts tried to protect and that Percy cried himself to sleep missing when he was in Japan. In the year Percy was born, Bob was tapped by community leaders to help develop a grassroots plan to stop Windward suburban development. "When I got to the community meeting at Waiāhole School—you know, I was asking for ten or a dozen people to talk with. Well, there were about twenty-five people there." Those gathered included all of the prominent local tenant farmers leasing McCandless Estate land, as well as landowners like Percy's uncles and his parents. "They said, 'What's going on? We've seen these limousines coming up and down this place, and there's this guy coming around interviewing us.'" Bob explained to the crowd that he had found a letter from Elizabeth McCandless Marks at the State Land Use Commission describing a massive development project. The Windward valleys were to look like Kaimukī, where thousands of spec homes were crowded onto six-thousand-square-foot lots. The interviews were being conducted for the project's Environmental Impact Statement. Immediately after the meeting, Waiāhole *kuleana* landowner Bobby Fernandez got word to the farmers in his valley, and Percy's uncle Arnold set out on horseback to inform everyone in Waikāne about an April meeting that Bob Nakata called to formulate a response. "And I swear," Bob recalled, "almost the entire adult population of those two valleys came to that meeting—about 250 people." The meeting gave birth to the Waiāhole-Waikāne Community Association, headed by Bobby Fernandez with Henry Roberts as his vice president. Words like "movement," "struggle," and "protest" fail to convey what these people undertook in deciding to stand up to the McCandless Estate and to the political establishment of development-addicted "New Hawaiʻi" represented by Joe Pao. Against tremendous odds, otherwise powerless people risked their subsistence farms, their livelihoods, the land of their ancestors. "We knew that the evictions were not just a threat," Bob said, "but that there were detailed plans in place," including warehouses for condemned possessions and even housing for the valley's children once they were seized by Child Protective Services. So when the words were spoken at one of the steering committee meetings, Bob recalls, they were as real as if someone had said them during wartime: "We're in a fight for our lives."

The association fought for the next two years, and the struggle culminated in a protest that blocked Kamehameha Highway for hours. Days before forced evictions were to be carried out, a number of forces converged to persuade Governor George Ariyoshi to meet with Elizabeth Marks, and the basis for a deal was struck: the state would buy six hundred acres from Marks. Just as Percy's grandfather had stood up to the McCandless Estate's dream team of lawyers, this simple community of local farmers, along with the help they attracted from such places as Legal Aid Hawai'i and the UH Ethnic Studies Department, beat three of the four biggest threats to common local land use: the colonial land grabber, the "New Hawai'i" suburban developer, and the entrenched careerist politician. Indeed, the same George Ariyoshi who had routinely entered into deals on real estate that he had the power to rezone and then resell at a tremendous profit was now standing against development. "It's still by far the best organizing I've ever seen in Hawai'i," Bob Nakata now says, deferring all of the credit to the actual stakeholders.

In listening to Bob explain the story of the struggle, I felt for a moment a sense of relief that the valleys had been spared—that Percy, Shane, and Charles had been allowed to grow up as their parents had. But those boxes overflowing with paper piled around Bob's office floor suggested to me that the story hadn't ended with the defeat of Joe Pao. If it had, Percy would not have had to tell his version of it from seven thousand miles away in the language of the men who were, at the very moment he struggled to make himself understood, working to carpet Grandpa's Hill with smooth Bermuda green fairways.

CHAPTER 3

HONOR

The Japanese culture, through sumo—it's so deep that it brings stuff out in you that you never knew you had. It's incredible the way they break you down and make you not want to give up, ever. And then you can see just a glimmer of their culture, the type of people that they are, the way they live, the way they keep their culture alive. We were lucky to be involved with their national sport. You can see the pride of Japan is a deep, deep emotion to always strive and never give up.

—Tyler Hopkins, September 22, 2006

The image struck Percy whenever he looked at the *sekitori*, in some ways just another big local guy with a warm, round Hawaiian face. Or Troy, another Samoan face from the Farrington High defensive line. What Percy noticed most around the local boys—even more than how at ease they all were in what to him was still such a strange language—was the tops of their heads. George and Bumbo were two guys Percy could have found on any football field back in Hawai'i. Except that in place of scratched and dented Kaiser High helmets they wore tightly twisted black topknots tied at the back and bent forward into sharp points over their prominent foreheads. These knots combined with their kimono to make them look even more Japanese, in a way, than the modern-day suit-wearing Japanese themselves. There was no doubt about it: these were real *sumōtori*. They were samurai.

Like anyone new to sumo, Percy could already see the sport as a cultural symbol linking the Japan of salarymen, bright lights, and electronic gadgets to a mythic version of a proud past, as rich in its own symbols as in the measured rituals preceding each bout, each tournament, each significant promotion and retirement. If he looked up when he stepped onto the *dohyō* in the Kokugikan—the hall of national sport—he would have seen that he was standing under a wooden Shinto-shrine-like roof that hung from the rafters, calling back to the days when *sumōtori* faced off outdoors, usually on the grounds of shrines themselves and often in conjunction with some kind of religious harvest or planting festival. He would have noticed that the referee scampering around the ring was outfitted like a Shinto priest. And later in his career he would see the *yokozuna* bless the ring wearing a rope adorned with five strips of folded paper—a homonym for "god" in Japanese—modeled on the rope stretched above the gates to Shinto shrines across Japan. As part of the prebout ritual, he would spread salt, the Shinto purification symbol, across the ring, which itself is blessed in a solemn ceremony two days prior to each tournament before ten thousand empty seats. And before charging at his opponent, he would hold his arms out to their full span—according to instructions passed down through generations—to indicate that he was an honorable man fighting without weapons.

None of this really mattered to Percy. Beyond the *banzuke*—the ranking sheet that defined their daily lives in ways that mean more to them literally than symbolically—the symbol that mattered most was the long hair, combed out and then oiled and sculpted into a style that hasn't changed in hundreds of years. Regardless of how far he rises, every *sumōtori* looks back on the day the topknot is tied as one of the proudest of his career. If he's a big guy, the size that to this point in famously conformist Japan has only drawn laughter and constant ridicule becomes a mark of honor. The topknot puts him in a special brotherhood that perpetuates the best of how the Japanese like to think of themselves: as disciplined fighters, as members of a strong and honorable nation, as people who practice relentlessly to perfect the smallest detail and who strive in the face of adversity to be the best. Even if the *sumōtori* has no hope of reaching the paid ranks, he is an *o-sumo-san*, which, as Percy once explained, is different from being a *rikishi*, as *sumōtori* are more commonly called. Percy had brought along a big friend from Takasago Beya to a bar in the Ebisu neighborhood one night in 2000, and I asked the guy how he'd done in the just-finished summer tournament. Percy interrupted to say it didn't matter, that an *o-*

sumo-san honored the sport by remaining a part of it long after his chances at becoming a *sekitori* had passed, teaching his younger stable-mates *sumodo*—the sumo code. Percy seemed to consider him more honorable than even the well-paid and well-known *sekitori*, who were separated too far by rank to ever speak much with the kind of rookies who most needed their instruction. Though no one in the crowded bar recognized this big *o-sumo-san* as anyone famous, the energy around us suggested that the topknot alone marked him as important. Just looking at it was enough to evoke for me one of sumo's more dramatic scenes—the tightly scripted retirement ceremony where men take turns mounting the *dohyō* (or a hotel ballroom stage, for lower-rankers), humbly receiving the gold-plated scissors from the referee, and taking a solemn cut at the retiree's topknot, until the *oyakata* makes the final cut, sending everyone into tears. When it's all over, the topknot is encased in a glass box and put on display the way a proud soldier might display his medals with a portrait of himself in his dress uniform, as Percy's was when I first met him that rainy day in Waimānalo.

"Sumo wrestlers, they look at us as the Lion King of everybody," he was telling me back then. "We the best of the best. I tell you, before I cut my hair, I was getting a lot of chicks." He shouted out a big laugh. "After that, no more. We used to go to discos—every ten minutes we could go home with somebody. Life was easy with the hair." The hair. Walk into a noodle shop in the Tokyo district of Ryogoku and sit among the slurping salarymen, and chances are that you'll see a big kimono-clad, topknotted *sumōtori* among them, and suddenly you're connected to Japan's past in the same way you would be caught between the bustling present and ancient Hawai'i deep in the Makiki *ahupua'a*, where you can stand beside the original rock wall of a working ancient *lo'i* farm and look out over Honolulu's urban sprawl.

Back when Percy was standing in front of an Azumazeki Beya mirror measuring out his growing hair, the idea of a non-Japanese competing in the national sport was still something new—if not insulting—to many Japanese, who had tolerated Azumazeki Oyakata's long career as an aberration rather than a Jackie Robinson–like opening of a door. Today sumo's top division may be clogged with foreigners from Mongolia and Eastern Europe, but this was 1992, when the Japan Sumo Association's failure to promote Oʻahu's Konishiki to the top rank became an international incident. (The association explained that the outspoken American lacked *hinkaku*—a strict kind of dignity said to be available only to Japanese.) Konishiki's heaviest rumbles came during Percy's very first year in Japan. A year later, Akebono became the first foreign *yokozuna*. And when in 1994 Oʻahu's Musashimaru scored sumo's first perfect 15–0 tournament win in five years, the association quietly enacted a ban on recruiting any more foreigners that would not be relaxed for another four years.

Right in the middle of all of this, when the paparazzi would lurk around every corner in hopes of catching one of the foreigners even remotely violating sumo's strict behavioral codes, Percy became what he considered a real *sumōtori*. It was September 8, 1992, when the Azumazeki Beya hair stylist was finally able to comb Percy's long hair down past his nose, soak it with sweet-smelling oil, tie it with white stiffened string, and fold it over Percy's forehead. He stood proudly in a long line stretching back to all of the men who had pounded their bare feet into the hard clay back into the late eighteenth century when sumo began to take on its current structure, and even beyond that, deeper into the peaceful Edo period, when out-of-work samurai put down their swords and began to compete with each other in street-side grappling matches to make a living. (This might have been where sumo's now-symbolic "no weapons" gesture originated.) When cultural distinctions were being pulled out to argue against the idea of foreigners even competing in sumo at all, Percy Kipapa from deep in Waikāne Valley could look into the mirror and see a topknotted man connected all the way to the two Japanese gods who grappled on the shores of Izumo to win control of Japan for a line of deities extending down to the current emperor.

What Percy felt now as he looked into the mirror was a deep sense of honor. He had the topknot just like the Kalima boys, just like his *senpai* Troy. Though still far, far down the *banzuke*, he was now visibly very much like even the *sekitori*. Percy had spent his brief lifetime looking up to his brother Kurt, and doing all he could to gain his big brother's approval. But the *sekitori*—Percy watched what Akebono did during practice, heard even the top-division guys respectfully greet him in the changing room at the tournaments, and saw him run through one opponent after the next with his mean slap to the head, right hand to the throat, push into the crowd.

And then there was Boss. He'd come here all by himself, nearly thirty years earlier, and look what *he'd* done. Look at the aura that descended over the practice area when he walked in, the hard charges that would follow for the rest of the morning. And Percy Kipapa—all the way from reaching into a fifty-five-gallon barrel for fists full of chicken feed, the roosters crowing at his feet—had come to follow Jesse, Konishiki, Akebono.

Two weeks later, he wanted nothing more than to go home. Long before songwriter John Cruz had immortalized the Hawaiian grandma in his local-boy anthem "Island Style," the epicenter of Percy's life had been Grandma Roberts. She had once brought Percy a coffee can filled with coins and given it to him without a word. Percy, she knew, looked up to his grown-up brother more like an uncle, and he used to watch in envy as Kurt would dump his loose change onto the table, separate out all the silver from the pennies, scoop up all the silver, and leave the pennies for Percy. The coffee can Grandma Roberts brought for him was filled with silver coins. From small-kid time, Percy had been taught to look for Grandma the moment the Kipapas arrived at any big family party. The car door would open, and out he would run, past his cousins, past the food table, to wherever Grandma was sitting so he could greet her with a kiss. However informal it may have looked, the ritual would always unfold the same way, as important and as choreographed as much of the sumo protocol he was now learning: kiss Grandma, then go down the line kissing all the aunties and hugging all the uncles. Other arriving kids would then run off and play, or make a plate of food, but not Percy. Although his mother always made a point to feed the big Kipapa kids just before going to such gatherings so they wouldn't shame themselves by attacking the buffet line, even had Percy's belly been rumbling he likely would have gone straight back to Grandma to see if she needed anything to eat or drink, or just to sit with her and listen to her stories. And then in mid-September, just at the start of Tokyo's fall tournament, Percy had begun to worry about Grandma, feeling in his bones that something had happened to her. He called home, but his parents had nothing to tell him. As it turned out, they were hiding some terrible news for fear of distracting him during the important tournament. They waited a week, until he had achieved his winning record, to finally tell him: Grandma Roberts had passed away.

"Ma, you hurt me so much, you neva tell me," his mother recalled him saying. She tried to explain why they had waited to tell him, but none of it did anything to make him feel any better, or any less far away from home. He was so distracted that his next opponent blew him straight off the *dohyō* and, as luck would have it, onto the lap of Azumazeki Oyakata, who was sitting beside the ring as a judge that day. Later, Percy took it upon himself to climb to the third floor and apologize to Boss and to let him know what was happening in his troubled head.

To his surprise, he found Boss to be sympathetic—though the fact that Percy was, after all, talking to another Hawaiian about the passing of his grandmother surely had something to do with the uncharacteristic reaction. Boss took the poignant moment to educate Percy about the kinds of cultural realities that keep Japanese baseball players from witnessing the births of their own children or attending the funerals of their own parents even if they're held only blocks away from Tokyo Dome. Sumo, with its long samurai history, was even worse. Boss told him of all the funerals and weddings he had missed over the years. He spoke of the day he'd spent as a young, homesick low-ranker riding Tokyo's circular Yamanote train line as it looped around the city for hours, wondering why he had ever come to Japan in the first place, and how it was then that he'd learned that one had to either choose the world or choose to devote oneself to sumo.

Percy thought about this for a moment, weighing the many vivid images of his loving family, of his deep green valley, against that of the *sekitori's* white practice *mawashi*. He told Boss that, given the choice, he would take sumo, and he would try his best.

He then walked downstairs and immediately called home to put his mother at ease, feeling a bit guilty over how he'd reacted to the news over the phone. He told her about his talk with Boss, and how one had to give up some things to do sumo.

"You did good," Percy's mother told him. "I'm proud of you."

And just as he hung up the phone, he jumped at the sound of the roar coming from the back room and ran to see what the *sekitori* wanted.

☾　☾　☾

THE NEW HAIRSTYLE DID NOT HELP PERCY much in the ring. Every one of the local *sumōtori* who'd come before him may have shown how a big eighteen-year-old guy fighting against the alternately scrawny and oafish fifteen-year-olds could march straight through at least to the top of *sandanme*—sumo's third division. The ones who wound up hitting roadblocks did so much higher up the *banzuke*. But Percy kept putting up a meager four wins per tournament. "For my first year and a half, everybody was in *makushita*," he told me, speaking of the Kalimas, Troy, Tyler, and two other Takasago Beya foreigners, Eric "Fats" Gaspar and Kaleo Kekauoha. "I was the only foreigner in *jonidan* [the second division] at that time. I felt so bad I wanted for quit." Though his winning records did eventually put him in *sandanme*, he debuted at that rank with his first loss, finishing 3–4. Whether it was the usual homesickness or his *oyakata*'s insistence on a technique he had trouble adjusting to, either way it didn't make sense. Percy's 4–3 trend stretched into 1993, and it dropped to a disappointing 2–5 finish in July's Nagoya tournament.

Things only got worse when he found himself behind the wheel of the car owned by Troy's girlfriend. Percy's *senpai* and the young woman sat in the back seat as they cruised around Nagoya. His first time driving on the left side of the road, sitting in the right side of the car, Percy found himself approaching a parked car on the side of a road as narrow as one of the Waikāne jungle trails where he and his boys had grazed the trees on both sides with a beat-up station wagon they'd been allowed to drive around back in the King Zoo days. This time Percy misjudged the space to pass—*See, I get bad eyes, so*—and wound up clipping the car's mirror.

"And then me," Troy recalled, "like one idiot, like one AKA *gangsta*, I told Percy fo' keep on going."

Not doubting the word of his *senpai*, perhaps already afraid of what Boss might do if they were to get caught and wind up in the news— Foreign *Sumōtori* in Car Accident!—Percy hit the gas and flew as fast as he could back to Azumazeki's Nagoya stable.

"You know I was on the phone," Fats told me, "you know the pay phones they get in Japan, the green phones. I heard one car screeching, brah, like picking up speed, taking the turn. I guess Percy was driving. Ho, he wen' pound one *mean right turn*."

As if things couldn't get any worse, Percy pulled up in front of Azumazeki Beya to find that the car he'd hit was right behind him. Worse still, it was a police car.

"I said to Percy," Troy went on, "'You betta tell 'em that eh, only you was in this vehicle. I neva like none o' *this*.' And then Percy was saying, 'Yeah, 'cause you know what, we all gonna get busted.'" Percy must have thought of all that Troy had done in helping him through his first lonely months in Tokyo, and he must have thought back to his blood-brother days with Shane and Charles, *we going die togedda*. Percy was no rat. No way Percy was going rat somebody out. "And I don't know how they neva see one five hundred pounda sneak outada passenger's seat and walk straight into the stable," Troy went on. "And then they neva seen my girlfriend—we all wen' sneak. I couldn't believe they neva seen none of us. So when the cops came, Boss came out, ho, he was *fuming*. I felt bad, but. And you know what was the good thing about Percy? He was a man of his word. He took 'um by himself, brah. He took 'um like a *man*. So I knew Percy was one bradda. Even when I told him 'Go!' he neva hesitated, neva questioned my word."

"P went eat that one," Fats said. "Perce wen' *eat* that one."

What "eating" it would amount to, no one could be certain. The last time anything as close to this bad came to happening in Azumazeki Beya was nearly four years earlier. Akebono's brother Ola had been dealing crystal methamphetamine on Oʻahu since he was fourteen, and sumo was a last resort for the talented athlete when he arrived along with Troy in 1989. But one *kawaigari* beating after the next had failed to break him into sumo's harsh codes, and Ola disappeared right in the middle of the Kyūshū tournament, only to wind up miles away in the care of one of Japan's more notorious *yakuza* families. When he did make it back, Boss met him with a ticket home. And this had been years before Konishiki had brought sumo into the international spotlight, years before Azumazeki Oyakata became the man in charge of the first-ever foreign *yokozuna*.

Percy called home the following day in tears, describing the incident (though leaving Troy out of it), and going on about how the last thing he wanted to do was come home. He'd hardly given his golden sumo opportunity a chance, and now here it was about to disappear. As Percy's father described the phone call, Percy's mother told him "to pray" and to ask Boss "to help him, and they continued to talk."

Percy heard nothing further and thought the situation resolved, as all of Azumazeki Beya packed up for the most grueling part of the sumo year: the summer exhibition tour. As part of my research for the book on Akebono, I followed the 1998 summer tour as it snaked back and forth across all of northern Japan, back to Tokyo, and then all the way up to Sapporo before snaking its way home, making more than twenty stops in just under a month. The routine seemed unbearable for the boys ranked as low as Percy was at the time of the car accident. I watched them stumble sleepily onto the *dohyō* to squeeze in whatever morning practice they could, then attend to the *yokozuna* as he trained, bathed, ate, and prepared for his afternoon bout. As the *sekitori* lined up for the ring-entering ceremony the lower-rankers set to packing up, with the whole operation rolling out of town before the sweat had dried on the last competitors. After an hours-long bus ride, the lower-rankers would scour the next town for a coin laundry, work well into the night, and start the whole thing again the next morning.

Only after a month of this nonstop work, in the stifling humidity of a hot Japanese summer, did Azumazeki Oyakata inform Percy that they were going to send him home.

Percy was devastated. He again apologized to Boss as best he could, and he begged to be allowed to compete in the September tournament, reminding Boss that the accident had happened almost two months ago.

"If this was any other *beya*," Boss told him, "you'd be gone in two *days*." But he did let Percy compete in one final tournament.

Percy fell behind with three early losses, and though he rallied to finish with four wins, there was no rejoicing. He climbed the stairs to Azumazeki Oyakata's apartment to perform the ritual of thanking his Boss for the fact that he was able to come through with a winning record. There he found the Hawaiian Godfather sitting alone in silence, staring back and forth between the telephone and Percy's passport.

CHAPTER 4

INVASION

It's like, if you eva go to Kāneʻohe, it's far, 'cause we neva used to need go Kāneʻohe—we neva need go grocery shopping, whateva. It was a strange place. It's like, "Wow, what is this?" 'Cause we neva used to leave Waiāhole, like Bob said.

—Shane Picanco, November 28, 2007

All the people at Waiāhole School came from around Waiāhole. But when we went to King Intermediate, now we in Kāneʻohe, where we met all different people.

—Charles Kekahu, June 16, 2007

NEARLY TWO YEARS INTO A LIFE of being beaten regularly, toiling in the lower ranks while showing no real hope of rising any time soon, and eating all the abuse dished out by every one of his *senpai*, one might wonder why Percy didn't just completely take the fall for Troy and go home. At the time, his father comforted him with the fact that he'd clearly given the sport an honest enough try to learn that maybe he just wasn't meant for sumo. And yet, here was Percy just about begging for the chance to stay.

The reason had a lot to do with why Percy joined the strange world of sumo in the first place. "Was right after high school when he came and told me they wen' offer him for go up to Japan," Shane told me. "I knew he was hanging around alladem kine guys, so I told him, 'Eh, go! Just come back and visit—you always going have your home here. You always going have Waiāhole-Waikāne, your mom's-them place.' I didn't bother him

49

during high school time mostly," Shane went on, "because he was with the wrong crowd, and I could see that change in him."

Just as Bob Nakata's "foreign territory" was working its way towards the Windward valleys, the boys began moving in the other direction, leaving the neva-wear-slippa world of Waiāhole School behind for King Intermediate in Kāne'ohe. And King Zoo, though it was only a matter of four or five miles away, may as well have been in another time zone. Thanks to the heroic efforts of the Waiāhole-Waikāne Community Association throughout the 1970s, it was as though some town-country demarcation line had been drawn right at the edge of Temple Valley. But at the age of twelve, right when kids have lost just enough innocence to be unable to "make friends" in that cute and instant way that an elementary kid can, the country boys were made to cross that line.

"It was rough," Shane recalled. "'Cause all the kids that I used to play sports against and used to fight on the field and everything—we were all in the same school, so we had to prove ourselves. And the kids was kind of punky, and we was coming out of the country, ah?" King was fed by five other elementary schools, none of which anyone would seriously call a "farming" school. "I'd say it was about a thousand kids," he went on. "The first week, as soon as we got there, we had to scrap. And Percy was really soft, so they would always pick on him 'cause he was the biggest. I was the youngest of seven brothers, so I used to really back Percy up. He neva used to want to get in trouble, so I was the one that used to fight for him. They would always tease him 'cause he had glasses, ah? You know how little boys are."

The taunts and insults immediately had the boys missing the "country" side of the line they'd just crossed, so it became a daily ritual to save a quarter from their lunch money and dream about Mama-san's Waikāne Store. "Every *day* we wen' go to that store," Shane said. Percy would stay on the bus an extra stop past Waikāne Valley Road just so he could walk into what still looks like the epitome of the rusted-tin-roofed country store, a brown-speckled Coca-Cola sign outside, and inside a shelf of candies, a glass-door refrigerator full of cool drinks, and an ancient white freezer—the long, low kind with a door on top that you lift to find a treasure trove of different ice cream bars stacked between the frost-caked walls. But Percy always saved his milk money for the four little pieces of sushi hand rolled by Haruko Tsutsui, who had come all the way from Japan as a little girl and opened the store way back in 1929. Mama-san, as she asked Percy to call her, once showed him an old black-and-white picture of her husband, who had since passed on: a skinny-looking Japanese guy wearing what looked like a fantastic apron with a picture of a mountain embroidered on the front. She called it a *keshō mawashi*, and explained that all the sugar plantations used to have sumo clubs that competed against one another.

"She adopted him," Mrs. Kipapa said. Percy's mother has a story from Percy's King Zoo days when his friend wound up helping himself to a few pieces of candy without bothering to pay. "He whack him," Mrs. Kipapa said. "He said, 'Why you steal from this old lady? Put 'um back!' She thanked him! When he went up Japan, she was so happy because her husband was one sumo wrestler." Mama-san had likely taken the time to show Percy her husband's *keshō mawashi* photo because of how easy it was, even then, to take one look at Percy's build and pick him as a future star of Japan's national sport.

But while Percy's size may have been admirable to someone who knew about sumo, it was otherwise causing him nothing but trouble. His sister Selisa knew that even as soft as he was, Percy would always be able to handle himself one-on-one. It was only when she heard that the entire Red Rag gang was set to fight him that she began to worry. "I was already in Castle, but it was big talk," she said, referring to Castle High School, a couple of miles away from King Zoo. "I like hurry up and catch the city bus before the school bus came." As usual, a smaller kid had challenged Percy to a fight after school. "Percy said 'Bring 'um, bring 'um,'" she recalled. But what Percy didn't know was that the kid was a Red Rag. "The guy had plenty kids from outside, you know—they not going King School. Older people. So after school, get this big bunch of guys out on the field, and here comes Percy walking up the cement ramp that comes onto the field. But behind him had only his two short friends, Charles Kekahu and Shane Picanco—that's all he had, that's his back-up. And had this *big* bunch of guys waiting for him."

"We was like 'Okay, let's *go*,' you know," Shane told me. "But Percy was like, 'I don't wanna get suspended, 'cause Ma gonna give me lickings.' We said, 'You betta do something cause they going be picking on you every day.' Then we work him up for scrap. And afta a while, then *we* started getting worked up fo' scrap."

So up the ramp they walked, and out onto the field, Percy and his two short friends against, as Shane recalls, "maybe twenty to thirty guys, the Red Rags." They could not have thought they would have much of a chance, but the three boys wouldn't have been in it for the win anyway. The point of such a brawl was to scrap, win or lose, and if you lost, to do as much damage as possible. The worst course of action, as Shane had pointed out to Percy in the first place, was to "back down." To guys from the Windward side, a hospital bed was preferable to backing down, because at least then you could say, even if through teeth that had been wired together, "Was thirty of them and only t'ree of us, an' we even wen' lick six-seven of those fuckas, but at least we neva back down, so."

But as Percy, Shane, and Charles approached the gang, something strange began to happen. They saw guys in the crowd turning towards each other with looks of surprise, fingers pointing back at Percy—all signs of confusion Percy might have expected had he brought along his own thirty guys. And suddenly only one of them looked ready to fight. When they got close enough, the Waikāne boys finally figured out the reason for the confusion when, as Selisa tells it, the biggest Red Rag in the gang turned to the punk who had first called Percy out and said, "Cuz, you talking about *that* guy? No way, cuz! You on your own—that's my friend! You can fight this guy—we ain't *even* getting involved."

The big Red Rag guy walked up to Percy and shook his hand. "Percy knew everybody else in the crowd," Selisa said. "And the guy couldn't believe it, 'cause they was supposed to be all one *hui*, ah? The Red Rags. He couldn't believe that nobody would back him up because they all know Percy: 'Eh, what's up, Perce!'"

Percy turned to his opponent and said, "Come on!"

The poor guy looked around to see his *hui* now surrounding Percy, and he *backed down*, saying, "Eh, it's all cool, it's all cool."

"The guy didn't want to fight with Percy after, but I caught the guy in the parking lot," Shane told me with a laugh. "Later they was acting up on the bus, so me and Charles, we caught them at Kahalu'u School without Percy knowing. They just wanted to fight the biggest guy in the school. They was trying for make him look stupid, for make themselves look tough. But they wouldn't bother him afta that." Shane then thought back to where he and Charles and Percy had come from in Waiāhole-Waikāne, where boys had the option to look for respect in ways other than joining gangs defined by violence. "We neva even know about Red Rags and Blue Rags and what was that," he said. "We neva even have time. It was just come home and work." He went on to say that he'd never even become friends with what Charles referred to as "Kāneʻohe people"—not after two years in King Zoo, not even after four more years at Castle High.

A state intermediate school record in the shot put meant that Percy would be heading even deeper into "foreign territory" instead of following Shane and Charles to Castle High. Though he'd never played organized football, the record drew the attention of Cal Lee, a coach of local note who offered him a football scholarship to St. Louis High School. Though it meant going all the way over the Koʻolaus and into Honolulu, Percy jumped at the chance. For starters, he would be given a shot at a real education, as opposed to dozing through classes in a Hawaiʻi State Department of Education school. He also knew of St. Louis as the state's most fertile college recruiting ground, where graduating senior football stars were routinely sent to big college programs, sometimes even going on to the pros. Percy's family was overjoyed, and they scraped together the money for his school uniform and for a set of strap-on sports glasses he could wear on the field.

Percy rose every morning as early as his grandfather used to—even before the chickens that swarmed around his bedroom window. He then walked down the pitch-black road to the highway, where he would wait for the first of three busses that would take him across the mountains and through Honolulu. "Minimum, hour-half," his brother Kurt told me, of a trip that takes a third as long in a car. "Three transfers. You've got to go downtown," and get off and wait, "then to Ala Moana," and get off and wait, "and then to Kaimukī. It was miserable." If he wasn't sleeping, Percy distracted himself by looking out at the thickening traffic, and when he reached the town it was light enough that he could see that this side of the Koʻolaus was as cut with valleys—Kalihi, Nuʻuanu, Makiki, Mānoa—as the Windward side. Two of them were split by highways that swelled to six and even eight lanes in places, lava-like ribbons spilling down the mountains and collecting at the foot of downtown's steel and glass high-rises.

Day after day, the same views would have ingrained themselves in Percy's mind—the tall buildings, the shopping centers, the overpasses on the parking lot that was the H-1 freeway, and most of all, the cascade of houses spilling out of valley after valley that had once looked like Percy's Waikāne playground. Builders had crept as far as they could up the steep edges of each valley, setting some houses, it seemed, directly on top of those below, and others so far back against the cliffs you worried a boulder could come tumbling down from above. As he looked out the bus window, 'āina—that which provides—and mana were not the words that would have come to mind.

The sense of respect Percy had gained from his country upbringing turned out to be just as hard to find as any feeling of mana was—even harder, if that was possible, than it had been at King Zoo, which was already "town" compared to Waiāhole. He only had to step off the bus and into the classroom at the Marinist-run "academy for young men" to be overcome by what can only be called culture shock. Everyone was dressed not just in shoes, but in shirts and ties. The roomful of young men seemed bent on learning as much as possible and getting good grades. Many had attended St. Louis during middle school, while Percy had gone to neva-wear-slippa Waiāhole School, where it had taken the teachers four years to figure out that he had astigmatism—an eye disorder that impeded his ability to read. Percy might later be thrown into a roomful of big topknotted guys barking at him in Japanese. And he might later be beaten to the point where he thought he was sucking in his last breaths in harsh tender-loving-care sessions. But at no point in Japan would he be made to feel stupid.

"My dad was in Kwajalein," Kurt told me, of a job Mr. Kipapa had been able to find on the distant Pacific military base, "and I was working, so I couldn't pick Percy up. Sometimes he would wake up on the bus in Kahuku," another thirty minutes up the Windward Coast. "The students were totally different. He was getting overwhelmed with school, with practice. He was only fourteen. Academic-wise it was night and day. I used to go down there and try to help him with his homework. They wanted to send him to a tutor, but he didn't want to go to a tutor 'cause it was double driving for him," again, on the bus into urban Honolulu.

The one place where Percy should have been able to find refuge turned out to be where he ran into the most trouble of all. One can easily imagine young Percy going far out of his way to buddy up to his new teammates, to revel in the idea of being a part of a fraternity in the way he would later feel after his topknot marked him as a member of the sumo brotherhood. Percy had long ago developed the ability to make friends instantly, but what he found among the team at St. Louis was that even his aloha would not be enough—this even before the natural hazing a freshman might expect turned mean the moment he was given a starting spot on both the offensive and defensive lines over two seniors.

"They were there all the years and this guy comes in out of nowhere," Kurt said. "I think it was the constant picking on him." His glasses, his thick Pidgin accent, the fact that he raised chickens and ducks and pigs—it was all on the table when his classmates were in the mood for fun at his expense. "There were a lot of guys that he didn't feel comfortable with." It finally reached the point where even Percy would not need Shane and Charles to *work him up fo' scrap*, when a fight broke out in the tight confines of the weight room and spilled out into the gym lobby, giving Percy the chance to take out a full year of bus-riding, class-failing, hazing-victim frustration with a single throw that sent his big opponent through a glass trophy case. As one might imagine, no meetings follow such flare-ups at an "academy for young men." The incident, perhaps almost to Percy's relief by the time it happened, put an end to his brief career at St. Louis. Years later he would have far less trouble assimilating to the distant and unforgiving ancient world of professional sumo. What his St. Louis experience made clear was that in urban Oʻahu there would never be any place for him.

WHAT PERCY DID NOT KNOW as he headed back over the mountains to Castle High on the Windward side was that the "country" he'd left behind had begun to change. Shane was one of the few who saw it. And though he couldn't pinpoint it at the time, "that change" he began to see in many of his Waiāhole-Waikāne friends would come to be traced back to 1976, around the same time that Bob Nakata and so many of the older generation were fighting for the valley's land. That year an army of federal drug enforcement agents, meticulously selected state and local star cops and detectives, National Guardsmen, and U.S. Army Green Berets descended upon the Big Island's Puna and Kaʻū districts. The mission had been planned extensively for well over a year. A rare consensus was reached on everything from its ultimate goals to the means of execution, which included keeping the whole operation secret for the first two years, after which its early success could be used as propaganda to fuel the war as it spread from island to island to root out the enemy wherever it existed.

The enemy was marijuana. For years, acres and acres of Christmas-tree-sized pakalolo plants had flourished under the tropical sun, nourished by just the right amount of rainfall to reach legendary levels of potency, and more or less left alone by local law enforcement due to the laughable lack of manpower relative to the scope of the problem. "Kona Gold" and "Puna Butter" had become famous nationwide, thanks to an export crop that brought Hawai'i some $10 billion annually in 1980s dollars—far more than either of the main cash cows, military appropriations and tourism. Growers sent themselves into fits of laughter imagining what might happen to a drug-sniffing dog assigned to Puna's Pāhoa post office, constantly loaded as it was with box upon box of pakalolo headed for the mainland. Other growers were reportedly confronting hikers in Hawai'i Volcanoes National Park with loaded shotguns.

The massive government response was called Operation Green Harvest. Herbicide was sprayed from low-flying Comanche helicopters. Crops were burned. Uniformed soldiers rappelled into forests, and left with bushels by the ton of green plants hanging from the feet of their helicopters. Houses were confiscated, land condemned, and tribes of dreadlocked hippies arrested. Green Harvest, as it continued to be known well into the 1980s and long after the statewide Operation Wipeout was launched, peaked in its effectiveness in 1987, a year that saw nearly two million plants confiscated and the price of pot in Hawai'i skyrocket from its mid-1970s average of $25 an ounce to an eventual mid-1990s cost of some $1,500 an ounce.

That same year, Percy Kipapa entered high school.

What "foreign territory" began to do to the Windward side in the ensuing few years could more accurately be captured by the word "transformation" than by Shane's more benign word, "change." While Percy was busy trying to assimilate into town life at St. Louis, the five hundred acres surrounding his home were fenced off by Azabu USA's Kitaro Watanabe, one of several Japanese golf resort developers pushing the tsunami of late-1980s bubble-economy money then washing over Hawai'i. While Percy's neighbor Ray Kamaka was locked in a fight with the U.S. military to clear his 187 acres of unexploded ordnance, and while State Senator Bob Nakata was fighting so hard to divert the billion dollars appropriated for the H-3 freeway into mass transit that he failed to campaign enough to get reelected, the Windward side was becoming another casualty in a national golf addiction that had already exhausted nearly every available space in Japan and then in neighboring Guam. North of Waikāne, Kizo Matsumoto bought both the Turtle Bay Hilton and Country Club and part of the Kuilima Resort. To the south, former Japanese professional baseball player Ken Mizuno took over Olomana Golf Links. When the Japanese investors had snapped up all but one course on Oʻahu where the public were welcome, they looked to open spaces, from the North Shore, where eight new courses were planned, to the Windward valleys. The owner of a pachinko-parlor chain, Yasuo Yasuda, bought most of Maunawili Valley. Billionaire Masao Nangaku grabbed some one thousand acres south of Kāneʻohe. And now Watanabe was on his way to paving Waikāne Valley Bermuda green.

Such purchases, and the deal-making required to plant golf courses in ancient tropical valleys, could not be done without the help of an updated version of Joe Pao. One such *seishō*—the Japanese term for someone who bridges the gap between business and politics—was Tom Enomoto, who was as much a caricature of the local-boy success story as of the politically connected operator. Not long after losing his construction-worker father at age thirteen, the Kalihi boy came under the wing of real estate magnate Harry Weinberg (some say "slumlord," others say "green mailer"), whose estate is now worth $2 billion. Enomoto started the first of a string of companies at age twenty-one. A quick learner, as he himself told the *Honolulu Advertiser*'s Jim Dooley in 1991, about "understanding how government process works," he reportedly went on to develop strong connections with Senator Dan Inouye and the Bishop Estate, developers Herbert Horita (the Ko Olina Resort) and Tom Gentry (much of central Oʻahu), political insider Larry Mehau, and Governor John Waiheʻe. Newspaper accounts of Enomoto at the time all echo the words of political commentator Robert M. Rees, who described him as "a powerful business leader sometimes called the 'stealth bomber' due to his ability to accomplish a great deal while remaining out of sight." Rees placed just three men at the decision-making center of "Hawai'i's Universe of Power": Inouye, Waihe'e, and Enomoto. Through an elaborate system of political action committees, as reported by the *Honolulu Star-Bulletin*'s Ian Lind in 1993, Enomoto was able to legally funnel more than a quarter of a million dollars to a short list of sitting government officials in the late 1980s, many of whom were not even up for reelection. At one time, Enomoto had two sitting legislators on the payroll of one of his companies. On the Windward side, he managed to bring together the landowner 'Iolani School, the Land Use Commission, and Masao Nangaku's Minami Group to turn hundreds of acres of steep, rugged jungle into the $100 million Ko'olau Country Club. It helped that William Paty, who also chaired Waihe'e's reelection campaign, chaired the Land Board.

"Enomoto, he's an interesting character," Bob Nakata told me. "He knows how to wheel and deal. I got involved in the banana farmers fighting H-3, and somehow that spilled over to the golf course, and he said, 'Let's work out a deal.' We were trying to stop the extension of the Department of Land and Natural Resources permit to finish the golf course. The construction was already 90 percent completed, so I looked at it and I said, 'We have no chance in hell of stopping it.'" Enomoto asked Bob and another Kahalu'u antidevelopment activist named John Reppun to sit on the board of a nonprofit he'd just formed called the Minami Foundation, which would be funded by donations of five dollars per round of golf, and an initial donation of a million dollars—money he found among the three million federal dollars Minami was paid for the H-3 easement across the edge of its property. Enomoto even arranged a deal that convinced the handful of banana farmers living on the property to relocate to the back of Maunawili Valley. "We actually should have gotten nothing," Bob said with a smile. "The Japanese must have had a lot of money. He probably told them, 'Just give him this, and let's get them out of our hair.'"

Bob could hardly have been understating things any more than he was. "A lot of money" amounted to hundreds of millions of dollars in credit that Japanese banks were throwing around at the time, and the sudden devaluation of the dollar against the yen. Former Legal Aid Hawai'i director Anthony Locricchio, who had also played a key role in the 1970s fights for Waiāhole-Waikāne before coming to represent the tenant farmers being forced out of other parts of Maunawili Valley the following decade, put it this way in a PBS interview: "For example, a hotel might sell to a Japanese interest for $30 million. Two months later, it would sell for $60 million. In four months, it would be $120 million. You would have had to rent out rooms at $500 a day and had 100 percent occupancy to meet the debt service. And for these excellent Japanese business people, there was a total ignoring of standard economics." And if the easy credit and the strong yen hadn't been enough, developers were able to sell hundreds of memberships back in Japan for around $250,000 each, according to Locricchio, before anyone planted a shovel. "What was going on in Japan at that time," he said, "was a golf epidemic."

"WHEN I WAS A KID, PAKALOLO WAS EVERYWHERE," Percy's brother Kurt told me. We were talking about an epidemic of a different kind that, at the time anyway, seemed unrelated to the epidemic that Anthony Locricchio was discussing. We were talking about what a state auditor, as early as 1990, had blamed on the organizers of Green Harvest. We were talking about crystal methamphetamine. About ice. Passing through high school thirteen years before Percy, the only ice Kurt had ever heard of was the kind he and his friends used to cool their homemade pineapple wine. "My uncle's neighbors used to grow pakalolo for medicinal purposes, or sell it to their friends, but it was neva one big thing. And then it was gone. First time I eva heard of ice was the nineties. When I was a kid there was pakalolo and that's it." Percy wasn't so lucky. When he came back over the mountains from St. Louis to finish high school at Kāne'ohe's Castle High, the ice pipe had replaced the joint as though what we've come to know as one of the most devastatingly addictive drugs ever concocted were as harmless as the mild hallucinogen that used to grow in the valley like weeds. "To me, ice is destroying our people," Kurt went on. "You see, people got choices, ah? Choices to do it or not. But you see your friend start doing it, eventually you going start doing it."

THE INCURABLE ADDICT WRAPPED UP in the "golf epidemic" that threatened Tony Locricchio's Maunawili Valley clients was Yasuo Yasuda, a Japanese of Korean ethnicity. The *seishō* who in 1985 helped him purchase his land, have it rezoned, and obtain the necessary permits and so on were a Kailua couple named Gene and Nora Lum, who, thanks to Yasuda's endless supply of cash, fared much better against that valley's tenant farmers than Joe Pao had in Waikāne a generation earlier. To clear the valley, the Lums worked with the City and County of Honolulu and a local "security" firm staffed mainly by Hawaiian *paniolos* (some of whom were off-duty Honolulu Police Department officers), handing out, as Locricchio recalls, "quasi eviction notices" and threats. As Locricchio told PBS, "They targeted the rancher first, we believe, as a lesson to the rest, as a 'Here's what's going to happen to you if you don't get out of here.'" The *paniolos*, who had thought to bring butchering equipment along, shot the rancher's prize bull and butchered it on the spot. Gene Lum, according to Locricchio, "later told the press that they had to kill the bull because it charged these riders who were there to protect the people. He did not tell the press that he pocketed money from the sale" of the meat. Two frightened children who hid under their house as the forced evictions happened were nearly bulldozed to death. A chapel was demolished. A ninety-three-year-old Filipino valley fixture who had to be hospitalized for months after being forced from his home died not long after. And a company called Pan-Pacific began construction as planned, resulting eventually in the Luana Hills Country Club, whose current Web site boasts "the perfect backdrop for golfers of all abilities searching for an escape" to a "verdant paradise" that is "teeming with Hawaiian royal history." In a look back at the late-1980s Japanese golf course invasion, Tom Enomoto, who had turned down the chance to be Yasuda's *seishō*, summed up what happened in Maunawili with this: "Really, really stupid things can happen when there's too much money pushing a project."

THOUGH NO ONE WAS EVER ABLE to total exactly what was spent on Green Harvest and its offshoots over the past four decades, conservative estimates reach into the hundreds of millions of taxpayer dollars. (Donald Topping, director of the University of Hawai'i's Social Science Research Institute, found that state agencies alone burned through $35 million in just one year, 1991.) Articles from the late 1980s laud the operation's success in a tone made naive by the passage of time—a tone that even spreads to the few pieces that begin to speculate on the possibility of Green Harvest's negative unintended consequences. For one example, in an October 1989 article entitled "Scarcity of Marijuana Here Now Has Users Just Saying 'Yes' to Ice," the *Advertiser*'s Barbara Hastings lets us know that "some treatment workers, who did not want their names used, said they believe crystal methamphetamine poses a greater threat to the young than marijuana"—a statement now obvious enough to lead one to wonder why people felt the need to withhold their names. "Sure, we see problems with pot," Hastings quotes one treatment worker as saying, "but nothing compared to what happens with ice."

If two full years after Percy entered high school, two full years after ice had begun accumulating victims, it is news even to an *Advertiser* reporter interviewing a drug treatment worker that ice and pakalolo are vastly different things, what can one reasonably expect a young teen to do—even one raised in what anyone would argue is the perfect, loving, supportive, and stable home—when he is surrounded by his boys, and everyone is partying and laughing and having a good time, and he is handed the pipe? The National Institute of Drug Abuse would later warn of a frightening 15 percent addiction rate for people who simply tried the drug once. But that warning would not be sounded for another fifteen years.

"SMALL MAN," MRS. KIPAPA SAID, recalling Azabu USA's Kitaro Watanabe, the golf addict who dropped more mid-1980s Japanese money on Hawai'i than anyone else. By the time she met him, Azabu USA had become Hawai'i's second-largest resort owner. Watanabe stopped in front of her house after touring the valley with an entourage of local fixers and executives from Pan-Pacific, whom he, too, had tapped to build his Waikāne golf course. The small man was surrounded by what Percy's parents now liken to a group of *tsukebito*—sumo's low-ranking attendants. Her husband, just returned from working at the military base on Kwajalein, had been hired by Pan-Pacific to patrol their property with the company Jeep they allowed him to park at the house. "Had guys up there stripping cars or riding motorcycle or whatever, so I just log 'um down, report 'um in," he said—easy work for the six hundred dollars a month they were handing him. Watanabe had asked to visit the family, making a show of having someone light his cigarette for him, ordering Percy to hand him a tangerine off the tree in his yard. "He had like six, seven guys," Mr. Kipapa said. "For the short time I was with that guy, I kind of visualize how he got to be where he is: the way he talk and the way he act and the way he presented himself. And then I watch these *other* guys that came with him. If the guy tell you jump, you *jump*."

Towards the end of his junior year, Percy joined his father's patrol effort as part of a Castle High School work-for-credit program. "He'd go up there," Mr. Kipapa told me, pointing up into the valley. "He'd check the fence so people don't go inside. He was like my gopher. The school was paying him. All I had to do was evaluate him. I was going to request to be in charge of the security when they made the golf course. That way I could turn around and hire Percy-them, and whatever of his friends I could find to be the security up here. But that was when everything fell apart."

When Pan-Pacific executives and local fixer Tom Pickard began meeting regularly with the Roberts family—Percy's parents, his Uncle Henry, his Uncle Arnold, and their wives—at the Zippy's restaurant in Kāne'ohe to discuss the planned golf course, the real reason for Mr. Kipapa's cushy job, the monthly handout, and the personal visit from Watanabe became clear: in addition to his five hundred acres, Watanabe also wanted the three-acre parcel of land up in the valley that Manuel Roberts had been awarded in State Land Court. "They was gonna do this, they was gonna do that," Mrs. Kipapa recalled. "When they make the golf course, they was gonna give us central air conditioning and block the windows because of the dust. All that kine promises. But *nothing written*. It's all *bullshit*."

"You know I listen, and I don't think I like the idea," George Kipapa said. "So after that I told the family, 'Eh, I think these guys is taking you guys for a ride.' I was not really opposed to the golf course, but the way they was talking: 'Eh, I'll give you this, I'll give you that,' but nothing was *written*. You know how they sweet-talk you, ah? We constantly had the meetings over and over for more than a month or so, maybe more."

"We was at a meeting and George put his two cents in," Mrs. Kipapa said. "And after the meeting Pickard said to him, 'Eh, you supposed to be with us, not for them—not for the family.'" Soon after, the six-hundred-dollar checks stopped coming, and someone came to take the Jeep away. "They put it in the way of, 'You know, your services will not be needed,'" Mr. Kipapa said. "I wasn't a 'Yes' person."

While the family was meeting to decide the fate of their land, Percy was participating in the kind of work-study program designed to teach kids the connections between school and community, to show them how the real world valued their education, to keep them away from drugs. As Percy half-heartedly "fixed the fences" or cut back weeds on the Azabu property's edges, he likely thought how his grandfather used to work the valley from sunup to sundown. Even before going off to Japan and gaining the kind of perspective that wound up highlighting the difference for him, Percy would have had the time to compare his make-work menial position to what his grandfather had done in cultivating his *own* fifty-nine acres with food for his family. "All that kine promises," was how his mother's story went, "but *nothing written*. It's all *bullshit*." Her distrust about a simple land transfer that could have brought the family a good deal of money, Percy knew, was rooted in how the story of his grandfather's land had actually turned out. What Manuel Roberts "won" in Land Court was six acres down by the highway, and those three acres farther up near the stream that Watanabe's people were spending so much energy down at Zippy's trying to pry away. The other fifty acres had been lost in a prior version of *all kine promises*, and *bullshit*. And what was left of those fifty acres—the part Watanabe didn't already own—had just been bought up by another developer. The Japanese company Hoyu Kensetsu was planning two additional golf courses on fourteen hundred acres adjoining Watanabe's land, and also eyeing ninety-five McCandless Estate acres along Kāne'ohe Bay for a hotel. Future golfers who stepped up to one of the Hoyu course's spectacular elevated tees—if the course designer were to work with the valley's natural features—would be greeted with the panoramic view that Percy liked to enjoy for hours from his special spot atop Grandpa's Hill.

In the middle of all this, someone handed Percy the pipe. Like Kurt put it to me so many years later, "People got choices." In 1990, words like "epidemic" and "fuckin' chronics" and "druggies" were more than ten years from making their way into the local lexicon. Percy would be long gone to Japan before Donald Topping looked back on Green Harvest's 1987–1988 peak—coinciding with Percy's first two years of high school—as "the exact years we see the introduction and rise and spread of crystal meth." Edgy Lee's shocking *Ice* documentary, the islandwide sign-waving efforts—all of that was thirteen years away. Back then, ice was the new thing. No one knew that you could get dragged down with a single hit. Percy had a choice, ah? A choice to do it or not. And he did it. At the age of seventeen, he took a hit.

❈ ❈ ❈

"NEVA IN MY WILDEST DREAMS," Percy's mother said, her eyes going wide at the sight confronting her in her own yard. A small car had pulled up, and out of one side came a wiry grandfatherly Hawaiian man with graying hair and steel-rimmed glasses. But out of the passenger side—you would never have thought such a big man could have fit into the car in the first place—came the man she had been watching on television for the past ten years.

"The Japanese ladies at work, they always used to talk about him," she told me. Takamiyama! Jesse! "When he came to my house I told him, 'Neva in my wildest dreams did I eva think I'd meet you in my house.'"

By the time Percy graduated from Castle, the dominant faces that the Kipapas saw on *Sumo Digest* were those of a chiseled Japanese man named Chiyonofuji and a mountain of a local Samoan named Konishiki who fought in Jesse's old stable. Jesse Kuhaulua had retired and was now known by the elder name Azumazeki Oyakata, and according to what Percy's father had been reading in the newspapers, he'd been busy recruiting local boys for his new sumo stable with the help of a retired firefighter named Larry Aweau. His star recruit, Akebono, had just made the pro ranks. Konishiki was dominating, having beaten all of the top competitors, and winning a tournament outright back in 1989. Even watching on TV, Percy could tell that Konishiki was scary—all power, charging forward with his hands flying into the faces of the much-smaller Japanese guys. And then here was Chiyonofuji, who could not have weighed even half of what Konishiki weighed, lifting the six-hundred-pounder *off the ground*.

Konishiki's brother, Junior, who was helping in the recruiting project, had first approached Kurt earlier that summer. He then offered to teach Percy some sumo basics, and soon Percy was driving his beat-up Mazda over the mountains to Nānākuli, its driver's seat ripped from its moorings and pushed all the way back to accommodate his giant body. When that arrangement ended in an unresolved game of phone tag, a meeting was arranged with Larry Aweau, who sold the Kipapas on Japan as a great opportunity for their big son, leaving them a biography of Jesse, Hawai'i's first sumo star. A week later Percy was holding his new passport, and a week after that his mother found herself serving her famous Portuguese bean soup to a national hero.

Boss took one look at Kurt, already nearly five hundred pounds of solid muscle, and asked if he was interested, but Percy's big brother had long since started a family. He and Larry went on to explain the sumo training structure and the *sumo beya* system. They deferred to Percy's father, who reminded Percy that he would have to learn to speak and maybe even write in Japanese, and that it wouldn't be easy to adjust to the harsh rules of this strange ancient life. Boss explained that Larry had already recruited several other local boys, for him and for three other *sumo beya*, who were working their way up the ranks. And then they handed Percy a five-year contract that would bind him to Azumazeki Beya, paying him next to nothing beyond his room and board until he rose high enough in the ranks to become the next Konishiki. Looking at Percy's big body, Boss intimated that it wouldn't take long for that to happen.

"Jesse told him: 'You see this car?'" Mrs. Kipapa recalled, Boss pointing to Percy's old Mazda. "'You go up sumo, you going have even betta car than this.' He said, 'You go sumo, you do good, you'll be happy.' And then just before he left, standing right over there, I still remember it clearly, he said, 'When you retire, we get you one job ova here, Panasonic.'"

"After we had our lunch," Mr. Kipapa recalled, "We sat around and talked, and I said, 'Percy, this thing is up to you. I neva had that kind of experience of going from high school to one different country. Not too bad you go to a neighbor island, but to go to a different country—not to the United States, but to Japan. And to me that's a long, long distance. And the thing is, communication, I don't know how you communicate. And the phone, you don't know wheneva you gonna get permission to use the phone. You'll be a guest of somebody else's house.' But both me an' my wife, we was kind of worried."

Larry Aweau went into high gear to close the deal, urging Percy to say "*dame*" in refusal of anyone else's recruiting efforts, taking him out to fancy dinners, and filling his head with dreams of sumo glory.

Percy spent the afternoon thinking about the offer while carrying rocks and pouring cement under the hot sun with Shane, who was supplementing his farming work with the small masonry company he'd set up after graduation. At one point, as Shane recalled the exchange years later, Percy stopped and said, "Ho, I cannot do this kine work." For a moment,

Shane was puzzled. For years he'd been dreaming of starting a company like the one his uncle, who had taught him the trade, had run. And here was his friend getting ready to dig out on him. But then Percy surprised him: "What if I do sumo?"

Shane thought again, having seen Akebono and Konishiki on TV and in the newspapers. "That's the best thing you could do!" he said, again thinking of the crowd his friend had fallen in with at Castle. "Right on!"

Percy talked on excitedly about meeting Jesse, about the new car he'd been promised, and even the job they promised after he retired. But then he admitted that when he thought of his family, and especially his mother, the whole thing turned into some kind of it-would-have-been-nice dream, and that he probably wouldn't go after all.

Shane looked at him wide-eyed, and then started, as he might have put it himself, *working him up fo' scrap*: "What you get for offer you ova here? We no more too much for offer. Whatchoo going *do?*"

Percy thought for a minute and then said, "I think I going."

"Go!"

"I was an all-star football player, everything," Percy told me that rainy afternoon we sat at his dining room table. "And came my senior year, I didn't play football, because I was all drugged out my whole fucking senior year. I got introduced to all that kine shit, and I fuckin' full-on partied *hard*. Go beach every day. I'd hang with all the chicks from Kalani—they had everything. So when I went up Japan, it was like detox. I used to challenge small guys and I couldn't beat 'em."

Detox. Percy's early records and Azumazeki Oyakata's growing lack of faith in his potential bear all of this out. "In one year's time, Percy was moving kind of slow" on his way up the ranking sheet, Troy explained. "*Jonidan*, Percy was there like four-five tournaments," while Troy, Fats, George, and Bumbo had each spent only a single tournament in that lowly division. Percy was struggling against scrawny little opponents fresh from junior high school, but no one knew why. No one knew that he was fighting more than any of this. Learning the language, adjusting to the ancient and cryptic codes of sumo culture—it all might have been easy were he not also trying to free himself from the monster. Given what we now know about ice, anyone not already struck down would be a fool to even go near a glass pipe today. But like so many people back in the late 1980s,

Percy had no idea what he was getting into. And unlike many of the future "chronics" who would wind up passing their children along to be raised by grandparents, the moment Percy got the chance to dig himself out, he took it, even though it meant parting with the tightest family on the island. Move to Japan? Become a professional sumo wrestler? A guy from the country, up in Waikāne? What was he thinking? Beyond a couple of greetings he'd learned at Mama-san's store, he didn't even speak the language. But Percy—he knew what he was doing when he left Hawai'i. Years later he would tell the *Hawai'i Herald,* "I was going nowhere."

CHAPTER 5

THE MINUTE MAN

You gotta actually jump in the ring to understand. Especially when you're talking about Percy's car accident. The next day you gotta go beat this kid up as respect to our boss. But when you beating somebody up, you pounding the shit outta them, you busting them up, they on the ground bleeding, breathing hard, you yelling at 'em, "Stand up!" and they trying to get up—afta a little while, you feel *something. All the guys who actually did get in the ring, was on the side of giving the* kawaigari, *was on the side of taking the* kawaigari, *there's this* respect. *In the beginning, you're like, "What, punk! You getting up?" But then after a while, you start turning into a fan. You get that feeling inside of you like, "You* Hawaiian! *Get up, boy! Get up! One more time!"* Easy for lie there and *just pass out. That's how you can tell if he get inside what it takes to match his outside abilities. 'Cause when you look at any of the sumo wrestlers coming out of high school, I can guarantee you me and Percy was the bottom ones on the totem pole abilitywise. But we had the same thing inside. And you know how when you growing up and your parents hit you, they say, "This hurts us more than it hurts you"—that's* exactly *what it is.* Especially *being from Hawai'i.* Especially *his brother-them live in Waimānalo. You no like be doing that.* Hurt *inside. But afta a little while when he start getting up, all* dirty, *hair hanging all over, you can see 'um in his eyes. You neva see him just sit down and cry about it. He got up.*

—Yokozuna Akebono, May 28, 2009

With plans all laid out to send Percy home, Yokozuna Akebono, who had just won his second straight tournament and third of the year, spoke to Boss. "I seen in Percy what I seen in myself," he recalled. "He reminded me of *me* when I first came up here. I was thinking sumo was gonna be a lot easier than it actually was. I thought you join some kind of club, you practice for a little while, and then you get to be on TV. I didn't realize there's a whole ranking system, almost nine hundred wrestlers, and when you come into sumo, you start at the *ass bottom*." Back then, Akebono had already seen too many local boys go home without really having a chance to adjust. "I told Boss, 'You know, don't make the same mistake.'" When Boss wouldn't budge, Akebono suggested a compromise—a severe one, but one that might at least keep Percy around. "I knew from watching other kids run away and come back, or steal," he told me, "usually what they did in sumo was, you give them *kawaigari*, and then you shave their head, and they apologize." Boss accepted.

"For you to cut your hair and walk around like that," George Kalima said, "everybody knows you did something that shamed you. You see somebody that's been there for two-three years, and then all the sudden he's bald again? He had to have done something, man. It's like taking a sex offender and putting a sign on him and telling him to stand out in rush-hour traffic. 'Cause the hair is everything. Losing your hair like that and walking around, that's like walking around with no fuckin' clothes on. You really think about it, man, Percy had some hard times in sumo."

It hurts to try and imagine the scene: Akebono reluctantly grabbing the topknot and hacking it off as everyone else stood around watching. And even as the scissors snipped away at the one tangible symbol of Percy's membership in the sumo brotherhood—scissors that would not have been gold-plated like the ones they use for a retirement ceremony—Percy said nothing, not even to Akebono, about the fact that all along he had only been doing what his *senpai* had ordered. When it was over Percy climbed the stairs to the third-floor apartment, the topknot held humbly in front of him like an offering, and bowed before the big Hawaiian Godfather, apologizing—or, more accurately, *taking the fall*. "Percy neva said one fuckin' word about Troy," Tyler Hopkins said. "Perce just took everything, just like a *real man* would."

What happened next became one of the more legendary acts of *gaman* ever to take place within the testosterone-soaked confines of Azumazeki Beya. After apologizing to his *oyakata*, Percy turned and walked back downstairs, still carefully clutching that brittle clump of shorn black hair. He may have thought back to the stories of his mother driving Grandpa Roberts into town to be grilled by teams of lawyers as he fought to save the family's land. Maybe he thought of Uncle Arnold, riding his horse across Waikāne to gather everyone for the fight against the developers. He must have thought of Shane, working him up fo' *scrap*, because that topknot in his hands—that symbol of his shame—he didn't throw it away or try to forget all of the ugliness of Boss giving up on him enough to want to send him home. No, he *kept* it. He put it in a safe place, and he saved it as a symbol of *pride*, as a symbol of a different kind of brotherhood. "I couldn't *believe it*," Fats Gaspar said. "Perce. He wen' *eat* that one. It was either go home, or cut his hair. He eat 'um. He not going squeal."

Percy was finished lying down. If he could eat this one, he could eat anything they threw at him. "My first years over there I was bullshitting around," he told me. "I was sick, or my body was in pain. But after my second year, even if I was sick I like practice. 'Cause every day after practice you gotta go upstairs and you gotta do Akebono's chores, and you gotta do yours. Then all the guys been here long time, they tell you what for do. And I used to look at them: 'Oh, you like tell me what for do? I'll get you back in the ring.' So next day I would look forward to go back in the ring. They used to tell me things, I'd be like, '*Hai!*'" And Percy would be thinking, "Yeah, I'll wash your clothes. Fold 'em up nice. Here you go. Wait till tomorrow: I'll kick your ass." The bamboo stick was finally working, having beaten a fighting spirit even into a young man as overflowing with aloha as Percy Kipapa. "That's the *old* style of training," George said, of the type of *kawaigari* beatings Azumazeki Oyakata relied on. "Bring the animal out. They brought the animal out in Percy."

After Percy worked through a knee injury at the start of 1994, the Yokozuna picked him as one of his closest personal attendants. When Akebono's family visited, the Yokozuna put Percy in charge. "That's how much I trusted him," Akebono told me. "With my own family." When he needed anything done, Percy got the call. "I don't think anyone else would've done it right," George said. "I remember one time Percy called me up. The Yokozuna wanted some CDs, so he sent him to Roppongi to get his CDs. Because he'd get it right."

"I remember we used to go out," Percy told me, "and these military guys, they come in every so often. They didn't know we talk English, and they were talking shit about us." It's not hard to imagine Akebono's anger growing at the typical sumo-fat-guy jokes coming from these haole boys. "So I walked straight up to the guys," Percy went on: "'What you say?' He seen that and every time he go out after that he tell me, 'Percy, we go.' The Yokozuna," he went on, "a lot of times the reporters and stuff get him in trouble. Plenty times the things I said got him outta trouble. Things my boss ask me are true, I lie to his face. I look right into his eyes and lie for Akebono."

"A lot of times the Yokozuna would go out dancing, people would like grab, punch, push," George said. "Dancing, you're having fun, all of a sudden this Japanese guy, got two girls with him, and he wants to show how tough he is. He's dancing, and he runs right into the Yokozuna: Bam! But of course he's not gonna do nothing, right?" Akebono was constrained by the behavioral demands of his exalted rank. "So we're all watching and all of a sudden, the guy slams into him *again*. And then Percy grabs him from behind, this guy flies up in the air and then bingo! Right up against the wall. I seen him knock out a few people sometimes. For Akebono. It happened so many times. The alcohol, they trying to be tough. And then you watch Percy take care of them."

It may have been one thing to take on little drunken salarymen, and even American military members, and still another to exact revenge on his immediate *senpai* during practice, or to trade wins and losses with Troy and John. But when they put Percy in the ring with Akebono later that summer, he lost all hope of ever becoming a *sekitori* himself. Still hovering well over a hundred spaces down between sumo's third and fourth divisions, Percy had been picked to help train the Yokozuna back from arthroscopic knee surgery. "Because of his size, it was easier for me to wrestle with him during my rehabilitation period," Akebono said. "He wasn't a pusher. He wouldn't slap, or jump on the side at the *tachiai* [the initial charge], so it was real easy for me to just practice getting back my *tachiai*." Akebono took Percy to school, charging forward and throwing him into the training area's wood-paneled wall in a spray of sweat, toweling himself off, squatting, charging, and throwing Percy time and again, sometimes for hours, slowly sapping Percy of all of his strength, and worse, his confidence.

"Fear, brah. Fear," George Kalima explained the task of sparring with Akebono. "Every morning. You know when the alarm clock rings, and you say, 'Fuck, I don't want to get up'? That's what's happening, brah. 'I don't want to get up, I want to play sick today.' 'No! Please!' 'Cause you gotta face one fuckin' mountain comin' at you. I know, brah, I know, 'cause once you hear something movin' around downstairs" in the locker room, "everybody's *shiko*-ing," doing their sumo leg lifts, pounding their feet into the clay. "Everybody's *shiko*, *shiko*, break one sweat, they're like, 'Oh, fuck, pretty soon the Yokozuna's going be coming up.' They know. If he's in a good mood? 'He'll want to practice, and we're gonna get our asses kicked.' That's probably what went through Percy's mind. And I'm pretty sure Troy and Big John were probably pulling rank: 'Oh, you go practice with him.' 'No, *you* go practice with him.' 'No, *YOU* go practice with him.'"

It's generally considered a great honor to practice with a *yokozuna*, and Percy certainly benefited from getting stuck with such sparring duties—particularly in light of what a great natural teacher Akebono was, with a nonstop string of technical advice always coming out of his mouth. But those of us who have never faced that five-hundred-pound mountain in the ring will never really know the pain and fear of which George Kalima, a solid four hundred pounds of muscle himself, speaks. "When you're stepping across the line," he went on, "his arms are so long, you get *scared*, brah, because the guy hits you before you even step over that line," a move that is supposed to look like a football lineman's violent charge. "He's hitting you in the chest or in the shoulders, and because he's got five hundred pounds, you're not gonna *move* him." Safely distant from the memory, George was able to laugh at his own futility against Akebono. "If he comes off with his chest or his shoulder, then that's another thing—you can work with it. But when he comes with the hands? The only way to go is try to go around him. You know, get on the side and try and throw him off balance. But you move forward and try and do the initial hit, and these two giant hands come up and stop you in your tracks, then all of a sudden your mind is wondering, 'What the fuck do I do now?'"

The tender-loving-care beatings had left Percy heaving on the hard clay in exhaustion, but this was much different. The point of tender loving care was to exhaust you, to see what you could handle. The point of these sparring sessions was to compete. Maybe if Percy had been able to catch the Yokozuna off guard on a single charge, or beat him out of the blocks and get a good hold *just once* and steer him out, it all would have been less depressing. But over the course of months, never did he even come close to winning a bout. Worse than that was the way Akebono so calmly dispatched of him, turning what seemed to Percy like frantic grappling battles into deliberate, slow-motion, choreographed dances: charge, grab, march out. Or the more painful version George described: charge, and then throw into wall.

"It's like a *makushita* guy practicing with a *jonidan* wrestler," George told me. "The initial hit, and the thrusts, I mean, you could *feel* that thing, brah. And because the Yokozuna was so tall, when you're hitting him, your head is hitting his chest. That five hundred pounds coming across the ring right into your head—it could pretty much break your fuckin' neck."

After weeks of the kinds of repeated daily beatings that George only had to face the couple of times a month the Yokozuna decided to visit Magaki Beya, Percy's phone calls home began to narrow down to a single topic: the prospect of walking off the *dohyō* for good. And this time his reasons had less to do with culture or with homesickness than with the cold assessment that he just wasn't any good at sumo. How could he expect to compete in the paid ranks, he reasoned, if he could not beat the *sekitori* even once?

And then it happened. He beat Yokozuna Akebono.

"His ass would be high," George said. "He would stand straight up, so you could fire up into him. But then Percy finally got his sumo—he'd grab you from over your back, and grab your *mawashi* and work 'um from there. He's *leaning* on you, and you've got four hundred and fifty pounds that you're holding up for a minute and a half. Everybody knew that if you gonna wrestle him, you betta be in *shape*. He's strong, he's big, he's hard to move. He was the Minute Man of Hawai'i," because inevitably his matches dragged on for over a minute—an eternity in the normally explosive sport. "If you lock up with him, you going get one fight."

"After Percy got into *makushita*," Troy recalled, "ho, that was it. Everyone found that Percy was hard for move. 'Don't grab Percy! Don't let Percy grab you, or you're dead.' He get hold of you, he just going *stay*. He not gonna even attempt for move forward or move back. He get you, and he just going sit. He going make you move him."

"Perce, he was like one spida web, brah," Fats said. "He'd *engulf* everybody, you know what I mean. He's not aggressive. He don't come flyin' out and start smashing. His one is just, he'd just wait. So once he grab you, you *in there*, brah, you know what I mean. He grab you, he just hold onto you like one spida web—you know how one fly get stuck in the web: whap! That's how Perce was. Now you going be fighting all the way until you get dis Hawaiian *back*, brah, but you *cannot*."

While fighting his way back into shape from the long injury layoff, Akebono himself had begun to move away from the same fierce, reckless hand-thrusting sumo style that Azumazeki Oyakata had been trying to drill into Percy for nearly three years now. Akebono had risen up the *banzuke* by flying forward at his opponents in matches lasting two or three seconds—a risky technique that had often caused the five-hundred-pounder to have to slam on the brakes or make abrupt cuts on the sandy clay surface when opponents managed to dodge his charge. Such cuts and stops were perilous to his now-fragile knee, so he spent his months away from competition honing the very technique that had come most naturally to Percy—that of wrapping up his opponent at the start with a strong grip on either side of the *mawashi*, and then methodically marching him out. As Akebono's most frequent practice partner through this months-long rehabilitation, Percy, with his own size advantage and his poor eyesight, finally found what all young *sumōtori* search for, and what all the veterans talk about the way a basketball player talks about "the zone." He found his "own sumo."

"We train five or six hours every day, and usually spend less than one minute in the ring," Percy told me. "But most of my matches was long 'cause I grab belt. I was neva like Chad—they wen' push. I felt more secure when I grab the belt, 'cause I used to use my weight as one advantage, and I used to outpower my opponents."

Percy's "own sumo" was what sumo commentators call *nagaizumō*, sumo that takes a long time. Some sumo purists look down on the tactic, as it turns a sumo match from a hard-charging battle of strength and Zen-like muscle memory into a test of endurance, and of wit, since things slow down enough to give a man time to plot his moves. But fans always seem to love *nagaizumō* matches for their pushes back to the straw boundary, nimble recoveries from the brink of certain defeat, impressive demonstrations of what is called "ring sense," and sumo's most obvious enactments of *gaman*. The translated term "sumo wrestling" irks a lot of true fans, but it applies perfectly to *nagaizumō*. If you watch on video a string of matches from Percy's peak, his grappling bouts stand out from the hard-charging contests of his peers, as he puts up with an opponent's thrusting attack, makes his catch, doesn't panic as he's pushed back to the edge, and then comes over the top with the hook, grabbing onto the back of his opponent's belt. It is a blind man's sumo. A close-up of one match catches his right hand creeping between his heaving opponent's arm and side as though it has a mind of its own, slowly crawling its way across the *mawashi* until it's finally in far enough to grab on with a vicelike grip. From there Percy takes a few steps back and forth to tire his opponent, and then slides him over to the edge, where the poor exhausted man steps out voluntarily and without any violence. Immediately after nearly every one of Percy's matches, the commentators give the time: "Wow—that was a minute and twenty-four seconds!"

"They say sumo is your personality—it's who you are," Tyler said. "And Percy's personality was of a nonchalant, nice, strong individual who didn't want to hurt anybody. That mothafucka could *hurt* you if he wanted to, but he'd rather take the long route. Percy had his own style and I think it portrayed the type of person he was in life—he was just a humble, happy-go-lucky awesome individual, and he didn't go anybody else's route but his own—that was *him*."

"I used to just blow him off the charge: boom!" Troy recalled. "Then when Percy found out 'this is how you stop Troy,' hoo! One time I just came up: boom, he grabbed me, so I tried for snap his hand off my belt, ah? Ho, then I could hear him *growling*. Ho, that growl came, then he came widdiz oddah hand: boom! I'm stuck. So I going try switch to my left hand, try get my lock in. I get my left hand in, okay, I figga I get Percy right here. Ho, I move? Brah, *no moving*."

Many years later one early morning, Percy and I walked into the churchlike silence of the Kokugikan to watch the lower-division bouts unfold before he headed into the changing room to sit with Akebono. If you get to the Kokugikan early enough, you can watch the *banzuke* unfold before your eyes, the scrawny fifteen-year-old kids flailing around on the same *dohyō* that the top-division stars will face off on later in the day. As the empty red seats begin to fill and the ring-announcer's sing-song calls begin to blend in with crowd noise, the fights become more serious, peaking in intensity not at the end of the day, but just before the television lights come on. On the day Percy and I were watching, the usual prebout ritual between two of the upper-*makushita* guys turned into a full-on stare down after several false starts, and when one of them came out of the charge too early, again, and followed through with an open-handed slap to the face that rang out to the rafters, it looked like we had a fight on our hands. The referee stepped between the men, and they finally did manage to time their charge correctly, right into one of the most spirited sumo bouts either Percy or I had ever seen. Percy found out later that the two had to be separated in the changing room after the bout.

If you ever go and watch a day of sumo, make sure to get there in time for the upper-*makushita* bouts, because these guys are literally fighting for their lives. With only seven matches to put up a good record, the losses count all that much more than they do a single step further up the *banzuke*, where the two divisions of *sekitori* fight fifteen times. "It's just half a rank on paper," Akebono explains, "but in the association, it's night and day. The *makushita* guy lives in a big room with all the rest of the other younger wrestlers. He gets not a salary but like a bonus every tournament depending on his win-loss situation, and that's it," a pittance for his endless toiling as a laundry-folding, cabbage-ripping, back-scrubbing slave. "Now if you move half a rank up into *jūryō*, you get a salary, you get your own room, you get your *tsukebitos*—the guys that serve under you—you get to look beautiful when you go in the ring, you start wearing expensive kimonos, you start wearing different kind of slippers—that's the difference of half a rank." On rare occasions, a *makushita* guy is pulled up to fight against a *sekitori* in a major tournament, and he may even win, only to trudge home to scrub the back of another *sekitori*. Depending on how many *sekitori* either retire or fall out of *jūryō*, twenty hungry *makushita* guys could be gunning for a single *jūryō* spot. It's a bit like twenty incarnations of Tiger Woods competing against one another, a single winner getting the green jacket and the Nike contract, with the rest of the field consigned to caddying for demanding, cheap retirees at some sweltering Florida country club.

And Percy walked right through it faster than even Akebono had, starting the year with a 6–1 record, and charging through the spring and summer tournaments right into the middle of the pack of hungry scrappers with a share of the eighth spot in *makushita* for July. Ferd Lewis of the *Honolulu Advertiser* visited Azumazeki Beya just before everyone headed for Nagoya, walking in to the sight of a heaving Percy being dragged around by his topknot in yet another tender-loving-care training session. "What we're trying to do is make him stronger and prepare him to make the most of it [in Nagoya]," the *oyakata* is quoted as saying. "He has been showing good improvement, but for him to do well, he has to get used to keeping his body low." By all accounts—including, at last, that of his *oyakata*—Percy was on the verge of making a name for himself. Azumazeki Beya sponsors were already handing him envelopes thick with cash. Other sponsors were lining up with promises of Rolex watches and more money, as though it were understood that Daiki would make it to *jūryō*. "The Nagoya tournament," Percy recalled, "I called my brother and told him, 'Ho, this tournament I feel invincible.' 'Cause the Nagoya tournament is hot. That's when your body no more that much pain. One week before the tournament, I fought everybody in the stable. I practiced with three guys for two hours straight. I stay in the ring, they just changing back and forth. I neva like lose. I do small moves, and they flying all over the place! I thought, 'I'm gonna kill somebody this tournament.'"

When Percy stepped up on the Nagoya *dohyō* to face the hungriest that sumo had to offer, there were no false starts, no angry slaps to the face. He treated upper *makushita* just as he had treated upper *sandanme*, working to keep his hips low, calmly catching each hard-charging opponent and letting them drive him back to the straw boundary, and then coming over the top with the hook. And then the Minute Man would lean, waiting it out as puddles of sweat formed on the *dohyō* while his heaving opponent was sapped of strength. As the wins piled up, he gained enough confidence to go on offense, to start *flyin' out*, as Fats might put it, and *start smashing*. "The last match I had was with this big, big bastid, Kanesaku," who later reached the top division, Percy explained. "He came straight for me and I forearmed him in his face and slapped the *shit* out of him. I was like, 'YEAH!'" And on the eve of his twenty-second birthday, Percy found himself standing alone with a perfect 7–0 record—a feat that not even Akebono had been able to perform.

At the time, he recounted the tournament much more humbly in a telephone interview with Ferd Lewis: "I was just trying to get some wins, one at a time. And the next thing I knew, I was going for number seven."

"He's changed a lot in the past year," Boss said at the time. "He's gotten stronger and tougher. He's got more fighting spirit. To tell you the truth, a year ago I didn't know if he could make it. But he's really come on." The perfect record was rewarded with a $25,000 cash prize. Even better, Daiki—Percy Kipapa—would become only the fourteenth non-Japanese in the long history of sumo to be promoted into its upper divisions, one of the strong and tenacious 5 percent of all the legions of young men ever to put on a *mawashi* and stomp their feet into the hard clay who could call himself, at last, *sekitori*.

"Percy had his own ways," Troy said. "Even though Boss wanted Percy for push—and he would in the beginning—he would always end up grabbing. But then once Percy knew how for bend his knees and get down low? Brah, there was no way you was going move that *mountain of Waikāne*."

CHAPTER 6

NO WEAPONS

May 16, 2005. While my wife and I were watching TV, our son Kurt, with his ʻohana and Akebono stopped by to inform us Percy was killed tonight, and asked us to stay away from the crime scene on ʻOkana Road in Kahaluʻu. We watched the TV news to get more information.

—George Kipapa, unpublished memoir, July 28, 2007

On may 17, 2005, the KITV Web site led with the headline "Former Sumo Wrestler Killed in Kahaluʻu Stabbing," which was accompanied by a picture of Percy's smiling face. I hadn't believed it when a friend had called from Oʻahu to say, "I'm sorry to hear about your friend." As I ran through a mental list of whom he could possibly be talking about, he said, "The sumo wrestler—the guy from your book." That narrowed it down, but when he'd said, "stabbed to death," Percy was nowhere near the top of the list.

"Who, Troy?" I asked him. "Ola?"

"No. Percy Kipapa."

Though Noriko and I had moved to Hilo, I'd just seen Percy a few weeks earlier when I flew back to Oʻahu for Bumbo Kalima's wedding, and he'd looked great. I went online hoping to find that it was some sort of mistake, or that the report would at least find Percy in "critical condition" or something, but no. He'd been "found stabbed to death at the wheel of an idling truck on ʻOkana Road," the brief report went on. "Kipapa and a friend had apparently just run an errand to the Kahaluʻu 7-Eleven. A half-hour after Kipapa was found, his friend showed up at a nearby hospital," saying he had been stabbed in the leg. The friend "was taken into custody after being treated at Castle Medical Center."

Everyone was feeling the same shocked disbelief, best summed up by Fats Gaspar, who told me, "Big P. Big P was a good bradda. He got caught up in the wrong fuckin' mix . . . Brah, people thought it was *me*. 'Cause Percy's name neva come out—all it said was 'sumo wrestler,' you know what I mean, got *stabbed*. You seen guys was blowing out my phone, brah, from all kine *angles*. 'Oh, Fats. We thought it was you.'"

"No one would think it was Percy," I said.

"Not *even*. No way. They would think it was eitha me or Tyla, you know what I mean. Perce. That would be the *last* guy. He was *harm*less. You know *that*. Fucka was one cruisa, kick-back. Oh man. I neva cry like that in a long time. Was hard. I was trippin' out."

The news came out in pieces over the first week. A few "Former Sumo Wrestler Found Killed" posts showed up on the sumophile electronic mailing list to which I belong. A brief e-mail from George Kalima explained how Chad's wife had called all the boys in Tokyo with the terrible news. A longer account appeared in the *Honolulu Advertiser*. Now they had a witness: someone had come forward and said that the blood-stained friend had made his way to her house and told her, "I stabbed Percy." When I called Bumbo, he happened to be driving his City and County refuse truck right past the road where Percy had been found. "He had stab wounds all in the back," Bumbo had since learned. The Windward coconut wireless must have been overheating with the news—dis wen' happen, dat wen' happen, see watchu get when you cruising wit' dat kine people, see what you attrac'. "I t'ink maybe they must've got into one argument at the 7-Eleven," Bumbo went on, "an' then Percy made him sit in the back of the truck, and that's when he wen' freak, an' start stabbing Percy in the back." There was also speculation that the friend's mother was "in cahoots," a theory that stemmed from a 911 conversation where she had apparently been overheard telling the dispatcher to "disregard" the call. In any case, he said, "No way dat one little punk going kill Percy all by himself."

☾ ☾ ☾

JUST ONE WEEK LATER, Mr. Kalima, Bumbo and George's dad, greeted me from out in front of his carport, his round, brown bald head sticking out from the round canvas hat with the top cut out that he always wore. He was sitting in a lawn chair straddling one of his dogs, pulling out ticks and squashing them on the driveway. Well into his fifties, Haywood Kalima looked the same as he did when I'd met him nearly seven years earlier when he was in Japan for George's retirement. He'd told me back then that he used to swim four hours a day out in the bay. His powerful arms looked like they still could have hauled that bull neck of his all the way out to Rabbit Island and back. "Get plenty beer in the fridge," he said. "Water too if you thirsty. You just missed the boys—they wen' take the kids to the movies." He asked about Noriko, and I told him she'd just started work at the hospital, so she couldn't make it.

"How long is George staying?" I asked him.

"He leaving next Wednesday—same day as us. We going Vegas." He looked up from what he was doing and said, "You know my wife an' me, we get enough for two tickets to Vegas, just one mont' collecting cans and bottles down the park. Some people shame, but since they started that bottle-can return, nobody like bring 'um down da kine, the redemption center—they just t'row 'um in the rubbish can. Every morning we go down there, sometimes thirty-forty dollars worth. One day we get fifty-two dollas—that's our record so far." He stood up and hosed the dog off and said, "I gotta go down the ramp an' start setting up for Sunday. We making one party for George, and so the cousins can all play together."

When he insisted that I change my ticket so I could come to the party, I told him I'd help go down to the ramp and help set up. "You still drinking Bud Light?"

"Nah," he said. "That stuff started giving me headaches. I switch to Keystone."

Mr. Kalima and his friends had rescued the small beach park at the Makapu'u end of Waimānalo seven or eight years earlier from rats and drug dealers, cleaning up trash and discarded concrete rubble, landscaping the area with *hau* trees and grass and *ti* trees, pouring concrete steps down to the ocean, and installing a small boat ramp. Mr. Kalima had personally gotten the mayor to resurface the pitted parking lot, and from then on whenever I passed it was full of family vans and old pickup trucks. When I got there he introduced me all around, saying, "He was up Japan widdus when George retired," and, "He wrote one book about Chad," and, "He stay up in Hilo now—he one professa," and I was greeted with hugs all around from retired City and County guys.

I pulled out a silver can and dropped the twelve-pack in the back of Uncle Bobby's truck, which everyone was standing around and using as a bar.

"Keystone?" somebody said. "That what they drink up in Hilo?"

"Mr. Kalima's trying to turn me on to this," I said.

"Whoa!" they all said at once, turning to their friend, "'Mista Kalima!'"

"You call that guy 'Mista Kalima?'" Uncle Norman asked me, teasing his good friend. Norman was bald like Haywood, with a bushy gray moustache and aviator glasses on his face.

"You know, Keystone getting expensive," someone said. "Used to be six dollas. Now it's what, six fifty."

"That's 'cause they know down at Bobby's that allayou start drinking 'um," Uncle Norman said. He was drinking Miller Lite. "The t'ing getting popular allofasudden, they raise the price!"

"Plus then they add the six cents," someone said.

"Ho, the t'ing only wort' six cents to begin wit'," Norman said with a laugh.

"You could return the cans and just get one free cold pack," Uncle Phillip said.

"No listen to these guys," Mr. Kalima said to me. "They all hard head—too much time in the sun. This one good beer." He took a long sip.

"You know Mr. Kalima's going Vegas next week?" I asked. "All on bottles and cans."

"I went Sandy Beach las' Monday, eighteen dollars," someone said.

"The Beach Park, sixteen-fifty," someone else said.

"Ho, my son an' his friends was ova last Friday, I set up one extra rubbish can for the empties—seventeen-somet'ing dollas."

"My wife an' me," Mr. Kalima said, "last week, fifty-two dollas one day—that's our record so far."

"Ho!"

Around it went, the Waimānalo old guard holding court on the topics of the day around the back of Uncle Bobby's truck. They discussed the remodeled bathrooms at the end of the park, the new fence. The progress of the grass that Uncle Bobby just planted along the curb next to the horseshoe pit. The canoe *hale* at the Beach Park, too far from the water. The accident last weekend in front of the ramp parking lot. And then the you-rememba-the-time-whens, all the way back into the 1960s. Later, Uncle Phillip came by to collect money from everyone for the party they were planning the following week, not for any special occasion—just something they wanted to do to get more neighborhood families down to their park.

"We just waiting for the sun to go behind the mountains," Mr. Kalima told me as the conversation went on around us. "Then we going start setting up. Norman-them already get the tent frame up, so." The shadow from the steep wall of mountains across the road had crept about a third of the way across the parking lot, leaving the tent frame, the row of portable toilets, and the tranquil aqua bay beyond bathed in the bright afternoon sun. The bay's natural postcard image made me think of George, home from prison-gray Tokyo, and I wondered if he'd be back from the movies yet. Then I heard someone say, "Ninety-two dollars, the fine!"

"I got one," I said, raising my hand. "Just today." The general conversation had shifted to the police department's Click-It or Ticket seatbelt campaign.

"Ho, welcome to Honolulu," Uncle Norman said.

"No, was in Hilo," I said. "This morning right after I went to the bank. And he was waiting, right in that spot. Because plenty people, they jump out of their cars at the ATM, and then jump right back in and drive off. I always wear my seatbelt, because after about a hundred yards, if you don't have your seatbelt on in my car the thing starts beeping, lights flashing all over the dashboard. But he got me inside of that hundred yards. He was *waiting.*"

"You'd think the guy would have something betta fo' do," Uncle Bobby said.

"Yeah, like going out and catching criminals," Norman said.

It got quiet for a moment. I could see the shadow from the mountains had stretched further across the hot pavement, now halfway to the beach.

"Yeah," I finally said. "The guy should have been out catching criminals."

❨ ❨ ❨

I FOUND GEORGE IN THE KITCHEN behind a huge bubbling pot looking relaxed in a gray tank top and black shorts, his hair peppered with gray and tied back loosely in a ponytail, his big body taking up most of the cramped kitchen. "Brah, you frickin' deadly wit' dat pen," he said. George has one of the most expressive faces I've ever seen. In one moment the brightest and most welcoming smile can cover it from top to bottom; in the next it can peel paint from the walls with his deep-set eyes and powerful forehead locked into a look of pure anger. Right now his vivid features were reading some combination of respect and appreciation.

"What?"

"That thing you sent me that you wrote about Percy," he said, picking up his spoon to resume stirring, "that thing eva make it into the paper?" I'd written a short piece trying to separate Percy's sumo accomplishments and his Daiki–Big Happiness personality from the horrible way he'd died, and I sent it to a friend at the *Advertiser*—but it had probably been way too sentimental for them. I'd e-mailed a copy of it to George.

"Nah," I said. "No matter, though. I just sent it in because I was afraid that was all they were going to say about Percy: that he was just some murder victim. But Ferd Lewis wrote a nice piece a couple days later that kind of did the same thing, so. Watchu cooking?"

"Pork stew and rice," he said. "You ready?"

Bumbo, Ipo, Kalani, Kari, and Bumbo's wife, Abbi, came out and greeted me before making plates and then sitting around the table in the carport. It wasn't long before we started trying to make sense of what had happened to Percy, whether or not anyone was going to do anything hot-headed and vengeful, who might have been involved.

"Cannot be over money," someone said, "cause now there's no way for them for collect the money."

"The madda wanted for kill him ova something, but."

"Would've been more easier just for shoot him."

"I t'ink they like people *know* how he wen' suffer. But I don't know why."

"That's one of the things supposed to happen with that stuff: frickin' chronics cannot even tell what's right and what's wrong. They don't even know what they did was wrong."

"I seen this thing about it on TV once," Bumbo said. "Was like one CAT scan or one MRI. Had one normal adult brain, all clear. Then had one pitcha of a retarded person's brain, had small black blotches here and there. Then the chronic's brain: big black spots with branches coming out, looked like one big black coral reef. The t'ing do permanent damage to your brain. Me, I'll just stick to beer."

The next morning, a mountain of a haole-Hawaiian man with cropped hair, no shirt, and long denim shorts down to his calves stepped down from a shiny black 2005 GMC pickup, the sun sparkling off of its 22-inch chrome rims.

"*Osssh!*"

"Yo, T!"

T had to weigh four hundred pounds. I figured he must be Tyler Hopkins, who'd joined Takasago Beya not long before Percy joined Azumazeki Beya, and who'd made it to *jūryō* around the same time as Percy did. As he made his way towards us, everyone stood to greet him, big slap handshakes and big hugs and how-*you*s. George introduced us and I kind of felt like I knew him already, so close was his experience to that of Chad, George, and Percy.

"That's one nice ride," George told him.

"Sale told me, 'Eh T, it's time we get you one new cah,'" Tyler said as we all took seats in the carport. He was now working for Konishiki (*Sale*—short for Salevaa), who'd gone high enough and lasted long enough in sumo to be able to build a postretirement career pitching Suntory whiskey and Hawai'i vacations on TV and on billboards across Japan.

"Ho, nah!"

"That's what I was thinking," T said. "So he take me down to the deala, we pick out the truck, and we sit down to make the deal. He pulls out two grand, cash, and he says, 'I get the down payment—you can take care a da mont'ly.' I look at him: ho, the mont'ly six hundred dollas!" Everyone laughed. "I can take care of 'um but."

"You can take care a da mont'ly!" George said.

"But Sale, he gotta take care so many people," he said. "Cousins, brothers, sisters. That's why he gotta keep moving, generate the money, he working for alladem."

"So you just get ova here?" George asked him.

"I just get in from Vegas," Tyler said. "Thought I'd come straight here, see if you was home."

"See, we had one *hui* up Japan," George said to me. "Percy, me, and Tyler. Chad, Konishiki-them already made it before us. So when we finally wen' make 'um, we went off on our own—eat together, pahty, go karaoke. You get this fucka in there, he neva stop singing." He pointed to Tyler. "We go in there, five, six hours sometimes."

"And P, he be li'diss," Tyler said, using his right fist as a mike and continually stopping to push his imaginary glasses back up to the bridge of his nose with his left index finger, singing, "'I shot the sheriff,'" eliciting Bumbo's machine-gun laugh along the way.

"Used to see him in the club li'dat, too," Bumbo said, shoulders bobbing, pushing his own imaginary glasses back on, "out on the dance floor."

When I asked Tyler why he'd retired, he said, "The back. I cracked two lower lumbar vertebrae. They were shooting me up with cortisone before every match. I think that's how come I went ten-and-five in my first *jūryō* tournament."

"Ho, everybody seen that, they was all fret-ting," George said with a smile, "everybody in *jūryō*. They seen you coming up, *charging*, they all saying, 'What wen' happen to this guy's sumo? This the same guy?' They all studying you, trying fo' figure out how to wrestle you all over again."

"They did that to me for two straight tournaments, and when I seen what that was doing to my body, and when I seen that it was all to line somebody else's pockets, I decided it was time to leave."

"Percy, too," George said. "They seen two more Hawaiians charging up, they all fret-ting. Right afta these two make *jūryō*, that's when we wen' set up our *hui*. Tyler, Percy, they was good friends because they always used to talk about how they would get beaten on back at their stables. T was Takasago Beya, and they used to fuck him up over there like Boss used to fuck up Percy."

Tyler shook his head. "*Kawaigari* afta practice," he said. "I stay on the ground, crying, puking, breathing hard. I look around and that small room's all full of thirty-forty big Japanese fuckas, dey all sucking up my oxygen, I think I going die right there. Sale stay *kicking* me in the ribs, 'Get up, haole boy!'"

"Just like Boss," George said. "I seen 'um one time in Kyūshū, they came down to practice with us. And all the *makushita* guys started going at it, and Percy was doing real good, pushing and slapping—that's what Boss wanted. But Boss was sitting there with one eye open and one eye closed and everybody *know* he was sleeping 'cause you could hear him snoring. So Percy must've went about ten bouts—that's pretty good, pulling off a run like that. 'Cause these guys in *jūryō* and *makushita*, man, they tough. You gotta start getting paid, so those guys are *hungry*. So Percy's going at it, and he's winning. He's pushing. And now Percy's tired, right? The eleventh bout he comes up and he decides to grab, because he's tired. And then Boss opens his eyes and sees him grabbing: 'Eh you fucka! I told you, you gotta push!' Boss stands up and runs into the ring and *punches* him: 'How many times I told you, you gotta push!' And he punches him again. And so Percy backs up, he goes into the corner, Boss starts kicking him and punching him. We're all, 'Whoa! Wait a minute! Percy's been pushing all this time and you were *sleeping!*'"

"One time he fought 198 bouts in one day," I said. Boss had once made Percy take on a university sumo club one day after an exhausting regular morning practice had ended. "It would have been 200, but he told me, 'I was so mad at my boss, I like hurt everybody I face.' Next day he had to do forty more bouts with John and Troy."

The two former *sekitori* just shook their heads.

"Chad used to come over for practice widdus," Tyler went on. "I had to do *butsukari-geiko* with him." I recalled the exercise where one guy charges into another guy's chest, sliding him across the ring like a football blocking sled. "I charge into him, I start tickling him, whispering in his ear, 'Chad! Please, Chad! Please! We braddas from way back, Chad, please Chad. Rememba Kaisa High School, Chad!' An' he listen—try not to t'row me down too hard." He took a puff from his cigarette and crushed it out. Then out of nowhere he said, "You heard they wen' arrest four more people?"

"Was da madda," Bumbo said right away, "and couple other chronics they got staying at that house. Da madda gotta be in cahoots."

"No way that one fucka kill P all by himself," Tyler said, "knife or no knife."

Bumbo explained his theory about the guy pinning Percy down with his legs. "The paper said he tested positive, but."

"But that don't mean nothing," Tyler said. "Still yet, don't make no sense even da madda wen' help. Percy was one strong fucka."

We all went on speculating on what could have happened, why Percy could have even been at the house, who else could possibly have had anything to do with it. It was maddening.

"Brah, read this," George said to Tyler, handing him a folded piece of white paper. He'd printed out the piece I'd written about Percy.

Tyler looked up at him in disbelief.

"Read 'um," George said again.

"Ho, Hawaiian, I just get in from Vegas, I been awake for *twenty-eight hours.*"

George lit another cigarette and passed it over. "He wen' e-mail it to me last week."

Tyler took the cigarette and shook his head and then leaned over the paper in his big right hand. "Ho, you wen' start right in wit' the '*mottai nai,*'" he said. It translates into "what a regrettable waste." He read a little further and took a drag of the cigarette and looked up at George. "When your madda getting back from work?"

"She stay inside sleeping," George said. "She work nights. Keep reading."

Tyler took another drag and leaned over the paper again, his concentration deepening as he went. "Brah, you not holding back," he said. "Ho: 'Look closely at the picture of Akebono being held aloft as the first foreign *yokozuna*: he's sitting on Percy's shoulders.'" He kept reading, his eyes going back and forth. And when he was about two-thirds of the way down the page, those eyes began to glisten, and well over. Reaching the bottom, he wiped his face and handed the paper back to George.

☾ ☾ ☾

HAWAIIAN MEMORIAL PARK. You drive by its sloping green hills dotted with red anthuriums a hundred times, but you never think about the next time you might have to drive through its gates. Today the place was buzzing with people, cars filling the small parking lot and then lined out along the two roads stretching out over the green hills.

"Man, I knew Percy had a big family, but," I said to Mr. Kalima.

He smiled and said, "They not all here for him—it's Memorial Day weekend." We waited for George and Bumbo and his wife, who'd stopped off at Bumbo's work to ice the coolers, for Kalani's family, and for Mrs. Kalima, who was coming straight from work.

When they arrived we all walked into the church together, and Memorial Day or not, it looked like all of those cars outside were in fact for all of these people—at least three hundred so far, half-filling the rows of pews, milling about towards the back room on the right where sandwiches were being served, or standing in a line that stretched about halfway down the aisle. Soft live Hawaiian music filled the church. Flower wreaths mounted on stands lined the altar area, each with a banner indicating Kurt's union, or "Takasago Beya" in black painted kanji characters. Off to the left Kurt's massive frame dominated the end of the family reception line of Percy's parents, his uncles and aunties, his nieces and nephews, each dressed in green-printed black aloha wear. A diamond stud in each ear, a close-cut black beard on his dark face, Kurt had emerged as Akebono's protector after having come to know him through Percy. Akebono's family now stayed with Kurt whenever they came to Oʻahu, the two having developed a brotherly relationship that, a few years earlier, had ceased to include Percy. "You know how they always expect the *yokozuna* for pay for everything?" Chad had asked me once. He'd been picking up bar tabs and dinner tabs for all the boys in Azumazeki Beya for more than five years. "Well the same thing happens when you go home, 'cause they know you get money. Well one time we went out with Kurt and his wife, and they neva let us pay. And you know Kurt-them, he has one big family for take care of, but he wen' insist on paying anyway. That's the only time anyone ever did that." Chad himself now sat off to the side in the adjoining courtyard, the church's sliding side doors having been opened wide to accommodate the overflow. "I always used to be on the side of him whatever he did," Percy had once told me. But then Percy wasn't at Chad's wedding, or his retirement ceremony—a fact evoked as much by the image of the Yokozuna's now-short hair as by the look on his troubled face.

I signed the guest book and was given a program, and as I approached the front of the line I could see that the music was coming from a small room off to the right that opened up into the church, where two people were playing live. A nice portrait of Percy smiled out at us from the table next to the podium. A white cardboard square stamped with Percy's red handprint and painted with the black kanji characters to spell out "Daiki" was propped up on a stand. Two glass display cases sat on another small table, one holding a straight, pointed topknot, the other the formal upturned flower-shaped topknot Chad had helped cut at Percy's own retirement ceremony. I had yet to realize that while that first topknot had been cut to shame Percy, it had become a symbol of pride, another incredible obstacle the boy from Waikāne had overcome way up in Japan. Indeed, everything the family had on display was rich with symbolism, right down to the photo on the program, Percy atop the *dohyō* facing an unseen opponent, arms spread out wide to indicate he was ready for a fair fight, and that he honorably carried no weapons.

And then there was the big white casket, open on one end with a white veil draped over Percy. Over the closed end the family had draped his sparkling blue-and-gold Pegasus *keshō-mawashi*. George lifted the veil and bent down to kiss Percy's forehead. The rest of the Kalimas in turn held onto Percy's arm and spoke to him briefly, and when I walked over to join them, I found that Percy wouldn't move. The laugh wouldn't come. The arms, still thick and still powerful looking, had finished working. He had, as Bumbo had said, picked up plenty weight—this was no "chronic." His full face sat beneath a black ski cap embroidered in green with the word, "Perce," making him look even younger than he really was, more like a joyful Daiki boy, resting before he goes out to play. But he wouldn't move.

I turned to the reception line: Grandma Kipapa, Uncle Henry, Mr. and Mrs. Kipapa, Selisa and Kirk, Kurt's wife Jolyn, Kurt, their sons and wives, all dressed in the same black background and light-green flower-print aloha wear. Mrs. Kipapa was now in Bumbo's arms. Kalimas were hugging Kipapas all the way down the line. I bent over to hug Grandma. Mr. Kipapa had the same round face as Percy, though his was framed with the gray of his hair and beard. He had that same nose, that same guttural Kipapa voice. He looked like Percy should have expected to look in another forty years. Percy's mother then turned from Bumbo's hug and met me, number four-hundred-something in line, and said, "You're the writer!" I'd met her only once, for about ten minutes, more than four years earlier when we went to look at the car in Waikāne, and here she was with a look of total recognition. "He used to talk about you all the time. He affected so many people."

"He helped me so much with the book I was writing," I told her. "No way I could have done it without him. He was such a great storyteller. He could pick out all the most important details."

"Somebody should have written a book about him, too," she said.

We hugged again, and I moved down the line of Kipapas before taking a seat outside in the courtyard. And for the next three hours, people kept coming. The reception line never dwindled to a length of less than halfway down the aisle, and the Hawaiian music continued, most of it live. Darren Benitez filled the church with his sweet high voice. Someone sang a song called "Pōmaika'i," which matched Percy's middle name as it appeared on the front of the program. A few of the people paid their respects and left, but most of them stayed, filling up the rest of the church and the folding chairs outside. Channel Two News came for a report, pulling Chad, George, and Tyler on the side for interviews. The service finally began with two songs from Kurt, and then Uncle Henry held his hands high and led us in prayer. Kurt somehow managed to make it through a song he'd written for Percy years earlier called "My Brother and Me." Percy's cousin Cynthia stepped up to the podium and read the eulogy—a brief, touching biography of a gentle giant who "loved his *'ohana* and loved people." A poignant slide show followed, Percy and his *'ohana*, Percy as a *sumōtori*. It all worked to shift the focus towards Big Happiness and away from the ugliness of his violent end. When it was over, I joined the line to stand before him one last time. That big, powerful body: *he put on plenty weight.* The black ski cap: Perce. That round, young face, the thick forearms. For some reason, from just below the elbows, a blanket covered the arms, hiding the hands.

"Look: he giving you his chest," Bumbo said, putting one hand on Percy's broad body, another on my shoulder. A *sumōtori* "gives his chest" during the *butsukari-geiko* training exercise, where he allows another *sumōtori* to charge into him and slide him across the sand-covered *dohyō*. "You can finally take him," he said with a soft laugh. Standing as I was right there in front of Big Happiness, I had to smile. Later as the church began to empty out, the musicians went into "I'll Remember You," the family gathering around the casket. The hundred or so of us remaining were invited to join hands and see Percy off with "Aloha 'Oe" and "Hawai'i Aloha," voices building into the first chorus. When it seemed the song was about to end, the guitarist would hang on a seventh chord and then start the whole thing over again. We got louder and louder, some of the shyer folks now joining in, when someone shouted, "Goodbye!"—they were closing the casket—and then one more verse, and then the final chorus, until we meet again.

"You going widdus?" George asked Tyler.

"I'll meet you out front," he said. "I gotta get the wreath."

We found Bumbo outside pulling beers out of the cooler in the back of George's rental car. "We going quick have one last one with Percy," he said, handing out beers to me, George, his father, and Kalani, taking three more himself, and leading the way back up to the front of the church. He offered one to Kurt, who declined, opened one for Percy and set it on the casket, and opened his own. I turned to see Chad sitting in the front row, that troubled look not having left his face.

"You get one for Hawaiian?" I asked Bumbo.

He turned and held out the extra bottle for Chad, who lifted his big body out of the pew and walked over to join us.

"To Percy!" everyone said together, clinking bottles with each other, Kalani, Mr. Kalima, Bumbo, George, Chad, and all of us taking care to include Percy's bottle without knocking it over. "*Osssh!*" Chad took what looked like a sip and then placed his empty bottle next to Percy's. Bumbo was right behind him, and then George, Kalani, and Mr. Kalima. I took a couple of tries and finally finished my last beer with Percy, and I could almost hear him laughing at me for taking so long about it. Bumbo collected the empties and we all walked away from the big white casket, a full open bottle of Budweiser sitting on top.

THE BLACK GMC WITH THE CHROME 22-INCH RIMS pulled up, with the huge "Takasago Beya" wreath of red flowers in the back and Tyler, now without his shirt, behind the wheel. Everyone double-checked to make sure we all knew where we were going, and I got in with Tyler. A song someone had played much earlier in the day was on a loop on his CD player: "Pōmaikaʻi." A sweet, high male voice sang out in Hawaiian of Pōmaikaʻi from Waikāne, and the chorus was structured around the familiar sumo greeting *Osssh!*, mixed with a chant of *Haʻaheo!*—the Hawaiian word for pride.

"This guy wen' write this song for Perce," Tyler said.

"The guy that played this morning?"

"That's him—Kevin Chang. Good friend of Percy's from way back." We were driving in a line behind George and Bumbo, Kalani and Kari, Mr. and Mrs. Kalima, heading through Kāneʻohe. Tyler's giant body was leaned way back in the truck's reclining seat as he expertly wove in and out of traffic, executing the whole operation with one pinky on the steering wheel and his right big toe dancing between the brake and the accelerator. He moved with more grace than men less than half his size. Tyler had also made it to *jūryō*, and watching his foot move between the pedals reminded me of a fact made clear every time I watched sumo practice: *sumōtori* only looked like big oafish guys until they started moving. Underneath the thin layer of fat, they were solid athletes. Sumo was a martial art, with seventy-something types of throws and pushes and countless other gripping and open-handed thrusting techniques, and to succeed at it you needed to be able to dance around the ring's edge.

Osssh! Haʻaheo. The song ended with "*He inoa no, Daiki-zeki,*" and then it started up again. We all turned onto Kahekili Highway, out past Windward Community College and the state hospital, and down into the country, the part where the summit of Puʻu ʻŌhulehule, way off in the distance, is framed by the big leafy trees overhanging the highway. I could have blinked and been sitting right next to Percy, who'd pointed out the mountain at this very spot back when we went up to Waikāne to look at his car. Right in the middle of that dream he'd shared of buying a lunch wagon and knowing all the best places to park it, he'd launched into the story about how that mountain was a part of his family, how he still hiked up the trails all by himself to find peace. That was where they were going to scatter his ashes in a couple of months, on his birthday.

We followed as George turned off the highway, and turned again onto another road parallel to it, heading back in the other direction. ʻOkana Road could have been any road off the highway on any part of Oʻahu: thick jungle stretching uphill to the left, corrugated iron-roofed box houses sitting in quarter-acre fields of overgrown grass off to the right, the odd car up on blocks out front, a pit bull chained to a carport post, the sound of roosters crowing even in the late afternoon sun—all the marks of country, less than five minutes outside Kāneʻohe. Except here the tension hung thick, the air clouded by the fact that we were approaching an ice den, and that if you closed your eyes you could imagine the road that night, its usual solid rural darkness cut by the blue and red swoops of the spinning lights atop a squad of police cars, and an ambulance that had arrived too late.

Tyler was on his phone to a friend trying to get the exact location, and then he said, "Oh, neva mind, it's right ova there. Somebody already put up one cross and some flowers." A driveway came down out of the jungle to meet the road, and just in front of it, off on the dusty shoulder in the shade of a monkey pod tree, someone had erected a makeshift cross out of two two-by-fours nailed together and anchored in a concrete hollow-tile block, surrounded by small pots of light-red anthuriums and white orchids. A piece of paper was stuck to the cross. When I got out of the truck and walked over, I could see what some child had carefully scrawled in crayon: "We Love You, Uncle."

Bumbo handed out beers and again we toasted Percy, each spilling some on the ground in the hope that it would somehow reach his wounded spirit. Tyler took the big wreath out of his truck and stuck one of its three legs through the fence bordering the road to keep it from blowing over. He stumbled a bit on the rough ground as he struggled with the wreath, and then caught himself.

"Whoa, big P!" he said.

"Watch out he don't pull you in there wit' him," George said with a smile.

And then the speculation started up again. Driveway here, truck found here, neighbor who called it in over there. The madda live here, or over there? If it's up this driveway, I don't know—can't even see the house, the thing just winds up the hill and into the jungle. They still looking for the murder weapon. The driveway, lined with head-high sugar grass on each side, you could throw a knife in there and never find it, t'row two-t'ree-four knives up there, never find it. Which way was the truck facing? And Percy was behind the wheel? Tell me how the truck could have been facing that direction if they just get back from 7-Eleven? Hadda happen up at the house. Which house? I only seen 'um on the Internet video, was all blurry. That house?

A car drove up and stopped in the middle of the road, one of the neighbors. "That's not really the spot," he said to us. "They found him on the other side of the driveway. I just moved everything over here to keep the flowers in the shade, ah? But happened over there." Everyone was full of questions for him, a nice country guy who didn't know Percy but seemed to understand our need to know—in fact, it was kind of strange how normal he was, living right here in what the papers had made out to be some drug-infested neighborhood. The truck had been found at the bottom of the driveway facing *away* from where we were standing, he told us. The cops had come back the next day and arrested four people on drug charges—not for anything related to the murder. All four of them were now out on bail.

George and I walked over to the spot where Percy actually was found, leaving everyone else talking with the neighbor. We spilled a little more beer. Percy had made it to *jūryō*, and was still well over four hundred pounds. He could *fight*. He was found behind the wheel. If he was facing away from where we were standing—that is, in the direction we had all driven to get to the spot on what turned out to be a dead-end road—then that means he didn't pull over from the road, because he would have been on the wrong side of the road, at night, shining his lights at whatever oncoming traffic there might be. Not Percy. No way Percy pulled over to the opposite side of the road, his lights facing into traffic. Which meant he was driving down the driveway. And then the guy freaks out and starts stabbing the person who's behind the wheel of a pick-up truck headed down a winding driveway towards the road? No way.

A few steps up the driveway the sounds around me grew faint. Up ahead the ribbed concrete pavement rose, and then turned into the thick green jungle to some hidden ice den, a crank factory out in the shed, I imagined, or right there in the carport, babies screaming and little kids zooming around on brand-new stolen bikes, a rusted-out swing set in the side yard, a screen door slamming to the point of threatening to bring the whole dilapidated operation down, remnants of flowers in a weed-choked garden by the front door, mangy dogs roaming about, one of them pregnant, a sparkling new Cadillac Escalade, black, with tinted windows, lowered over bright chrome rims, parked at the top of the driveway. I wanted to walk up and make sure this was what I'd find at the end of that driveway. Or if I didn't, if I just found some regular three-bedroom country house, a worn buzzing refrigerator full of cold Heinekens in the carport, a lovingly tended garden and a nice, shy little kid running inside to announce I was coming—even if I found that, I just wanted to ask them why the fuck they killed Percy.

I walked back down to find everyone listening to Percy's sister Selisa, who'd come to collect the "Takasago Beya" banner from Tyler's wreath to save for her mother. "They bashed my brother's head in," she was saying. "I know they did it up there." She pointed up the driveway. "That's why we had to put the beanie on him today—his head was all bus' up, like with one baseball bat. And his hands: my brother was fighting them. We had to cover up his hands because they were all mangled, he had a chunk of muscle *this big* missing, right above his wrist. And the fucking cops." She rolled her eyes, growing angrier as she spoke. "I asked them: 'Where are my brother's glasses? You know my brother cannot see anything without his glasses.' They jus' look at each odda." She mimed a stupid look. "I ask them: 'Where's my brother's watch? My brother had a Fubu watch he wore *all the time*, he *never took it off*.' They look at each odda." She gave the look again. "An' they not going do not'ing, they already get this guy for take the fall for them. Just yesterday I seen the madda in the store, just going about her business, just another day, like nothing eva happen. They probably going end up letting him out, too—he's pleading temporary insanity."

"Yeah, the paper said the guy had thirty-one priors already," someone said.

Thirty-one prior arrests? *Thirty-one?* Meanwhile the cops were all out on stakeout for the mad criminals driving around without their seatbelts.

And then the clincher: he'd only been able to kill Percy because he was out on bail. Only a couple of weeks earlier he'd been locked up for pulling a gun on his girlfriend, and then he was out. The story just kept getting worse until we said our good-byes and promised to meet at the party the family was throwing at Kurt's house. When everyone drove off, Tyler and I resumed speculating. Had to happen at the house, Percy wen' fight alladem off, five, six guys maybe, stabbed in the back, stabbed in the heart, hands all mangled, *still* manages to get in the truck, and he's dead by the time he gets down the driveway, slumped over the steering wheel turned to the left, the truck rolling to a stop just off the road and idling until a neighbor calls the police. Not some random, freaked-out drug killing at all. Five guys hold Percy down. But Percy, he wasn't just some big guy from the valley. Percy made *jūryō*.

"I don't know if you know," Tyler said as we pulled back out onto the highway, "but in sumo training, get what you call *kawaigari*. Tenda loving care. At the end of practice, they kicking you, making you cry, you can't even frickin' *breathe*." He turned away from the road to face me, eyes wide, and said, "They *fuck you up*. This not football practice, the coach yelling at you, making you do sprints. Nah, they kicking you, yelling at you, berating you, hitting you with the bamboo stick, the baseball bat. They stuffing the salt in your mouth, everything—you wish you could die right there. And I mean, you wish you could *die*, anything just to make it end. And it takes you to one whole different level, one whole different world, where you find out you can take things you never thought anyone could take. Percy wen' go t'rough alladat. Plenty times. You don't just make it to *jūryō*."

By the time Tyler pulled back into Hawaiian Memorial so I could get my rental car, we had it pretty much figured out. The victim tested positive for methamphetamine. *He wen' pick up plenty weight.* They put a knife to his throat and make him suck on the pipe 'cause, hey, what's one chronic killing one nodda chronic, anyway? That just leaves one less chronic—the guy did us a favor. But Daiki, *he's in his no-weapons pose, arms spread out wide, ready for a fair fight,* he struggles free, and they come at him, blade after long, polished blade. Daiki meets them with pistonlike hand thrusts, right into the oncoming blades. *Where are my brother's glasses? You know my brother cannot see anything without his glasses.* So one of the blades gets through. *I neva could get the push down, 'cause, see, I get bad eyes.* Get plenty pig farmers up here, and look at where they wen' stab him: up here, just above the heart, where all the stuff is, the critical veins and arteries. And then they pull *over* and *down*, right down the middle to his stomach—that's exactly how you gut one pig. Percy knows he's hurt. He runs for the truck, pulling out his phone and hitting 911 on the way. *Had the madda's voice on the 911 tape, she tell 'em, 'disregard.'* Multiple stabs in the back as he runs for the truck, and then the bat, a full swing to the head just as he gets behind the wheel and points it down the driveway. If Percy went down, we were sure, he went down fighting—and more than just one guy.

"Dat fucka taking the fall for somebody," Tyler said.

CHAPTER 7

ZAPPED

I seen this thing break up families. I let the people know: I'm not a bad person—I just got caught up. And at the wrong time in the wrong place when you're having problems, you meet up with the wrong person, and anybody, in any high achievement can get onto this drug. It's not for low-class, no-class, or just Hawaiians. This thing will hit you. In your hospitals, in your schools. It could be the people in your doctor's office. Everywhere.

—Lori Ryder of 'Okana Road, Kahalu'u, August 7, 2006

At percy's funeral I'd found myself wondering how it could have happened in Kahalu'u, of all places. How could Percy have been killed in Kahalu'u, so close to that valley of his where people still grew their own food, where so much was still done as it had been done since his grandfather's day? When I learned more about how the community had been able to band together and fight off suburban development, and then stand up to a tsunami of Japanese resort developers, it came to make even less sense. The place seemed to have been on a permanent neighborhood watch since before Percy was born. How could ice have taken hold the way it had in such a place?

"This was supposed to be like Hawai'i Kai," a Waiāhole-Waikāne Community Association member named Bernie Punuciel told me at a 2007 Waiāhole Beach Park cleanup. About thirty of us were cutting grass and whacking weeds in the twenty-acre field fronting the two valleys, a collection of retired folks fighting the good fight along with subsistence farmers who traded their taro with other farmers for vegetables. After thanking me profusely for simply showing up, one of the farmers had handed me a

99

gas-powered weed whacker and handful of nylon replacement lines. Citing an aversion to using chemical herbicides, he'd instructed me to search for two types of troublesome weeds and grind them to bare ground. During a water break I listened to Bernie's stories of the association's history, all the while looking around at the deep green valleys and the mountains beyond. And though I'd driven past the area hundreds of times over the years, for the first time I could picture the postcard views as someone like Tom Enomoto might: a golf course over here, a subdivision up that ridge over there, a strip mall and gas station right here next to the highway. And the bay may have been a bit muddy from stream runoff, but it was as peaceful as a lake. "The marina was supposed to go right there," Bernie told me, pointing just up the coast. Standing where I was less than thirty minutes from the city center, the green untouched emptiness of the valleys suddenly struck me as a kind of miracle.

I walked out across the big field, lowering the weed whacker, gunning it, grinding a weed into a cloud of dust, and moving on. There were no showers or restrooms, or even a sign designating the park, and the task of maintaining the place—keeping the cane grass near the ocean's edge cut short so "druggies" couldn't congregate there, towing the occasional abandoned car from the jungle off to the right, and even cutting the huge field's grass—had fallen to the community association. They hung a sign beside the highway every month or so to announce a "cleanup," and let the hard workday evolve into a potluck party under the big tent someone had put up the day before. The buzz of the weed whacker put me into a rhythm, my mind wandering as I worked up a sweat under the morning sun. I felt like I was *doing something*, even if it was only one weed at a time. The idea was for the surrounding grass to move into the bare spot left by the weed whacker; even though the weed would probably grow back, if you stuck to it for a few months the grass would eventually take over. But when I stopped and looked back over the vast field of grass now dotted unevenly with manhole-cover-sized patches of brown dirt, hundreds of dark green clusters of weeds still left to grind, the image came into clear focus. I couldn't even keep my yard free of weeds back in Hilo. And once a month, when they weren't busy working their own farms, these folks had four hours to maintain a place where families could go barbecue on a Sunday, where fathers could take their sons fishing. The weed whacker was just

another weapon in the same battle—the public presence, the community recreation space, and the effort to rid their community of ice, one dealer at a time. Twenty acres.

Compared to the scope of the problem, this well-meaning attempt to reclaim even part of the Windward side from ice could not have looked more hopeless—a feeling that only deepened once I learned exactly what the community was up against. Before Percy left for Japan, the drug distribution network in place since the 1960s had endpoints. But when ice fell into the vacuum left by Green Harvest and Operation Wipeout, its overwhelmingly addictive quality combined with its low price to break the network wide open, like a deadly disease once restricted to the veins and arteries but now free to infect the tiniest capillaries. From 1991 to 1998 while Percy was sweating his way through ten thousand practice matches and struggling through hundreds of tender-loving-care beatings, back at home ice was working harder and spreading faster. A former dealer explained the web to me: "Seventy-five percent of the people that do drugs are low-level chronics," he estimated. "You get one big dealer—this guy's been running twenty years, so this guy's running with every hardcore line there is. He controls his community by giving one guy just enough so that he can sell three tiny little papers, and giving another guy just enough, so they think they're all playing. He don't give nobody the load, and he's got fuckin' a network like you wouldn't believe. I know of like maybe six to twelve families that have been dealing for twenty years," between Temple Valley and Waikāne. "And say there's fifty people that drop off of each of them. And that's not even close to it, 'cause you got kids whose parents do it, and then they pick up a little baggie and they put something in it and smash it, and they sell it, and then the second kid wants to smoke it, and he wants to get some more so he goes out and finds some other guy to sell to. How many people live there?" Another former dealer told me that "when it comes down to selling ice, just about everybody who do 'um sell, to support their habit. They going buy something and then sell some just to make their money back."

"The t'ing came from Kāne'ohe," Percy's best friend Charles Kekahu said. "Right when I was in Castle, eleventh and twelfth grade, the t'ing started coming. 'Cause nobody used to do that, and from Kāne'ohe, the t'ing came down to Kahalu'u, and the t'ing wen' *zap* Kahalu'u, slowly eventually migrating." Zapped. And then Waiāhole got zapped. And then Waikāne. Kualoa. Kaʻaʻawa. Punaluʻu. Hauʻula. By decade's end, that's how so many communities across the state got zapped, meticulously torn apart more effectively than any invading developer ever could tear them apart. Ice was no longer something that high school kids did when they partied with their friends, or something that the kind of toothless losers we could always look down upon as "druggies" or "chronics" did. It began to reach into parts of Hawaiʻi where no one had ever expected to even consider the mention of drugs. Perhaps the very height of unself-conscious admission to the drug's statewide grip came to me a few months before Percy returned from Japan, when I walked into the second-grade class where I would be student teaching and found that one of my students had been named, on purpose, "Crystal." Like many kids in the class, she was being raised by her grandmother.

Anecdotal evidence now abounds of the lawyers and doctors and other professionals, who at first couldn't believe how "productive" they could be thanks to ice, telling their stories in rehab clinics. The drug even took down a former deputy prosecutor named Gary Modafferi, who as the head of Hawaiʻi's biggest drug prosecution unit had almost certainly racked up a thick stack of convictions for Green Harvest and Operation Wipeout pakalolo offenses before switching teams in 1994 to join the more lucrative ranks of the criminal defense lawyers. It is not difficult to imagine any number of scenarios that led to his first puff from the glass pipe. Was he arguing one case and preparing for several more, gulping down gallons of coffee to get himself through a string of twenty-hour days in his new job? Did he feel the need to be more productive? Modafferi almost certainly thought he would be able to "use" ice in some kind of benign medicinal way. But as most of us in Hawaiʻi now all-too-painfully know, and as he would come to find out with his addiction and then his 1998 conviction, he was wrong.

If an addict did come to the point where he admitted he needed help, he was essentially given the message that he may as well go on using ice and, more than likely, dealing it. Treatment options statewide were close to nil, with even Hina Mauka, the largest facility statewide at forty-five beds, in a financial shambles. "In '94 when they were looking for money during the economic downturn," former Hina Mauka CEO Andy Anderson told me, "they took a million dollars away from the Department of Health," which funds drug and alcohol treatment centers such as Hina Mauka. "And nothing was increased in the Department of Health budget for addiction treatment for the next ten years." Anderson—not to be confused with the 1980s local politician of the same name—was hired "as a guy to get this place out of trouble" in 1996. "We were ready for bankruptcy," he went on. "We couldn't put people in the beds because they didn't have the ability to pay. Their health insurance wasn't covering it. We had to turn people away. I think we had thirteen clients when I got here, out of forty-five beds, and some of *them* were outpatients. There were no resources to pay staff and keep the doors open, so we couldn't just say, 'Yeah, we'd be glad to take you.' The heart said 'Yeah, we want to do that,' but we knew if we did that we would have to shut down."

It all may have been enough to let ice spread past the point of control: the spectacular lack of official public concern at the root of Hina Mauka's financial woes, the unheard-of addictive power of ice combined with its low price and wide availability, and the collective sense of denial perpetuated by the local news media. University of Hawai'i journalism professor Beverly Keever, for instance, named the Drug War as 1991's most "conspicuously underreported story," telling the *Honolulu Weekly* that "the scattered coverage is there, but it is never put together critically as a whole." The stories that did emerge were swept aside or ignored, such as Attorney General Warren Price's speculation in the late 1980s that Green Harvest would cause "a shift to other competitively priced drugs," or Donald Topping's detailed cautionary study from 1995, "Drugs and Crime in Hawai'i." Topping kept elaborating a year later in a *Honolulu Star-Bulletin* op-ed piece that introduced the word "epidemic," pointing out that ample evidence of similar unintended consequences existed long before Green Harvest began, such as proof of a 150 percent rise in morphine use when alcohol was prohibited in the 1920s, and a National Institute of Justice report clearly linking the lack of what they called "pakkol" (pakalolo) to the increased use of ice in Hawai'i as early as 1985. And nearly two years before Percy returned home from Japan, Topping cited the work of Patricia Morgan.

In the very first substantial ethnographic study of ice use in Hawai'i, conducted for the National Institute on Drug Abuse while Percy was in high school and published in 1990, Patricia Morgan and a team of researchers concluded overwhelmingly that ice "replaced marijuana, which had become scarce and expensive due to eradication policies." To back this claim she points out, among other troubling statistics, that 86 percent of the study's interview subjects began using ice after 1984, just three years before Operation Wipeout's triumphant two-million-plant peak. Morgan's team further found that while the users they examined in San Diego and San Francisco overwhelmingly preferred to snort or inject ice, "92 percent of the Honolulu users are primarily smokers." In other words, when pakalolo started disappearing, in the context of a social circle at a house party the glass pipe replaced the joint. A drug with a wide range of types of users—from the fully functioning stoner on down through the weekend partier, from the experimenting college kid to the famously never-having-inhaled former president of the United States—had been replaced by one that could zap an entire island, and Donald Topping was screaming it out right there in the Sunday paper nine years before Percy was killed.

Though there can be no excuse for the way Topping's warnings were ignored on an official public level, if the army of community activists in Waiāhole-Waikāne wasn't listening, it was partly because the land battle had never really ended. While Percy was crying himself to sleep in Tokyo, they were busy going up against the kind of money and connections that had led to a chapel being bulldozed a few miles south, in Maunawili. If Kitaro Watanabe could spend the equivalent of nearly half the cost of the H-3 freeway on Hawai'i real estate in less than two years, it might take involvement on the scale of the Waiāhole-Waikāne Community Association's traffic-blocking protests in the 1970s to stop him from eventually teeing off across from the Kipapas' home. And as for connections, the community need only look further up the valley, where Hoyu Kensetsu, and its local subsidiary, SMF Enterprises, were requesting to have part of their fourteen-hundred-acre property "downzoned" from agricultural land to the more restrictive "conservation" zoning. As Pat Tummons of Environment Hawai'i pointed out in a 1991 *Honolulu Weekly* commentary, usually it would work the other way around, with the developer fighting for land to be shifted into a less-restrictive zoning district rather than gambling that the Department of Land and Natural Resources would place it into a conservation subzone that permitted golf courses.

The unusual move made the community suspicious, particularly in light of the fact that the Japanese company's *seishō* was Tom Enomoto. All they really knew about Enomoto were such stories as the one where Ian Lind of the *Honolulu Star-Bulletin* found that Governor John Waiheʻe had used tens of millions of federal dollars designated for airport use to instead purchase 120 acres from Campbell Estate, then avoid the state-law-mandated bidding process through a "complex escrow transaction" to provide Enomoto's company with a below-market lease to construct a new Hawaiʻi Raceway Park. Or the story that Enomoto had not only managed to quietly set Minami USA boss Misao Nangaku's thousand-acre golf course project in motion; he'd even gotten an ʻIolani School building named after Nangaku—the same "Japanese businessman and philanthropist" who had famously dropped $157.7 million on a Vegas hotel only to tear it down. Although Enomoto had been advised by Waiheʻe reelection campaign chair Bill Paty to step away from Minami USA—Paty told the *Honolulu Advertiser* that the connection would cause the governor "political headaches" and that Enomoto had "swallowed hard" before complying—the Koʻolau Country Club was completed. They may also have known that Paty also chaired the Board of Land and Natural Resources, which virtually assured a favorable subzoning for Hoyu Kensetsu's golf course.

Though the odds seemed impossible, the community fought on, even after Waiheʻe's reelection had passed, thereby freeing Enomoto to involve himself with Hoyu Kensetsu, and even after the company won its downzoning gamble with BLNR approval in 1992. The Waiāhole-Waikāne Community Association publicly called for a "master plan" to control further Windward development—a move that delayed Hoyu's plans enough to dissuade them altogether from buying the ninety-five bay front acres, and that also presented a united front announcing that the same strong-arm tactics that had cleared Maunawili Valley would not work in Waikāne. And then all at once, it seemed, Japan's spectacular 1980s economic bubble finally popped, sending Hoyu Kensetsu into bankruptcy. By decade's end, Azabu USA/Watanabe's five-hundred valley acres and the ninety-five bay front acres lay in the hands of the City and County, who had bought it all and then designated the first as the Waikāne Valley Nature Preserve and the second as a park. The empty Hoyu land passed into the hands of an "entity" called Waikāne Investments, and Tom Enomoto busied himself with projects on the now-booming Leeward side. But the "intensely private" man who had refused to let the *Honolulu Advertiser* investigative reporter Jim Dooley take his picture when they met kept a hand in the land that included Grandpa's Hill.

WITH THE GOLF COURSE BATTLES NOW OVER, the community might have finally turned its attention to the ice problem. Instead, several groups of Windward community activists found themselves pitted against a dream team of Bishop Estate lawyers. "I was fighting Waikāne development, fighting H-3, getting involved in the water fight," Bob Nakata told me, shaking his head in wonder as though he were talking about someone else. "When I look back I think, 'How did I hold myself together?'" Pooling their efforts into an organization they called Windward Parties (not to be confused with Joe Pao's "Windward Partners"), the groups saw the impending closure of the last of Oʻahu's sugar factories in 1995 as a chance to have Lincoln McCandless's Waiāhole Water Ditch plugged, thus sending the life-giving fresh water back to the valleys and out into Kāneʻohe Bay. "By the late sixties," Bob said, "Kāneʻohe Bay was dying," thanks to the combination of runoff resulting from Kāneʻohe housing development and the fact that the fresh stream water had been slowed to a trickle for half a century. In the 1970s, taro farmers Charlie and Paul Reppun sued the Board of Water Supply for drilling yet even more wells in the back of Kahaluʻu to service the new Kāneʻohe subdivisions, and managed to force the state to restore some of the water to their parched taro patches. And the Reppuns did not stop there. In 1992, with help from the Sierra Club, they managed successfully to argue that even rain-soaked Windward Oʻahu should be designated a "water management area"—meaning it could then be regulated by the Commission on Water Resource Management, which normally protected drought-prone areas on the Leeward side. And now the Reppuns and Windward Parties were arguing that since the McCandless water wasn't needed for sugar, according to Bob, "The water should come back."

Leeward developers thought otherwise, envisioning artificial waterfalls fronting the entrances of their newly planned gated communities. Bishop Estate spent heavily from the dollars they had been entrusted to spend on educating Hawaiian children to fight to keep the ditch open, reasoning that suburban and resort development on the former sugar land was more important than reviving traditional cultural practices such as fishing and subsistence farming for the disaffected Hawaiian friends Percy had left behind when he went to Japan. But the battle-seasoned community still somehow managed to get half of McCandless's water returned to the valleys. "We succeeded to a greater extent than I thought we would," Bob said. "They returned the water, the salinity in the bay started to rise, the bay has become much healthier, the coral is growing, the clarity of the water is much better. And the colors in the bay are much more vivid now, so it's going to be harder now for them to take the water back the other way."

Meanwhile, ice kept spreading, the drug war having become a lot more complicated than spotting an unmistakable grove of bright green plants from a speeding helicopter flying hundreds of feet up. By the time Percy Kipapa returned clean and sober to Waikāne in 1998, the local dailies had switched from trumpeting plant counts to talking in dollars and pounds, with one 1999 *Honolulu Advertiser* article detailing the year-long effort to "gather enough evidence" to arrest eleven people for operating a 30-pound/$580,000 per *week* import operation where ice was hidden inside Harley Davidson motorcycles and motorcycle crates. In this single bust we can read the entire Hawai'i ice epidemic writ large. The figure 580,000 multiplied by 52 comes to just over $30 million dollars—nearly all of which, unlike pre–Green Harvest pakalolo money, left on the next flight out. By the end of the 1990s Hawai'i had effectively replaced a $10 billion export business with a comparable import business, arguably resulting in the kind of economic strife that leads many people to begin using drugs in the first place. One *Advertiser* retro-piece on Green Harvest from 2000 quotes Big Island detective Marshall Kanehailua pointing out that many pot growers were "not bad people. You've got guys who grow just to try and make their mortgage." The $10 billion dollar impact extended far beyond those who grew, dealt, and smoked pakalolo. In a Green Harvest feature from 1990, the *Advertiser's* David Waite has Board of Land and Natural Resources chair Bill Paty pointing to a lack of business at a family-run store in Volcano—located in the exact kind of rural setting where ice first began to infect Hawai'i—as progress: "The clerks told me that a lot of growers used to come in and buy out the store. Now, they're a lot more selective. They don't buy everything in sight."

Thirty pounds is equal to 13,636 grams, the weight unit by which ice is typically sold. If a gram typically yields thirty doses, then the thirty pounds that this particular group was bringing in weekly was good for 409,080 doses, each of which lasts around fourteen hours. Over the course of just the single year that these particular smugglers were under surveillance, that comes to well over twenty-one million doses, any one of which may have sent even the most good-hearted and upright gotta-be-more-productive professional into a spiral of addiction. These thirty pounds were seized in a single operation more than twelve years deep into ice's invasion, a full nine years after a state auditor admonished Green Harvest for failing "to assess the negative impact of reducing the marijuana supply, such as driving users towards more dangerous drugs," four years after Donald Topping started speaking out, and three years after Joan Conrow's *Honolulu Star-Bulletin* Sunday feature, "Marijuana's Scarcity and Rising Price May Be Keys to 'Ice' Boom," quoted the state audit, Topping, and Patricia Morgan. Nine years—a span that includes Percy's entire tenure in Japan. Waite goes on to paraphrase "law enforcement officials" as pointing out that the "handful" of "large-scale methamphetamine smugglers" they caught in "the early days" of Hawai'i ice use "were replaced by dozens or even hundreds of smaller scale smugglers" like the subjects of this one story.

Although the drug predates World War II, in this context ice's "early years," according to the incredibly well-researched and documented *Yakuza: Japan's Criminal Underworld*, began in Korea—the place where Japan's most powerful crime syndicates centered the import-export business that allowed them to deepen the Hawai'i roots they had first planted in the late 1960s. Authors David E. Kaplan and Alec Dubro tell us that "Japanese police believe that meth [ice] sales amount to one third of *yakuza* income." They cite Japanese criminologist Masayuki Tamura pointing to the ice trade as "the cash engine that allowed Japan's big syndicates to expand nationally." They estimate that some 70 percent of mid-1980s *yakuza* ice was manufactured in Korea, a place naturally hospitable to Japan's organized crime groups in part because unlike official Japan, which doesn't even allow third-generation Koreans to carry Japanese passports or to vote, *yakuza* groups have always readily accepted ethnic Koreans into their ranks. Pounds of Korean-made ice would make the short boat trip across the Sea of Japan, from where much of it, as the FBI's William Baker told the *Honolulu Advertiser* as far back as 1986, continued on to Hawai'i.

Two "large-scale" Hawai'i-related busts from "the early days" illustrate what Tamura meant by the *yakuza*'s move to "expand." One came in 1985, when federal agents arrested Masashi Takenaka and Hideonomi Oda, to whom Kaplan and Dubro refer as "two of the highest-ranking bosses of the Yamaguchi-gumi"—Japan's most powerful *yakuza* syndicate. Posing as Hawaiian Syndicate members, the federal agents caught the bosses agreeing to a deal that would send handguns, machine guns, and rocket launchers to Japan, and—so the bosses thought—fifty-two pounds of ice to Hawai'i. Another emblematic "large-scale" bust involved the collaboration between local-Hawai'i/Japanese CPA Francis Matooka and ethnic Korean Cho Sam Ha, who were arrested for trying to smuggle 117 pounds of ice in 1987, the year Percy entered high school. And while he was away in Japan, Percy's island became such an attractive import destination that ice began hitting it, as Fats might have put it, from all kine angles. The "dozens or even hundreds of smaller scale smugglers" that David Waite had described were now rushing in not just from Japan and Korea but from Mexico, from California, and even from within Hawai'i, where some desperate addicts were trying to concoct their own ice on their kitchen stoves from dangerous blends of over-the-counter medicines and other chemicals. Considering how effectively Japanese ice was able to begin "zapping" Hawai'i while Percy was in high school, how completely it was able to finish the job while he was away learning sumo's ancient codes of Japanese honor, and how busy even the most effective community activists were while the problem quietly festered around them, what is most notable in all of these cases—even the Yamaguchi-gumi case, which was a setup, and such a bad one that two godfathers were allowed to walk—is that anyone was caught at all.

CHAPTER 8

GAMAN

I wrote to him at least twice. While I was up there with him, he was talking about going to school in Japan, and I was encouraging him to do that. When I came home, I tried to tell him to find more ways to educate himself there, living there and gaining skills there. I told him that a year before that, two of my other friends—one of them was murdered and one committed suicide. One of them was a Hawaiian kid who actually became my friend at Oregon where I went to college, ironically—not here—he had followed his girlfriend up there to go to school with her. I wrote him the same kind of letter: I just said, "Don't come home, man." He had a similar background to Percy, and he came home and he died. So when I told Percy about that, I was pretty serious about it.

—Kevin Chang of 'Āhuimanu, January 2, 2009

THE ROAR COMING FROM YOKOZUNA AKEBONO'S ROOM made Percy jump, suddenly ready to rush in and open the windows, or run downstairs for a cold drink, or head out to the video store—whatever he was asked. He almost got to his feet, too, when it hit him just as suddenly that he was now alone, also in his own room, and that someone else would attend to the *yokozuna.* They had promoted Percy to *jūryō,* and now his practice *mawashi* would be just as white as Akebono's. On formal occasions his dress robe would be just as black as the one Boss wore. At the tournaments, he too would fight the full fifteen days, and help consecrate the *dohyō* by filing in with the other *sekitori* and clapping his hands to alert the gods, dressed in the most beautiful piece of clothing he'd ever seen: his *keshō mawashi*— the royal blue apron hemmed in gold, stitched in front with a snow-white

Pegasus in flight, and the two kanji characters spelling out "Daiki." And right now it hit him that he could let out a roar of his own and have one of the boys walk all the way over to McDonald's and bring back a bag of Big Macs while he sat in his *own* room and watched whatever he wanted on the TV he'd just bought with part of his bonus for taking the July 1995 *makushita* championship.

"The attitude was changing towards me," Percy told me. "'Oh, *sekitori!* You made 'um. Arrite!'" He thought back to that first day he'd met most of the local boys, back on the sumo train to Kyūshū when they laughed at the sight of him trying to balance on those wooden slippers. Four and a half years of cooking stew and rice, cleaning toilets, hanging out thirty-foot lengths of canvas *mawashi*. Now he'd blown past Tyler, George, John, and Kaleo, while Fats, Bumbo, and Troy had already gone home. As for the rest of his brothers in Azumazeki Beya, Percy could see how most of them had been trying to make him stronger and more disciplined over the years. But he could also see when *senpai* had abused their power. Usually it was the *senpai* who were never going to make it who staked their identities on being above anyone else. The one Azumazeki Beya brother fitting such a bill was Tsuji—he of the swinging frying pan. "I neva whacked him back," Percy told me. "He came up to me and grabbed my head and went, 'Poom!' So when I came *jūryō*, I gave him the *kawaigari* of his life. I pushed him one hour straight. I beat his ass up so bad. And when I was finished I went up to him and went, 'Poom!' Ever since that he gave me respect."

Then there was his wallet, now bulging with brown-tinted ten-thousand-yen notes, over seven grand worth. He'd be getting that much every *month*, that and more: the phone was ringing three or four times a week, his sponsors or Boss's sponsors or Akebono's sponsors inviting him to this party or that restaurant opening. Weary and full of pain from a day's practice, he would lift his aching body from the futon, put on a nice kimono, and take one of his boys along with him to the party, where they'd feed him all the high-end sushi or steak he could eat, and then fill him with beer and *sake*, happy just to have Big Happiness in their presence. All he had to do was talk with them. He knew his own big laugh always got everyone else laughing. And at the end of the night someone would hand him an envelope. The first time he opened one of these, he couldn't believe what he was seeing: five crisp brown ten-thousand-yen notes. Almost five hundred bucks. Sometimes the envelope would be even thicker: a thousand, maybe. They were *paying* him to party.

"Fats had his own, I had my own *kōenkai*," or group of sponsors, as Tyler explained sumo's patronage system. "Say they're businessmen. In business, they'll have the same emotions that you'll have in the ring so they'll keep on striving to make the money that they're giving you to sit down and enjoy a good meal of sushi and yakiniku, and drink to your heart's content. As long as you go in the ring and you give that same 150 percent, they're content, because when they see you on TV, there's actually a connection between you and your sponsors. It's like they're with you."

Above and beyond the money was what any newly wealthy twenty-one-year-old would consider his main source of gratitude for a private room: it was a place to entertain the endless parade of groupies waiting to date a new *sekitori*. "A lot of life up there was good fun," Percy said. "I had two girlfriends before I went up there, but after I went up there, I said, 'Oh, this is the life.' You could make one movie about all the girlfriends I had. They'd say, 'Oh, you Akebono's brother?' I'd say, 'Whateva. I'm Akebono's brother.'" It was a life Percy enjoyed for months, until a woman named Yayoi swayed gracefully out from the crowd. "Sent down from heaven above, brother," Tyler recalled, "on a ti-leaf petal, right into Percy's arms. A little hula girl. She was a beautiful girl. She was in love with him."

In his off-hours Percy would invite George and Tyler over to his room and tell them about it all—the women, the money, the respect—and the boys would go home energized. "After I made 'um," Percy told me, "Tyler made 'um, George made 'um. I guess they got jealous." Years later, Percy's father pushed an old box of videotapes across his kitchen table, duct-taped shut for my flight back to the Big Island. One of the videos captures the 1996 New Year's *jūryō* ring-entering ceremony, where Tyler follows George to enter from the east side, and Percy enters on the west side. Later in the day, as Percy steps up for his bout, George stands to offer the ceremonial water to Percy's opponent, and Tyler can be seen up the tunnel in the background waiting his turn to enter the arena. "All being near the *dohyō* at the same time," Tyler said, "that *mana*, the power that was there, was awesome, ah? 'Cause it looked like a *movement*. It was like, 'Oh, who are all these guys? There's so many of them!'"

"When we made *jūryō*," George told me again long after the funeral, "what we did was we made our own group. We'd go out and party ourselves, go out to a karaoke bar for hours, drinking, call our friends. There was no pressure. We were all at the same rank. We didn't have to feel inferior to anybody else." Out would pour all the stories of growing up on the Windward side, but now with more of a sense of satisfaction since the boys could look over the long road they'd endured and see that somehow they'd all become *sekitori*—and who really knew what that meant except for the three of them? Percy's climb had even been commemorated in song, with Kurt having written "My Brother and Me"—his soft voice trading phrases with his ukulele in awe of what Percy had been able to do up in Japan, but still longing for the day when Percy finally comes home.

"I was real, real touched by the song that his brother made for him," George said. "I mean, that song hit *all* of us, 'cause we all got brothers too. When we heard that song for the first time, brah, some of us got teary-eyed. You always miss your family a lot. I know he missed his family a lot. He didn't want to show it—how he felt that his brother made the song for him—you know you gotta act tough. But he was feeling 'um just as bad as us."

"Most of the time it would be the locals," Percy told me, acting tough, just as George had described. "Me, George, Tyler. When we used to go out, nobody would come around us. After a while people know not to bother us—we'd mark our territory, piss in our bushes. 'Don't come in the lines—we beat you up.' We all used to go out after the tournament."

"And if he didn't get injured," Tyler said, "Fats, he'd be right there."

If he didn't get injured. The words are almost a sad joke to someone familiar with the most martial of the martial arts. While I was working on the research for this book, iron man Hideki Matsui broke his wrist while diving for a ball in the vast Yankee Stadium outfield. He then underwent surgery, rested for several weeks, worked with personal trainers at the Yankees rehab facility in Tampa, played a few minor league tune-up games, and was back in the Yankee lineup in time for the playoffs. But what happened to Fats is a story of *gaman*—how injuries figure into the sumo rules and how striving through pain is taken to levels that can cause permanent physical damage and mental trauma. Fats stands just over six feet and looks solid, with the big shoulders and thick arms of an NFL linebacker. Unlike most high-school wannabes, his NFL dreams were grounded in the reality of an All-American career at Kailua High School. But a torn ligament at an Arizona junior college sent Fats home just as the Hawai'i sumo boom was gaining steam, and he was easily recruited into Konishiki's stable.

"It was either sumo or become one cop," Fats said. "'Cause Chad went. We all grew up widdhim. And when he made *jūryō*, I was thinking, 'I think I *can!* I'm more athletic than this guy!'" And he did, straight up to the top of *makushita*, a single winning record from becoming a *sekitori* and from going who knows how much higher. "I was moving the pace," he said. "I was just as fast as Konishiki. Brah, he used to tell me that: 'Fats, you're moving up just as fast as I was moving up.' Coming from *him*, he telling *me* that." Fats relied on a head-first charge drawn from his football experience: less than wrestling, he was driving a big offensive lineman back into the quarterback. And he was doing it without pads, without shoes, his head protected by nothing more than the tightly wound samurai topknot.

Then in the 1993 New Year's tournament he came out of his crouch into the onrushing four hundred pounds of George Kalima, perhaps the best offensive lineman Kaiser High has ever seen. "I attacked my opponent with my head," Fats said, "and my opponent came with his hands, you know the push, and my head was just in the wrong position at the wrong time. That was just bad timing. And when we hit, I went down so fast. I was coming with my head like a ram, and I was just trying to push him straight back, but that neva happened, it just happened so fast that I went down, and that was it."

Five of sumo's fifty-odd *oyakata* sit around the *dohyō* in their formal black robes as judges for each bout, and of the *oyakata* officiating the match that day, Fats found himself lying on the clay looking into the eyes of Azumazeki Oyakata, he of the 1,231 consecutive upper-division bouts, the walking definition of *gaman*. "He was looking at me, he telling me, 'Get up!' I told him, 'I cannot, I cannot.' I was just one dead fish, brah. One fish outta watah. I couldn't even stand up, I couldn't feel nothing. My whole right side started to curl up—my fingers, my toes, my legs. I was like, 'Oh my gosh! What's happening right here?' My feet was turning in, just all on its own, I not even doing notting. In football you get stingers, yeah? I caught those. Whateva. This was one *different stinga*, brah. One stinga where I got scared."

"He took some time and they have these guys who come out and help you up," Tyler recalled, "and a lot of wrestlers, they'll be pampered and they'll grab their shoulders like you see in football in America. But Fats denied everybody's help and rolled himself off the ring. And then he got up. And the next day he was practicing again."

"I sat out, 0–7," Fats went on. "I *gaman*ed. I tried to dig deep, but I couldn't already. I wen' try to handle for *three more years* afta that. T knows. One day he wen' hit me hard. Boom! My whole frickin' right side just went *out*. I jus' wen' walk back, right into the wall. He said, 'Ho brah, what's the matta?' I said, 'I don't even know. I don't even know what's wrong.' That was it. One year in *makushita*, sayonara."

When I asked Percy—then all of twenty-five years old—about his own fall from sumo royalty, he couldn't trace it to any one dramatic moment the way Fats could. In fact, he still looked as though he could easily have handled at least half of the *sekitori* I'd just watched compete for the past three months. And then he launched into a long story that captured the way sumo's routine, all by itself, could physically grind you into an old man—especially when it was carried out by the same iron-man boss who had instructed Fats—who should have immediately been immobilized to avoid permanent paralysis—to "Get up! Get up!"

"What a lot of people don't understand is that Boss wasn't a technical wrestler," Akebono told me. "All they taught him was just come out and pound guys. He did that for twenty years. So then when he became an *oyakata*, everybody in his stable used to push, because that was the only way he knew how to wrestle." All of the bone-shaking charges where four- and five-hundred pound bodies crash into one another behind the full force of each man's tree-trunk legs, getting thrown to the rock-hard clay time and again for so many years—Boss may have been able to withstand it during his own active days. But it was catching up to Percy, a collection of nagging injuries sending him back to *makushita* after less than a year. And though he opened July 1996's Nagoya tournament with two straight wins, Percy's day-three opponent managed trip him onto his back, right onto the ring's raised straw boundary. "I hit that, I saw stars," Percy told me. "I had one bad back already—from wrestling alone we get pain. But I never felt pain like that in my life. I went home, sleep, the next morning, I couldn't get up my back was so sore. So I told my boss I cannot practice." Boss asked if he wanted to withdraw, but Percy clung to the hope of reclaiming his private room. "I said, 'No, I'm gonna try wrestle.' So I went to the doctors. They wen' shoot my back up with cortisone. Felt all right. I went to the tournament, I locked up with Chiyotaikai, saw stars again. Pain just came back, just like when you get one sore tooth an' you bite on it. My whole body got all shocked, one jolt, so I just walked straight back. I lost every fight after that. Part of me was telling me to drop out, the other part was telling me, 'Stay in, or you're gonna drop *down*.'"

Part of Percy's motivation to get back to *jūryō* was a certain hula dancer. After Yayoi had led him to forget about the postpromotion parade of sumo groupies, he'd begun to consider marrying her, picturing one of sumo's media-event weddings, tables full of wealthy sponsors bringing tens of thousands of dollars to Azumazeki Beya. But now without his *sekitori* status, he knew a wedding would be worth nothing to Boss, so Percy soldiered on to November's Kyūshū tournament. "That's when my back was so sore, 'cause got cold, ah?" he told me. "And I neva went to the hospital. I just *gaman*, fight the pain. 'Cause that's what my Boss was teaching me: '*Gaman*.'" After two easy wins, Percy found himself paired with a former university sumo champion named Tosanoumi. "I never lost to one college *yokozuna* before," he said—a modest feat that had earned him the nickname "College Yokozuna Killer." "So I told myself, 'Oh, I cannot lose to him.' I was so pumped, ah? When I came out of my charge I blew him straight back." To better keep his balance—Percy explained that Kyūshū's cold air causes the ring's thin layer of sand to dry up quickly into a slippery hazard—he dragged his feet across the clay surface as he charged. And then under the full weight of his forward momentum, his foot caught on the white painted line in the middle of the ring, causing his knee to lock up, and then to bend backwards. "And the guy just pushed me down," he said, of Tosanoumi. "Right away the guy was saying, '*Daijobu? Daijobu?*' [Are you okay?] The next morning I tried to stand up, my leg wouldn't bend. I had jeans on, and it was swelled up just as big as the jeans, my knee. I blew my inside ligament, and my middle ligament was ripped almost half way. The cartilage shattered into thousand-something pieces. So they had to operate."

Unless it's happened to you in some equivalent way, it's hard to really know how a professional athlete feels upon being taken down by an injury. Athletes—their bodies are not just what they do; their bodies are who they are. Witness the countless vows to "heal fast," or the trouble Michael Jordan and Brett Favre and so many others have in giving in to age. What you see is fear rooted in a loss of identity—a loss compounded for men who actually fight for a living. When the rules of the sport dictate that the longer you are out, the further you drop in rank, it's not an exaggeration to imagine Percy taking his doctor's recommendation to sit out for at least six months as a kind of death sentence for Daiki. That would leave Percy, alone in a hospital bed way up in Tokyo, far away from where he knew he really belonged, picturing himself walking up Waikāne Valley's narrow jungle trail and looking out across Kāneʻohe Bay from atop Grandpa's Hill. As Thanksgiving and Christmas came and went, not only could Percy feel the strength begin to melt from his now-idle muscles, he could close his eyes and imagine Kurt's yard at Sherwood's crowded with the people he missed the most. If he talked much to Akebono, he would have gotten the kind of everything-happens-for-one-*reason* reassurance with which the Yokozuna had talked himself through his own knee injury two years earlier—an ordeal that had taught Akebono to begin thinking about life after sumo.

Percy's thoughts would then have turned to Yayoi, who stuck with him through his lonely hours away from the ring. He filled her with stories of his valley, how his grandfather had fought for the land, how he and Shane and Charles used to hunt for rations. He couldn't wait to show her the family's land, but he also knew that could only happen in two ways: if he retired, or if he could ignore the pain screaming out from his knee and his back and then pound his way back to the paid ranks. Ingrained as he was with *gaman*, Percy chose the latter, stepping right back into the ring not after six months but for the very next tournament. To accelerate the healing process and to dull the throbbing pain, they had pumped his back and his newly repaired knee full of cortisone, testosterone, and other chemicals he couldn't recall by name. Whatever the doctors had concocted, it had him feeling, as he explained to his father at the time, "real good." Far from having to shake off any rust, Percy blasted right through the 1997 New Year's Tournament. Forty-three steps down from the top of the *makushita* division, he was paired with a progression of opponents who'd either been beaten down from above, or who were on the way up but lacking his experience. He breezed to his second perfect record, his second *makushita* championship, and a trip back up to *makushita*'s top ten—a single solid tournament from *jūryō*, and the altar.

The championship also put an unexpected amount of money back in his pocket—enough so he could take Yayoi and her mother to Hawai'i during the post-tournament vacation. Percy arrived on his mother's birthday with a bunch of red roses, kicking off a whirlwind five-day tour of his home island, with Kurt's wife Jolyn managing to hook up a deeply discounted ocean-front room, through a friend who worked at the Sheraton Waikiki, for Yayoi and her mother. It's not hard to imagine the Kipapas pulling out all the stops in welcoming Yayoi with loving hugs, food, and— as much as the language barrier allowed—stories of Percy growing up. They'd planned trips to Waikele shopping center, the swap meet, to the beach with Kurt's family. Percy organized one night out after the next with his friends, arriving home at dawn and then watching the morning drift away talking story with his mom and dad. And he certainly would have taken Yayoi up to Grandpa's Hill. He even found the nerve to extend his stay a couple of days *before* calling Boss for permission—a little act of rebellion that further underscored the difference between local-boy freedom and sumo enslavement. Though his recent championship may have pushed the thoughts of life after sumo far away, this trip home would wind up planting the seed.

If there were a moment when that seed began to take root, it would have to come during one of those lonely times back in Japan when his worn-out body was not performing. The visions of Waikāne had always pulled hardest when things went badly—the knee operation, the back pain, the humiliating fallout from the Nagoya car accident. But the pull was never stronger than midway through 1997, when Percy awoke to find himself once more in a hospital bed. As far as he knew, he had just arrived in Nagoya, eager to make good on the two recent 3–4 finishes that had sent him trickling out of *jūryō* range. And now here he was again, watching a clear plastic bag drip its liquid down the tube someone had stuck into his forearm. The doctors, as Percy recalled, were "confused." First they said appendicitis. Then it was gall stones. Then kidney stones. Then, all three at once. When the word "operation" came up, his eyes widened as he adamantly told them, "I no like operate over here, I no like operate over here," thinking back, as he told me later, to his knee operation, where "they did so much t'ings to me in the process of operating: they give me enema, all kine stuff, for a *knee* operation—I neva heard of that before." When he called home, as his father put it, "We prayed to Jesus to remove his pain, and that he may not have surgery, and that he be released from the hospital." It's easy to picture Percy with the phone buried in his thick fist, praying with his father, and then continuing to chat with his mother about family news until a smile finally came to his face, and even his laugh shouted out as the *'ohana* back home passed the phone around. The stories they traded would have comforted Percy at first, but then they would have wound up underscoring how short his recent stay had been, how he'd hardly had time to visit everyone. That final click at the end of the conversation was an exclamation point as strong as it had been during his first weeks in Japan, cutting him off from the very people who would have been surrounding his bed had he been at Castle Hospital.

If the Nagoya doctors could be forgiven for their confusion, it was because some six years into this brutal sport Percy's body had turned into a broken-down 522-pound bloated science experiment. The process had been put in high gear after Percy's Kyūshū knee injury, apparently in an attempt to "speed" his healing so that he might more quickly fight his way back to *jūryō*, a word that roughly translates into "money." "After I wen' blow my knee," he told me, "I started going to the hospital constantly. And every tournament, I would go to the hospital and they would shoot my knee, and my back. The week before the tournament I'd do the same thing. The week *of* the tournament I would do the same thing. The week into the tournament I would do the same thing. It was testosterone and some kind of steroid. And I was getting bigger and stronger after I blew my knee, but my body wasn't keeping up 'cause I couldn't get enough rest. And all the sudden I started getting mean pains in my stomach. I started pissing blood, coughing blood. I'd wake up in the middle of the night, *mean* rage, so tense. I would go downstairs, I don't know what for do with myself, all confused."

Some six months into this routine, Percy traveled to Nagoya to begin training for the July tournament, when suddenly, he said, "I woke up in the middle of the night again, the pain was so intense I couldn't stand up. I couldn't sleep, I was sweating so much. So this guy came up for deliver fish, he asked me if I like go hospital. Fuck, I don't remember jumping in his van. I don't remember arriving at the hospital. When I woke up I had an IV in my arm." Percy watched on television as the opponent with whom he'd been paired stepped into the ring alone, squatted in postbout form, and was acknowledged by the referee as having beaten him. Over the next two weeks this happened six more times, as the number in the loss column next to the characters for "Big" and "Happiness" grew to a perfect seven. And as the lonely hours passed, the hospital room might have been where Percy began to really see what had been happening to Big Happiness all along. Sure, the hospital bed was a renewed death sentence for Daiki, whose climb back to *jūryō* would now have to start all over again from who knew how far down. But now he was seeing that even the "Big P" happy-go-lucky identity that had earned him his sumo name was also dying—*I was so mad at my boss, I like hurt everybody I face*—and had in fact been slowly dying since that very first *kawaigari* beating, administered mainly because Percy had "too much aloha." He was beginning to see that Big Happiness had turned into a restless, pacing, confused monster plagued by night sweats, lack of sleep, and a *mean rage*. So when he gathered the nerve to stand up to Boss and just about demand to be allowed to go home for his operation—instead of back to work on the sweltering month-long summer exhibition tour after another enema or whatever the Nagoya doctors had in store for him—it was because at least back in Waikāne he knew who he was.

That much is clear from a home video, taken not long after Boss did allow him to go home, where Percy and Kurt jam into the front of a Jeep and scramble up and down Waikāne's deep jungle trails, with a friend in the back seat offering a running commentary on how the great Daiki enjoys his spare time, proudly shouting out "HAwaiian!" The whole 'ohana went to the hospital to watch Selisa give birth to the first girl among the Kipapa grandchildren, Brandee. Percy couldn't stop walking back and forth with the baby cradled in his arms. Kurt later took him to the recording studio to watch his group cut their first CD, which was centered by "My Brother and Me." One afternoon in the breezy shade of Sherwood's he and Kurt detailed the pimped-out bright-red dream truck Kurt had restored, right down to its sparkling chrome rims and DAIKI vanity plates. They drove off to change the title and get it registered, stopping for some sushi on the way home so he could show it to Mama-san. The way people turned to look at his new ride would have made him feel like he had in Japan when they'd tied his topknot for the first time. It would also have gotten him thinking about life after sumo, but in the more practical sense of what he was going to do with the rest of his life careerwise: pulling up at a meeting for his new business, or handing the keys to the valet at the Waikīkī hotel that made the right offer to have Daiki managing its staff and greeting its Japanese guests. And at the end of the day when he cruised back up the Windward side, one look at the truck and everyone would *know*: Percy Kipapa had gone up to Japan, and he'd made good.

When Percy was finally able to return to Japan, he found himself ranked so far down that even without a single loss—a ridiculous goal, he knew—at least a full year separated him from the good life he'd enjoyed in his brief time as a *sekitori*. A more realistic goal, even for someone not suffering as Percy was with his weakened, broken body, would be to climb back up to *jūryō* in two years—two years of cortisone shots, of night sweats, of mean rages, of *I like hurt everybody I face*. "From 522 pounds, I went to 315," Percy said. "So I asked the doctor, he told me, 'Oh, you still got gall stones.' He asked me, 'How's your back?' I told him, 'Oh, it's still sore.' He told me, 'Betta for you retire, you know, if you like lead one healthy life.' I told him, 'I don't like die in Japan.' Plus my mom and dad was giving me one scare 'cause they getting old themselves. I said, 'I'll go and talk to my boss.'"

I like quit, I no like quit. Part of the dilemma has to do with how hard it is for any *sumōtori* to confront his *oyakata* with thoughts of retirement. The middle of the *banzuke* is clogged with guys who have no hope of ever reaching the paid ranks, many of whom are just afraid to admit defeat to such a strong father figure. George Kalima has a story of having to fly his parents to Japan for a meeting with his boss just so he could retire, the family-values appeal aimed at countering the *oyakata*'s inevitable response:

gaman. Stick it out for another year (because, although I won't say so out loud, I don't want to lose the lucrative monthly stipend the Japan Sumo Association pays me for each man in my stable). Just over two years earlier, Percy's *senpai* Troy, body deteriorating from diabetes, had run away rather than face Boss about retiring. "And Chad neva like me retire 'cause he would be lonely," Percy said of Akebono. "He told me, 'What, you going leave me here hanging?'"

"He was my savior!" Akebono told me. "Whenever I had my stress: 'Perce! Let's go drink!' His room was right down the hall from my room. He was somebody I could talk to who knew half the stress I was going through. You know, being up there in *jūryō.* I mean he might not have known the stress of being a *yokozuna,* or the stress of fighting for championships, but he knew the stress of the everyday grind we gotta go through, of dealing with Boss, of dealing with all these politics" that come along with having to tread lightly as a foreigner in Japan's national sport.

"It's my body we're talking about," Percy told the *yokozuna.* "I know we're friends, but this is my body. I cannot be over here all your life." So up the stairs Percy climbed to tell Boss what the doctor had just advised him. "He said, 'No! You wrestle,'" Percy told me. "'You wrestle till Chad retire. I like one more local boy here.' I look at him: he's over here thinking for *himself.* That wen' piss me off. That wen' click right there because I was just home for so long—I got some American blood back into my body." What "wen' click" was how no one seemed to care what sumo had done to Percy. And while he could forgive Chad for simply wanting him around as a friend, in Boss's insistence he saw nothing but money. The whole thing had been about money—especially the more than two years Percy had spent competing in the most exciting matches of the day, when a packed paying house watches some twenty upper-*makushita* boys claw for a single spot in *jūryō.* Like starving college football stars worn down for the purpose of attracting the 800,016 booster dollars needed to pay a big-name coach, no one in *makushita* saw a dime of the spoils. "I was like, 'Boss, I gotta retire, 'cause my body not working right.' He said, 'You can wrestle.' I said, 'I cannot.' Then I show him my scars. Plus I still gotta go operate for gall stones. Plus my knee. And my back."

This time they used the gold scissors. At the Azumazeki-Beya post-tournament party, Percy was seated on a hotel ballroom stage, and a roomful of his sponsors, his sumo brothers, Yokozuna Akebono, and Azumazeki Oyakata each took a turn snipping a piece of his topknot as one of the highest honors a *sumōtori* can receive. Though he didn't rise quite as high as Akebono had, Percy twice had done what Akebono would never be able to do: finish a tournament with a perfect record. And those perfect records had come in *makushita*, where the stakes are highest. He had done it all thousands of miles from one of the most loving families in Hawai'i, in his second language, all before reaching the age of twenty-four. And maybe that was when those two words were first spoken, there at the haircutting ceremony where a *sumōtori*'s career ends in the most visibly permanent way possible. When Azumazeki Oyakata made the final cut and held the topknot aloft, maybe that was when someone first said *mottai nai*. What a regrettable shame, this strong man's career has to end at such a young age.

CHAPTER 9

FOREIGN TERRITORY

I think when Perce came home it was such a shock, but, in the same way it was for me. My body was bus', I couldn't take any more cortisone, I was taking uppers, downers, steroids. And everything was supposed to be good now. But for me, from high school I was a full-blown ice addict. I stopped in Japan for five years, cold turkey, just to do sumo. I had no other choice. And then when I got to jūryō, everything seemed cool now, ah? I had money, I had rank. And then I just lost everything. The injuries, that was the main part of it.

—Tyler Hopkins, June 17, 2007

PERCY'S FATHER SAT WAITING FOR ME, a big stack of photo albums on the carport table in front of him. "It's just some pictures we took over the years," he said after greeting me and sitting back down. "And there's some pictures people sent from Japan, and some papers I collected regarding his sumo career." I flipped through one of the albums and picked out Percy in his fourth-grade class picture: the tall kid in the back with the glasses and the big smile, green Waiāhole Valley in the background. A young bull of a Mr. Kipapa digging the *imu* for Percy's first-birthday luau. The lady-killer shot from his middle school yearbook. Percy in a kimono standing next to Akebono, serious looks on their faces. The odd photo of Kurt or Selisa showed up, but the four thick volumes were clearly devoted to Percy. One might have expected a grieving parent to put together this sort of memorial, but the wax had long since lost its stickiness on most of the pages,

124

and photos were sliding out everywhere. Percy's father had been waiting for me as anxiously as his laid-back demeanor would allow, because he had been preparing all of this material not since Percy's funeral, but since his son had first set off for Japan.

That much became clear when I got to the three-inch binder at the bottom of the pile. Mr. Kipapa had taken pages of blue-lined loose-leaf paper, a ruler, and a black ballpoint pen, and blocked off boxes to create a neat monthly log of Percy's entire sumo career. One entry read, "Jan. 1 31 93 ENTRY HATSU BASHO (SANDANME RANK 92 W-4 L-3)"; another read, "FERD LEWIS INTERVIEWED PERCY IN TOKYO & PHOTO IN ADVERTISER." A handdrawn graph followed, marking the days of each month that Percy called home. The proud father had cut out newspaper articles in Japanese and English and carefully pasted them onto the next several loose-leaf pages. Another homemade graph sketched the careers of the rest of Hawai'i's *sumōtori*, and the next listed their tournament-by-tournament records ("The Akebono File," "The Sunahama File," etc.). Mr. Kipapa had then handdrawn a double line of columns and listed, line by line, the dates where Percy was mentioned in the newspaper. "This is some of the things I wrote down," he said. "What I did was I just kind of keep track of these guys, the local guys. I didn't know what the hell I was doing," he said with a laugh. I recalled spending hours trying to track down the results of Akebono's earlier bouts. The fact is, despite my years-long obsession and the three-hundred-page book that resulted from it, I still can't accurately trace all of the numbers of his career, and here was Percy's entire record laid out right before me. "I wasn't too much interested before Percy went up," he went on. "I was not the kind type who would spend time on sports."

And as if this homemade Daiki encyclopedia weren't enough, all the stats pages were followed by an inch-thick stack of loose-leaf completely filled with brief diary entries detailing every single telephone call that Percy made from Japan, or that the Kipapas made to Percy, for his entire career. Flipping through the pages, I imagined Mr. and Mrs. Kipapa passing the phone between them, laughing with or reassuring their homesick son, and then Mr. Kipapa sitting down at the kitchen table, putting on his glasses, opening his green binder, and writing down an entry like this one, from just before Percy's second tournament: "Mon. Jan. 6 Percy called My

Love and said he hurt his leg in practice and Jesse was mad because the tournament starts on January 12, Sunday night. Percy told My Love he felt hurt, he wanted to come home, and My Love told Percy to hang on and rest your leg, and we will be praying for you, and Percy said OK, he would try." Even when they couldn't get through to him an entry would appear, such as this one: "Mar. 25 My Love called Percy but he was not home. They told her out-go, Percy out-go."

"It's just some of the highlights," he said.

"Did you write this as it happened?"

"I wrote that in the month of September, before he went up," he said, pointing to the first entry. "Even when Jesse came over, I started writing. It only get highlights, though," he said. "I don't think I put it into the right da kine."

The log begins with the heading, "Percy in the Sumo World," where Mr. Kipapa tells the story of his six-year-old son getting picked by Uncle Ray as a future sumo wrestler the day the family is working together to resurface their driveway. It skips to the summer after Percy's graduation, when he's "discovered," and the meeting with sumo recruiter Larry Aweau and Azumazeki Oyakata is arranged. The entries follow meticulously not only for the first couple of years, when one might expect the family to begin to get used to having Percy so far from home, but all the way until the injury that sent him back to Hawai'i for good. Flipping through the pages, I thought about how I used to call my family once a week when I went away to college, and then later after I'd moved to Hawai'i. Three or four years later I'd call every couple of weeks. Now more than twenty years later, I hardly ever talk with my sister, although I love her very much—it's just that you get used to being apart. But here was Percy calling home for six and a half years, and none of the phone calls are separated by more than a couple of days, right up until the end, with entries such as, "Percy called and asked if Charles had dropped off some flowers. My Love said yes, and Percy said it's for you and Selisa and Jolyn for Mother's Day." Another: "Percy called Kurt's home and talked to My Love too, and Percy told My Love he just mailed a box on July 27th. He sent clothes for Kurt and some things for Selisa and kids." And this: "Percy called John at Rosie's home and continued talking with him and 'ohana." "Percy called and asked My Love if she can call Kurt so he can talk on the same line and wish Joe Happy Birthday." "Percy called and talked with Selisa and said he might come home in February for Bronson's party. He must try to do good in January and win at least 5 matches." Clearly, Percy didn't just miss his *'ohana*—he seemed to feel a bit guilty for being away.

Though the phone log's last page ended the Daiki encyclopedia, I found the green binder's inside-back-cover pocket stuffed with clean white sheets of blue-lined loose-leaf paper. I could imagine Mr. Kipapa opening to the back of the binder and taking out a new page as needed, clicking the three rings open, and adding it to the chronicle of his son's life. But the permanent blankness of the remaining pages was now written on the father's face, speaking as loudly as the rest of the binder and all of the photos put together.

❆ ❆ ❆

AS HIS FATHER RECALLED, much "rejoicing" accompanied the return of Uncle Percy, of the best friend of so many of the Waiāhole-Waikāne boys, of Mrs. Kipapa's "baby." You can see right there in Mr. Kipapa's phone log many of the faces of the hundreds of friends and relatives who showed up at the welcome-home party. You can hear Kurt and the boys playing music, see Percy proudly carrying his newborn niece, smell the big foil pans of kalua pig and chicken long rice that Joe and Kurty-boy seamlessly rotated onto the big banquet tables next to the house at Sherwood's. I can see the smile spread across Mrs. Kipapa's face, her husband sitting next to her taking the whole scene in. For a while it wouldn't even have mattered to Percy that in the end he'd returned without Yayoi, who had left him the moment his topknot was cut.

The party went on for hours, eventually drifting into a circle of Percy and his boys, with Percy shouting out his laugh to punctuate one incredible story after the next, and all of them looking at him with great pride. For each of them he had a *tegata*—the beautiful handprint painted with the calligraphy of his sumo name; a picture of the great Daiki dressed in his *keshō mawashi*; and a ceramic sake set, also emblazoned with the kanji for "Daiki." At some point the conversation would have turned to what Percy planned to do now that he'd returned, and the possibilities seemed endless. He had some money in the bank—tens of thousands from his retirement bonus plus all the envelopes that the Azumazeki Beya sponsors had handed him at the retirement party. Maybe Percy could start a restaurant or a bar or something, or maybe some kind of small tour company—a fleet of limousines to take the Japanese around the island. Even hotels: anyone who could go all the way to Japan for six-plus years had to be able to run right through any training program they had for their managers. And what about the Hawai'i Tourism Authority? How many guys on the whole Windward side—or in the whole state, for that matter—could speak the beautiful Japanese that poured so fluently from Percy's mouth?

The future looked so good, in fact, that Percy felt he could take his time and wait for just the right job to come up. As his mother recalled, "He told me 'Ma, I been working seven days a week for almost seven years now, I like take some time for rest.'" And for the first few weeks, "rest" meant an occasional look at the want ads, and then a ride up the Windward Coast, or down to Waimānalo, where he was having a house built for his mom and dad. At stoplights everyone was still turning to check out his ride, and he must have laughed at how far he'd come from that little Mazda with the ripped-out seat, all the way to the pimped-out red truck with the chrome rims. Daiki was rolling. Daiki had money. He knew that the Japanese, whom he'd grown up watching buy nearly every available inch of land on his island, had the power, and he imagined that they were waiting for him.

But as he drove back through Kahalu'u, Percy would have begun to notice that he wasn't the only one who had changed over the past six-and-a-half years. You can hear his thoughts as he waits at the intersection of the old Kam highway and the Kahekili cutoff waiting to turn north: *Look at all those frickin' druggies!* Right there under the banyan tree, a cop car parked right across the street at 7-Eleven. Sure, the odd messed-up-looking person could always be seen under the tree ever since Percy's bus used to pass by on the way to King Zoo. But now more than twenty people milled around, skinny shirtless guys with stringy hair and long black beards, their skin browned from days walking the streets under the hot sun; tattooed women with holes in their smiles hanging around them. And this was right in the middle of the day, right next to the guy who sold cut ginger and pickled mango from his step van. And while Percy could look down on the chronics as he schemed to build his postsumo career, on some level he had to know that even from behind the wheel of his dream truck, even with a brand-new house under construction, the distance separating him from those toothless smiles was not as far as he would have liked. He may even have driven by the banyan tree and been afraid, because even though sumo had succeeded as a way to "detox" his system, the pull of ice wasn't something that you could ever really be "cured" of. Years later Tyler Hopkins, whose life parallels Percy's in every significant way, recognized the same fear, saying "I see my addiction as a gorilla in a garage doing push-ups every fucking day. And I'm walking, and he's in that garage doing push-ups, 'cause he's just fucking *waiting.*" *I-like-quit-I-no-like-quit*—the words seemed to ring even louder in Percy's head now that he had come home, except now they were tinged with regret, and amplified every time he drove past the banyan tree. So a few weeks later when Tyler called with an offer to work with Troy greeting incoming Japanese visitors at the airport for ten bucks an hour, Percy accepted, probably thinking the work was beneath him but eager to get something going until the right job came along.

To his surprise, Percy never felt more secure in his decision to quit sumo than at the end of his first busy day at the airport, when his new Japanese boss pulled him aside and handed him an envelope. Mrs. Kipapa's retelling of the story caused me to picture Percy throwing the envelope on the passenger seat of his truck, thinking back to the days of *jūryō*, when blue-suited salarymen would come up to him after practice or at a post-tournament party. They would bow and say *"ganbare"*—try your best— and then slide him envelopes stuffed with brown-tinted ten-thousand-yen notes. Sometimes they would invite him to preside over some restaurant opening or company party, where he would fill the room with laughter for a couple of hours, eat and drink to his heart's content, and be handed one of those elaborately folded decorative Japanese envelopes. He would often wait to open it until he got home, where he would tip his *tsukebito* from the four hundred, five hundred—sometimes a thousand dollars nestled between the stiff paper folds. True, today had only been his first day at the airport, but if the envelopes kept coming, the tourist cattle call wouldn't be such a bad job after all.

Percy hadn't felt that way earlier in the morning, when he found himself getting out of bed in the dark, just as he had in his early sumo days, just as he had back when he used to face the interminable bus ride over the mountains to St. Louis High. After pulling into the airport parking lot (where parking alone would cost him an hour's pay) he joined the herd of uniformed imported corporate wives and *yakuza* mistresses swarming the Japanese arrivals area in part-time jobs designed, it seemed, to keep them from dying of boredom in their Diamond Head homes. Spilling through the terminal doors was a flood of money. What did they charge someone for a package tour from Japan, anyway? A thousand per person? More? Five thousand? And the place was already as crowded as Tokyo Station. That he had been more likely to run into another local person on the streets of Tokyo than there at the airport suggested his new job was so specialized that few in Hawai'i could face this sea of aloha-shirted humanity—assemble those on the list handed to you by an anxious little boss, and then lead them to the proper tour bus—all for ten dollars an hour. Although Percy may not have had to scrub anybody's back in the shower, if you took away what they took out for taxes and added in the way his boss kept running him, it was worse than being Akebono's *tsukebito*. All for Japanese tourists getting off of Japanese planes, greeted by Japanese workers from Japanese tour companies, sent to Japanese hotels and to shop in Japanese stores—Percy quickly saw that beyond his meager pay, none of the money even stayed in Hawai'i.

Big Happiness would have tried to make the best of things, though, joking with the Japanese in a way that the robotic corporate wives would never think to do, at home in their language and perhaps even a little nostalgic for the life he had recently left behind up there. His laugh shouted out now and then across the crowded arrivals area, and before long someone asked to take a picture with him, perhaps just excited upon stepping off the plane and into "paradise," perhaps surprised to actually see a real live Hawaiian up close. Soon a line formed—a line long enough that Percy's boss pulled him aside to do nothing more than stand for pictures. So for a while Percy could even imagine that he was in *jūryō* again—and indeed, some of them even recognized him as Daiki. And then at the end of the day, Percy's boss had made it all real by handing him the envelope now sitting on the seat next to him as he waited in line to pay his way out of the parking lot. It really was a bit like *jūryō*, or at least *makushita*, where the pain of a meager monthly stipend could be softened by cash-stuffed envelopes offered in the name of *gaman* and *ganbare*. Sure, just like in sumo his unique talents were being exploited to line someone else's pockets—much like Hawai'i itself was being exploited by all of these Japanese companies for its unique tropical beauty. But Percy did have the envelope, which seemed to indicate that if your name was Daiki, they were willing to spread some of the wealth around.

He probably would have reached for the envelope when his turn at the gate arrived—why dig for your wallet when you have a pile of cash sitting right next to you?—and when he opened it—I can picture it now—his eyes widened in such shock that he had to sit for a moment, never mind the waiting parking-lot attendant or the cars behind him. And then it probably caused him to laugh, and shake his head, and maybe even say it out loud: "Five fuckin' dollas." He probably shook his head again, and even said it again as he shifted in his seat to reach for his wallet: "Five fuckin' dollas."

The next day after rising in the dark, and parking his truck, being run back and forth like a *tsukebito*, and finally checking in his final busload from among the camera-snapping flood of money, Percy ripped open another envelope right there in the arrivals area, pocketed the five-dollar bill, turned to Tyler and said, "That's it. I quit already."

☾ ☾ ☾

WELL AWARE OF WHAT MIGHT COME of a twenty-four-year-old son back from the glories of a professional sports career, still idle and now surrounded by the chronics proliferating under the Kahalu'u banyan tree, Mr. Kipapa changed his mind about the planned move to Waimānalo and had Percy go instead. "I asked him to stay at our new home so he could spend time with his brother Kurt," who lived minutes away in Sherwood's, he told me. "We would go and stay with him on the weekends, but I didn't want him all the way up here." The change in Percy's home ground wasn't restricted to Kahalu'u's tweaked-out welcoming committee, either, as Charles Kekahu explained to me—it had spread right into his backyard playground. "Lot of new people, new faces, so it like wasn't our town anymore," Charles said. "Kahalu'u started to come over to Waikāne—they invade the place. Before, Waikāne Valley Road was private-like. Only certain people from Waiāhole would come: Fernandezes, Demby-them. They stay Friday-Sataday, they put up tent, drinking. But that was all country living, ah? From ten years old all the way up, I know everybody, or they know me. But by the time Percy came back from Japan it was different—people were coming not only from Kahaluʻu, but from Kāneʻohe. If he went up there, he would hardly know anyone."

Over in Waimānalo, Percy immediately started turning his new house into a museum commemorating his sumo career: huge framed pictures of him in action on the *dohyō*; the two glass boxes containing his topknots; various unfolded Japanese fans and draped cloth banners depicting the two kanji characters for "Big" and "Happiness." Behind the framed photo of Daiki accepting the certificate for his first *makushita* division championship, he could see a hundred *kawaigari* sessions, getting thrown to the hard ground and beaten with the stick and kicked in the ribs, drowning from lack of oxygen. In the radiant blue, gold-stitched apron hanging next to it he could hear the raspy screams of his boss, *What kine sumo is that!* And he could hear people calling him *sekitori*. In that first cubical glass case, he saw a speeding car, an angry boss, two police officers, his *senpai* Troy sneaking into the stable undetected; he could feel the weeks of uncertainty as Boss stared back and forth between his passport and the telephone. So far from the neva-even-wear-slippa world of Waiāhole School, from the running-wild days at Castle High, more than anything that room made Percy feel like a success.

If Percy was thinking that somehow the job would just come along to match his truck and his new house, that first you needed to *look* like you were rolling if you were ever going to wind up an actual player, then one of his former sponsors, a man named Shiroishi, would indeed have confirmed for him that that was the way things worked. Not long after Percy settled into his new home, Shiroishi called him to help open a new restaurant in Waikīkī, and for the rest of the following year, the job became Percy's obsession. Every morning he lifted his still-aching body out of bed, hobbled to his truck on his bad knees, drove into town, found parking, walked to the huge second-floor space that Shiroishi had leased above the International Marketplace, and poured himself into every aspect of setting up—everything from ordering the furniture and tableware on down to designing the floor plan for a place that would seat over three hundred people. Percy hired the floor staff. He helped design the menu. Through a friend he managed to obtain a cabaret license from the Honolulu Liquor Commission that would allow live music. He hired Kurt's band to play, and through Kurt he was able to book other prominent local musicians. They called the club "Breathless," and when Shiroishi returned to Japan for other business, he made Percy the general manager.

"Opening night Percy and his partner mixed in with the crowd of people," Mr. Kipapa wrote years later, "listening to music and getting to taste all the food and look at the setup. There were lots of flowers from Percy's friends. His partner thanked him again for everything he'd done."

"I wouldn't go home until it was light out already," Percy told me when he was visiting Japan the following year, where I was still living as I worked on the Akebono book. "I'd look at the sales receipts, add up the credit card transactions, count all the cash. And then I'd count 'um *again* just for make sure I get 'um right. You know people talk, ah?" At the time, I was working at the restaurant that George Kalima had opened in Roppongi just after his retirement. Percy and I were trading restaurant stories while I waited out the last table so we could close and go out drinking. "I used to watch everybody," he said, and then he launched into a story about catching one of his bartenders giving away drinks to a hot-looking girl at the bar: "I look at 'im: 'She's all right, ah?' He tell me, 'Yeah!' I put my arm around him and I tell 'im, 'I'm glad you think so, bradda, 'cause you going have a lot more time now for spend with her!'" And then he shouted out his laugh. It's hard to picture a better fit for Percy's talents than something like managing a Waikīkī restaurant, combining as it did not only the cooking and organizational skills and Japanese language that sumo life had taught him, but also the hospitality he'd been raised with and that he'd cultivated during Azumazeki Beya sponsor functions. And despite the tremendous monthly cost of leasing such a huge space, Breathless was able to turn a profit.

And then after less than a year, Shiroishi pulled the plug, and Breathless went dark.

PERCY AND I HAD BEEN ABLE to trade our restaurant stories that night in Roppongi because Shiroishi had arranged to fly him up in summer 2000 to film a TV commercial. Percy seemed happy to have returned, for the first time since his retirement, to the place where he had essentially become a man. An early-morning arrival to visit Azumazeki Beya brought back memories of sneaking home after a night out partying, and everyone there—especially Akebono, who complained loudly about how his current attendants compared to the always-attentive Percy—was thrilled to see him. "*Mottai nai*," the boys kept telling him, looking enviously at his big, strong body, "*Mottai nai*." Later at the Kokugikan one of the bosses said the same thing before asking Percy to carry his bag for him so he could get in free through the side gate. Percy and I sat at a table at the back of the arena's lower level and bet one-hundred-yen coins on the lower-division bouts. (I did all right, but by the end he'd taken about twenty bucks off me, which he used to buy us lunch.) And the blue-coats, the legion of retired lower-rankers hired by the Sumo Association into security and usher jobs, didn't stop coming up to greet him for the next two hours. "It's been a while," they would each say with a huge smile, "Are you back in Japan to stay?" Then they would look him up and down from head to toe and say, "*Mottai nai*." "Look at that perfect sumo body of yours," the two words said. "It ought to be up there fighting on the *dohyō*." They clearly meant it as the highest compliment, and Percy took it that way, with great humility, turning the conversation to whomever it was there in the blue coat, knowing some little detail that told me he'd taken the time to get to know all of these guys. I knew that Percy had "only" made it to *jūryō*, but here were these guys who *knew* what it meant to pound your feet into hard clay day after day for years all coming up to pay their respects like he was Konishiki or Akebono.

If the trip to Japan did anything besides put a few thousand dollars in Percy's pocket, it gave him the perspective to step back and make the cold, hard observation, more than two years into his move back home, that other than from his family or people like Shane and Charles, the same level of respect just wasn't there. *Eh, Perce!* was what they had all been saying. *I thought you was in Japan! What? You back? I thought you was going do sumo like da kine, Akebono, Konishiki-dem.* Percy may have thought to try to explain the *banzuke*, and what it means to reach *jūryō*. He may have thought to sit them down and fully explain *kawaigari*, or let them in on what it feels like to stand in a roomful of big fucka's babbling away in Japanese—not even the three local guys will speak English, and you can't understand a word they say. Cortisone injections, *gaman*, the pain of a blown knee—where would he begin? *I give you credit, going all the way up there, what? Seven years? I give you credit, brah. You eva wrestle Akebono?*

"When I came back, I was really down and out because I told myself, 'Now, I'm a big nobody over here,'" Percy told me. "But the thing I get over everybody else: I went to Japan. I learned the language. I learned the culture. And I'm one out of a million from Hawai'i who went sumo. Like when I joined, had seventeen guys that I joined with, and I'm the only guy who became a *sekitori*. When I started . . . " and he went on to tell me about detox, as if to emphasize how far he'd come from Castle High School, how incredible it was that he'd made so much of himself. In my memory of the conversation, he talks about this almost casually, as though he's just conveying information. But now when I listen to the tape, I can hear it. He's trying to convince himself that it mattered at all.

"Kumau, he's a wrestler from my stable," Tyler told me. "He's from Saitama. He was *jūryō*. His sponsors opened him his own restaurant and everything. They got him a bankroll and everything—set him up. All he had to do was get up in the morning and go down to the docks and buy his fish. Another guy from George's stable, he retired, he went back to Nagano, fuckin' right into a fuckin' real estate firm, manager position already."

"The boss will get you a job someplace," George said. "A lot of the wrestlers from our place ended up getting jobs at the companies of these people who supported the stable. And what did they do for the foreigners? Nothing. We get out of sumo, that's it."

"So what?" I asked Tyler, "Someone in Hawai'i is just supposed to give you guys jobs?"

"I mean, it's just a given in Japan," he went on, "that they've seen what you've been through, you tried, maybe you made a little bit of rank, and maybe you have a little bit of something in common that you can talk about with somebody who enjoyed sumo and maybe you can sell something. You gave it all you had. You didn't make *yokozuna*, but you did sumo for us, for your family, and for Japan. But for Hawai'i and America it's a little bit different—athletes are paid so well. Sumo is not that way."

"Well they always called you guys 'Ambassadors for Hawai'i,'" I said. "What does that mean? Who did you have to smooth the way for?"

"Linda Lingle came," he said. "Cayetano came. Fuckin' President of the United States, bro, coming to the boys from Hawai'i and meeting them because we were American sumo wrestlers."

"So the governor and maybe some HTA [Hawai'i Tourism Authority] people come to Japan and meet with, say, people from JTB [Japan Travel Bureau], and they take them to practice at your stable, or you eat with them, whatever. What do you get?"

Tyler laughed. And then he said, "Konishiki is the epitome of that, and he never got what he was worth. I was with him when he had to speak at the American embassy. He's done more shit privately for Hawai'i than anybody. But he wants to help Hawai'i."

"Just before he left," Mrs. Kipapa told me, recalling Jesse Kuhaulua's surprising recruitment visit years before, "standing right over there, I still remember it clearly, he said, 'When you retire, we get you one job ova hear, Panasonic.'" For the years Percy was sacrificing for the dicey shot at sumo stardom—years he might have spent in college, or working his way towards a pension in some job like City and County Parks with Kurt—he was promised a future even if sumo did not make him rich.

"Are you *sure* he said that?" I asked, thinking anger might be clouding her memory.

"He said that," she insisted. "Just before he left my door. I can still remember it. He said 'When he retire, we get him job over here. Panasonic.'" And then there was that beat-up Mazda with the seat ripped out and pushed as far back as it would go to accommodate Big P. "You go up sumo, you going have even betta car than this" is what Boss had promised him, according to Mrs. Kipapa. For a while Boss had been right, too. The red dream truck with its gleaming chrome rims, its pounding subwoofer under the seat, its DAIKI license plates—to Percy, that truck was a loud statement to the kinds of people who used to put him down for his humble country roots during his brief time at St. Louis High. All by itself, it made him *somebody*. But the visions of rolling up at the Waikīkī hotel, handing the valet the keys before he goes into work? Not long after Percy returned from the trip to Japan where they were all telling him *mottai nai*, he had to trade in the dream truck for the old Cutlass, because for him anyway, that job didn't exist. Then a maintenance job fell through. A stomach virus kept him from an interview to drive limousines. And the rest of the time, it was rejection. After Percy had pulled me over to the side at my wedding and apologized, in tears, for not coming with a gift, I wrote him a resume and a cover letter connecting his accomplishment in Japan to his experience opening and running Breathless, and even found a few jobs in the Sunday paper that seemed to suit his abilities, but still there was nothing. Not even Hawai'i's version of the blue coat.

"I used to always tell him," Kurt said, "'Perce, you come back, you just another fat Hawaiian.' That's what people portray, they judge you. My brother looked for jobs all over."

"I would have been trapped like Percy was if I came home," George said, "trying to get a job. If you weigh four hundred pounds, you're automatically a liability to any construction firm you approach. Nobody wants to hire you."

Whenever I see George home visiting, I joke with him that he looks like he's just been let out of prison. He sits in his father's carport looking out at the steep green mountains like a tourist, in deep envy of Fats, who lives with his wife and daughter down the road in the house his family was able to pass down to him. That same aura of relief washes over Akebono when he comes home and stays with Kurt in the Kipapa's homestead house and repeatedly postpones his return to Tokyo. "I'm not saying I'm not going back [to Hawai'i]," Akebono told me. "But for now, economically, it's just easier to stay here. We cannot live this life back home." George's brother Bumbo, who rose to *makushita* faster than Akebono before a shattered knee sent him back to Hawai'i, graduated from Windward Community College and got a good job with the City and County. He is happily married, but he and his wife and four kids all live in the room in his parents' four-bedroom spec home that he shared with George as a child. Fats gives surf lessons to Japanese tourists. After overcoming an ice problem of his own, Troy now works the graveyard security shift at the Likelike Drive Inn. And then there's Tyler, still trying to rebuild his life while that gorilla in the garage keeps doing push-ups. Back in Japan, George and his wife run a successful hula school and a production company that flies in such local musical talent as the Makaha Sons and the Brothers Cazimero. For years George had been scheming for ways to run the business from Hawai'i, but he gave up recently by sinking his roots with the purchase of a Tokyo home. "Worst thing about it," Akebono said, "is that actually we've lived here longer than we lived in Hawai'i."

The image of the once-majestic Akebono allowing himself to be dropped to the canvas on national television time after time, first in his brief K-1 kickboxing career and later as the bad guy in Japanese pro wrestling, raises a sad question: if the former *yokozuna* has to resort to *this*, then what could Percy or Tyler expect to do after stepping off the *dohyō* for good? Listen to Kaleo, who rose all the way to the top *makushita* spot before injury sent him back to his parents' home: "Get a lot of guys like that, all the ex-guys—you name it. Buddah John, T—they's all big guys. They not gonna find one regula job." Now listen to George: " . . . trying to get a job. . . . you're automatically a liability to any construction firm you approach." In defining the employment opportunities available to young Hawaiian men, George conflates the words "job" and "construction" without even thinking about it. Like a *reflex*.

❨ ❨ ❨

AT SOME POINT THE SUMO MEMORIES Percy had displayed in his living room began to weaken in their ability to awaken his pride. As good as he was at being the cheerful Big Happiness, every joint in his big, bruised-up body would scream out on rainy days, triggering regret that he'd come home to find himself as alone as he'd been during those miserable first three years at Azumazeki Beya. Part of what had sustained him in those early years was the thought that he would come home a winner. And a look around the room proved that he had. The two glass cubes on the shelf, the two topknots—the second one, sculpted into the up-turned ginko-leaf shape that only *sekitori* are honored to wear, had put him in the elite class of Akebono and Konishiki, he knew. But sometimes when he looked at it now, he recalled not just the joyous day on which he was first allowed to wear it in that style, but the day that it was cut, and another immediate and powerful result. "When he was in sumo, he had this girl that he was kind of attached to," Mr. Kipapa told me, "Yayoi. She stayed over here one night—that's how we got to meet her. Percy really liked the girl, and the saddest part was when he had the injury he neva want to quit sumo, 'cause that stuff wen' kind of change his life—the girl." An admitted "player," for once Percy had found love, floating down from heaven on a little ti leaf, as Tyler had put it, and until his topknot was cut, Percy was sure she had found it too. And then only a few months later, he spoke to me about the whole thing with nothing but bitterness. "Before I came back here I was engaged," he said. "When I was in sumo, that's when she wanted for get married. And when I retired she neva like get married. Bitch. She would've taken half my retirement bonus."

And then there was the first topknot—the one they had cut to shame him. That he'd bothered to save it suggests that he knew even at the time that he would get past it, that he would *gaman* his way to coming out on top. Just a look at that first topknot would bring it all back, and at first it had filled him with pride at what he had been able to overcome. But now, winner or not, and forced to see that winning hadn't been enough, still in his mid-twenties he had to admit that what they'd taken was his trust, and what he'd given was his body. "My pain thing?" Tyler explained. "Goes up to the fuckin' ceiling, brah." I had recently spent the night at Tyler's so our sons could play together and was awakened by the sound of the big man crying out in agony, three rooms away, simply because he'd rolled over the wrong way. "So I don't know when I'm *in* pain. I've been beaten fuckin' half my life by one fuckin' overweight *solé* who I always thought hated me. Percy went through worse, brah." A year or so after Percy's murder trial, Japan was shaken by the news of a seventeen-year-old sumo recruit's death at the hands of his *oyakata* and his *senpai* after a *kawaigari* session invoked to punish one of the boy's many attempts to run away. Among the personal items returned to the boy's parents was his cell phone, broken in half. Knowing what I'd learned from Percy and the rest of the local sumo brothers, I couldn't see what the fuss was all about—a *kawaigari* session getting out of hand was inevitable, and as Noriko pointed out, it had probably happened before, only to be hushed over with a cash-stuffed envelope.

Tyler's own introduction to sumo life came with the soundtrack of blood-curdling screams, as he and Fats and Kaleo were kept awake past four o'clock one morning listening to a group of mostly drunken *sumōtori*—a tournament had just ended, so many of their *senpai* had been out partying—try to extract a confession of stealing from one of the young boys. "They beat him all night," Tyler said. "We were trying to sleep, and the hours go by, and the more guys came home later, the more joined in—they grab a bat, grab the bamboo stick. This boy got fuckin' *tortured*. And finally at three, four in the morning, they let him go to the bathroom, and he jumps out the fuckin' window. He landed in the cemetery next door and he tried to run. We heard this fuckin' wailing and screaming and shit.

The next day his legs were black and blue all the way down to his Achilles tendons, his ass was all swelled up. I neva heard screaming like that in my life. And the more guys came home, they just fuckin' sat there and smoked their cigarettes and watched this poor fucka get tortured."

The *keshō mawashi* with its shining white Pegasus flying through the royal blue sky: that was supposed to have made it all worthwhile. The beatings, taking orders from fifteen-year-old kids, taking the fall for Troy after the car accident—it had all been worth it, because Daiki had become one of only *fourteen* non-Japanese ever to become a *sekitori*. But the day had to come when the *keshō mawashi* began to evoke the real memory about how his final step to sumo stardom had played itself out. The Japan Sumo Association and NHK television had made a big enough deal of the historic promotion, inviting Daiki to a quiet studio set up in a Kokugikan back room for a reflective one-on-one conversation. I found the interview buried in the box of videos that Percy's father had given me, and I could imagine Mr. Kipapa looking on with incredible pride at his son on Japanese national television dressed in a formal kimono, his hair styled in a samurai topknot above his big gold-rimmed glasses, conversing freely in the difficult language about the highlight of every *sumōtori*'s career—even those who go on to rise much higher, including his own *oyakata*. The interviewer compliments Daiki on his beautiful new *keshō mawashi*, on proud display as a backdrop to their interview. They then cut to a taped interview with the great Yokozuna Akebono, who speaks softly and proudly of Daiki's early struggles, and his great accomplishment. And then they cut to an interview with Azumazeki Oyakata, the great Takamiyama, the man who had also come all the way from Hawai'i so long ago and become the walking example of *gaman*. Jesse had trained the first foreign *yokozuna*, and now he had another new *sekitori* in his stable. Sitting in his suit and tie, obviously having been summoned specifically to discuss Percy's promotion, the big man is surrounded by an aura of respect.

"Do you have anything to say about this wonderful happening?" he is asked from off camera. An inset appears in the screen's lower-right corner to show Percy looking on from his own live interview in expectation, hoping to savor the one time in his life when the strict and overbearing but well meaning father will finally say, "Well done, son. You did it."

"I'm afraid I don't have anything good to say," the Oyakata says. "His charge is slow, so he always winds up doing that *nagaizumō*. He's got to work a lot harder."

The interviewer then offers this: "He did come all the way from Hawai'i, and struggled for nearly four years adjusting to sumo."

"Yes," the Oyakata admits. "He did try hard."

Down in the lower-right corner, Percy's face has long since dropped, the words clearly hitting him like bullets, and now he's struggling valiantly to keep that Daiki face of his from falling any further on national television.

The camera cuts back to Percy's interview, and the man interviewing him (we can't see him), perhaps taken aback at how hurt Percy is so obviously trying not to appear, offers this:

"Well, that was some stern advice from the Oyakata. But what do *you* think of your charge?"

Percy, as Fats might have said, wen' *eat 'um*, struggling to answer the uncharacteristic question with, "Yes, I've got to keep working on my charge. In *jūryō* everyone's charge is faster."

After throwing out a few more questions to try to change the subject, the interviewer mercifully ends the conversation with the clearly dejected new *sekitori*. Percy manages a smile as they congratulate him again and wish him luck in the upcoming tournament.

Three and a half years later, the wound had deepened. As Percy told me, "When I made *jūryō*—everybody who make *jūryō*, they have one interview, you know, the first interview in *jūryō*. So they show the sumo wrestler and they show the *oyakata*. Oh, he came out and he said, 'Daiki, you gotta do better sumo. You no more good sumo.' He told them, 'He gotta practice his charge more betta. He gotta be faster off his charge. He made 'um, but he still gotta practice harder.' He told them in Japanese. You see that on the TV, the reporters are looking at me like, 'How your boss?' I went back in the locker room and Chad just told me, 'Ah, fuck what he said.'"

"Percy, him, he probably kept a lot of things to himself," Kaleo told me. "I mean if he was hurting, he wouldn't tell anybody. He not going let nobody know if he's hurting, or if something's wrong. If something's wrong, he just going back up in his own corner and just wait it out."

BY NOW PERCY KNEW THAT THE HAWAI'I VERSION of his *keshō mawashi* was not available to him—that if he was going to put his unique set of skills to work, it would always mean serving the kinds of people who had turned his twenty-five-year-old body into that of an old man, all so someone like Boss could get rich. It would mean being the kind of ten-dolla *tsukebito* he'd been at the airport getting ordered around by some skinny corporate version of the frying-pan-wielding Tsuji, but with no way up the corporate *banzuke* no matter how hard he worked. If watching Hoyu Kensetsu buy up the fourteen hundred acres that included his grandfather's land, or watching Azabu USA buy the five hundred acres surrounding his house and then try to buy off his father for six hundred dollars—if this had not shown him the extent of the Japanese reach into his home island while he was in high school, then the always-observant Percy would have learned during his time at Breathless that nearly every hotel in Waikīkī was Japanese owned. He would have learned that Kitaro Watanabe's Azabu USA also owned the Hyatt and several other hotels statewide, and that Kenji Osano's Kyo-Ya owned all four Sheratons in Waikīkī. And after his time in sumo, Percy would not have needed Japanese crime experts David Kaplan and Alec Dubro to point out that Osano's hotels were *yakuza* "landing spots"—it would have been obvious to him.

"He speaks Japanese," Kurt said. "I told him try use that, but he no like work for Japanese."

"He said, 'Japan made me hate, and lie.'" Percy's mother said. "'Ma, I'm going tell you now: I not going work with the Japanese. I had enough.'"

Few former *sumōtori* have more respect for sumo and all of its ancient traditions than Tyler Hopkins, but of his own promotion to *jūryō* and sumo stardom he says this: "I found out that once you do a pull-up and you look up [into the world of sumo's paid ranks], it's all fuckin' politics. It's all fuckin' bullshit, brah. So you've been bustin' your ass for bullshit. *Now* the game begins. Now how good can you play the fuckin' game? And you look: 'What the fuck is this? This is all bullshit!'" Keep your mouth shut. Know your place. Turn your head at the first sign of corruption. And, often for no apparent reason, get beaten to a pulp during morning practice.

"Percy grew up over here," George Kalima told me. "You're growing up in your room in your mom and dad's house, you don't know what the world is like, and then you come over here and you notice that everybody has two faces."

So Percy waited it out, trying to keep himself busy by doing side jobs with Charles Kekahu, or cruising up to Pounders. The long drives up past Waikāne, and then around that spectacular bend at Kualoa Ranch, through the little country beach towns all the way up the Windward side would have been trips back into the memories of Percy's youth, when Kurt used to take him along with his family for a day at the beach, and then later when Shane and Charles would join him in a convoy of the cars they'd fixed up together, Percy sitting nearly in the back seat as he drove his little beat-up Mazda through Ka'a'awa, the green, misty valley opening up to his left, the emerald waves breaking way out on the outside reefs to his right, and the people fishing with their long poles stuck into metal pipes in the sand all the way up through Hau'ula.

But then the drive home along the breezy coast would kick him awake as rudely as one of his *senpai* had back in those first dark Tokyo mornings. There was Country Stop—the little store in Kahalu'u where a deal was likely going on outside even now as he drove by. From the highway you could now see the brown bay water, the Waiāhole-Waikāne Community Association having pulled acres of hau bushes along the shore. There was the banyan tree, the surrounding gravel parking lot crowded with stringy-haired, toothless druggies. Farther along, 'Āhuimanu was filling up with houses, the once-empty slopes of Temple Valley Cemetery now dotted with faded anthuriums and bronze plaques. Temple Valley Shopping Center across the street had exploded in size. Big green signs pointed to H-3—the slab of concrete carrying cars toward his precious valley through the funnel of Kahekili Highway, now six lanes wide and landscaped just like the freeways in Tokyo with three-story concrete walls and chain-link fences. Percy knew that people had been fighting against H-3 since before he was born, and that they'd mostly given up the year before he'd entered high school. The twelve miles of bridges and tunnels had cost more than a billion dollars, and the highway was finally finished while he was away learning the meaning of "tender loving care." Farther on through traffic-choked Kāne'ohe, past the Ko'olau Country Club and then the Pali Golf Course, through the long wait at the Pali Highway intersection, past the

Luana Hills Country Club, Olomana Golf Links, and into Waimānalo. Percy would pass by the turn into Sherwood's, trying to avoid Kurt, who by now was losing patience with him for failing to get his life underway nearly three years since coming home from Japan.

"I think he always used to try to prove to Kurt that he could do this or that," Charles Kekahu, who was with Percy almost daily during this time of his life, told me. "I'm sure he always wanted the approval, ah? And I'm sure they all loved him so much that they wanted him to do good, but I don't know if he really wanted to do that. He like his simple life. But by the time he came back, everything changed already. T'ings was fast paced. Everybody getting smahta—not people doing simple t'ings anymore. Still had Waikāne and stuff, but wasn't like when we was growing up. You come back seven years later you get all kine people bullshitting each odda, you don't know what's true or not. I know he was disappointed. Deep inside I still think he wanted to become big in Japan. Somehow, he wish he gave it one more chance. To be this, and then come back to *this* and it's not the same."

A return to a "simple life" that no longer exists, one that may have only ever existed in the homesick corners of his imagination. A sense of defeat, and worse: his own *mottai nai* feeling of regret: What if I'd stayed another year? Another two years? I'd just won the championship again, with another perfect record. Why didn't I stay? Such thoughts would inevitably be followed by anger, because he knew exactly why he hadn't stayed. The life was destroying his body, clearly. But worse, it was destroying his sense of what was right. *Japan made me hate, and lie.* That afternoon Percy and I spent together at the Kokugikan betting on the lower-division sumo bouts—a lot of things came up in those couple of hours. One of them was that he'd likened the Sumo Association to *The Firm*—the John Grisham book where the young lawyer scores what he thinks is the ideal job, only to find that he's "learned too much" and will never be allowed to leave. But in looking back and knowing what Percy came home to after getting out of sumo—all of that mysterious talk sounds more like he was trying as hard as he could to convince himself that he'd done the right thing in getting out.

I forget how many copies I made of the cover letter and resume I wrote up for Percy, but there were still quite a few of them left among the materials Mr. Kipapa gave me along with the photo albums. And the red truck—even after he'd sold his pimped-up dream vehicle, his attempt to trick out the Cutlass with chrome rims and a four-inch lift seemed about as half-hearted as what his job search had become after three years of trying.

"Her and I, we are concerned parents," Mr. Kipapa told me. "But me, I only going talk once. I'm not going repeat this and that. I told them, 'I'll tell you the truth: I knew a lot of guys who into this kine drugs, this and that, but I neva was curious. Like how you see wet paint and you put your finger on top to find if it's wet? I wasn't curious.' But my advice to him when he came back from Japan was, 'Don't get yourself too deeply involved in something that you'll get hard time getting out of.' So he preferred not to talk to me—he'd prefer to talk to her. Once he see me coming like that, boom, he's gone! For the short period of time he was living here, we try to encourage him: 'Why you no like go work?' But he neva like the idea of us getting on his case, so he just put himself in the room, and I leave the burden to my wife."

One evening Percy's good friend Kevin Chang and I lingered over dinner at a Waikīkī noodle shop discussing how he had grown up with Percy, taking kung-fu lessons at the Kualoa-Heʻeia Ecumenical Youth (KEY) Project as kids, attending King Zoo and then Castle at the same time. They developed that unique local-boy expatriate bond during the three months Kevin spent in Tokyo not long after Percy's promotion to *jūryō*—an experience that inspired Kevin to write the song looped on Tyler's CD player the day of the funeral. Kevin went on to earn a law degree and work for the Trust for Public Land—a nonprofit that raises money to buy Hawaiʻi agricultural land and protect it from development—and currently works for the Office of Hawaiian Affairs. After Kevin took me through his own high school years with a sense of relief that he'd made it unscathed, we tried to figure out why Percy had, at some point, stopped waiting for the phone to ring. We piled on all the disappointments he'd faced upon returning to his precious valley—his fiancée left him; people treated him like a well-at-least-you-wen'-try failure for not becoming the next Akebono; the place had changed so dramatically; Breathless had closed; he'd been rejected repeatedly in his search for work. But for someone as resilient as we both knew Big Happiness to be, we knew that even that long string of let-downs wouldn't have been enough to defeat him. And then Kevin said something remarkable—one of those observations that, once you hear it, seems so obvious you wonder why you hadn't already thought of it. All he did was place Percy's painful homecoming in the context of what he sadly called a "typical" local-boy identity.

"The big, lifted four-by-four with the tinted windows and the chrome rims, all the tattoos, the mean looks, the pit bulls," he said, "these guys are obviously all trying to compensate. They've been castrated on their own home ground. They know on some level their lives have been taken from them and reduced to doing some menial work to make someone else a lot of money. They may know what was taken from them over the course of generations, like Percy knew about his grandfather's land. The trucks and the tattoos, being all bad—badder than the next guy—that 'ainokea' sticker on the bumper, even turning to drugs, or worse, to dealing—that may be the only way these guys have left to assert some kind of man-hood. They've been castrated and they know it. I know some guys, guys from high school, guys as big as Percy that we both grew up with, they're too afraid to pick up the phone and *order a fuckin' pizza* because they've been so convinced that they're stupid. That's why we need the pit bulls and the trucks, and why we can only express ourselves through violence. Somebody needs to articulate what that feels like. Somebody needs to say it honestly."

What separates the local sumo boys from the typical tattooed four-by-four driver, among other things, is that they were all away long enough to gain the perspective to see just what Kevin saw in the twenty-two-inch chrome rims, even when it was their own reflection. "We achieved so much and came out with so little that everything else doesn't really mat-ter," Tyler told me, concluding a story about his brief stint with Percy as a "ten-dolla whore" greeting tourists at the airport. "It's all about *getting fuckin' high.*"

CHAPTER 10

THE ICE IS BROKEN

The chronics who go up there [Waikāne Valley], to them it's just one hideout. Back when the t'ing started twenty years ago, nobody was aware, 'cause all along that beach area, that used to be hau *bush, and had compartments, where people used to go in and go fishing. From Waiāhole Poi Factory all the way down to Mama-san's store, that used to be* hau *bush. They used to park their boats on the water—the wooden boats. The compartments was where they used to pull their trucks in, and, you know, they set up their family, and go out on the boats and catch crab. Wasn't hiding compartments. And people slowly started migrating down that side. Afta Kāne'ohe figga them out, afta Kahalu'u figga them out, they start migrating down that side and go into the compartments, you know what I mean? Then the community got together and cut everything down—you see 'um all flat now. And now they been discovered, so where else they going go? They just going go up in the valley.*

—Charles Kekahu, June 2007

Tyler wanted me to start this book with the car story, because when I told it to him he said it really captured the way Percy would go out of his way for people, the little things that would go wrong along the way that he'd optimistically brush aside and work to correct. He said it really showed what kind of guy Percy was. By the time I'd told the story to Tyler at Percy's funeral, Noriko was working as an ICU nurse at Hilo Medical Center in a language she hadn't been able to speak four years earlier. She always pointed back to that day we'd run into Percy in the Waimānalo Shopping Center parking lot as a big reason why she had succeeded. Right in the middle of the most uncertain, depressing, lonely time she'd ever been through, she saw it in his face that she would be able to make it. Percy, who at the age of eighteen had gone to the cold and brutal world of Japanese sumo, was telling her, yeah, it's tough to be so far away from home, you *should* be sad right now, but you'll make it. He reminded her that she hadn't lost her ability to laugh, and she thought back to his big Daiki face whenever she did get homesick.

So when Noriko saw his concern a few months later that we didn't have a car, she was eager to jump into his and take a ride up to Waikāne Valley, where he was storing a Chevy Corsica he'd fixed up a couple of years earlier. By then we'd come down with the worst sort of rock fever, our existences reduced to the five-mile radius our bikes would take us, or to the day-long project of catching the city bus. We'd been thinking about buying a car for a couple of months, but I'm useless with any decision dealing with anything mechanical, and our budget was still limited to the thirteen grand I was making as a UH graduate assistant and the cash I took home waiting tables on the weekends. So when someone we trusted said he had a running car for eight hundred bucks, we were quick to agree to take a look at it.

Percy talked nonstop all the way from town about how great the car was, how he and his friends had lowered the body, how fast it could go, even over the Pali, even with big guys like himself driving it. And then when the big green mountain came into view, for a while it was as though he'd forgotten all about the car, and the real reason for the trip was that he wanted to let us in on the secret of the beautiful place where he'd grown up. "My fadda always used to tell us, you see that mountain, that's your home," he said. On he went with stories of growing up in the valley raising chickens and goats with Kurt and Selisa, his family's long history in the area, the land they owned back in Waikāne Valley. We passed 'Okana Road, the banyan tree, the Hygienic Store and the 7-Eleven, Waiāhole Beach Park. And then Percy turned off the highway straight into the thick jungle, onto a dirt road I'd driven past a hundred times on my way to the North Shore without a thought that anyone lived in there, and soon the canopy of leaves suddenly opened out into the most beautiful valley I'd seen since I'd gone camping years before on the Nā Pali Coast.

He turned into the dusty driveway of a little tin-roofed country home, and the first thing he did was go inside to get his mother so he could properly introduce us. We were his "friends from Japan." She greeted us warmly, handing us an armful of fruit and inviting us to come back and visit any time. You could immediately see where Percy's "too much aloha" had come from.

He led us through a flock of clucking chickens and over to where the car was sitting under a huge grapefruit tree in the corner of the yard, going on about how he used to race his friends in it. "But you gotta watch out," he said, reaching across the windshield with his long arm to clear away a handful of leaves, sending a cloud of mosquitoes into the soft afternoon sunlight. "You get up to eighty-ninety, the front end starts to wobble." The car didn't look bad—except for one long scratch down the side, with a good washing and waxing it might match the tight racing tires he'd put on the front, making it look kind of sporty. But when he opened the driver's side door, we were all hit with the powerful, sour smell of mildew.

"This thing been sitting for months," he said. "Plus get one small hole in the roof in the back, on the odda side, but we can fix 'um up, no problem. MaGaiva! I telling you, this one fast car."

Noriko opened the back door and jumped back with a scream as three giant spiders scurried out onto the grass, sending Percy into a fit of belly-rolling laughter.

"That's life in the country," he told her in Japanese.

With each step in the process she looked more and more uncertain, but even with all the mold and the puddle of water in front of the wet sponge of a back seat, this was a running car that fit our budget. All I was thinking was that I'd spent my last miserable blazing-hot afternoon waiting at some bus stop.

But when Percy squeezed in behind the wheel and turned the key, nothing happened. Whatever was under that leaf-covered hood didn't even attempt to start with a "click," let alone the laboring *whrrr* of a car trying to turn over with a dead battery.

"Ah, my fuckin' sista!" Percy said, reaching down to pop the hood. He had to use both hands, the handle to pop the hood lying at his feet at the end of a sheathed steel cable: one hand to hold the sheath, and one to pull the handle. "Her friend's car—the battery died. I bet she wen' take my battery."

He lifted his big body out of the driver's seat and then jammed his big fingers into the tiny crack between the hood and the grill, fiddling around as he explained that the lever to free the hood had broken off, and that there was a trick to freeing the spring lock that held the hood down, "Li'dis."

A few more bugs scurried across the now-sunlit engine, which was packed in tightly all the way to the car's maroon-painted edges, making the empty space where the battery was supposed to be look like a canyon. Adding everything up, including the hole in the roof, the puddle in the back seat, the handle to pop the hood, the broken lever, and Noriko's near heart attack over the spiders, plus the driver's seat Percy had ripped from its moorings so he could push it back far enough for him to fit behind the wheel, my first reaction at the missing battery was to be relieved. Looking back, I could see that we'd somehow committed to buying the car the moment Percy had driven us away from our apartment in town. But that empty space next to the engine was going to get us off the hook.

And then Percy looked at his watch and said, "We go Kāneʻohe. Still get time for buy one new battery." And within the hour we were driving back towards Waikāne, a new battery from Napa in a crisp brown paper bag at my feet, the mountain now a dark silhouette against the pink and yellow sky off in front of us, and Percy going on about how he wanted to buy a plate-lunch wagon—he knew just the right places to park it for breakfast and for lunch, where to get the stuff to make the food, that it was a cash business and how he was going to make a killing at it. I recalled some of the stories he'd told me about managing the restaurant in Waikīkī, and I knew from his experience in sumo that he knew how to cook. To me a lunch wagon seemed a few steps down from what Percy was really capable of doing given his experience and his perfect Japanese, but on he went and couldn't have been more excited.

IN THE FADING TWILIGHT he installed the battery, all the while telling us stories about how he and his friends used to work on cars back in high school. He let the hood slam and got behind the wheel again, and this time the car roared to life. We could see his beaming face through the windshield, the wipers now on and clearing fallen debris as he slowly rolled forward, hand-sized leaves clinging to the front tires.

He left it running and got out proudly, saying, "See? I tol' you this was one good car!"

I got behind the wheel and he opened the rear door to help me Ma-Gaiva the seat forward and anchor it as best he could, jamming a piece of wood under it and reassuring me that he had the actual seat mount some-where back in his garage in Waimānalo. The seat rocked back and forth a bit, but it would be good enough to get me home.

In front of me the dashboard was lit up like a Christmas tree, urging me to get the engine checked, add coolant, turn off my high beams, add wiper fluid, get gas, and three or four other things I can't remember that looked pretty important. It also told me the car had over ninety thousand miles on it.

"No worry," Percy said, of all the warning lights. "That t'ing neva work since I got the car."

Noriko gave Percy a hug and got in next to me, and off we went, Percy following behind all the way into Kāne'ohe and the first gas station. I had to grip the wheel extra tightly to keep my seat from rocking back and forth too much, and the sleepy engine coughed and stalled once at a light, but we managed to make it over the Pali and home. The next day Percy drove us to Satellite City Hall at Windward Mall to change the title. He drove us to State Farm (where the agent knew him) to help me get insurance, and then on to the police station to get an abstract of my driving record that the insurance agent had requested, and finally, to the bank, where I took out eight hundred dollars and handed it over. Back in Waimānalo the seat mount he'd ripped out was nowhere to be found among the rusting bolts and brackets in the big box he hauled out of the garage, but he did manage to MaGaiva a more secure anchor for me, sitting on his driveway, leaning in through the open driver's side door, and bending a steel support beam from the bottom of the seat to jam into a hole on the floor, beads of sweat pouring down the sides of his face, his glasses fogging with the effort. Though the seat still swayed a bit, it was the perfect distance from the pedals for me. We left the Hawaiian-warrior-helmet charm that Percy had carved "Kipapa" into hanging from the mirror. Noriko made aloha-print covers for all of the seats with a bolt of cloth she found on sale at Fabric

Mart. I put another three hundred bucks into the brakes, another eighty into a new tire, coaxed it through inspection at another friend's service station, and proudly parked our new car in space number 21 at the Diamond Head Surf apartments.

That car freed Noriko and me from our little five-square-mile prison, taking us camping on the North Shore, to watch Henry Kapono or Jake Shimabukuro at Aloha Tower (where I used the valet, no matter what), back and forth to school and to Noriko's new job at the hospital, and then back and forth to physical therapy and the doctor when she blew out a disk in her back lifting big patients. The car took us to weddings and birthday parties in Waimānalo, on circle-island tours for visiting friends and relatives, back and forth to Kaplan, where Noriko was studying for the RN licensing test. The battery died once. It needed a new muffler later on. The hole in the roof got bad enough so that we had to bail out the car after heavy rainstorms, and the windows stopped rolling up, too. We finally sold it when the water pump went, just before we moved to the Big Island. But for three years we lived right on the poverty line, a graduate student and a nurse's aid, and that maroon Corsica was our BMW.

Tyler had a good idea to start the book with the car story, but that made me uneasy because when I told it to him I avoided telling how it ended. About a week after I'd handed Percy eight crisp hundreds, he showed up at my apartment again asking for more money. He told me about new tires he'd had to buy for his own car, money he'd owed a friend, his trouble finding work. He said he needed two hundred dollars, and that he'd asked another friend first, who'd *given* him forty rather than lend him anything. I explained to him that I was still in school and Noriko wasn't working yet, and then I had him drive me to the bank anyway. Along the way I hated myself for thinking what people had been saying about Percy since I'd first heard about him, and for recalling in vivid detail a conversation we'd had up in Japan—"Just 'cause I used to do that stuff long time ago, everybody like talk about me like I'm one drug addict. Every time they see my truck go by they like look at each odda and say, 'There he goes, probably going for buy drugs.' But you tell me you going look at me, look at my size, an' tell me I doing drugs. Fuck, I wish I could be that skinny!" I withdrew two hundred dollars and gave it to Percy. I told him I needed the money back by the end of the month so I could pay my rent. And just before I got out of the car I clasped his hand with one hand and hugged him with the other and, essentially, said good-bye.

I said good-bye because I knew that I'd never see him again, that he'd never come up with the two hundred dollars, and that the shame of owing it to me would keep him from calling or dropping by like he'd been doing for the past few months. I knew exactly where the money was going, and while I was so busy trying to not judge Percy for that fact, I was trying to hide from myself the fact that I wasn't going to do a thing about it. No, it was worse—I was wishing Percy's problem away. Even worse, I was wishing *Percy himself* away, all the while trying to justify it with internal excuses about my own busy life. I was *hoping* Percy wouldn't call again, that he'd somehow get help from somewhere else, that he'd kick the habit on his own. I ignored the whole thing out of convenience, which is probably what I was doing when I didn't tell Tyler how the car story ended. It's what we were all doing in the Kalimas' carport all those hours we spent trading stories about Percy, all the while knowing he'd had a serious addiction all along, but tip-toeing around it in our recollections not because we wanted to avoid soiling his memory but because we were ashamed to admit we knew all about it and ignored it or even blamed Percy for it, which is probably what Kurt did, too, what Chad did. What everyone did.

❨   ❨   ❨

ONE NIGHT AT THE END OF MARCH 2003, two years before Percy was killed, Kahaluʻu's then-KEY Project executive director Bob Nakata, along with Hina Mauka Treatment Center CEO Andy Anderson, community leaders Mike McCartney and John Reppun, and Kahaluʻu pastor Keith Ryder, all waited outside an empty KEY Project Center wondering if anyone was going to show up for the first town-hall meeting ever called to discuss what all of us all over Hawaiʻi had been trying to ignore for fifteen years now. Ice was somebody else's problem—the "druggies" and the "chronics." And if it was someone down the street, if it was one of our friends or even one of our cousins or sons, we hushed it over and tried to wish it away just like I had done with Percy. But Anderson, Nakata, and Ryder knew that it was long past time to bring ice out into the open. After directing Kalihi Valley Housing for all of the 1990s, Bob Nakata had returned to Kahaluʻu to head KEY Project and to run for the State Senate. "In the 2002 election I became aware of how *pervasive* the drug problem had become," he told me. "I knew it was there, but I really became aware when I went down to campaign at coffee hours in Kahuku, Lāʻie," all along the Windward Coast. "Samoan women. I said, you know, tell me what you see as a problem. They said 'ice.' And they wouldn't shut up about it."

"And these aren't necessarily community activists," I said.

"No. And they started to talk about it. And, you know, I didn't campaign enough, that's why I lost the election. But another factor in the loss was that I started to pay more attention to the drug issue than to campaigning. I had already started visiting the evangelical churches because I wanted to know more about the drug issue. Every Sunday I would go to a different church, just getting to know more people, getting to know more about the drug problem. I was telling the church people, 'Let's start paying attention to the needs of the poor people here.' That's how I got to know Keith."

Keith Ryder is a man who found Jesus. However you feel about evangelical Christianity, the story of his conversion is nothing short of miraculous. The son of noted syndicate boss Roy Ryder, Keith was "following in his father's footsteps," as Bob Nakata puts it. "I was telling Bob, I feel somewhat responsible," Keith told me, "because I know when I was a young boy, it was only alcohol, and we used to bring back the drugs and start selling them" back in the seventies: pakalolo, acid, and cocaine. Then one night when he was in his late twenties, Keith stormed from his regular living-room card game with the intention of scolding his ten-year-old son for making too much noise. But when he entered his son's room, the boy dropped to the floor and curled up in a fetal position, shaking in fear. Hating the pit-bull monster he had become, Keith went to church the very next day for the first time and has devoted his life to God ever since. Though he still carries the bulk that would have impressed his father's former colleagues, that bulk is now dressed in the black of a Christian minister. Unless you're a dealer, you'll usually find a soft smile above his goatee, and you get the sense that if he's trying to get people into his church, it's as much for practical reasons as for spiritual ones: he wants to give them hope and purpose so that they stay away from drugs.

"As a minister, I was asked to sit on the board for KEY Project, and that's where I met Bob and other community leaders," he told me when I asked about the 2003 meeting. "And one of the issues that we were facing as a community with the problem of ice was denial, even though the evidence was all around us. Family was starting to fight against family, within our immediate families, within our extended 'ohana, our calabash cousins—everybody started to fight. The way we always dealt with the problems in our community was to blame the other guy for doing it. And then it would come back to you: 'Oh, but your family get the chronics,' 'Oh, they're the dealers.'" So he and Bob started a coalition of churches, and the idea for a town-hall meeting began to take shape.

Like many of us only recently willing to admit we're only a handshake away from someone who's been taken down by ice, Keith knew all about denial. "I had gotten away from that world," he said. "I really didn't know what ice was until we started to see some really gruesome-looking people walking around the streets." We'd all already seen enough before-and-after pictures of the worst kind of chronics, so it was easy to pretend that the problem was limited to them, that normal-looking people like the former deputy prosecutor in charge of the city's drug program, for instance, had not gotten caught up in it. But when Keith began to see these "gruesome-looking people" start to proliferate under Kahalu'u's banyan tree, and that the tree itself had come to symbolize the drug problem, he started to look around more closely, and what he saw was that denial—especially when it's strengthened by the tight web of family relationships in places like Kahalu'u, Waiāhole, and Waikāne—was not *part* of the ice problem, it *was* the ice problem.

"I found out one of my cousins was one of the biggest dealers in Kahalu'u," he said, indicating the first of several cousins on both sides of the law that appear in his story, confusing it in a way that actually helps illustrate the extent of the problem. "She was ground level, but she caused a lot of damage. See, it's not the big-time guys—it's the ones on the street. That's the ones that's causing all the damage." He found out that his cousin and her brother, "who had just gotten out of prison," he explained, were dealing on an old barge anchored off the little park below St. John's by the Sea church. "One night I went down to St. John's, and I knew my cousin was on the barge. She would come down during the day, she would park her truck right on the boat ramp, and they were open for business. And all of a sudden you had traffic coming in and out, and kids were playing in the park. When I got down there and I saw that I said, 'Ho, this not happening. Not *here.*' Cause if my aunty was alive—she lived right next door to the park—she would *neva* allow this.

"I see all of this happening," he went on. "So this is my solution: 'You guys want to play that game?' I went back to my church and I told them, 'We're gonna do our prayer service down at St. John's in the park, and we're going pray that God closes down this business.' So that's what we started to do. Before you know it, other churches were going down there with us." They attracted the attention of Carol Chang from *Midweek*, a free publication mailed weekly to every residence on Oʻahu. "So I took her down there, I told her this is the barge where they're selling the drugs. My cousin who's a police officer lives right there. Nothing being done, it's right in front of his house. So she writes the story. Now my other cousin who just got out of prison, he's selling for his sister, he comes up to me, he tells me, 'Eh, you read the article in *Midweek?*' I said, 'Oh yeah. Did *you* read it?' 'Yeah.' I said, 'Well what did you think?' He said, 'Oh, you made it seem like we selling drugs down here.' So I looked at him and said, 'And what, choo not? That's the truth. They neva make it *seem* like. And that's why we out here. If you not going listen to what I'm telling you, then I gotta go talk to somebody else, somebody bigga than you to take care of this problem.'"

"So your prayers were answered," I said.

"Our prayers were answered!" he said with a smile. "Here's the deal: we called the DLNR to make a complaint against this barge. Now instead of the DLNR coming down and citing them and getting them to get rid of the barge, one of the top guys from DLNR comes from Waiāhole. He knew it was there all along. Better yet, he knew it was my cousin's. So instead of doing his job, he told my cousin, 'All you gotta do is go register the barge. Nobody can kick you out, you just gotta have a registered numba on toppa the barge.' He give 'em the address and everything for the place they gotta go. Now he has the barge registered, so it can legally be in the water. So instead of thinking of doing your job and doing what's best for the community, you're still thinking, 'But this is my family,' 'We go way back.'" It would take months and many more phone calls to finally get rid of the barge, which, by the end, had a pier connecting it to shore for the convenience of its customers.

If such small-town connections defined the ice problem, they also presented a map towards its solution. "In December, the year I lost the election," Bob Nakata recalled, "I'm at the Windward Health Center. Hina Mauka is right down the street, so here's Andy Anderson doing the same thing, standing in line. He asked me if I would sit on his board at Hina Mauka." Bob declined, having already committed to KEY Project the fund-raising skills he knew Anderson needed. Then Anderson brought up the idea of a community meeting. "And he named a few people: Mike McCartney, John Reppun. But I didn't think Andy was going to charge ahead as quickly as he did. In January he called me and he said, 'Okay, Mike has said that he would emcee the event.' He had talked to John, so there we were, off and running."

A recovering alcoholic for the past forty years, Andy Anderson may not be an evangelical Christian, but he's as religious about the value of substance abuse treatment as Keith Ryder is about Jesus. When I called to set up an appointment to discuss the 2003 "ice storm," as he called it, he set aside an entire morning to talk with me at Hina Mauka. He told me that during the fall of 2002 he went to Kaua'i to give a presentation on treatment and addiction at a Princeville meeting of about 150 business people, health care workers, police, and environmentalists. After some introductory remarks, Kaua'i mayor Bryan Baptiste broke the room into groups, telling them, as Anderson recalled, "'In this part of the auditorium we're going to have people meeting about health. In this corner we're going to have people talking about ecology. In this corner we're going to have people talking about agriculture.' And then he said, 'And in this corner we're going to be talking about drug abuse.' And that was okay," Anderson went on. "I was prepared for that. I wasn't prepared for having 120 people come over there. I've been in this business for forty years, and up until that point, you didn't get that many people who want to talk about drug abuse. It totally blew me away."

With his large audience around him, Anderson took a deep breath and launched into his usual presentation, but he was quickly interrupted. "People didn't want to hear that," he said. "What they wanted to do was vent: 'Why aren't the police doing more?' 'Why isn't treatment doing more?' 'What can we do?' 'Why can't we get rid of the dealers?' 'Why can't we do something about these people with addictions?' And that opened my eyes. I remember, 'Wow, if we could make this happen in other places!'"

Just after returning to Kāneʻohe, Anderson ran into Bob Nakata, and the strategy sessions followed quickly to draw as big a crowd as possible. They all went back and forth on what to call the meeting, leery of mentioning the "I" word for fear of offending the very people they hoped to attract. But then Anderson spoke up: "Let's lay it on the line: town meeting on ice. Let's keep it to the point." For the next two months they got the word out, with a blizzard of flyers falling upon the neighborhood bulletin boards, the schools, the churches, and the community mailboxes from Temple Valley to Waikāne.

"Still, you can do all that and then have maybe forty people show up," I told Andy.

"We thought we would have a dynamite crowd if thirty people showed up," he said.

They had their emcee. They had a panel of experts on drug treatment, education, law enforcement. U.S. Attorney Ed Kubo. Alan Shinn from the Coalition for a Drug Free Hawaiʻi. Lieutenant Governor Duke Aiona. Now all they needed was an audience. "We were standing out there in front of KEY maybe half an hour early, just a handful of people wondering who was going to turn up," Bob Nakata recalled. "And at that point it was mainly the agency types who were there. But closer to seven, people started coming in. It was amazing." They just kept coming, over two hundred and fifty people—and not just "the same old faces" from the Waiāhole-Waikāne Community Association or from previous KEY Project functions. People came from everywhere. Sixteen years after ice had begun its invasion, the masses put aside their fear of shame and took a moment from their overly hectic lives to reach out for help.

"But the reason for the great turnout is tragic," Bob explained. "About ten days before the event, a young man from one of the large Hawaiian clans here hanged himself."

"One of my cousins up in Waiāhole Valley," Keith said. "He had had a problem with drugs. In and out of jail, dealing ice, had problems with his girlfriend, he made it known that he was not going to go back to prison. He was threatened by his girlfriend that she would turn him in. He was missing for about a week. He hung himself pretty close to the house. He climbed about thirty feet up into the tree so nobody was looking that high, but his brother ended up finding him."

"That event provided the emotional push, and it lowered the resistance to talking about the issue," Bob said. "So not only did we have a great turnout, but there were people saying, 'Oh, this was my cousin,' 'This was my nephew.' This is almost an intended pun, but the ice was broken, and people started talking."

"And the thing was," Keith went on, "we had set it up so that we had a panel of experts, but that's not what the people wanted to hear. They didn't want to hear from the experts. They wanted to know what we were gonna do as a community, and how we were gonna handle it. And so that night we seen the meeting kind of shift and turn. I stood up to share with our panel of experts that it was important for them to be there, but it was more important to be there to *listen* to what people are saying."

"And then the uncle of the young man that hung himself," Andy Anderson went on, "he shared what happened, and that opened up the floodgates. And if you're aware of the culture here, families don't open up as far as 'sharing their dirty laundry' goes. Tremendous, tremendous shame, guilt, remorse, and anger started pouring out of everybody there, because that's what families that have addiction go through—they think they're responsible, they're ashamed, they're angry because they're put in this situation, you know, 'What did I do? Why didn't I raise him or her right?' They go through all that kind of thing, and actually the truth is, they did everything they could. After one person shared, then somebody else shared, and then somebody else, and somebody else, and all of a sudden, here it is out there in the open. The meeting went on for three hours. And we huddled up during the meeting and said, 'We've gotta call another meeting.' We attended twenty-one or twenty-two of those town meetings on O'ahu."

"And the very thing we were trying to avoid was what almost happened," Keith said, "where all of a sudden there was some pointing: 'Oh, but you guys, and you guys,' and we kind of hashed all of that out because we weren't there to put the blame on anybody else—we were there to accept that we have a problem, and we're not gonna deny it anymore." Grandparents talked about the "missing generation"—how they'd lost their own kids to drugs and were now parenting their grandchildren. Parents talked about

losing teens to addiction. Addicts stood up and admitted their own problems. The word "addict" even began to lose its negative connotations. For
once, addiction wasn't anyone's fault, or something to hide and be ashamed
of, because none of it was personal: ice had infested every neighborhood
from Temple Valley to Waikāne and beyond, and it had taken down whoever stood in its way.

And for a while, it worked. In 2003, two full years before Percy was
killed less than a mile away from KEY Project, *Advertiser* reporter Eloise
Aguiar quoted U.S. Attorney Ed Kubo as saying, "I promise you will see
the faces of law enforcement agents out there." Steeped as we all were by
then in the election-season tradition of sign-waving, Keith Ryder suggested
that everyone line Kam Highway from the banyan tree up to Country Stop
with signs shouting their message to dealers. And for the next several weeks,
the phone at KEY Project was ringing off the hook. "We had people from
all around the island calling us saying, 'Can we join?'" Bob told me. "And
it was getting big, so we started telling people, 'You know what: do it in
your own community.'" So two months later, people lined Kam Highway
not from the banyan tree to Country Stop—a stretch of a mile or so—but
from Kāneʻohe all the way to Waialua—the entire Windward Coast *and*
the North Shore. "We were running around like crazy," Bob went on. "So
you get the spark from the suicide, and then Keith provides another spark.
And then around the state, other islands they started doing it. The way that
thing caught fire!"

The fire spread both upward, causing Lieutenant Governor Duke Aiona
to set up his ice "summit" later that summer, and downward, leading the
people of Kahaluʻu to form a neighborhood watch. "Our base station was
at the elementary school," Keith said. "We went through the process where
we were recognized by HPD. We got the walkie-talkies, the banners, the
signs. And it was working. One night we got into the back and parked at
the dead end. There was a car, so we began shining our lights into the car
because they shouldn't be back there. When they saw us they started taking off and heading back out to the main street, so we followed them to
make sure that they went all the way back out. They made a short detour
at one of the parks because they thought we were police officers, and two
girls ran out of the back seat. We knew they were running out to probably

dump the drugs, so we just sat out there and waited for them to get back in and go out on the main road. But it works."

So the ice was broken, and while those of us on the edges of what we could all now call an "epidemic" may have been shocked and even frightened by what we were now having to admit, those who had been living for years with the reality of an addicted son, or a daughter who dealt, or of having to raise a grandchild named "Crystal" had to have been shot through with a sense of hope. People were making *noise*. A *Honolulu Weekly* cover story cited the National Drug Intelligence Center in pointing out that Hawai'i led the nation in per capita ice use by a wide margin. The *Pacific Business News* cited a Columbia University study setting a one-year price tag at $437.8 million for things like corrections and ER visits and other facilities drained by ice users. A Waiāhole Beach Park cleanup drew over a hundred people. More people were volunteering in other community areas only peripherally related to the drug campaign, all working together, as Bob Nakata was quoted as saying at the time, to "take back the streets."

By the end of September, the noise had grown so loud that eleven local television stations had no choice but to give up hundreds of thousands of dollars in commercial airtime to simultaneously broadcast Edgy Lee's documentary *Ice: Hawai'i's Crystal Meth Epidemic*. The film's narrator, Matt Levi, somberly hammers the ice-is-EVERYBODY'S-problem message for an hour straight with shocking pathos appeals: our *'āina* being contaminated by toxic waste from clandestine ice labs; law enforcement storming a house to arrest a man smoking in front of his four frightened, neglected children; a tour of an actual user's house given by a jaded Child Protective Services worker who's seen it all before, every room strewn with dirty laundry and other flotsam of complete dishevelment; a meth lab exploding in a giant ball of orange fire, leaving the remains of a charred child's doll. It's all interspersed with statistics delivered by the somber faces of our leaders—Honolulu Prosecutor Peter Carlisle, U.S. Attorney Ed Kubo, the presidents of our most respected private schools, the Department of Education superintendent, the Honolulu Chief of Police, and Hawai'i's highest-paid state employee by several hundred thousand dollars, a football coach named "June"—all drilling into us the fact that the astronomical costs of ice are paid for by us, the taxpayers. The addicts are after your cars! They're going to rob your house! "You better wake up," Big Island Mayor Harry Kim says sternly. "Wake up before it hits you in your head like a two-by-four."

If shock value was the goal of *Ice*, it worked, both Honolulu dailies running features the following day that shouted admirably about the "buzz" the film had created. How could that chronic mother have abandoned her husband and those two beautiful kids? My god—Timothy McVeigh, the Oklahoma City bomber, used ice! Hitler used it eight times a day! There's the Baskin-Robbins killer! There's the Xerox employee who taped the shotgun to that hostage's head a few years back! Listen to those violent crime statistics! And that woman in silhouette—she's a *teacher?*

The very first user we see is a back-lit belligerent "Maui teacher" who's "not hurting nobody" and defensive about her use, telling the interviewer of her kids, "They get everything they need. They get fed. They get showers. What the [bleep] else do they need?" And, "The [bleep] you talking about? Abuse? I just party." The parade of recovering abusers that follows seems centered around the words, "I chose"—"I chose my addiction over my kids."

As I watched the documentary for the first time, this "I chose" mantra made me think of what Andy Anderson, a recovering alcoholic who does not appear in Edgy Lee's movie, told me about the range of his choices back when he used to drink. "Addiction is a brain disease," he said. "The brain is dramatically impacted by reducing the ability to say 'No.' A lot of people think that addiction is simply something that, 'If you drink like me, that won't happen.' When I was in my drinking days, I always got lots of *very* good advice from friends: 'Why don't you drink like me? Just have a couple of beers and go home.'"

"You just don't know when to stop," I said with a laugh, as though beating alcoholism were that simple.

"Well, hell, if I could figure that out I wouldn't have a problem! It's always a case of 'Hey, get in my shoes for a minute.' They're well meaning, make no mistake, but they're giving you suggestions and advice on something they know nothing about."

Edgy Lee is so busy trying to scare us that she never asks us to empathize with any of the users she presents or to draw distinctions between varying levels of addiction—two tactics that could have gotten more of us to try to get our addicted friends and relatives into treatment programs as opposed to locking our doors and checking our wallets whenever they came in sight. And as for treatment expertise, the film turns not to someone like Andy Anderson but to a fifteen-year-old recovering addict who pronounces, against years of peer-reviewed research by psychology Ph.D.s, that no addict can get help "if they don't want to." Deep within all of these slap-to-the-head images and somber pronouncements, drowning in reams of statistics, are two narrated sentences that get lost: "We need to understand that addiction is a disease. It is less a moral weakness than a medical condition requiring treatment." And no one heard them. What came through loud and clear was that sure, ice is *everybody's problem*. Now if only the cops would go and lock up all of those frickin' chronics, and if only all the druggies would "choose" to stop. Drug addict? You just don't know when to stop.

"Our mission is to reduce stigma about all addiction," Andy told me. "The best way to reduce stigma is when you come up to somebody who is walking around clean and sober and isn't afraid to say so. When all of a sudden, you're having coffee somewhere and someone says, 'Oh, this is almost as good as the coffee at the NA meeting I went to last night,' then you know you're getting someplace." Andy and I did not talk about Edgy Lee's movie, but only a few minutes into watching it I could tell that its explosions were not helping Hina Mauka's mission. "Probably what makes ice so different is the extreme violence that comes out of it that doesn't happen with too many other drugs," Andy told me at one point. "Like where you have somebody taking people hostage with a shotgun to the head, or some of the real horrific stories that the press sensationalizes. It's sensationalism when you put an addict on the front page with no teeth. We've got a great rapport with a lot of the press, but there are some that are out there to make this sensational, because you don't sell TV time unless it's sensational. We know that that happens, and it's not a good thing."

"I didn't know—and I don't think Percy knew—how much help there is out there," Tyler Hopkins told me. It had taken his sumo brother's violent death to get Tyler to even begin reevaluating his own years-long relationship with ice. "I went into Hina Mauka and I told these guys, 'I don't have a problem.' But I learned some shit in there that was fucking outstanding.

In medical terms, they call it a 'disease.' In 1935, they defined addiction as a disease. For me—and this is pertaining to Perce, too—I'd always thought it was just being weak. Period. And you gotta be strong, and you gotta push hard." He may as well have said, "You gotta *gaman*." "Because I've always been in sumo, or I've been around guys who don't show that emotion." Or, as Kevin Chang would have put it, around tattooed guys with pit bulls who best express themselves through violence. "But I found out it's not a 'weakness.' It's a disease, and if you don't change one thing—which is *everything*—it will break you down."

Two years after Percy Kipapa's dead body tested positive for ice, I asked his mother what she knew about his addiction. She had to stop and think about it, and then she finally said, "When we were staying in Waimānalo, in the early morning somebody would come: 'Percy, Percy.' And my daughter would say, 'Ma! Must be he's calling Percy for drugs.' But probably, I was in denial at that time. Until one day we ask him, and he said, 'Yeah, I not going lie. I do it. When it's there and it's free.' He neva pay for not'ing. You know what, if he did have to pay, he would be stealing my jewelry! [Ice addicts] don't care who they hurt. He said, 'You know Ma, the t'ing just grabs you.' But he neva did take anything from us. And I thought, 'Is he really on it, or what?' 'Cause I hear so much bad things about 'um. I hear people experience the family or friends that's on drugs, they say, 'I don't know her anymore,' 'I don't know him anymore.' 'He's violent.' But Percy was none of that."

By the time *Ice* was aired, Mrs. Kipapa had her son back under her own roof, and she certainly would have noticed "that change" in him that Shane had seen back in high school if she hadn't been led to think such a change had to include explosions in her kitchen, belligerent behavior, and the disappearance of anything of value from her house. Percy hadn't even complained when the family decided that Kurt's big foster family needed the Waimānalo homestead house more than he did. He may have slept late much of the time, but when he was awake and around he would be Uncle Percy joking with the kids, or MaGaiva Percy making repairs around the house, or Percy heading up the trail to Grandpa's Hill.

I finally got to see Percy's valley a bit over a year after the funeral, when George was home from Japan and the Kipapas took us to see the memorial they'd constructed at his favorite place—the spot on Grandpa's

Hill where they'd scattered his ashes on his birthday a couple of months after the funeral. Kurt and Jolyn and their kids and grandchildren joined us, along with Selisa and her kids—all of us piling into four-wheel-drive trucks that swayed back and forth as they negotiated the big ruts in the narrow jungle trail. I've since hiked all the way up to the spot—a much different experience where you can feel the deep valley's silence gradually envelop you as you walk back in time, leaving the noise of the real world's problems behind. It was a walk Percy would take daily, even in the middle of the night, where he would build a small fire to keep the mosquitoes away and sit for hours looking at the stars. The trail opens out onto an area called "The Flats," revealing the kind of tremendous tropical green vista that, other than in Waikāne, one can only see nowadays from behind the wheel of a golf cart: a stream cutting through the valley below, the blue ocean way beyond, all traces of civilization obscured by trees and surrounding peaks.

"He talked about this all the time up in Japan," George said. "All the time." I told him about the day we'd bought the car, how excited Percy had been. *That's all Roberts land back there*, he'd kept saying.

"There's a place down there he used to go for swim," Selisa said, pointing in the direction of a babbling stream below. "That was his *lomi* spot. He used to massage everybody, he had like one big couch over there. He had a nice area, his own pond and stuff. After he moved back from Japan that's where he used to go." She pointed out a shack far below, nearly hidden in the jungle between where we were standing and the curtain of greenery at the back of the valley. Percy had helped their cousin Manuel build it not long after moving back from Waimānalo, and when they were finished, Big P tested it out with a big jump. "My cousin go, 'Ho wait wait! No do dat!'" Selisa said with a smile. "He go, 'No worry—now it's Percy proof.' If he can jump inside li'dat, then no worry. Percy wen' Percy proof 'um already!"

And the days drifted by, Percy getting back to nature, cruising with Manuel and Manuel's girlfriend Willidean, or, as they all called her, Dean. "Percy would come up to our place and talk story with us," Dean told me. Dean would play guitar, and out would come the sweet, high voice of Big Happiness. "He was always singing," Dean said. "We would try to harmonize. We was living up there and he was working with Manuel. We'd always keep each other company, yeah?" The three of them would regularly work for a Filipino woman in Waiāhole, building a garage for her, cleaning her yard, cleaning her house. "Sometimes we would get tired of going work and stuff, but Percy would say, 'Come on, we just go, and we push this day through.' We always had fun," she went on. "We had barbecues, we'd call our friends. We were always in the mountain. I mean, that was our backyard."

During the time-warp walk up to Grandpa's Hill, it's impossible not to think of Manuel Roberts and imagine the vast, empty area fenced off and cultivated with rows of cucumbers, or picture the big man standing up to the McCandless heirs. Percy knew his family had fought off the biggest threats Hawaiians had ever faced—land developers who tried to control massive areas of the islands, first for sugar, and later for golf courses, resorts, and gated subdivisions for retired mainland haoles. His neighbor Ray Kamaka had even taken on the military, to whom he'd leased 187 acres for the Waikāne Training Facility. When the lease expired, Kamaka sued them to clear the tons of unexploded ordnance they'd left behind. Instead, they condemned the land and offered him the "fair market value" of $700,000. Kamaka would fight the settlement and lose, but there were the three acres that remained of Percy's grandfather's land, still intact right there below him.

Tyler once told me about how he and Percy used to meet in a little park up in Tokyo around the corner from Azumazeki Beya. "We used to sit on the swings and talk," he said. "He told me all about Waikāne Valley. He said, 'You gotta come check it out, brah. We get land up there.' He told me about the *mana* that still lives in that valley, and how the people were trying to save the land. When I finally went to his house, he said, 'Hey— right there's the gate that I used to tell you about.' Up in Japan when you learn about a foreign country's culture and you learn to respect it, you respect your own culture that much more. And then you kind of get mad at America and you say, 'Hey, why am I learning about cowboys and Indians when I got my own history over here?'"

Three acres. Sitting up on Grandpa's Hill day after day, Percy had a lot of time to meditate, and his time in Japan had given him the perspective to see the three acres in the kind of complexity that Tyler explained to me. Sure, he was proud of what his grandfather had been able to do in hanging onto even that sliver of land. But in telling me how his family was one of only two *kuleana* landholders left in the valley, Percy was also being his happy-go-lucky, make-the-best-of-things MaGaiva self, because he also knew that not three, but *fifty* acres of that land he liked to look down upon was supposed to be his. And now he really knew who had been trying to get their hands on it over the years. *Japan made me hate, and lie*, is what he was telling his mother around this time. By now he knew that Kizo Matsumoto, who had bought the Turtle Bay Hilton and Country Club and part of the Kuilima Resort, had been deported because of his ties with Japan's most notorious *yakuza* group, the Yamaguchi-gumi. He knew that Yasuo Yasuda, the man behind the Maunawili Golf Course, had been deported on a similar visa violation despite his lawyer's denials of *yakuza* connections. He knew of Olomana Golf Links owner Ken Mizuno's *yakuza* ties. Back in high school he'd even met Azabu USA's Kitaro Watanabe, the man who'd tried to buy his father off for six hundred dollars. By now he wasn't surprised that Watanabe had since been connected to the Kobayashi-gumi *yakuza* group and arrested in Tokyo, and that his company had gone bankrupt, which was really the only reason Percy's backyard remained the way it was just before Grandpa began to clear it, fence it in, and plant his cucumbers and sweet potatoes.

Such thoughts certainly filled Percy's head whenever he looked out over the valley now so many years into his *at-least-you-wen'-try* return from Japan. They may have lingered on his way down the trail, on that long walk back into the noise of the real world—a place that had nothing for him. And then one day he reached the bottom to find someone waiting for him, someone else, as it turned out, so far out of the mainstream that he hunted to keep himself fed. Perce being Perce, he began to talk to the guy, a dark-haired local man whose light skin and Mediterranean features would have caused the word "Portagee"—Portuguese Hawaiian—to register in Percy's mind. He found out that they'd both gone to Castle High School, though a couple of years apart. The guy shared his country-boy feelings for the quiet wilderness that lay ahead up the trail—a bit of information that would have led Percy to go on about his family's land, how he loved to hike to this special place up there, that there was a river with clear mountain water where he liked to cool off—all the things Percy had told me that first time he'd driven me to Waikāne, the most important being, in this case, that he had a key to the gate. As a pig hunter, the guy would have taken an interest in the fact that Percy had a key, so he would have been just as friendly right back. His name was Keali'i Meheula, and as a pig hunter, he would have been carrying a knife.

CHAPTER 11

THE USERS

Ice is a scourge in our communities that must be treated as any in-fectious disease. Ice is a public health crisis that must be fought by identifying the sources of the infection, preventing the spread of the disease, and treating those who are sick. At all times, the safety of the people of Hawai'i must be protected. Those who reap profit from the spread of the ice epidemic and the misfortune of the afflicted must be punished.

—"Final Report of the Joint House-Senate Task Force on Ice and
Drug Abatement," Hawai'i State Legislature, January 2004

THROUGHOUT THE SUMMER two years before Percy was killed, the nine representatives and the nine senators sitting on the Hawai'i State Legislature's Joint House-Senate Task Force on Ice and Drug Abatement did the kind of work that would renew a faith in government even among the most cynical haters of politicians. The task force convened "informational briefings" with experts from law enforcement, education, and treatment. They held public hearings statewide, during which they listened as concerned community members and affected families vented their frustrations. They conducted site visits at treatment centers across Hawai'i. And if they were unsure about any of their findings, rather than pretend to have the answers, they sought out the experts and consulted the relevant scholarship—pages and pages of it stacking, as they note in their report, "40 inches high." The resulting 188-page document, "Final Report of the Joint House-Senate Task Force on Ice and Drug Abatement" lays out highly specific plans for programs related to treatment, prevention, law enforcement, and partnering with insurance providers, local communities, and

businesses to achieve its main goal, highlighted in bold: "THE SOLU-
TION TO THE ICE EPIDEMIC IS TO PREVENT THE FUTURE
GENERATION FROM SUBSTANCE ABUSE AND CURE THE
PRESENT GENERATION OF ICE ABUSERS." The report is appended with pages of statistical evidence, community recommendations,
and summaries of testimonies ranging from such prominent experts as
Honolulu Prosecutor Peter Carlisle and U.S. Attorney Ed Kubo to the
head of the Department of Health's Alcohol and Drug Abuse Division,
with every relevant treatment center director, judge, law expert, and sociologist in between.

After a comprehensive summary, the report details the history of the
rise of ice in Hawai'i, pegging the start of the "ice epidemic" at 1997—the
year before Percy came home from Japan for good—and tracing the anti-
ice fight's birth to the "first ever" Hawai'i Regional Methamphetamine
Conference in 1999. A Big Island "summit" in 2002, a House Committee meeting in 2003 leading to ice-related laws passed by the legislature,
and Kahalu'u's 2003 town hall meetings fill out the timeline, which ends
on the hopeful note that Lieutenant Governor Duke Aiona "convened a
Hawai'i Drug Control Strategy Summit" which "resulted in an action
plan." The task force's findings, including the reams of statistical break-
downs regarding such things as ice use according to ethnicity, percentage
of treatment patients addicted to ice, and number of estimated users statewide (thirty thousand), are abstractions that quickly conjure the concrete
image of Percy. When the John A. Burns School of Medicine's Dr. Barry
S. Carlton concludes that there is "never normal experimentation with ice
because of brain change after a single use," in my mind I see the pipe being
passed to Percy in high school for the first time. When Carlton defines
effective treatment as requiring that the user's "peer group must change
in order to support a client's sobriety," I hear Percy telling me how sumo
was "detox" for him, or Tyler telling me he quit "cold turkey" for five years
up in Japan. When the report cites a 1998 survey concluding that "ice
was emerging as a dominant drug of choice, particularly by young male
adults, 18–34 years old," I hear Kurt warning, "Perce, you come home,
whatchu got here? Honestly?" I hear Kevin Chang talking of pit bulls and
tattoos. When I read that "the numbers of Hawaiians who are affected by
substance abuse is disproportionate to their population," I recall that every

addict or relative of an addict I wound up interviewing for this book is Hawaiian. And when I see, all over the place, evidence not only that treatment works but that *forced* treatment works, I wonder why we never did anything.

What also stands out is the high number of near admissions that Green Harvest was a mistake. While the report spends several pages making the case that marijuana use among Hawai'i's youth is still a problem that needs addressing, it does so only after making absolutely clear that ice, as Andy Anderson put it to me, is a "different animal." Immediately following the brief history of ice section is a section headed "ICE IS A PO-TENT, ADDICTIVE DRUG THAT HAS SERIOUS, HARMFUL EFFECTS ON THE USER," which asserts that "treatment providers, law enforcement, and government officials report that crystal methamphetamine causes behavior and addiction that are unique to the drug and unlike anything that society has experienced with other substance abuse addictions such as alcohol, cocaine, and marijuana." The *Journal of Addictive Diseases*, the *American Journal of Psychiatry*, and the National Institute of Drug Abuse are all cited in further detailed description of the effects of ice use. The report repeats several times that ice "can create addiction with just one use." Appended expert testimony summaries tend to disagree outright with any notion that Green Harvest could ever have been considered progress. Dr. Fred Hoschuh, a thirty-year Hilo ER veteran, "disagrees that marijuana is a gateway drug," and even Honolulu City Prosecutor Peter Carlisle recommends that "law enforcement focus should be shifted away from marijuana eradication to theft crimes and hard drug use."

Andy Anderson took Carlisle's sentiment a step further when he and I discussed Green Harvest's tremendous price tag, extending as it does to some unknown number in the hundreds of millions of dollars. "You know what my question would be?" he asked me. "Why the hell couldn't we put all of that money into treatment?" He then went on to answer this question himself: "But see, there's too much money invested in law enforcement, because how many jobs do we have in law enforcement especially for interdiction? Seventy to eighty percent of the federal budget on drugs and treatment is being spent by the federal government on interdiction." If all of that money funded treatment, Andy's logic goes, you could grow all of the marijuana plants you want, and roll crate-loads of ice off the container ships in Honolulu Harbor right there in plain sight, because no one would be interested in using any of it.

The task force's report essentially granted the wishes of Andy Anderson and treatment providers statewide by making its strongest funding recommendations for treatment programs rather than interdiction. Pie charts scream out the gap between how many addicts the state was treating and how many more were not just in need of treatment but actively seeking it and being turned away. Other sections clearly spell out what "treatment" entails, and what the recidivism rates are. The report cites U.S. Department of Health research that overwhelmingly proves that "treatment" and "incarceration" are not at all the same thing, stating that "treatment focuses on changing behavior, particularly the cognitive behavior approach. Incarceration does not change behavior, and illegal drug use and abuse in prison continues without treatment." The appended summary by University of Hawai'i law professor David Bettencourt flat-out says that "drug law enforcement does not work," citing a U.S. Department of Human Services survey. And the task force could have been speaking for Andy Anderson in citing the California Department of Alcohol and Drug Program's finding in 1994 that "for each dollar spent on treatment, the savings were $7.14 in future costs, primarily in costs avoided due to the reduction in crimes." In response to the report, the Hawai'i State Legislature acted immediately by coming up with a package of treatment programs worth over $14 million—an increase in the Department of Health's Alcohol and Drug Abuse Division budget of 1,300 percent.

Governor Linda Lingle, whose total 2004 budget proposal for substance abuse treatment, transition skills training, sex offender treatment, and job development amounted to a total of $430,000, greeted the final report's January unveiling with this: "We can't simply throw money at the problem and think it's going to be solved." For some reason she intentionally muddied the waters further by falsely comparing the package to the disastrous Felix Consent Decree of the early 1990s, where money was indeed thrown at a public education problem without the kinds of accountability measures the legislature had included in Act 40—the omnibus bill drawn up in response to the final report. And then the governor took a hard swing at the political softball the task force had thrown in allocating all but $75,000 of the multimillion-dollar package for treatment by saying, "It's simply not fair to expect law enforcement to be an important part of dealing with this issue, and not give them the tools that they need." It would not take much of a cynic to conclude that Lingle, who had delegated the ice problem to Lieutenant Governor James "Duke" Aiona, was deliberately trying to drag the issue out for as long as it took for the lieutenant governor's own task force to come up with a solution for which she could take credit. When Act 40 landed on her desk in April, the governor vetoed it. When the legislature overrode her veto in May, she let the bill become law without signing it, indicating that she was in no hurry whatsoever to release any of the money.

"They didn't invent it," task force chair Senator Colleen Hanabusa would say in a *Honolulu Star-Bulletin* look back at the political scuffle a few months later, "so they don't want to fund it."

❨ ❨ ❨

THOUGH THREE YEARS HAD PASSED since I'd handed over the two hundred dollars and watched Percy drive away, I could hear his voice every time I put a fresh bath towel on the seat of my maroon Corsica. The windows would no longer roll all the way up, and the driver's seat had become a sponge that never fully dried out. I'd hear him reminding me that *Dis one good car*, and it was—it still got Noriko and me wherever we needed to go. If I wound up in Kāne'ohe for some reason, the only familiar landmarks that ever jumped out at me would be the State Farm office, the police station, and the Napa store where we'd bought the battery. Back home, hard at work on finishing the book on Akebono, I'd often read over the transcript of our first interview. I guess on some level I thought about Percy every day. I'd start to wonder about him, but then I'd easily push away any kind of worry with images of his resourcefulness. If I hadn't heard anything, I figured, he must be doing all right. If George was visiting, or if I ran into Bumbo, the topic of Percy was sure to come up, but no one had heard from him. When I ran into Kurt one evening at Sherwood's, that was the first thing I asked him: How's Percy? Is he doing okay? Is he working? This was when I first found out that he'd moved back to Waikāne, and that was all Kurt could really tell me.

Now, in light of how things turned out, I picture Percy at that time spending his days up on Grandpa's Hill, or with Keali'i Meheula—the pig hunter he had become friends with after meeting him at the Waikāne Valley gate a couple of years earlier. I see them stalking the valley and gutting huge feral pigs in another version of the kind of pit-bull local boy compensation act Kevin Chang would later so eloquently describe to me. And I picture Percy heading up the Windward Coast in that gold Cutlass he'd been driving when I last saw him, still searching for that idyllic past. Maybe he was wondering what had happened to the place over his long six-and-a-half years in Japan, and probably he was in the kind of intense physical pain that Tyler still talks about, likely feeling even more like "one big nobody" than he had back when I'd first interviewed him not long after his return home. But still, Perce being Perce, he would be doing what he could to make the best of it.

On the way through the little town of Hau'ula he would pass the roadside stand where a man known as "Honeyboy" sat in the shade of a monkeypod tree selling flower leis and cookies to the tourists. Honeyboy looked like he'd stepped right out of an Elvis movie, the rotund happy Hawaiian who smiled like it really did make him happy to add that special touch to a tourist's visit. And it was worth the long drive just to see one of the few things that hadn't changed in Percy's time away. Just drive up the Windward Coast, and there he was, sitting in the shade next to the bus stop, the little wind swells of the bright blue ocean washing up on the sand behind him and receding across the sand with a hiss. If it were summer he would be surrounded by kids, as always, handing out homemade cookies like the town grandpa.

"And get kids who is adults now, like in their forties, yeah?" Honeyboy's brother recalls. "They remember Honeyboy from when they were small. And Honeyboy, jus' like any time he get seed, *lee hing mui*, mango seed. The same thing he used to do to that fadda—give 'em seeds when they was small—he doing that to *their* kids. Everybody all know Honeyboy from way back."

Percy would have learned that Honeyboy had worked for the Grayline tour bus company, and that he'd set up his lei stand because he missed the warm feeling of welcoming visitors to his island. "You know the tour bus drivers all knew him, yeah?" Honeyboy's brother said. "They not going stop for just anybody. They stop, talk story with him, and the bus driver tells everybody, 'Ho, he's selling leis.' Ho, they go off: 'How much you selling the leis for?' And him, he always laughing, ah? And two hours li'dat, the leis is *gone*. That's his side money, yeah? The leis he used to sell was from Mrs. Beppo—the lady who sews the leis. For instance, like ginga leis, or pakalana leis—I think the pakalana leis was like eleven dollas, yeah? And the ginga leis was like seven dollas or something like that, but half of that was his. You sell 'em eleven, you split 'um down the middle, you get yours and he get his."

Like Percy, Honeyboy knew everybody, and Honeyboy's brother is full of stories to prove it. "And him, he like da kine, yeah?" he said. "Pies. He no catch the city bus. He stands right where he sells leis. And he know the cars, too, yeah? And they *stop* for him you know: 'Where you going Honeyboy?' 'Oh, I going da kine—Ken's Bakery in Wahiawā, I going get pie.' 'Ho, I'll take you!' And they take him all the way to Wahiawā," a good forty minutes away from Hau'ula. "But he used to treat them, like, go eat, and they go cruising. And he comes home with his pies."

Needless to say, in June 2004 the whole Windward side was shocked at the news that Honeyboy's shirtless body had been found floating facedown in the shallow surf just behind his lei stand. They were shocked further when someone came up with the theory that it might have been done on purpose—somebody might have *killed Honeyboy*, of all people. A crowd of Hau'ula neighbors gathered at the small town's beach park, every one of them full of questions. What was Honeyboy doing in the water? He hasn't been in the water since we were kids—he doesn't swim! Why wasn't he wearing his shirt? Honeyboy *neva* took off his shirt! Where is the plastic case he kept around his neck? The one where he kept all of his money—Honeyboy *neva* took that thing off! What about that huge bump on his forehead? How did *that* happen? Dr. Shlachter was called from up the road in Kahuku to officially pronounce Honeyboy dead, and according to at least one concerned Hau'ula resident at the scene, and to Honeyboy's brother, the doctor had no doubt that foul play was involved. (Dr. Shlachter later denied to me that he said this.) The responding HPD officer, Sergeant John Lambert, hastily concluded that Honeyboy had simply fallen off of the three-foot high rock wall fronting the ocean, and, as the medical examiner would later conclude after an autopsy, drowned.

He reported Honeyboy's floating, shirtless body with the single bloody lump on the forehead as an "unattended death." There was no further investigation.

Percy was among those who knew that there should have been one. But unlike the concerned Hauʻula residents, he also knew exactly where to look.

☾   ☾   ☾

A MONTH AFTER HONEYBOY WAS FOUND floating in Hauʻula, Governor Linda Lingle still had not released $11 million of the $14.7 million dollars that the legislature had approved for Act 40 back in April. (The State Judiciary had the power to release the other three million, and they had done so right away.) In an interview for a Maui radio program at the time, Lingle had this to say: "Treatment doesn't work, and it's very expensive."

Treatment program directors from across the state—the same ones who had worked so hard to make their cases to the task force the previous summer—immediately began flooding the Department of Health's Alcohol and Drug Abuse Division with phone calls. They knew that when the governor makes such a pronouncement on such a complex issue, average citizens, busy with the details of their daily lives, would assume that she is informed. Andy Anderson, after pausing to make sure he was "pretty well simmered down," aimed higher than the DOH. He called the governor's policy advisor, Linda Smith, to ask for clarification on Lingle's comment.

"And so she started explaining, 'Well that's dadadadada, and the data says,'" Andy told me, "and that's when I stopped her. I said, 'Where are you getting the data from?' She didn't have an answer. I said, 'Have you looked at the data your own Department of Health is putting together for all the treatment agencies?'" He handed me a copy of appendix C from the Alcohol and Drug Abuse Division's report to the legislature—a document titled "Adolescent and Adult Substance Abuse Treatment Performance Outcomes" for fiscal year 2004. Appendix C lists percentage rates for such things as "no emergency room visits" and "no arrests since discharge" incurred by treatment patients in the six months following their releases, and it was readily available to the governor, who does not hold any advanced degrees in medicine or psychology and whose undergrad-ate degree is in journalism. "Let me explain how we gather the data," Andy told me. "Every single person we bring into treatment, whether they be adolescent or adult, we have to give the data for the treatment to the Department of Health. Not a problem. Because they're paying for it, which is right up front. And this is what we've been giving them for the ten years that I've been here, for all adolescents and every adult that we treat in our program."

"No arrests since discharge," I read, "79 percent. Not bad."

"Pretty damn good, I think," he said. "Read the rest of them. Read 'em."

"Employment/school/vocational training," I went on, "92.7 percent. Stable living arrangements, 91.6 percent," and on it went. "What they want to do is throw them in jail," I said.

"And keep them there for a year for $40,000." At the time of our conversation, the total cost for an inpatient at Hina Mauka was around $15,000. "And she has no idea of what people can accomplish if they get treatment and they get turned loose in the community ready to go back to work."

"And bring in four more people for treatment. You're not going to bring in four more people to jail."

"And you know the best thing they're going to do?" he asked me. "Two things: they're going to remain clean and sober and they're not going to get arrested, but the most important thing they do is they pay taxes, and that's a positive asset compared to being a liability before."

At the end of August, Bob Nakata held more town meetings at his church, calling the situation a "crisis." The *Advertiser*'s Karen Blakeman covered the first of these meetings, quoting Hina Mauka's Alan Johnson as saying, "There is no reason that money can't be released." Blakeman then called the governor's office for a response, only to find Lingle away on the mainland. Blakeman was instead connected to Chief of Media Relations Russell Pang, who told her, "The administration is in the process of evaluating the programs because we want to be sure they can produce measurable results."

In September Bob Nakata responded with a long letter to the *Advertiser* pointing out that these "programs" Pang was talking about were already evaluated annually for national accreditation purposes, that the money to fund the legislature's proposals was there all along—"The General Fund tax revenues for the calendar year 2004 through August have grown by 17.3 percent over revenues for the same period in 2003"—and that statistics from the City Medical Examiner's Office showed "an average of more than one ice-related death a week on Oʻahu alone"—a statistic that did not include Honeyboy, whose death had been classified by Sergeant John Lambert as "unattended." Andy Anderson was also quoted as saying at the time that Hina Mauka had space for eight to ten new patients, but no way to fund their treatment.

In October 2004, Lingle finally released the money.

"This is when [Alcohol and Drug Abuse Division chief] Elaine Wilson called me and said, 'You know that was a hell of a bold thing you did,'" Andy Anderson recalled, "'because that's what triggered the money.'" When I asked Andy how many people he'd had to turn away from Hina Mauka between April, when Act 40 was completed, and October, when the money was finally released, he thought back and said, "We probably turned away anywhere between seventy-five and a hundred. And there was no reason to delay that money. No reason at all. And there was also start-up money for new adolescent programs."

"And once adolescents pass through that window," I speculated, "the chance to save them is gone." I thought, I've looked into the vacant, glassy eyes of twenty-year users, their lives now come to nothing, who could have been saved had such a program been in place years ago. Who, really, were those "adolescents"—the bouncy skateboarding kid, the giggling and talented teenage girl—in fall 2004? Are they now smoking up in the valley, mom and dad raising their new baby? Are they doing time? Dead?

"And for her to come out and say treatment doesn't work and it's expensive," Andy went on, "that was an ultimate disservice to the community after what had just happened." He was talking about the twenty-one statewide town hall meetings where people had first become desperate enough to even find time in their lives to attend a meeting, and then put their shame past them to just about beg for some way to treat their sons and daughters, and maybe even themselves.

"You turned away at least seventy-five people in those four months," I said. "How did that feel? Turning someone away."

"It felt absolutely horrible," he said. "That was terrible."

"Someone who finally even *admitted* they had a problem."

"I *know*," he said. "I'm a recovering alcoholic, forty-six years, and I *know* that. And I've worked in this business forty years. It's terrible when you have to turn them away. People at the front desk would always call me out to explain it: 'You see, our lobby is full, and we're full.' And the major difference is we're able to treat people and get them clean and sober and send them out into the community. But that incredible pain that would come when I would have to talk to an angry mother or father, or a tearful mother or tearful father. . . ."

When this big Vietnam vet choked up, obviously *seeing* the memory of a real mother or father he hadn't been able to help, rather than just offering me some abstraction to make his point, I thought of the recovering addict I'd interviewed a week earlier who'd told me, "It started to, like, I couldn't make it through the day without it, and stuff like that, and I was saying, 'Oh my god, I'm getting more worse.' And I used to pray that some way, somehow, that I could just wake up and get myself out of it." She wound up, somehow, on the lucky side of the treatment statistics, having graduated from Hina Mauka a year after the money was finally released. Though in her late thirties now with no life to look back on, she's now so full of hope it makes you want to cry in thanks. What if the money hadn't been there to treat her once she finally became desperate enough to seek help? Would hers have been the kind of *someone please help me* face that Andy had had to look into and say, "I'm sorry"?

☾ ☾ ☾

HAWAI'I RESIDENTS ALSO TURNED ON their televisions that summer to see a hulking convicted felon with a long, flowing blond mullet and blond beard that together evoked an image of the Cowardly Lion on steroids. He dressed in black high-heeled boots, tight black pants, a black vest, and wrap-around mirrored shades, with a can of mace and a pair of handcuffs clipped to his belt. Together with his hefty bleached-blonde wife and two twenty-something sons who all could have come directly off the set of a Jerry Springer show—spouting out the worst kind of haole Pidgin, badly mispronouncing local names, and peppering his twangy midwestern speech with "da kine" and "HOWzit, brah?" and "'kay,'kay,'kay,"—he had come to Hawai'i to make his fortune, and there he was on the screen tracking down some wayward brown person with the hope of setting him on the straight and narrow.

Duane Chapman was his name. Or, as he preferred to be known, "Dog" the Bounty Hunter. Convicted in Texas on a murder charge, Chapman turned his "second chance" into a career of chasing bail jumpers. Under the guise of "helping the people" and "cleaning up the streets," he dreamed of fame and much bigger paychecks. He opened a chain of bail bond offices, including Da Kine Bail Bonds in downtown Honolulu, and began to cultivate a kind of super-hero catching-the-bad-guys image and even some notoriety long before first appearing on TV. His long-term plans began to fall into place when he flew down to Mexico in 2003 with his associates and, most importantly, a video camera, to "hunt" for the well-known heir of a huge cosmetics fortune who had been convicted of rape. The resulting footage started a bidding war between CBS and A&E for a series of Dog the Bounty Hunter shows set mostly in Hawai'i— Chapman's "decompression chamber." "Dog sat out at Makapu'u Point for days doing the investigation on his cellular phone," his wife is quoted as saying at the time of the negotiations. And then, to evoke the show's other major hook: "He pieced the entire investigation right where he feels closest to the Lord."

A&E won the bidding war at the start of 2004, with Chapman saying, "I am so very happy about this deal, and at the bottom of my heart, I promise I will make Hawai'i proud." The drill quickly became familiar to viewers: the Chapmans drive past some postcard tropical scenery and speculate to build dramatic tension for the impending chase, and they bicker with one another about some trivial family matter to create a sub-plot to the chase story. They enter a poor neighborhood and Dog knocks on a door, melting into a patronizing we're-here-to-help-your-daddy tone when he addresses the little kid who answers. Then the chase is on. To apprehend the fugitive, Chapman and the rest of his haole associates employ a technique they call "Hawaiian Style," which he defines as follows: "Just like sumo, we grab them quick and get them down." (Chapman fails to elaborate on how such a scrum has anything to do with either sumo or Hawaiian culture.) It ends with the crying bounty in the back of an SUV, the now-benevolent Dog giving the guy a cigarette and convincing him that everyone's on his side. "That's the ride to jail, their last ride, when I lecture them," Chapman explained to the *Honolulu Star-Bulletin*, going on to offer a sample lecture: "Even if you make a mistake you can change, but I tell ya brother, if you insist on making mistakes, we're goin' to get ya every time." The assumption is that Chapman is *helping* the bail jumper, and giving him a chance to learn his lesson in prison. If all goes well, Dog gets the jumper's grudging thanks. If it's an adult with a teenage son, the Dog promises to give the kid some "side work" pulling weeds in his Kahala yard while mommy or daddy is away in jail. And then we all hold hands and pray.

It took over a year for anyone to point out the flaws in the show, so intoxicated were we all on the fact that "Hawai'i is on TV! It's like a free ad for tourism! Great for the economy!" But University of Hawai'i sociologist Katherine Irwin and political scientist RaeDeen Keahiolalo Karasuda finally did so in an *Advertiser* op-ed piece, pointing out that "eight out of ten of Hawai'i's drug addicts do not receive drug treatment services while incarcerated," and also that "the majority return to society without rehabilitation, and two-thirds return to prison within a few years." They underscore the oft-cited statistic that Native Hawaiians fill over 40 percent of Hawai'i's prisons, and then make the natural connection between what Chapman does when he's "closest to the Lord" and Hawai'i's long and troubled missionary history, saying that "now, criminal justice agents and this reality TV show tell us that the key to public safety is to incarcerate Native Hawaiians—at a rate double that of any other ethnicity in the state."

The major irony of the law-and-order hook in Chapman's show is that most if not all of the "fugitives" that the Chapmans throw down "Hawaiian Style" were put out on the street by Chapman himself in the first place, who posted their bail through Da Kine Bail Bonds. A *Hawai'i Business* profile on Chapman later explained how bail-bonding businesses work: someone is arrested and charged and stuck in jail, not yet convicted and awaiting trial. A judge sets a bail price, which is usually far too high for the arrestee to afford. The arrestee's family scrapes together ten percent of the bail, which they pay to a bail bondsman such as Chapman. The arrestee is then freed into Chapman's custody, and Chapman must guarantee that he appears at his court date. The article then quotes Bill Kreins of the Professional Bail Agents of the United States as saying, "You don't write every bail that walks in your door. For the ones that you do write, you can minimize your losses with the collateral you're holding."

Da Kine Bail Bonds is all about losing money.

"I hate to say this, but I was a legend in my own mind," Chapman is quoted as saying in the *Hawai'i Business* profile. "I knew I could make it, but I also knew that I needed something else besides bounty hunting. Wesley is our bookkeeper, and he was like, 'Boss, we aren't making it!' I told him, 'Wesley, we can do it, if we can get a television show.' And of course, we did. On the other hand, there wouldn't be a television show if it wasn't for Da Kine Bail Bonds."

Chapman declined to reveal to the *Star-Bulletin* what he was paid for the show's first season, saying it was "not much," but he then went on to joke about how much money he now has to throw around to get information on the streets. "Money is the root of all snitches," he said. "Information that used to cost us $100 is now $1000."

When the people he is chasing are his own clients, though, I can't imagine Chapman having to dig too often into the snitch fund. If one were to follow Bill Kreins' advice about weeding out potential flight risks, one would come close to what he cites as the industry standard of only 10 percent of bonds failing to show up for their court dates. The failure rate for Da Kine clients, according to *Hawai'i Business*, is *three times* this industry standard. But as it turns out, that's all part of the business plan: look for potential flight risks, post their bail, and hope they run so you'll have material for the real cash cow—the television show. Chapman's wife doesn't even attempt to hide this feed-the-TV-beast formula, saying, "I always say I write bonds to support my husband's bounty hunting career. If they have a pulse, I'll write a bond."

❨   ❨   ❨

TWO YEARS AFTER KEITH RYDER HAD BEEN QUOTED in the paper as saying he wanted to let "all the dealers and the users know that we're going to start turning them in," the very face of Windward O'ahu's anti-ice campaign turned on the television to see his own sister's driveway roped off with yellow police-crime-scene tape, and a flood-lit reporter with the swirl of blue-and-red emergency vehicle lights lighting up the background telling him that a former sumo wrestler had been stabbed to death.

"That's the truth," Keith told me, shaking his head. "While we were dealing with this problem, I continued to confront my family, and that's the stuff nobody's hearing. I approached my brother. I approached my sister—I was confronting her daily: 'You guys not doing drugs?' 'No we're not.' And through the whole time nobody is telling me that my sister is a dealer. But I *know*. I hear it on the street, but when I confront them they always deny it to me. So I told them, 'If you get caught, that's your problem, and if I gotta turn you in, I will.' I had a meeting with Ed Kubo and the DEA [back in 2003], and I gave them a list of names of all the people who were dealing in our area. I was fed up. So the first thing happens is my brother gets caught," Keith went on. "The night he gets caught, I'm up here at Windward Community College because we were having a town meeting. Ed Kubo is on the panel, and also Peter Carlisle, and I'm present to speak out against the problem of ice in Kāneʻohe." At this point a cousin of Keith's walked in and informed him about his brother's arrest. "That night immediately after we're done with the meeting, I see Ed Kubo. I said 'Oh, I just wanted to let you know that I just got word that my brother just got caught by your people, and I don't expect you to do me any favors.' I just wanted to let him know because here I am supposed to be out in our community and now my family is getting caught, you know what I mean? And then not long after that incident, I gotta see on TV that my sister's house is being raided."

From the start of 2005, ice-related deaths took off on a pace that would shatter the previous year's three-year high of sixty-seven (which, again, did not include Honeyboy's "unattended" death), ultimately reaching a total of eighty-five. To close out 2004, helpless parents of addicts had seen HPD Officer Harold Cabhab Jr. arrested for trying to steal an incoming ice shipment with the intent to turn around and sell it. Grandparents raising the Missing Generation's children then watched Governor Linda Lingle breeze through her State of the State address without the word "ice" passing her lips once. Tireless activists may have thought that all of their sign-waving had been for nothing when they watched veteran HPD Officer Robert Sylva arrested for dealing. Cousins of dealers would later have to watch HPD Officer James Corn Jr. arrested for taking a thousand dollars to protect a deal that sent nearly a thousand doses worth of ice onto the streets. And addicts who were finally ready to step forward and admit that they had a problem—and Percy very likely may have been one of them—saw the impulse to turn things around evaporate when Lingle's proposed 2005 budget treated Act 40's $14.7 million, as Hawai'i Substance Abuse Coalition chair Claire Woods put it to the *Honolulu Star-Bulletin*, like "a one-time shot."

"Providers are very concerned," State Senator Rosalyn Baker, who chaired the Senate Health Committee, told the *Star-Bulletin*. "But they don't want to say anything publicly because the administration, rather than the Health Department, has been reviewing which programs get funding. They don't want to say anything publicly and get their programs blacklisted."

Lingle referred the controversy to the public relations expert Russell Pang, who told the *Star-Bulletin* that Act 40's $14.7 million was in fact "a one-time appropriation and allocation." Pang promised that "the Lieutenant Governor will discuss his proposals" the following day, including a "drug control and substance abuse initiative that we will submit to the legislature this session." Governor Lingle's refusals to sign Act 40 into law, and then to release the funding for it, seemed to mean that she had a task force of her own that was putting together a much better and more comprehensive solution package than the exhaustively researched 188-page document the legislature's joint task force had labored to produce. Her people must have been out trying to substantiate an argument for more spending on law enforcement, or compiling better peer-reviewed research on the value of prevention efforts. Maybe she had her own team of psychology Ph.D.s, medical professionals, and corrections experts putting together an argument for more prison space so that more frontline dealers could be swept off the streets.

But while the legislature's joint task force had been busy conducting site visits and community meetings and other research, Lingle handed the problem over to Lieutenant Governor James "Duke" Aiona in the way a president might hand over a highway beautification project to his First Lady. Aiona had addressed a Kahalu'u town hall meeting around the same time with this statement: "A winner makes commitments, a loser makes promises. This community is a winner because it has made a commitment to battling ice. *Imua* Kahalu'u." After his 2003 media-event ice "summit,"

Aiona and his Hawai'i Drug Control Action Working Group worked for sixteen months to address the ice crisis at the highest level of government, finally delivering their "Hawai'i Drug Control Plan: A New Beginning" in January 2005. And the seven-page document could not have looked any more like the result of a Flip-Chart Meeting—the kind where people "break into groups" and are handed different-colored magic markers and big flip-chart pages, and told to "throw out ideas" that all wind up condensed into one big flip-chart page as each group's "spokesperson" explains their list, and such things as citing relevant peer-reviewed scholarship, if indeed anyone had even bothered to do any research, are clearly not appropriate.

Aiona's groups would have used three colors of magic marker—one for each "prong" in the Three "Prong" Approach of "prevention," "treatment," and "law enforcement." They would have "thrown out" such abstractions as "moving forward," "coordinated effort," and "comprehensive approach." But the two words undoubtedly emerging from Aiona's own small group looked to have steered the meeting. They were not "crystal methamphetamine" or "ice crisis." They were "underage drinking." Someone then apparently strung all of the ideas together to form something like the following excerpt, found under the heading "Information Dissemination," which is typical of the plan's circular way of stating the obvious:

> "Currently, there is an absence of a comprehensive and integrated data infrastructure, data reporting methods, and data collection within State agencies. Logic dictates that a better informed community contributes to informed policy and informed resource allocation. Thus, it is necessary to create an appropriate data information system to disseminate findings and develop priorities for funding."

And as for concrete solutions to the crisis that had been festering for over twenty years, the plan offers such suggestions as a media campaign "featuring role models" like shark-attack survivor Bethany Hamilton, decathlete Bryan Clay, and American Idol finalist Jasmine Trias to "counter attack illicit drug use and underage drinking."

When the "Hawai'i Drug Control Plan" was finally delivered to the legislature, Judiciary Committee Chair Sylvia Luke did not need a flip chart to come up with such phrases as "mish-mash," "underwhelming," and "disappointing." Nowhere on page 1 do the words "ice" or "crystal methamphetamine" appear. Neither do they appear on any of the report's other six pages. But the phrase "underage drinking" appears thirteen times, following the dubious logic expressed on page 4 that alcohol is a "gateway drug"—an assertion that drug addiction experts have repeatedly proven false. Though the plan also mentions "illicit drugs," the overwhelming weight it places on "underage drinking" suggests that Hawai'i's number-two elected official—the same man who loudly tried to ban the sale of alcohol at Aloha Stadium—was using the ice crisis as an opportunity to push his own tenuously related political agenda of coordinating public policy with his religious beliefs on the evils of drinking. But most of all, the plan sent the clear message, to thousands of sign-waving citizens who were ready to be led, that leadership would not come.

"Compare it with what the legislature did," Andy Anderson told me, speaking of Aiona's plan. "One is an eighth-grade model, and the other is a long-overdue road map for how to get us out of what we just experienced, and treat people. All that summer [2003], the legislature went to every drug treatment agency in the state, met with all the communities in the state, and the families of people with addiction, as well as recovering people, as well as doctors, as well as the mayors. Everybody. There's no comparison. It's over a hundred pages, and it's well-documented research. On ice. Specifically on ice."

"When you had your first town hall meeting back in 2003," I said, "you just came right out and called it a meeting about 'ice.'"

"And there was a lot of opposition to that [in the preceding strategy meetings]," he said. "They wanted to water it down."

"Sonny from Kapolei did not go to an underage drinking meeting," I said.

"They knew we were going to talk about ice."

"That's *why* he went."

"That's right," he said. "And the neighbors who were suffering because they have an ice house next to them, and the ones that are suffering because their kid's in Hālawa for ten years for ice—those are the people that showed up."

"And then they wait sixteen months for this," I said, holding up Aiona's report.

"And it was pitiful. That's what I thought. Pitiful."

Bob Nakata had to pause for a long time to search for a diplomatic way to agree, so reluctant is he to criticize anyone. In his own reserved way he told me that Aiona "has sincerity, but he doesn't have the strength of personality to be very effective. It's a harsh judgment, but."

So two years after Hawai'i had finally shed its denial about ice, what little that had been accomplished had happened so slowly that the blazing fire of community activism had all but died by the time I ran into Percy at Bumbo's wedding that spring. I was sorry I'd lost touch with him, and I was happy just to see him—to let him know that he could forget about the damned two hundred bucks, and how was he doing, anyway?

"I stay up in Waikāne now," he told me. I'd had to park far away from Uncle Bradda's house, where the reception was being held, and Percy was squeezed in behind the wheel of a pickup truck and giving me a ride— he would double-park up by the house since he only planned to stay long enough to congratulate Bumbo. "I stay taking care my madda—she was sick for a while," he said. I thought about George, home for the wedding— and, as usual, looking like a man let out on furlough, knowing that he had no real choice but to return to Japan. Percy's mother would later tell me about how Percy had continued to answer want ads—another limousine company, an entry-level management job at the Duty Free Store in Waikīkī—and come home empty handed time and again. She'd follow these stories with anecdotes about Percy's wondrous ability to fix everything around the house—to "MaGaiva," as he would have put it— everything from the plumbing, to masonry, to carpentry. "He'd sit down and think, and he think, and he'd *do* it," she told me. "I stay taking care my madda" was Percy's way of telling me that some four years after I'd tried to help him, he had yet to find a job.

I told him how useful the car had been to us right up until we'd moved to Hilo. I told him that the book on Akebono was finally finished—how prominently he appeared in it and how I'd get him a copy as soon as it finally came out. He asked me about Noriko, and I explained that she couldn't come to the wedding because she'd passed her nurse licensing exam and just gotten a job at Hilo Medical Center. We laughed about how lost she'd been when he'd first run into us in the Waimānalo Shopping Center parking lot years ago.

We walked into the crowd that was growing under the huge tent in Uncle Bradda's yard, and shouts of the sumo greeting began to ring out: *Osssh!* Bumbo and George walked up with big hugs, and a circle formed, with old sumo war stories spilling out. I walked away to put my beers in the cooler, and even from across the crowded yard I could hear Percy shouting out a laugh. We all begged him to stay, but he said he had a family party to go to, and that he had to get the truck back to somebody. And that was it.

ONE NIGHT A BIT OVER A MONTH LATER, the Kipapas' phone kept ringing with calls from Desiree Kaeo—Keali'i Meheula's girlfriend. "She would call and say 'Where Percy?'" Mrs. Kipapa told me. "So I tell 'em, 'Don't call Percy. Call the cop,' 'cause Meheula was on a rampage. She called here a couple of times 'cause she wanted Percy for call Meheula." Court records explain that Desiree frantically began calling "people from the church" to help Meheula "because she knew he was 'smoking ice'" and had gone into a fit accusing her of "fooling around." Her phone calls caused him to change into "all-black shirt, pants, shoes, wearing a black beanie cap," load up two hunting rifles, turn off all the lights, and tell Desiree, "We see what happens to anyone come up here." Police arrested him later that night, April 30, 2005, at Whitney's Bar in Kāne'ohe. The following morning he was charged with terroristic threatening in the first degree, and his bail set at $11,000.

The next night Percy looked out on the road and saw Willidean's truck pulling up outside the gate. He walked out to her with a smile on his face, got in the truck beside her, and soon they were singing, harmonizing as they always did, the hours flying by. "Ho, what time now?" Willidean asked him as the sky began to lighten.

He looked down at the Fubu watch on his wrist and told her the time, and kept looking at the watch for a long moment after. His father had given him the watch, and the previous week he had been foolish enough to part with it for the first time ever, giving it to Willidean's friend Rosey for collateral because he was too ashamed to be owing her money. Willidean had talked Rosey into giving it back to him the same night. Now Percy looked up and said, "Ho, Dean, t'anks, ah? Nobody would do anything like that for me."

"Nah, Perce," she told him. "You my bradda, you know me. No worry."

He looked at her again and said, "You know, Dean, if I tell you something, you promise you not going say notting?"

Dean was put off by his uncharacteristically serious tone, thinking, as she told me later, *Oh, why, you not going t'row one pass on me! You my frickin' bradda, you my nephew-kine, yeah?* "Why, Perce?" she finally asked him. "Whatchoo getting at?"

"Nah, nah, nah, notting like that," he said.

"Ho, *brah!*" Willidean said with a laugh. "I ready for say, 'Brah, get the hell outta my truck!'"

"Nah, nah," Percy said, but he wasn't laughing. He looked away and then he told her, "You know what, I'm not afraid to die."

Not afraid to die?

"Whassamatta you, Perce," she said. "Why you talking stupid?"

He didn't respond.

"No make li'dat, Perce, *no make,*" she said, worried now.

He finally turned to her and said, "Whatever happens a week from now, tell my cousin-them that I love them."

"Whatchoo talking about?" she said.

"If Keali'i come out, I don't know what going happen." He explained to her some things that Keali'i Meheula had done, and gotten away with, and told him about, and that he'd been holding all of this inside him for almost a year now, and had never told anyone until this moment—not his mother, not his father, and not his Uncle Stanley, an HPD cop. "Promise you going take what I tell you to the grave," he told her.

"Perce, whateva you tell me not leaving this cah," she said.

He made her understand that Keali'i had threatened him since he'd been put in jail, and that he was certain that Keali'i would "do something" if his family managed to bail him out. Willidean had a hard time believing that Keali'i would hurt Percy, knowing them as close friends. But she also knew Keali'i as someone whose life was controlled by ice. Some ice users, she told me later, "get emotional, I mean real dramatized. Some is happy-go-lucky. Some like keep to themselves, they no like go out nowhere.

Some is like, as soon as they get, they like do something for get some more and some more. Keali'i, he would be spooky. I always felt uneasy around him. I neva trust him, period. When he smoke, he get paranoid"—a state of mind which, as Percy explained, was being compounded as Keali'i stewed behind bars knowing that Percy knew enough to get him locked up for a much longer time. "Percy was crying, too, when he told me," Willidean later recalled.

As Percy unloaded his secret on Willidean, the sound of someone's truck approached from down the road. It was Joshua Wilson, coming up from Waiāhole Beach Park. Josh had grown up in Ka'a'awa, and been a friend of Percy's since they were kids—first at church, and later when they wound up together at King Zoo. Lately they'd been seeing each other up in the valley, or at Josh's place across from KEY Project in Kahalu'u, almost every day.

"Eh, Percy, how come?" Josh said with a laugh. "Venda, she like kill you, ah?" Venda Meheula, Keali'i's mother, was a known ice dealer in her forties who had been convicted back in 1998. For years she had been what to many appeared as unnaturally inseparable from her son, and she was now, as Joshua was saying, in a rage of her own.

Percy looked at Josh for a long time, and then said, "Nah, Josh."

"That's what she told me: that you was trying for go there widdher." *Go there with her!* Perce was putting the moves on Keali'i's madda!

Percy thought for a moment and then said, "That's not the reason why."

"Whatchoo mean that's not the reason? That's what she told me: thatchoo was trying for go there widdher."

Percy turned to Willidean and said, "See Dean. That's not why. I told you."

She was silent, uneasy.

But not Josh: "How come? How come, Percy?"

"Nah, I no like say notting."

"Why? 'Cause you was trying for go *there*, ah?" Josh kept messing with his big friend.

"Nah, Josh."

"Why? How come?"

Finally Percy gave in and said, "You gotta promise you not going tell nobody." Nearly a year earlier, he went on, Venda and Keali'i had shown up at his house laughing about how they'd gone up to Hau'ula and waited, waited for Honeyboy to come out, and how easy it had been to get him over to the wall and roll him, to take the little plastic container he wore around his neck, and guess how much they found in it? So we rolled him, they told Percy, and threw him into the water and ran. Percy got angry as he told the story, telling Josh and Willidean how he'd come down on Keali'i, *How could you do that to Honeyboy, of all the people on this island, to Honeyboy.* Keali'i and his mother didn't stop laughing the whole thing off until later that afternoon, when they found out that Honeyboy didn't know how to swim, that he had drowned. And suddenly the story turned from something to brag about into a secret to be protected at all costs. For nearly a year Percy, as Troy might put it, *took it like a man*—he not going squeal. But this was *Honeyboy*, and the secret had been eating away at him daily. And now his friend was bouncing off the walls in jail with anger and paranoid fantasies, making the whole tragic situation even worse than it already was.

"He straight out said that when Keali'i come out," Josh would say later, "Keali'i going kill him."

PERCY'S MOTHER WAS SHOPPING in Kāne'ohe when the sweet sounds of someone strumming a ukulele came out over the store's sound system, matched by the sweet high voice of Kevin Chang singing, "*Oh, Pōmaika'i, Pua o Waikāne . . . Osssh! Ha'aheo!*" Kevin had written an ode to Percy celebrating his Waikāne roots and commemorating his odyssey in Japan, and here it was playing on the radio. Mrs. Kipapa could not wait to tell her son.

"I said, 'You know what, Percy, you know that song Kevin made? They played 'um on the radio.'" But his reaction surprised her: "He look at me, he wasn't impressed, like 'Oh yeah! They played the song?' He wasn't thrilled about it."

And what he said next surprised her even more. "You know Ma, I'm not afraid to die. Are you?"

"Yeah, I like live as long as I can," she told him. "I like life. I love people."

"I'm not afraid to die," he told her.

Her recollection reminded me of Kaleo's observation about how if something was bothering Percy, you could tell, but you could also tell that he would keep it to himself. I asked Mrs. Kipapa if she thought Percy was depressed. "He was always joking around with the kids," she said. "He's always happy-go-lucky, so it's hard to tell. When friends come around, he joke around with them. But when I think about it now, well, yeah. I went to Foodland and I heard 'um. I came home and I said, 'Percy, guess what. They playing the song he wrote for you.' He just put his head down. He neva say notting."

PERCY HAD FALLEN OUT OF TOUCH with Tyler just as he had with the rest of his sumo boys. Tyler had been busy working for Konishiki, setting up weddings and house parties for Japanese tour groups at the big man's beachfront estate out on the Wai'anae Coast, and then more recently drifting into oblivion on a massive drug binge triggered by the sudden passing of his uncle. Tyler had been ignoring his phone for weeks, cut off from everybody, when out of nowhere he picked it up to see Percy's name flashing on the caller ID screen.

"Everybody's calling me up, I don't answer the phone, I see 'Kipapa,' and I fuckin' *laugh*," Tyler told me. "He *knows* me, ah? This guy, we've been through the fuckin' dirt together. So I answer the phone: 'Hello?' And he goes, 'T-boy.' I go, 'Yeah.' 'I saw your cousin today.' I said, 'Who, Todd?' He goes, 'Yeah.' And he goes, 'By the way, what are you doing?' And then he laughs! I said, 'I'm not doing anything. Why, what are you doing?' He goes, 'Ah, I just wanted to tell you I love you.' I said, 'Oh yeah? Well you know what Perce, I love you too, brah.' He goes, 'No, really cuz. I love you brah.'"

CHAPTER 12

THE TRIAL

*He got up in the morning. He came inside here, and I could see he
was kind of hungry. I was doing some paperwork, sitting down and
watching the TV. So he sat down. I ask him, "Is there any special
program you like watch?" He said "Nah, nah, I just watch whateva
you watching." But I wasn't actually paying attention 'cause I was
doing some paperwork, so I told him, "You hungry, you go cook.
Don't expect me to cook for you, or you gotta wait till your madda
come home." He said, "Where she went?" "She went Kāne'ohe." So
he went back to his room, and then came back and sat in the same
chair. So I put my paperwork down. I figure to myself something's
wrong. So I ask him, "Percy. Is there anything troubling you?" He
look at me and he tell me, "What?" "Is there anything bothering
you?" He tell me, "Why?" You know the first time was all right, but
this is the second time. I neva wait for the third time, so I ask him
if something's wrong. He tell me, "No, no, no." He stood up and he
went. Until that evening, he went. The reason I was telling you the
word "regret" was 'cause I gave him the opportunity to correspond
with me. The thing is, I don't know, to me something was troubling
him. But I didn't expect anything bad about it.*

—George Kipapa, June 7, 2007

B<small>Y THE THIRD AFTERNOON</small> of Percy's murder trial, seating in Judge
Karl K. Sakamoto's tiny courtroom was getting harder to come by. And
though both families were starting to line up outside the locked door a
good fifteen minutes before each recess was set to end, the potentially
volatile scene remained surprisingly calm throughout the trial, with Kurt's

193

big tattooed sons, for instance, even going out of their way to make space for the defendant's family. A low roar of separate conversations filled the air, but, as if out of some unspoken respect for the fact that it might lead to conflict, none of it touched upon the events of the case. And then right after lunch that day, Wednesday, the ebb and flow in the cramped hallway brought Tyler Hopkins within inches of Keali'i Meheula. The defendant was dressed in a new blue suit and a blue tie, his hair cut neatly and jelled, his round face shaved clean, and his thick neck exposed above the collar of a white oxford shirt. For a long moment Tyler appeared to forget where he was, finding himself looking straight down on the man who had killed Percy. He seemed to have tuned out the noise around him as he stared into that exposed neck, right there in front of his eyes.

"T!" I called to him from across the noisy hallway.

Against Deputy Prosecutor Glenn Kim's strenuous pleas, Judge Marcia Waldorff had granted Meheula bail nine months earlier, after giving him "instructions" to "stay away" from Percy's family and potential witnesses. Kim had quickly moved to have bail revoked, arguing that Meheula "was already out on bail when he killed Mr. Kipapa." Kim went on to argue that the rest of the family and other potential witnesses were scared. Meheula's state-appointed attorney, William C. Domingo, came back with what turned out to be the winning argument: "He's already been out on bail for a week, and he hasn't hurt anyone yet." Duane "Dog" Chapman had been happy to post the $150,000.

"How's *that?*" Keith Ryder told me. "My sister was scared." One could easily imagine Meheula going after Keith's sister Lori—a witness in the case—or Willidean Makepa, or Josh Wilson, and then jumping bail. I'd spent the last several months dreading the thought of seeing Meheula's face on TV as he gets the "lecture" in the back of Chapman's SUV: "Even if you make a mistake you can change, but I tell ya brother, if you insist on making mistakes, we're goin' to get ya every time." I could imagine Chapman's wife waddling into Mrs. Kipapa's yard with a TV crew in tow, dressed like an American flag, designer sunglasses perched on her forehead, and twanging out in haole-Pidgin: "Eh, Aunty! HOWzit!"

"And you know, this is Hawai'i," Mrs. Kipapa told me, "and a lot of people know Hawaiian people, and the wife makes *ass* out of them: 'You druggie!' You know, she *yelling* at 'em, and condemning them, all that kine—it's really bad. I'm going tell him, 'Thank you for letting all those crooks out so you can be on TV and catching them again.' They always end up praying, but bad heart." Her husband added, "Lot of things in life you say there's two sides: right, and wrong. When you come down to it, the Dog, he's gotta make a choice, and his choice that he made, was he look at himself in the mirror, and he only seen himself: how he going make the next million. He neva worry about the other person."

"I was scared and mad at the same time," Mrs. Kipapa said upon hearing of Meheula's release, "'cause you don't know if he's coming up here nighttime. He had thirty-one prior arrests. *Thirty-one prior arrests*. It really was stress. My daughter used to come home crying. She said, 'Guess who I just saw?' She said, 'I wanted to bang him like that, but I had the kids.' I said, 'No, let the law, and the Lord take care.' I tell you, it took a good ten, fifteen years off my life knowing he was out. But what could we do?" Mrs. Kipapa stewed in anger, knowing that as her son's ashes washed farther into the soil deep in the back of Waikāne Valley, the man who killed him was allowed to walk in the jungle and hunt pigs, star in a wedding attended by all of his loved ones, and kiss his new wife both good night and good morning. "And you know what I was really mad about?" she asked. "Come Thanksgiving, come Christmas, that kine, he was *enjoying*. That really, really made me mad."

On Monday, the trial's opening day, Percy's mother and I had been sitting on the hard wooden benches that line the hallway when a muscled, young Portagee-looking man walked by wearing the kind of blue suit that defense attorneys like to dress their clients in. Only after he'd taken a seat at the far end of our bench did she turn to me and say, "Hey, that guy looks just like Meheula!" Of course it was Meheula. The disheveled, spaced-out, greasy-haired, pot-bellied chronic we'd all seen a year earlier in the newspaper had spent a good deal of his freedom preparing for his trial, because frankly he looked great. He'd clearly been working out regularly. He had gone through the treatment program at Sand Island. And as we would learn on the trial's second day when he carried a leather-bound Bible with bright-gold trim, he'd found the Lord. Based on what he'd done to reconstruct his identity, any jury could be forgiven for thinking he'd "turned himself around" and "gotten the help that he needed," and thus convict him for the lesser charge of manslaughter if not acquit him altogether.

What Duane "Dog" Chapman had done by bailing Meheula out had not yet led to any further "mistakes," but it had led, with Meheula's determination and hard work, to the real possibility that he would get away with deliberately plunging a knife into Percy's heart.

It had taken Glenn Kim to talk me out of the heroic must've-been-five-guys version of Percy's death that the sumo brothers and I had all constructed after the funeral. A couple of weeks before the trial I'd phoned the prosecutor's office to find out exactly when the trial was starting, expecting to have to punch my way through a phone computer menu and then get the date from some secretary. Instead, someone answered the phone and put me on hold, and suddenly I was talking to Kim himself. I felt a bit embarrassed to disturb him just for the date of the trial, but he put me right at ease even before I identified myself and explained that I taught at the University of Hawai'i at Hilo and wanted to fly over.

"I used to teach American literature," he said, telling me about his Ph.D., which turned out to be from Harvard. "And then I went into law."

"That's quite a jump," I said.

"Not really—what we're dealing with here is language." He went on to calmly tell me that they'd selected the jury and that they would start either on Monday or Wednesday two weeks later, explaining that each judge has a day when they do some kind of administrative work and do not hear trials, and that the judge in this case had his "off" day on Tuesdays. I had never met Kim before, but his pace of speaking and his tone were such that it seemed he'd been expecting my call, and that he had nothing better to do than talk to me.

"I hate to take up any of your time at all, Mr. Kim," I told him, "but do you know anything about sumo?"

He said he didn't know all that much beyond what a casual fan who's seen a few matches on TV might know, so I gave him the one-minute version of what we'd all concluded as we stood in front of that driveway following the funeral: mainly, that one guy couldn't have killed Percy all by himself.

Before he started talking I could just about hear him nodding over the phone, and I realized someone else had already volunteered this version of events—and probably a hundred others. "He had Percy in a very vulnerable position," he told me, "physically, emotionally, and every other kind of way.

And he's not a little guy—he does weigh over two hundred pounds. He's also an experienced pig hunter."

"He knows how to handle a knife," I said.

"The attack was vicious, and lightning quick," Kim told me.

"I guess you can imagine us all standing around and driving each other crazy with speculation," I told him, and he understood. He invited me to call back next week when he would have a better idea as to when the trial would begin.

"Please come up and introduce yourself at one of the breaks," he told me.

"I will, absolutely, Dr. Kim."

He laughed. "Call me Glenn."

Outside the courtroom I was telling Mrs. Kipapa, "This guy specializes in ice cases. He's good." Among other cases, Kim had gained some notoriety by convicting a pregnant woman for manslaughter because she had tested positive upon giving birth to a dead baby.

"You know he told me, 'It's all right if you cry, Priscilla,'" she said. Kim would call upon Mrs. Kipapa as his first witness, to establish Percy's character.

Kim's opponent, William C. Domingo, walked past us into the courtroom—a stocky, balding, and even under these circumstances, *jovial* Filipino guy, a good bit under six-feet tall, wearing small, round gold-rimmed glasses and an unbuttoned sport coat. I would later meet him in the elevator and find him, as Kim's assistant described him, a nice guy. Although an awkward silence followed when I told him that I was a friend of Percy's, with an understanding smile he admitted that the whole thing was sad. Although he had the advantage of defending the only witness to the stabbing—that is, without Percy around his client could make up his entire testimony—Domingo began working for every possible advantage before the trial even began. Indeed, he became concerned when he saw the hallway packed with more than twenty Kipapas, each wearing a black T-shirt emblazoned with the words "In Loving Memory" and photo of a smiling Percy visible from across the room, and in Kurt's case, with the words "Let God Be the Judge" stretching like a billboard across his big back. "He's in there talking about a mistrial," Kim's assistant told Jolyn. Domingo's argument was that the T-shirts may already have swayed the jury unfairly, since some members walking around outside might have seen the display. After Jolyn calmed her passionate sons, the Kipapas all agreed to turn their shirts inside out, and we walked in.

The courtrooms in the Honolulu Civic Court building are small and square—not much bigger than a high school classroom—and paneled in a dark-toned synthetic wood. The judge's bench rises up in the far corner, flanked by the clerk's stand and the witness stand, which faces the audience head on. On the right, the jury box takes up a good part of the room, leaving a living-room-sized area for the defense and prosecution tables, the stenographer's desk, and a very small area in between. Add to this clutter four rows of hard synthetic wood benches looking on from behind a waist-high wall, a TV camera between that wall and the jury box, and a collection of spectators and journalists, and the room becomes cramped. Fill three and a half of those rows of benches with big Kipapa bodies, all wearing inside-out black T-shirts, and the heat and tension become silent players in what is about to unfold. Domingo must have known this when he brought up the T-shirts. What he did was turn a loving and grieving local family into what looked like some kind of menacing, tattooed, black-shirted gang—an image he would later try to put to work.

WHEN GLENN KIM FACED THE JURY to begin his opening statement, I could see what he'd meant about the overlap between his old profession and his new one—he had what educators call a "teacherly presence." He was built like a distance runner, standing just over six-feet tall, with the long slimness of his body accentuated by the buttoned gray sport coat hanging tightly just below his waist. His black hair looked salon-cut, and his glasses were wide, taking up much of the middle of his slender face. One is compelled to pay attention to him because he clearly pays attention to himself and to what's happening around him in equal proportion. And as a former college instructor, Kim knew that paying attention in a warm and crowded room in two-hour stretches for several consecutive days would not be easy for anyone.

His statement recapped Percy's entire life, speculated on the events of May 16, summarized his strategy, and anticipated the defense's strategy—a bogus self-defense claim centered on a stab wound to Meheula's leg—all inside of twenty minutes. Kim's mastery of tone, the smooth and deliberate movements of his long arms, and the way he handled the pace of his delivery turned it all into an enthralling story for what appeared to be a quintessentially *local* jury—a term that means much more than that they lived in Hawai'i. Cultural theorists use *local* to describe the typical pastiche of multiple cultures and ethnicities I saw seated in the jury box, and the common values that unite them. Kim appealed directly to at least four of these values. Percy "lived with his mother and father, his sister and her children, up in Waikāne"; he was a "big guy" who won a scholarship to St. Louis; after the great Jesse Kuhaulua "saw potential in him" and recruited him for sumo, Percy "worked very, very hard" and he made it to the rigidly traditional sport's paid ranks; and Percy was given the sumo name "Daiki"—Big Happiness—because he was full of aloha. In other words, Uncle Percy—living with Mom and Dad just like so many people we know because skyrocketing real estate costs have made multigenerational homes the norm here in Hawai'i—was not big for nothing; he was a hard worker, big for a *reason*. He was like *us guys*. Some other lawyer could have come off as manipulative, if not racist, in the big-lazy-Hawaiian-exceeds-all-expectations sense, perhaps buddying up to the jury or throwing in some Pidgin. Kim did none of this. Using tone and gesture and pace, he conveyed an us-guys sense of common understanding totally appropriate for addressing a local jury, as though he were immediately giving them credit for being aware of what it might mean to grow up in Waikāne, or what a big deal it would have been to be admitted to a prestigious school like St. Louis. In so doing, he was hitting on the most important local value: respect.

Kim then described Percy's two-year relationship with Meheula, from the day Percy provided Meheula with a key to the gate to the trail up Waikāne Valley and straight through to the truck on the night of the murder. "While he sat in the driver's seat," Kim began, his voice now slow and deliberate, Percy was "stabbed twice in the abdomen. He received a cut wound to his right thigh. He sustained cut wounds to both hands." Kim paused. "And his chest [was stabbed to the depth] of at least five inches." He paused again. "Percy was in fact *driving*." Kim's voice was rising now. "The attack was quick, and vicious." He turned away from the jury. "And the person who stabbed him was the defendant." He pointed directly at Meheula, pulling off a gesture that would have seemed melodramatic if not for his professorial tone. After explaining his plan of action, Kim began to acknowledge the fact that the scholarship-winning, hard-working, aloha-filled Uncle Percy was not without his flaws, when he told the jury in a let's-level-with-each-other way, his palms open, that "ice was involved."

Whether he'd planned to do so from the start, or whether he figured he had to make some adjustments upon hearing Kim's strategy, Domingo reserved his opening statement.

MRS. KIPAPA DWARFED THE BAILIFF, a short local Japanese woman in her twenties, as they made their way to the witness stand. Percy's mother was wearing a bright flower-print *muʻumuʻu* top, her short gray hair tied up in the back, glasses on her round, expressive face, which was now, as she stood with her right hand raised to be sworn in, full of sadness. After having her state her name, Kim walked Mrs. Kipapa through a series of difficult questions almost apologetically and full of kindness. He asked her her name, where she lived, and how long she'd lived in Waikāne.

"From the *mahele*," Mrs. Kipapa said. She was leaning forward, focused on Kim, who was standing at a podium in front of his table facing the witness stand.

"The *mahele*. You mean, for generations?"

"Yes."

"Do you have a husband?"

"Yes."

"What is his name?"

"His name is George Kipapa."

"Do you have any children?"

"Yes."

"How many children?"

"Two, now. I used to have three."

"What are their names, the two you have left?"

"Kurt, and Selisa," and then Mrs. Kipapa started to break up. "And Percy," she managed through tears. "He was my baby."

Kim let her gather herself, and then asked, "When did he die?"

"Last year. May 16th."

Kim delicately steered her out of this emotional territory, beginning a series of questions to elicit the biography of Percy he'd given in his opening statement, taking the audience through the scholarship at St. Louis. "He didn't stay at St. Louis?" Kim asked.

"From public school to private school, it was hard for him to keep up with his homework and play football." The tears had stopped, but the big woman's voice continued to waver. Kim then led her through sumo, how Percy was reluctant to leave home, how he won two tournaments and made it to *jūryō*, what his sumo name meant, and why he had been given it: "Because he was always smiling."

He asked if she knew Keali'i Meheula, and asked her to identify him. She pointed, "He's right over there. Wearing a suit." Her voice had stopped wavering.

"Could you tell us what happened on the night of May 16th?"

"It was nighttime. Somebody picked him up. And I never saw him again."

Of course, any mother testifying to the character of her dead son is going to speak highly of him, and she is going to cry on the witness stand. The main reason Kim must have picked Mrs. Kipapa as his character witness was that she could not have more clearly fulfilled the jury's image of "Aunty," of the big Hawaiian maternal figure, of Percy's madda. Slipping "How many children do you have?" into his list of initial identification questions certainly helped, but Kim's purpose was achieved just by having Mrs. Kipapa on the stand at all. This is where Percy came from, all the way back to the *mahele*.

Domingo declined to cross-examine.

Kim then called Lori Rodrigues—known around Kahalu'u by her maiden name, Lori Ryder—of whom I knew at the time only as one of three people arrested at the 'Okana Road house, which the newspaper painted as a working meth lab. In my imagination I'd had her lumped in with whomever else might have been involved in the Percy-was-mobbed scenario we'd all come up with after the funeral. Now in her mid-forties, she spoke in a soft, raspy voice, and slowly. Kim, who was calm and polite throughout ("May I call you Lori?"), established how long she'd lived in the house (nine years) and with whom (her boyfriend and three children—ages twelve, seven, and five), how long she'd known Venda Meheula, the defendant's mother (about five years), how long she'd known Percy and the defendant (about a year and a half before the murder), and whether or not she was home at the time of the murder (she was), and whether another witness named Donna Freitas was also there (she was). Lori testified that Venda Meheula came to her house between 6:00 and 6:30 on the night of May 16 and stayed for around three hours. Keali'i Meheula appeared twice, first kicking the door open shortly after Venda had arrived and then leaving without a word, and then returning about an hour later, holding a knife and covered in blood, saying that he had just stabbed Percy. When Lori asked him why, she said he told her, "He's always stealing my stuff" and "He's fooling around with my girlfriend." She directed him to the bathroom to take a shower, and at Venda's suggestion she called an ambulance. Venda left, and then Donna left to check on Percy. Venda later returned, and then left with Keali'i, who had not taken a shower and was still holding the knife. Donna returned much later that night in fear. "She came in the house, locked the door, locked all the windows. She was shaking." The following day Lori called detectives to give them a bloody towel she'd found in her bathroom.

At the point when Lori spoke of Meheula returning to her house the second time, Kim asked, "Did you see any injuries? Was he limping?" She answered "No" to both questions. When she got to the part where Meheula appeared at her door with a knife in his hand, Kim had her estimate the size of the knife by holding her hands a good twelve inches apart in front of her—a dramatic gesture that would resonate for the rest of the trial.

The word "ice" was never spoken the whole time Lori Rodrigues was on the stand, despite the fact that she'd been arrested. Her face gave her away as a user, but her tone and her demeanor made one empathize with her, like she was one of those addicts who gets sucked up by the drug, and everyone hopes she can turn herself around. Her voice came out in soft, measured tones that suggested she was not out to take sides or put away some drug-dealing criminal, but rather a woman who was trying to do the right thing, and who was even courageous for doing it.

Given the circumstances of the case, it must have frustrated Domingo that in his cross-examination he, too, could not utter or elicit the word "ice." What he appeared to be doing was asking many of the same questions Kim had asked in an effort to get an inconsistent answer, at one point even referring to her as "Donna." When this didn't work, he turned to her account of Meheula's second appearance at her house that night, asking, "Did he also mention something about his nieces?" to which she replied, "He mumbled something." He established that Meheula was in the house for about twenty minutes, and then said, "He didn't threaten anyone?" He didn't.

Cross-examination is, by nature, threatening if not predatory. It did not work in Domingo's favor that, having reserved his opening statement, this exchange was basically his introduction to the jury, who by now knew Deputy Prosecutor Kim rather well. Whatever empathy Lori had been able to build was only bolstered by what clearly looked like Domingo's attempts to catch her in a lie—which, to be fair, must be a common tactic in cross-examinations. But this was William C. Domingo's chance to create a first impression. Respect? Other than the cops and medical experts that Kim would call on to go through the forensic evidence, here was one of only six witnesses that would be called in the entire case—including Meheula himself—and Domingo got her name wrong.

AFTER A SHORT RECESS Kim called Donna Freitas, a stocky forty-three-year-old woman in baggy Levi's and a yellow polo shirt whose hair was cut like a boy's. She took the stand, and when Kim asked her to state her name she paused for a long time, clearly frightened just to be speaking before a roomful of people, let alone testify with the accused staring her down from across the room. For a second the long pause made you wonder if she had something to hide. And then Kim said, "You have a speech impediment, don't you Ms. Freitas." He said it as an understanding parent might, as if he were acknowledging that she needed her glasses to drive.

"Yes."

"Could you describe your speech impediment for the jury?"

"I stutter," she managed.

"And it causes you to pause, as well as stutter."

"Yes."

Without a hint of pity or condescension, Kim then assured her that everything would be fine. He invited her to take as much time as she needed to answer his questions, and to let him know at any point if she was having trouble. And with that little exchange, Donna Freitas went from a suspicious character who potentially knew more than she would say, to a hero simply for speaking in front of a crowded courtroom, television cameras and all.

Kim established that Freitas had known Percy for "about a year, year-and-a-half" before the stabbing, that she'd met Venda Meheula at about the same time, and that she'd first met the defendant about six months before the stabbing. When Kim had Freitas go through the events of May 16, the point of the "witness exclusion rule" became clear. No one on the witness list other than Meheula himself was allowed in the courtroom—including even character witnesses such as Percy's mother. So the fact that the testimonies of Lori Rodrigues and Donna Freitas essentially matched carried far more weight than it otherwise would have. According to Freitas, Meheula's first appearance at the house that night "was just in and out," and he was acting "weird." An hour or so later he returned. "He said that he stabbed Percy." Meheula had no wounds on his legs. The knife, she said as she held her hands out in front of her, was "about twelve or so inches." Most important, when Freitas asked him why he'd stabbed Percy, he told her, "He was stealing my stuff," and that "He was fooling around with my girlfriend."

From here Freitas said she left the house to check on Percy, taking her car because the driveway is so long. "About three-quarters of the way down I seen the mom walking back up. She asked me where's her son at? I said I didn't know. I seen his truck. It was parked middle-of-the-road-like. It was facing up." No longer so nervous, her words were now full of grief. "I didn't see him inside, so I went straight up the road." Not finding anything there, she returned and parked. "I walked up to the truck. I seen him."

"Who did you see?"

"My friend Percy. He was on the driver's side." From here, Donna Freitas would refer to Percy as "my friend Percy" as though it were his proper name, her speech impediment causing the three words to come out as one—adding even more poignancy to what she was saying.

"Did you hear any sounds?"

"Yes, I heard sounds."

"What did it sound like?"

"Like a gurgling sound."

"Did you believe he was still alive?"

"Yes," she said emphatically.

She then said she returned to her car and tried to call 911 but failed, finding her cell phone battery dead. And as she sat in her car trying to call, "out of nowhere" Meheula and his mother appeared, "an' he tried to get in my car on the passenger side."

"Was the door open?"

"It was locked."

"Could he get in?"

"No. He wen' hit my window."

"Did he break your window?"

"No. His mom Venda came around the driver's side" and opened the door. "He just came climbing inside right over me," and ended up sitting in the passenger's seat, still carrying the knife, which was now wrapped in a shirt and pointed at her.

"Did you want him in your car?"

"*No*," she said.

So with a long bloody hunting knife pointed at her, Donna Freitas was forced to drive to Kāne'ohe, where Meheula's sister lived. "He was saying things like, if it was the right thing he had done . . . He seen his nieces crying . . . He said he wen' go hurt his nieces . . . He was saying t'ings like, oh, his family is gonna find out—myfriendPercy's family. He said we going die." When she said this I looked around at each of the three rows of wooden benches on either side of the aisle entering the courtroom. Other than the four journalists and the three younger women and the tattooed kid with the earring occupying the bench directly behind Meheula, the benches were stuffed with huge, black-shirted Kipapas—all with sullen looks on their faces. Had Percy been there himself he might have looked as frightening to someone who didn't know him. "He neva even *blink* the whole time," Freitas was saying. "I really, really, *really* thought I was going be next." Kim then established that where she dropped Meheula off in Kāne'ohe was nowhere near the fire station. He further established that Meheula was not injured, and was not limping. Then, Freitas said, "I drove straight to Lori's house, locked all the windows, locked all the doors. I was really scared."

Kim turned to two pieces of forensic evidence. He first asked her to confirm that a seat cover in a photo he showed her was in fact the one taken as evidence from the passenger seat of her car. The second appeared to be a photo of Percy behind the wheel of the truck after he'd been stabbed. Kim showed both photos only to Freitas.

"Tell us what you see in this photo."

"Myfriend Percy," she said, and she started crying.

Kim then spent some time with Freitas discussing a sketch she had made of the knife for the police, which had been submitted as evidence. So after some thirty minutes of questioning she had admirably recovered, having come off strongly as just a regular working-class person trying to do the right thing. Even as Percy's friend, she didn't come off as being on anyone's "side," partly since, after all, Meheula claimed to be his friend as well. I could imagine someone with her insecurities having a need to feel included, just as I could imagine Percy taking particular care to make her feel comfortable.

Domingo began his cross-examination gently enough, asking Donna Freitas how long she'd known Venda Meheula, and whether or not she knew if Percy, and then Meheula, had a job. (She didn't know.) He then worked to soften the idea of Meheula as a threatening presence that night by asking, "Was he yelling?" She told him no, that "he was out of breath," and that his eyes were "really wide open, bulging-kine." And then Domingo's larger objective became clear: the "stealing my stuff" and the "fooling around with my girlfriend" statements were going to hurt a possible self-defense claim by providing Meheula with a motive, so he called Freitas on the fact that both in her statement to Detective Coons on May 17 and at the May 23 preliminary hearing, she failed to mention either of these things that Meheula had apparently told her. When she said she could not recall being asked what Meheula had told her on either occasion, Domingo submitted the transcripts of her statements as evidence, inviting her to read them.

Judge Sakamoto took this as a convenient time to call a recess, instructing Freitas to read through the documents during lunch. Out in the hallway I said goodbye to Mrs. Kipapa, who by now was exhausted—sitting outside the courtroom and wondering must have taken even more of a toll than actually watching and listening. Jolyn asked me what my T-shirt size was, and then she and her daughters-in-law rounded up most of the kids who had been waiting out in the hallway with their grandma, leaving me with Kurt, his sons, and his cousin to speculate together on how things would turn out. "It's hard for me," Kurt said at one point. "That's my brother they're talking about up there." One of his little adopted kids came running up with a white plastic bag filled with cool tall cans of iced tea and happily handed them out to everyone, apparently having been sent up by Jolyn, and then ran back down the hallway. Caught up as I was in my analysis of what was going on—of what appeals each lawyer was using; of the makeup of the jury; of the lines of questioning, and so on—I'd been able to distance myself somehow from the fact that when they said "Percy" and "Percy's blood," they were talking about the same man who'd been the life of the party at my wedding. Not so, Kurt. "And he's just sitting right there," the big man said of Meheula.

Outside it was typically beautiful, with a nice breeze countering the bright sun. Across the street from the courthouse the downtown Honolulu crowd of professionals filled the bustling buildings of Restaurant Row from the upscale Sunset Grill down to the Asian plate-lunch place where I found a plate of noodles for four dollars. Among the mostly haole and Japanese corporate lawyers and real estate agents in their suits and skirts and designer aloha wear, I saw Donna Freitas sitting on the edge of a planter staring intently into the stack of white papers Domingo had handed her—an image that would come back to me when Bob Nakata praised Chris McKinney's novel *The Tattoo* for capturing the Windward side's "sense of extreme isolation." Right in the middle of what Bob Nakata called "foreign territory," Donna's eyes narrowed in concentration. There across the street in the Circuit Court building's courtyard a group of black-shirted Kipapas sat with white styrofoam boxes in front of them. A few of the jury members were sharing lunch in the opposite corner. Further beyond, the kid with the tattoos and earrings and what looked like Meheula's sister, mother, and father were all sitting and waiting. Everyone looked as out of place as Percy probably used to feel when he got off the bus at St. Louis. The trial should have been held in Kahaluʻu. But then, as Keith Ryder's stories of the strong family ties between cops and drug dealers would later scream out, it would have been impossible to find an impartial jury.

Donna Freitas took the stand again after lunch, and sure enough she had made no mention of Meheula telling her that Percy had been stealing his stuff or fooling around with his girlfriend, either in her statement to

Detective Coons on May 17 or in her statement at the preliminary hearing on May 23. She seemed to be trying to say something about not having been asked about those statements on either occasion, but Domingo steered her to statements she'd made about what Meheula had told her about his nieces. "He said that he," meaning Percy, "had hurt his nieces."

Kim followed up with this: "Were you ever directly asked why the defendant killed Percy Kipapa?"

"No."

"No further questions, your honor."

Kim spent the rest of the afternoon calling on police officers, detectives, and HPD evidence specialists to interpret such forensic evidence as clothes recovered from inside the truck, a knife sheath, a pair of machetes, and the truck itself. His performance came off as professional and extremely meticulous, taking on the form of a routine that began with Sergeant Duke Zoller, the first officer to arrive on the scene. Kim first made it a point to establish the fact that Zoller was a sixteen-year HPD veteran, and then asked the sergeant to go through his actions on the night of the stabbing. Zoller then proceeded to deliver his testimony in perfect copspeak ("Upon arrival I observed the truck . . ."), coming off immediately as the kind of professional, respect-for-the-law cop we all know from TV. Kim pointedly elicited five pieces of information from Zoller: upon arrival, Venda Meheula "was standing in the driveway"; the truck was registered to the defendant's father, Harold Meheula; Zoller found a black leather men's wallet "on the step panel" of the passenger side of the truck, and when Venda Meheula claimed it as hers he "proceeded to give it to her"; he saw a large rubbish bag on the passenger side floor, covered in blood that was dripping out onto the road; and he found an open can of Dr. Pepper on the bed railing behind the passenger window.

Kim retrieved four of the cardboard-framed photos from the neat pile on his table. As Zoller described a photo, Kim would place it on an overhead scanner, the image appearing on a television screen next to the witness stand. The Dr. Pepper can. The front bumper of the red GMC, documenting the license plate. And then there he was, Percy sitting behind the wheel of the truck, slumped over, his head facing down so you couldn't see his face, his shirt off, his body covered in blood. This was the photo that had made Donna Freitas cry.

A moan suddenly rang out, and I turned to see the giant body of Tyler Hopkins, his face red with anger, his eyes boring holes into the back of the defendant's head.

Meheula, who to this point had been following intently, was now looking down at the table in front of him.

WHEN KIM CALLED THEODORE COONS, the homicide detective assigned to the case, his routine continued: establish the witness's authority (Coons had been on the force for twenty-five years and had been a detective for fourteen); have him recount the events of May 16 (and in Coons' case, May 17, when he returned to the scene); and have him talk the jury through a series of photos. Coons described driving up 'Okana Road: "It's rural, it's dark." He added to the *there was blood everywhere* argument, having found a "transfer stain"—on the truck's front bumper. The Dr. Pepper can "was sweating." And Percy was found with his foot on the brake of what Coons identified as a standard transmission truck, in first gear, with the ignition on. The first set of photos were of the truck and the scene from various angles, again, apparently to establish that *blood was everywhere*. "It's very *dark* out there," Coons explained, so he had returned the next day to photograph the driveway. "It's a *long* driveway," he said, and Kim had him walk the audience through the four shots he needed to get the whole driveway from beginning to end, thereby loudly implying that someone whose leg had been stabbed could not have made the climb. A photo from May 16 depicted the eerie sight of a woman's handbag hanging on the mailbox at the end of the driveway. Coons explained that Venda Meheula claimed the bag as hers, and allowed him to search it before returning it to her. Inside the bag he found "the defendant's wallet," which he "recovered as evidence." Coons had also recovered an empty "Sawg Specialty Knife" sheath for a blade of seven and a half to eight inches in length.

Kim then had Coons identify the defendant ("He's heavier now, but . . ."), and then describe him after he was taken into custody on May 17. "He had a minor scratch on his hand," and no injuries other than the knife wound to his leg. Coons' arrest photos elaborated the descriptions from the overhead scanner. There was a close-up of the knife wound, which, already stitched, looked like a small dog bite, maybe an inch long and parallel to the leg. The other photos showed Meheula, pasty white without a shirt, his hair longer and disheveled, the round pot-belly that accounted for much of his two hundred pounds making his arms look skinny, the same sullen look on his face that he wore today. His pale white skin was totally free of bruises.

Domingo cross-examined both Zoller and Coons, in both cases trying to bring into question whether the crime scene had been contaminated (it had not), and then testing each man's credibility with detailed questions about the scene, some of which clearly lacked relevance (Zoller could not recall the year of the truck), and others Kim might have asked himself (Coons did recall that the truck's parking brake was not on). Domingo appeared to be looking for a way to diffuse the biggest bomb that the two testimonies had just dropped: if both men were telling the truth and remembering events accurately, then Venda Meheula had lied to a police officer at the scene of a crime she knew to have been committed by her son.

IN CALLING THE HPD EVIDENCE SPECIALIST Walter Fung, Kim shifted deeper into his "teacher" identity. After his usual four or five questions establishing the witness's authority, Kim used Fung to demonstrate how blood samples are collected and stored, and to define the phrase "chain of custody," which refers to a record kept of the investigators and evidence specialists and so on who have had access to a particular sample. In around ten minutes, Kim made the point that the blood evidence he would later submit would indeed be sound evidence.

When his turn came, Domingo asked Fung, "Did you specifically collect any evidence from Mr. Kipapa?"

"I collected a leather pouch with a pipe in it."

Domingo asked what such a pipe is used for.

"It's used for narcotics."

Domingo asked where it was found.

"I believe it was in his left front pocket."

Domingo asked if anything else was found in the pouch.

"No."

"Did you test this pipe?"

"No."

"Did you find any latent finger prints on it?"

"No."

Domingo finished, again, without having used the word "ice," suggesting that it's not so easy to say that Kim "lost" in this exchange, having admitted during his opening statement that "ice was involved," having presented someone with the appearance and voice of Lori Rodrigues as an upstanding citizen doing her part for the state, and in light of the fact that he would go on to freely refer to Percy as a user. As the trial unfolded it was becoming clearer that cases involving ice were no longer as clear-cut as they may have been even four years earlier, before the Kahaluʻu anti-ice campaign—especially in cases like this one where both the victim and the accused were users. Sadly, the odds were good that everyone sitting in that jury box was no more than a few handshakes away from that former school friend who had to refinance his house, or that mother around the block whose kids were taken away, or even one of Hawaiʻi's thousands of functioning addicts. Ice had taken such a hold that it was no longer possible to simply dismiss someone as a "druggie" or "chronic," even in a courtroom. Where there used to be judgment alone, now the judgment was mixed with pity.

ON WEDNESDAY MORNING the parade of evidence specialists and medical experts continued, as Kim worked to establish that *there was blood everywhere*. Back in teaching mode, he called Mary Sullivan, an HPD criminalist for the past six and a half years. Again, Kim would have been the kind of teacher who had "presence"—not the kind of babbling lecturer who puts students to sleep but rather the kind who displays the sort of infectious curiosity that has them on the edge of their seats awaiting the next detail. Today, at least half the jury were clutching state-issued flip-top notebooks and pens, and all of them—including a few who looked like they hadn't clutched a notebook since high school—were putting them to use.

"What *is* DNA?" Kim asked, approaching the interaction with the genuine curiosity of a beginner, using a tone that made it okay for the rest of us not to know much about science, and inviting us to be curious about how DNA identification actually works.

"It's a blueprint of a person," Sullivan said. Kim had her succinctly explain how, even with the smallest of blood samples, she can "copy" DNA to the point where she has enough of it to determine a person's "blood profile," and how each person's blood profile is completely unique. Kim had her explain how she comes up with the blood profile, making sure to have her point out that she found no blood on the seat cover recovered from Donna Freitas's car. He had her walk the jury through a huge chart listing several blood samples (from the pavement, from the plastic bag in the truck, from the front bumper, etc.) and the blood profiles she'd come up with. All of the blood profiles on the list matched that of Percy "except for the blood taken from one item"—Meheula's shorts.

Domingo did not cross-examine.

Thanks to Kim's initial questions, we all learned that Dr. Gail Suzuki, who performed the autopsy on Percy the day after he was killed, is a local girl. He asked her about her bachelor's degree not because it had any bearing on her authority in this case (zoology), but because she got it from the University of Hawai'i at Mānoa. She then earned her medical degree from the university before participating in a five-year pathology residency program. She had been a Honolulu deputy medical examiner for four years. Dr. Suzuki explained that Percy's 430-pound body had sustained one stab wound to the chest, two stab wounds to the abdomen, "incise" (that is, cut rather than puncture) defensive wounds to the hands, an incise wound to the right thigh that did not penetrate, and a stab wound to the right thigh penetrating to a depth of just under four inches. Stab wound "A" to the abdomen went three inches and did no organ damage. Stab wound "B" to the abdomen went a half inch deeper and grazed the liver. The stab wound to the mid-left side of the chest penetrated the heart to a depth of five inches, going straight in. Percy had one V-shaped cut on the back of his right hand and three small cuts on his right fingers, all wounds "consistent with warding off an attack," she said.

Everyone pretended not to hear the sound of another groan filling the small room, and I turned to see Tyler sitting behind me, his face red with anger.

Kim then had Suzuki walk through ten autopsy photos, as meticulously and efficiently as he'd had Sergeant Zoller walk through the photos of the truck. Throughout, Meheula stared a hole into his Bible. The chest wound, now cleaned up, looked like a small bite, just over an inch long. The wounds in the abdomen were also much smaller than I'd expected, one right next to the other. There was a shot taken of the chest wound from farther back that included Percy's face, his eyes closed, the corners of his mouth turned down. Tyler lifted his big body out of the wooden bench and left the room. The back of Percy's big hand looked scraped and cut, in a V shape. The wound on his left finger looked like what happens when someone cuts himself accidentally in the kitchen. "The cause of death was stab wounds of the chest and abdomen," Dr. Suzuki said.

Kim slowly acted out what particular motions might have caused the wounds, first by swinging an imaginary knife across his body with his right hand into an imaginary target sitting next to him, asking if the wound to the chest was "consistent with this motion." (It was.) He elicited the fact that it would take a person sustaining such a stab wound to the chest several minutes to die. "Does the fact that he ingested crystal meth change your opinion as to the cause of death?" Kim asked the question almost matter of factly, without making excuses for Percy's drug use, or Meheula's. His delivery, and indeed all of his references to drug use up until his closing statement, suggested the words, *Look, we are all going to have to accept the reality that ice is so deeply imbedded in Hawai'i that the mention of it, particularly in a murder case involving one man who admitted to using and another who tested positive, doesn't even really matter.*

"No," Dr. Suzuki answered. Kim had her explain the idea of "defense wounds" in more detail. "You tend to ward off blows," she said. Kim asked if it were possible that the wound on Percy's left hand could have resulted from grabbing at a knife. It was, she said.

In his cross-examination, Domingo went to work on the idea of "defense wounds"—a pivotal piece of evidence in the case if Kim were correct in assuming Meheula would plead self-defense. "You couldn't tell who was the aggressor," he said.

"Correct."

Could Percy have "struck out at something," he asked, to get the wounds on his hands?

"Hmm. It's possible," she said.

"Are you familiar with the term 'shock'?" Domingo suddenly asked her.

Dr. Suzuki was taken aback. "Shock" did not seem to have anything to do with the discussion of stab wounds, or, for that matter, with her expertise as a forensic pathologist. Domingo asked her several questions about the behavior of someone who is in shock, about the kinds of high-level stress that cause shock, and so forth. Throughout, Dr. Suzuki appeared to be giving qualified answers along the lines of "as far as I remember from back in med school," and then Domingo gave up. It all came off as a last-ditch effort to help build the kind of "under extreme emotional stress" argument that can get a murder charge reduced to manslaughter in the state of Hawai'i. I imagined that if someone as meticulous as Glenn Kim had been representing Meheula and wished to make such a case, he would have called his own witness—one with years of experience and proven expertise in diagnosing "extreme emotional stress" who would be able to clearly list possible causes of such stress, and so on. But this sudden shift to talking about "shock" looked like a spur-of-the-moment decision on Domingo's part: I've got a doctor on the stand, so let's see if I can make use of her.

This little exchange had the effect of making Kim, by comparison, look even more deliberate, precise, and *prepared* than he already did.

"Your honor," he said, "the state rests."

WHICH BRINGS US BACK to that cramped little hallway with everyone trying to be heard over the roaring surf of conversation, and Tyler staring right down into the exposed neck of the man who had killed Percy. I couldn't believe what I was seeing, only ten feet away. Tyler's face was reddening, his eyes widening as if the rest of the bustling room had disappeared around him. And while it was hard to imagine that Tyler would *do* something, right here in front of everyone, right here in the State Circuit Court building, well—what did it take, anyway, for one man to kill another? Did it take a year of stewing in anger? Did it take the sight of a series of autopsy photos depicting the best friend you ever had? Did it take an opportunity of proximity such as the one in which Tyler now found himself? It would be so easy, too—a fact that Tyler himself must have been thinking. All he had to do was lift a hand, one of those battle-tested hands of his, and grab that neck, and then lean into the paneled wall with the force of his five hundred pounds.

"T!" I called out again over the crowd noise.

It's hard to say if Tyler would in fact have acted in that moment. He had, after all, been drilled for over seven years with sumo's lessons in honor, in fighting a fair fight. So at last he finally turned and looked at me, dazed. He shook his head a bit as if to clear the cobwebs, and then squeezed his way towards me. By the time we entered the courtroom and sat down, beads of sweat were dripping down the sides of his face, his mighty chest heaving.

DOMINGO BEGAN HIS OPENING STATEMENT with an emotional appeal for regarding Keali'i as a nature lover who liked to hunt pigs and give the meat to his friends. Meheula met "his good friend Percy" two and a half years before the night of May 16, and they became friends because of their common love of Waikāne Valley, their interest in hunting, and their use of ice. "They would smoke ice together" up in the valley "for days at a time," Domingo said. On May 16, Venda and Keali'i came to pick up Percy because "Percy wanted to score some ice." They were surprised to find him "different, kind of distant." As Domingo walked the jury all the way through the stabbing and on to Meheula's arrest at Castle Hospital the following morning, he had the entire room hanging on his every word as he painted a Percy who *wasn't himself* and a confused Meheula lost in a dreamlike state after realizing what he had done. "Keali'i looks over and sees what he's done to his friend," Domingo said, facing the jury, "and he starts crying."

Domingo's strong opening statement led me to wonder why he'd waited until now to deliver it. Perhaps it went back to the T-shirt incident from the first morning—there can be no getting around the fact that the image of the big, black-shirted Kipapas packing the courtroom was frightening, and Domingo had let it hover there long enough to become a powerful unspoken reason why Meheula would flee the scene of an "accidental" killing. Or maybe Domingo wanted to make sure that Kim could refute the theory that Percy had stabbed Meheula before he abandoned Meheula's leg wound as a piece of his self-defense claim. In any case, Domingo would rely not on the idea that Percy wasn't the great guy we all thought him to be, as Kim had anticipated, but that Percy *wasn't himself* that night. The wink-and-a-nod meaning—which Domingo could not come out and say since his own client was an admitted habitual user, not to mention the one who went wild with an eight-inch hunting knife—was that Percy, starving for drugs that night, had to get his way *or else*. To Domingo, ice clearly did matter—perhaps more than anything else—because he was creating a version of Percy that perfectly fit a layperson's image of that stop-at-nothing chronic we'd all been warned about repeatedly in Edgy Lee's movie and other media: that is, Percy was an ice fiend.

DOMINGO'S FIRST WITNESS was Venda Meheula, the defendant's mother. In walked a woman of medium height and build wearing a black-and-red aloha-print dress, her longish brown hair feathered out in a style that might have come out of my mid-1980s high school yearbook, her face tanned and a bit worn. She came off as one of those forty-something women who used to trade socially on their stunning natural beauty, and who then try to hang onto the looks that got them by in their twenties. Under questioning from Domingo, she said she'd known Percy for two years before he was killed. "He's a friend of ours," she said evenly. And of Percy and her son, "They were good friends for a long time."

"Do you consider Percy a good guy?" Domingo asked.

"Yes. I got along well with him," she said. She seemed remarkably comfortable on the stand, leading me to wonder if she'd been there before. On the night of May 16, she explained, "My son was getting ready to go to a program." He had asked her to help him move some things to a friend's house in Pearl City where he would be staying, and when she said that she couldn't help him, they decided to ask Percy. "That was somebody who he trusted," she said. When they picked Percy up "he was fine," she said. He sat in the back of the truck. He wanted to go back to Lori's house to buy drugs, so Keali'i and Percy dropped Venda off at the house to "score some ice." At the house, according to Venda, "there were a bunch of people. Donna, Lori, and a bunch of people." Lori and Donna "were smoking ice."

Keali'i returned to the house around half an hour later, shirtless and out of breath, holding a knife, having stabbed Percy. When she asked him, "Why? Why, boy?" he told her that Percy had threatened to kidnap his nieces, and "had threatened to kill him." Venda then "ran down to render aid" to Percy.

"Was there any mention of 'Percy is ripping me off,' or 'Percy was fooling around with my girlfriend?'" Domingo asked. (There wasn't.)

Domingo asked if she'd been carrying a can of Dr. Pepper when she went down to find Percy.

"When I ran down, I had it in my hand."

He asked about her purse.

"It was under Percy's arm," she said. When she found him she told him, "Relax, boy. Don't worry. Aunty stay wit you—you'll be okay." She then ran all the way back up the hill to make sure someone called 911, and when she came down the second time, with her son, "We ran into Donna." She then told the jury, "My granddaughters were being threatened," so she asked Donna to drive Keali'i to his sister's house.

"There was no problem," Domingo said. "She said she would take him."

"Donna opened the door and let him in," Venda said.

"Where was the knife at this point?" Domingo asked.

"I don't know," she said. "I stayed there with Percy, just rubbing his shoulder. I was comforting him."

"Was there any response?"

"He just nodded," she said.

"No further questions."

By now Glenn Kim had clearly established a few important parts of his identity with the jury. He was full of deep respect—for the court, for the jury, for the witnesses, for himself—which meant, of course, that he never tried to get away with anything—even with presenting all of the available blood evidence long after he had clearly made his case that *there was blood everywhere*, for instance. And now he was about to cross-examine a woman who had lied to either Sergeant Zoller or Detective Coons about the black wallet in her purse. So, for lack of a better term, Kim let her have it. Referring to the statement Venda Meheula made to Detective Coons on May 16, Kim said from his place at the podium, "You didn't tell him *anything* you just told the jury. Do you want to see your statement?" He drilled his point home with a series of questions picking at the story she'd just told, all of them beginning with the same words. "Did you tell him anything about *a bunch of people* at Lori Rodrigues' house?"

"I think I told him . . ."

"Do you *wanna see your statement?*" he asked, clearly irritated.

"If it isn't there I must not have said it then."

"Did you tell him anything about *going to buy ice?*"

"I don't know . . ."

"You *wanna see it?*" He held up a sheet of paper.

"I must not have said it."

The line of interrogation went on for five more questions. Then Kim said, "The detective even asked you, 'You sure you're telling the truth?' And you said, 'The whole truth, and nothing but the truth.' Do you remember saying that?"

"No."

"You *wanna see it?*"

"If it's written there, then I must have said it," she said.

"The truth is that you said nothing about *ice*, or anything like that, right?" he said.

"Because of the rage, I didn't know," she answered.

Kim then raised his voice, saying, "The fact of the matter is that you were *protecting your son.*"

Through a series of questions on the order of "You mean you didn't think to call the detective the next day with this important information?" Kim established the fact that Venda Meheula had been far less than cooperative, and then, eight days later when she was called and asked for more information, she volunteered an eight-page statement that Kim was clearly implying was fabricated. "You *lied* to that first detective, didn't you."

She denied lying. She denied smoking ice that night. And then Kim led her into what were really a series of declarative statements he wanted her to agree with:

"You never saw Percy smoking ice that night, *right?*"

"No."

"He was 'fine,' right?"

"No."

"He was *no different* from his normal self, *right?*"

"Right."

"You asked Donna Freitas very nicely if your son could get into her car, *right?*"

"Right."

"And she said, 'No problem,'" he said. The fact that his words were now dripping with sarcasm explained in an instant the "witness exclusion" rule that had barred Venda Meheula from hearing the testimony of Donna

Freitas. Kim was about to hang her out to dry, and she was the only one in the room who didn't know it.

"Right," she said.

After another "You wanna see it?" exchange, Kim asked, "Did you score the ice?"

"I did."

"Why didn't you tell the detectives?"

"I don't know." She'd clearly long since had enough of this.

He asked her what she'd done with the ice, and she explained that she'd hidden the pipe and her ice "under a tree" and "to this day" never went back to get it.

Kim then brought up the wallet.

Directly after picking up Percy they had driven to a Kahaluʻu country store called Tang's to buy cigarettes, she explained. "When we went to Tang's store, my son gave me his wallet," she said.

"That wallet wasn't sitting on the side rail of the truck, and you didn't ask the officer for it?"

"No."

"No further questions."

OF THE THREE WITNESSES Domingo was relying on to prove that *Percy wasn't himself* on the night of May 16, two were Meheulas—one of whom had just told the jury that Percy was "no different from his normal self" when they picked him up in Waikāne. So a lot would ride on the testimony of Maydell Pakele, who had known Percy for about a year and who had seen him that evening outside Tang's store. "Percy was sitting in the back of the truck leaning against the cab," she told Domingo. She said she greeted him, but surprisingly he did not respond—he usually greeted her with his big smile and a "How-you, Aunty?" "He was not himself," she told the jury. "He looked like he had other things on his mind."

Kim's tone had switched entirely when he stood to cross-examine Maydell Pakele. Her testimony apparently matched the statement she'd made to the detectives the previous year, so Kim was relaxed, and as full of respect as he'd been while questioning the evidence specialists. "He wasn't hostile to you or anything?"

He wasn't.

"He wasn't crying . . . ?"

He wasn't.

"You weren't worried that anything really bad was happening with him, or you would've investigated further, right?"

Of course.

And then Kim asked this: "What kind of guy was Percy?"

Maydell Pakele then brightened up, launching into the kind of he-would-go-out-of-his-way-to-help-*anyone* description of Percy that Mrs. Kipapa might have made herself. Percy was "lovable," she said.

Kim then referred to her statement to the detectives, asking her if it was correct that, on the same occasion, she saw Meheula "pacing back and forth" in the parking lot.

"Correct," she said. "He looked like maybe he had something on his mind, too."

AS HIS FINAL WITNESS, Domingo called Keali'i Meheula. The defendant stood at the witness stand in his nice blue suit, was sworn in, and sat, leaning on his elbows into the microphone. His shoulders slumped just enough to make him look saddened by the whole affair. His eyes focused intently on his attorney, whose questions he answered evenly, as if according to a script, telling the court of his sister, his cousins, his nieces. Three years earlier he had a roofing job, but since then he had been unemployed, picking up the odd carpentry or mechanic job, and hunting pigs in Waikāne Valley with "my friend Percy. Percy Kipapa." He said that he and Percy had met three years earlier in Waikāne. "He seemed like a good guy," he said. They soon became "good friends." They would "go hunting once in a while." They would "smoke once in a while, smoke ice." They would talk for long stretches. "We talked about his sumo career and how he won the tournaments and how he wound up getting injured."

Domingo then turned to the night of May 16. "I had just got kicked out of my house by my wife," Meheula said, referring to Desiree Kaeo, whom he'd been able to marry while out on bail after killing Percy. "I was planning on going to ATS"—the Salvation Army drug treatment program. "I was planning on leaving my things at my friend's house in Pearl City." In reading an account of this exchange, one might be forgiven for calling Meheula on how conveniently dramatic and tragic this little piece of information was, and therefore for thinking he had to have made it up: *Immediately before* heading into treatment, all goes terribly, terribly wrong for a guy who wants to clean up his act? But with the perfect slump of his shoulders, the resigned and weary tone of his voice, and his even delivery, Meheula appeared to be pulling it off. You felt sorry for him.

He went on, about Percy: "He had called me a couple of days earlier to tell me he had parts for my Nissan truck."

Domingo asked how Percy acted when they first met that night.

"We shook hands."

"Was that normal?"

"No. We usually shake hands and give a one-handed hug." It was also unusual that the 430-pound Percy sat in the back of the truck. "He usually would squeeze inside widdus."

Meheula's mother drove them to Lori Rodrigues' house "to buy drugs." Domingo asked some detailed question about what had been said in the truck, and Meheula thought for a moment and said, "I can't recall. I tried to block all of this from my mind." At Tang's store, where they stopped to buy cigarettes, "I seen May Pakele and her husband." After five or ten minutes, they drove to 7-Eleven "to call Lori." At Lori's house, they parked "on the second level" of the driveway and walked up the rest of the way to the house, where Meheula and Percy were not allowed in.

Domingo asked if that made him angry.

"No," Meheula said. "I just felt kind of left out." He and Percy then got in the truck and started driving, Meheula behind the wheel. "He asked me where we was going," Meheula said, "and I told him, 'I don't know.'"

According to Meheula, Percy then said, forcefully, "You don't know? Then get the *fuck* outtada driver's seat!" At the 'Āhuimanu stoplight Percy got out and forced his way behind the wheel, Meheula arguing the whole time, "Nobody drives my fadda's truck!" Percy headed "towards the country," and "the whole way to Waikāne, he was silent."

Domingo asked if this was normal behavior.

"He would always make jokes," Meheula said, but not tonight.

Percy turned onto Waikāne Valley Road and parked the truck where they normally parked, about twenty yards from the highway in a dark place. "He started snapping at me," Meheula said, "telling me why was I talking shit about him ratting on me." The "ratting" referred to Percy possibly telling his uncle, who was a police officer, "about my drug sales in the past." Meheula admitted to having started telling people that Percy was a "rat" "about six months prior" to May 16. As they were arguing, Percy's cousin pulled up and asked if everything was all right, and Percy said, "Nothing I can't handle." And then, "Out of the blues, he said he loved his niece. I said, 'Why did you bring that up?' And he said," Meheula paused, "I can't think of it right now." Domingo coaxed him forward. "He said, 'How do I feel about my nieces?' I heard him mutter something under his breath . . . I heard like key words like 'pay them a visit.' I thought he was planning on kidnapping my nieces."

Frightened, Meheula asked to be driven back to 'Okana Road, and Percy complied. On the way, out of nowhere he shouted, "I should just wrap this fuckin' truck around this pole!" He then "veered off to the right," coming only inches from a telephone pole. "I was afraid," Meheula said. "I thought I was gonna die." Percy yelled out, "I should just kill the both of us!" Then Meheula told the court, "I begged him to pick up my mother."

"What did he say?"

"He didn't say a thing."

They drove on, and then in a low voice Percy said, "That bitch betta have something for me."

"How did that make you feel?" Domingo asked.

"I was angry," Meheula said. "Because that's not like him. He usually talked with respect about my madda. I was afraid for my madda."

Domingo asked what happened next. Meheula paused, struggling.

"He did pull over," he said. "The left side of the road."

Domingo then produced state's evidence number 40—the Sawg knife sheath—and handed it to Meheula, who identified it as the sheath for his "skinning knife." The eight-inch blade had sat on the seat between himself and Percy. "I knew it was there," he said.

Domingo asked him what he intended to do with the knife.

"Scare him outta my fadda's truck," Meheula said. "My intentions wasn't to stab him. Ever."

Domingo asked him to reenact what he'd told Percy.

"Get the fuck outta my fadda's truck!" he yelled, wielding the black sheath. "He told me, 'Fuck you!' and he hit me."

Domingo asked if he hit the knife.

"He hit the knife, and he hit me, too."

Domingo had Meheula step down and sit in a chair directly facing the jury, as though he were sitting in the passenger seat of the truck. Meheula sat, that world-weary look on his face, his shoulders slumped in sadness, and again acted out the get-the-fuck-outta-my-fadda's-truck threat, and then acted out Percy reacting by backhanding him in the chest. "And he hits *hard*," Meheula said. "He hit the knife, then me." Percy then "grabbed me by the throat" with his right hand. Domingo directed him to demonstrate with his own hand on his own throat where Percy's hand had been, pointing out that the thumb was directly over the Adam's apple. Domingo then established that Meheula was five foot ten and weighed only two hundred pounds when all of this was being done to him by a "430-pound former professional sumo wrestler." Meheula, still sitting in the chair facing the jury, "felt like my eyes was just gonna come out." Domingo asked what he did next. "I thought I was gonna black out, so I just swung that knife wild." Still a bit slumped over, he imitated an absurdly half-hearted motion of a man going "wild" with a knife. It looked like he'd never held a knife in his life. Domingo asked him why he'd stabbed his good friend. "I thought I was gonna die. I couldn't breathe. I couldn't speak. I just swung the knife wild." And then? "He hit my hand down, and then it went into his thigh." And next? "I opened the door, and I ran." Domingo asked what he was thinking. "I can't believe I had just done that." Done what? "I had stabbed Percy." Meheula said he'd run away because "I wanted to get help." And next? "After that had happened, it was just like a dream. I was praying it was a dream."

Domingo then walked Meheula, now back on the stand, all the way through this "dream" sequence until the next morning at the hospital, where he was surprised to have been arrested. Along the way, he said, "Donna had told me to go around" the car and she willingly drove him away. Meheula "feared the Kipapa family. I feared their retaliation." And then, still in this dream state, he wound up running, and then "as I was running, I had hit myself." Realizing he was still holding the knife, "I just threw it." At the fire station "they were asking me all kinds of questions. I was feeling sick. I couldn't think straight. I remember them calling an ambulance and taking me to the hospital." And the restraints and sedation at the hospital? "I told them that they didn't have to strap me down—that there was no reason to strap me down. I remembered struggling for about thirty seconds and then I blacked out." The next morning, "I felt dizzy, like I woke up from a dream."

Several times throughout this story, Meheula could not remember certain details. Twice Domingo tried to refresh his memory, and on both occasions, Kim jumped up and objected, "Leading, your honor. The witness says he doesn't remember."

Finally, Domingo asked Meheula what he thought of Percy.

With deep sincerity, Meheula said, "I considered Percy one of my best friends."

Domingo then said, "You're responsible for your good friend's death."

And Meheula broke down, leaning forward into the microphone and covering his face with both hands, sobbing.

Domingo then said, "Would you have anything to say to Mr. Kipapa's family at this point?"

And Kim pounced, as angry now as he'd been at Venda Meheula for lying to the court. "Objection!" he said. "That was totally uncalled for."

THE FOLLOWING MORNING we all entered the courtroom to find Glenn Kim sitting in his seat like a boxer waiting for the opening bell. Given his slender physique and his polite, sophisticated demeanor, I sincerely doubt that he's ever been in a fight. But this morning he looked *ready*.

At 9:30, Meheula was on the stand. Kim greeted him evenly: "Good morning, Mr. Meheula."

"Good morning, sir."

Kim then referred to the night of May 16, 2005, and asked, "Did you stab Percy Kipapa multiple times?"

"Yes, sir."

"You weren't *dreaming* when you did this, were you, Mr. Meheula?"

"It felt like I was dreaming," Meheula said.

"You *knew what you were doing*, didn't you, Mr. Meheula."

"No, sir."

"When you *plunged the knife into Percy Kipapa's chest*, you knew what you were doing, *right?*"

Meheula paused for a long time. "No, sir," he finally said.

The fact that he was clearly lying led Kim to change the subject. He asked how many times Meheula and Percy had smoked ice in the past.

"Too many times to count."

"And had you and Percy ever had any problems before?"

"We had our arguments, our ups and downs," Meheula said.

"In any case, the two of you found it a pleasurable activity—that's why you did it, right?"

"Yes, sir."

Kim then asked if "in *all* those times," there had ever been any problems between them at all like those Meheula described from the night of May 16.

"Not really, sir," Meheula said.

Kim then asked if Meheula had smoked ice on the night of May 16.

"No, sir."

"You're *denying* that you used ice that night?"

"Yes, sir."

Kim then deepened his can-you-believe-*this* tone, and brought his line of questioning back to the Kāne'ohe fire station, where Meheula had been asked if he'd taken any medication. "And you said, 'Yeah, ice. A couple of hours ago.' And now you're denying that you smoked ice that night?"

"Yes, sir," Meheula said.

Kim let the exchange speak for itself, going back to work on the *Percy wasn't himself* claim. "*You* went to pick *him* up that night, right?"

"No," Meheula said. He then repeated verbatim the line from his testimony the day before, about how Percy had called him "a couple of days earlier" with parts for his Nissan truck.

When they went to pick him up, Kim went on, "He was pretty normal, right?"

"No, sir." Meheula tried to explain how Percy was different.

"He wasn't yelling at you?"

"No, sir."

"He didn't go psycho?"

"No, sir."

Kim then took his questioning to Tang's store, then to the 7-Eleven, and finally to 'Okana Road. A couple of times Meheula got mixed up in the chronology of events—"I'm sorry, you lost me back there, sir. I got confused." So Kim, even in the heat of his questioning, apologized and then made sure Meheula was caught up to where he was in the narrative. And then he asked, "Why would you get back in the truck and drive away if your mother was inside buying drugs for you? Wouldn't you wait outside? Is she supposed to just stand out there and wait for you to come back?"

Meheula did not have an answer.

Kim made sure to elicit from Meheula that Percy was fine at the traffic light where Percy supposedly forced his way behind the wheel, that he was calm all the way to and from the 'Okana Road house. And then suddenly Percy snapped, Kim said, "out of nowhere!"

"Yes, sir."

On dark Waikāne Valley Road, Kim had Meheula remind the jury how frightened he'd become—frightened of Percy, frightened for his life—so that he asked Percy to go back to 'Okana Road. "And he *does* drive back to 'Okana Road," Kim said.

"Yes, sir."

"You begged him to drive you back to your mother, and he *complied*."

"Yes, sir."

Back to 'Okana Road. Kim again had Meheula explain how he was frightened for his life, and that he wanted to get back to the house, and how he wanted Percy to pull over. "You guys are *right* by the driveway," Kim went on. "And you order him to pull over, and according to you, he *does*." Kim let that one sit for a moment, and then asked, "Up to that point that night, had he ever hit you?"

"No, sir."

"Had he ever threatened you?"

"No, sir."

Kim let that sit for a moment, and then he had Meheula explain his interest in killing feral pigs with knives. "You had experience with knives," Kim said.

"Yes, sir."

"Percy knew that, right? He'd seen you use a knife, right?"

"Yes, sir."

And then on the night of the 16th when "you threatened him, Percy saw the knife, right? That was the idea, right? For him to see the knife, right?"

"Yes, sir."

"And what is your testimony?"

Meheula went through the get-the-fuck-outta-my-fadda's-truck part, and then said, "He swung his fist."

"You said he hit you *hard*," Kim said, asking Meheula again to explain exactly how terribly hard he'd been hit in the stomach. He then produced the photo taken of Meheula, shirtless, on May 17, and he walked right up to the stand, one might say, for the kill. "This is you, right?"

"Yes, sir."

"You see anything on your stomach?" he asked, so wrapped up in the moment that it came out in the unmistakable Pidgin tone of a father scolding his son.

"No, sir."

Kim then produced the black Sawg knife sheath, and he asked Meheula to act out what he had done to Percy, whom he said he had stabbed "three times." Standing behind the witness stand with the sheath in his right hand, Meheula swung across his body once at chest height, and then pulled all the way back and adjusted to aim his next two swings, which followed more quickly one upon the other at stomach height. The pace was that of one long deliberate stab followed by a quick one-two to the stomach, with all three stabs hitting the precise spots on the imaginary victim where the autopsy photos had revealed the three stab wounds on Percy's body. It was as though Meheula had the photos on a teleprompter in front of him as he acted out the motions, which were certainly not "wild." Fascinated, Kim had him demonstrate the "one, one-two" motion again, and then let him sit.

Next Kim turned to the Percy-was-choking-me claim, leading Meheula down a path that allowed him to indulge in all of the my-eyes-were-bulging, I-thought-I-was-gonna-die imagery he could come up with. When Kim even began helping him out with questions like, "Did it feel like he was going to break your windpipe?" you could tell what was going to happen. And sure enough, once Meheula had dug himself into a hole, Kim produced the close-up taken on May 17 and approached the witness stand. "Is this you?" he asked.

"Yes, sir."

And in the same scolding Pidgin tone as before, "Do you see *any* mark on your throat?"

Meheula thought for a moment. He wouldn't make the same mistake twice, so he pointed to the photo and said, "There."

"Right," Kim said, walking back to his podium. "We'll let the jury decide on that."

Kim then led Meheula through the rest of the attack with a string of "Is it fair to say" questions to account for the wounds on Percy's hand ("So he grabbed for the knife at that point with his left hand?") and his leg. After Meheula stabbed Percy's chest, the testimony went, Percy's hand dropped from the defendant's throat and on the way down, "He hit my hand"—the one holding the knife—"and it seemed like it went into his leg, sir."

"Right," Kim said. "Yesterday you said 'thigh.'" He gave Meheula the chance to say whether or not anything else had happened that they'd missed, reminding him that it had been dark that night, and that he'd been fighting for his life, and that the events must have all gone by quickly. Meheula had nothing to add.

Then Kim walked away from the podium, saying, "Mr. Meheula, you've just accounted for every single wound on Percy Kipapa's body, no more, no less. Don't you find that *interesting?*" In a murder case with no witnesses, the state, arguing on behalf of a man who is no longer around to tell his story, must construct a plausible chain of events using the clues available in such forensic evidence as photos of the scene, autopsy photos, blood evidence, and so on. Kim had just made clear the fact that the *defense* had also very likely constructed its story the same way. Meheula's story was *too* precise, *too* accurate to have possibly happened. Hadn't Meheula, after all, been "dreaming" that night?

Next, Kim moved on to Donna Freitas and her apparent willingness to drive Meheula to his sister's house. "She was fine with it," Kim said.

"Yes, sir," was all Meheula said.

In moving on to discredit Meheula's dream run through Kāneʻohe and the "realization" that he'd stabbed himself in the leg, Kim made use of his own lanky frame. First he had Meheula step down in front of the jury. He had Meheula point to where he'd discovered he'd stabbed himself on the leg—a point just below where his fingers reached while he stood with his hands at his side. "Is that the *one* time the knife hit you?" he asked.

"Yes sir."

"You were running with your hands down *here?*" Kim asked, acting out the motion of running with the knife. With his shoulders hunched over, he ran in place—his hands brushing against his thighs. Had Meheula been the one demonstrating with his stocky frame and slumped-over shoulders, the motion would have looked perfectly natural. But Kim looked ridiculous. "Wouldn't somebody normally run like *this?*" He went into a perfect marathoner's form, hands held high.

"I was kind of running/walking," Meheula said.

Kim then moved on to the issue of the hospital and the arrest, and he asked, "Do you remember calling Lori Rodrigues while you were in custody and telling her that what she was saying was hurting your case?"

He didn't remember.

"Even according to your own version of the story," Kim said, "you're the one responsible for the escalation of events." And at 9:50 he turned to sit, saying, "Nothing further, your honor." His examination had taken twenty minutes.

THE COURT RECONVENED AT 1:15 for closing arguments. While Judge Sakamoto read aloud from the five or six pages that made up the jury instructions, the chances for conviction became, despite Kim's apparent victories in cross-examining every one of Domingo's witnesses, much less certain. The instructions placed the burden of proof "beyond a reasonable doubt" squarely on the prosecution, with "reasonable doubt" defined as being based on facts, not "suspicion, not probability, not opinion." Further, the jury "must not be influenced by pity towards the defendant, or passion against the defendant." They were told to weigh "direct" evidence and "circumstantial" evidence, and they were to decide how much weight to give each piece of evidence. In judging a witness's credibility, they were invited to consider "appearance," "candor" or lack thereof, "interest in the case," and "intelligence." "It is testimony that has convincing force upon you that counts." When the judge read that the verdict must be unanimous, things became even less certain, particularly in light of the splendid job that Meheula had done on Wednesday: couldn't there be at least one jurist who'd been swayed enough by the tears to consider at least the *possibility* of big Percy choking the defendant? The rules then defined second-degree murder: the prosecution must prove, first, that the defendant "intention-ally or knowingly" did what he did, and second, that he knew it would kill Percy. The jury was instructed that intentional intoxication could not excuse murder, but could be pointed to as a reason for aggressive behav-ior. "Self-defense is a defense to the charge of murder," Judge Sakamoto went on, meaning that if Kim could not prove that Meheula did not act in self-defense, Meheula would walk. Sakamoto then defined self-defense, stating that the defendant must "reasonably believe" that deadly force is "immediately necessary." If the jury did find that the defendant com-mitted murder, then they were required to consider "extreme mental or emotional disturbance." Should the jury find, unanimously, that Meheula was under extreme mental or emotional disturbance, and that there was a "reasonable explanation" for this disturbance, they were to find him guilty of manslaughter.

In order to get the murder conviction, Kim would have to get the jury to discount Meheula's entire testimony. Since the burden of proof was on him, he was allowed to deliver his closing argument first, and he was al-lowed to reserve some of his allotted one hour to rebut Domingo's closing argument. "Don't worry," Kim assured the jury. "I'm not going to take even near an hour." He started by addressing the jury rules. "There's at least one thing we can say we know for sure about this case." He was back into his teacher mode here, but now he was giving them credit for know-ing what he was talking about, like a professor addressing a class of gradu-ate students who've done the reading. "It's not a whodunit." He pointed out that we at least know, even according to Meheula's own testimony, that the defendant stabbed Percy Kipapa to death on the night of May 16. "He also did so intentionally, or knowingly," Kim said, taking a moment to emphasize the "or" in the jury rules. "It's not even in dispute that he at least *knowingly* stabbed Percy Kipapa." Kim then reminded them that Percy was stabbed repeatedly, six times, implying that something like one stab might be considered an accident, but not six. "That's murder in the second degree," he said.

"And what is the evidence for self-defense in this case?" he went on. "His *story*." Kim paused, letting the hint of sarcasm drip in to the mo-ment. "So let's look at his story," he said, promising that he would not go "into every little detail," and praising the jury for having been so attentive throughout the trial. He touched on a few of the Percy-wasn't-himself details, but having dissected it all earlier in the day, he didn't insult the jury's intelligence by saying much. "If you believe him, you're probably going to acquit him," Kim said. "If you think he was *lying*, you've got to convict him." Kim paused again, moving over to the front of the courtroom between the jury box and the witness stand, and said, "You *know* what kind of guy Percy was." He echoed some of the earlier "Daiki" testimony, specifically citing Maydell Pakele, who'd called Percy the kind of guy who would go out of his way for everybody. He cited Venda Meheula calling Percy a friend. And, "ironically enough, even the defendant" referred to him, convincingly, as his "best friend." And then all of the sudden, out of nowhere, this wonderful guy turns into a psycho who wants to wrap a truck around a pole?

"He's lying to you," Kim said. "Why? Unless he can convince you that Percy was acting like a monster that night, self-defense goes out the window." He walked to the center of the courtroom, turned and faced the jury, and said, "The dog ate my homework." He paused. "Now, this is a murder case, and I don't want to make light of the important decision that's facing you. But let's think about that boy who comes to school without his homework. The teacher calls on him, and he gets caught. At that point, the boy has two choices. He can tell the truth, or he can lie, and try to get away with it." He went briefly into the anatomy of a lie, pointing out that a lie has to be based on certain facts—in this case, the wounds on Percy's body. "He has to come up with a story that accounts for every single one of those wounds," he said, reminding the jury of how Meheula had been able to "remember" in such great detail "every single stab wound on Percy's body, no more, no less," despite the fact that, as Detective Coons had noted, it was *so dark* out, and despite the fact that the defendant was supposedly fighting for his life. "I find that interesting," Kim said. Again, he trusted that the jury had seen enough earlier in the day that he did not have to revisit Meheula's discussion of the stabs again, or of the lack of evidence of aggression on Percy's part. "You look at the picture," he told them. "You look at his throat."

It was certainly clear to everyone that Venda Meheula was lying, having been nailed beyond any doubt lying about the wallet twice. So Kim took the corresponding accounts that Meheula and his mother had made about Donna Freitas' willingness to let him in the car, and then lumped the clearly-lying mother together with the might-be-lying son. He pointed out that *either* Donna and Lori, *or* Meheula and his mother, *must* be lying about how Meheula got into the car. "Ask yourself who has the motive to lie in this case," he said. Kim steered the jury further into how you make a lie like this one stick. "You've got to dirty the victim," he said. " 'Percy took drugs all the time.' 'Percy wanted to go and buy drugs.' " Kim pointed out that the evidence for such behavior came from Venda and Keali'i Meheula, and *not* from Donna Freitas and Lori Rodrigues.

Kim again acknowledged the serious task facing the jury, perhaps knowing that there might be someone sitting there who might feel okay getting away with just voting for manslaughter, since, what the hell, the guy will go to prison anyway, and the other guy was on ice too. Kim, who'd spent the past week setting the example for meticulous efficiency with every photo he introduced and every question he asked in that courtroom, told the jury this: "Do your job in this case." Kim, who had not tried to get away with leaving out the mention of a single speck of blood evidence even though he clearly had an overwhelming amount; who brought every evidence specialist who even touched the truck to testify on the stand; who had asked not a single irrelevant question, even while cross-examining Domingo's witnesses; who had, if nothing else, *done his job*, told the jury this: "Do your job in this case. Convict him for what he did to Percy Kipapa." His closing statement had taken less than fifteen minutes.

Domingo faced the jury like a TV lawyer, at times smiling, at times moving around to lean on the side of the podium. He began by referring to *Star Trek*—not the Captain Kirk version but the one with Jean-Luc Picard, making a joke at his own expense about the fact that he and Picard shared the same lack-of-hair style. He went further into a detailed description of a particular episode, explaining how Picard's character was on trial for something, and that this futuristic courtroom had "holograms" that could re-create events. He seemed to be building up to the point that Meheula, like the Picard character, was "innocent until proven guilty." He then brought up *The Da Vinci Code*, and asked for a show of hands as to who had seen the movie, apparently trying to make some connection between this case and the difference between a book and a movie. Everyone looked confused.

He then pointed towards Meheula's story and said, "And Mr. Kim is right: if you believe Mr. Meheula" then you cannot convict him. Kim's major attack on Meheula's story, he pointed out, was that it was too accurate, and therefore must have been fabricated. "Here's a novel idea," he said. "Everything Mr. Meheula said matches the evidence *because that's what happened*." Domingo then returned to *Star Trek*, this time the original series with Mr. Spock, where a premium was placed on "logic." "It's a blitz attack on a 430-pound professional sumo wrestler inside the cab of a truck with a knife," he said, asking who in their right mind would do such a thing in such a place. Since Percy and Meheula were hunting up in the mountains all of the time, Domingo reasoned, sometimes with guns, why didn't Meheula "take him into the mountains? Shoot him!" When Domingo concluded, what he'd been trying to do with the initial *Star Trek* discussion became a little bit clearer: he was setting himself up to perform his own hologram. He raised his voice, shifted into a mean, threatening tone, and said, "I should wrap this fuckin' truck around this fuckin' pole right now." He paused, and then in an equally threatening voice he said, "Get the fuck outta my fadda's truck!" And then he yelled loudly, "Fuck you!"

Before Domingo was even seated, Kim was walking back in front of the jury to instantly rob the moment of its melodrama by calmly saying, "Those would have been powerful words if they had actually been said." Stopping to face the jury—his palms open as if to say, "Let's be real, here"—he said, "Both of them were on ice." Here Domingo asked to approach the bench. Court records later showed him complaining that his client had denied smoking ice on the night in question, and Kim was forced to rephrase his assertion. "Both of them were on ice," he went on. "The defendant denies it, but use your common sense. And it was the *best* time to kill Percy. He was trapped." Kim spent some time depicting the giant Percy, the wheel of the truck jabbing into his stomach, unable to get his hands up in time. His voice rose in anger as he went on, "If Percy had been outside of the truck, if he'd been able to move around, don't you think things might have turned out differently?" He let the question settle, and said, "So not only does the defendant plunge a knife into Percy's heart," taking him from his family, leaving him unable to give his version of the story, "but then he gets up here and *assassinates Percy's character* in front of his whole family, turning him into some kind of psycho monster." He paused, and then finished: "Nothing you can do can bring Percy back to his family. Do your job," he said again, asking them to at least provide the Kipapas with "justice. And convict him for what he did to Percy Kipapa."

THE NEXT DAY, FRIDAY, we all waited—a collection of Kipapas and Meheulas alternately pacing the Circuit Court building's vast atrium of a lobby, or stepping outside to the courtyard, or sitting on the benches along the lobby wall, all speculating on what the jury might be talking about, recapping the various arguments and performances, wondering how long it would take them to decide the defendant's fate. The weight of such a decision aside, we figured the jury probably wanted to get on with their lives, and we hoped the deliberations wouldn't drag into the following week.

"He could still get acquitted, you neva know," Kurt told me. "But he gets convicted, he'll probably serve twenty, twenty-five years, that's good enough."

Mr. Kipapa had studied the makeup of the jury, and he concluded that if the haole woman had been picked as the foreman they would come to a decision quickly, and it would more likely be to convict. In addition to being haole, he reasoned, she was a bit older than most of the jury, and she looked like she'd been to a few meetings in her life. The implication was that no one else in the room would find it appropriate to take charge, to run things, and to force people to back up their assertions in the same way that the more direct-looking woman probably would.

His analysis got me thinking about Glenn Kim's performance, and how it had resonated with the kinds of values we like to think make up "local" identity. Percy's family, all the way back to the *mahele*. The humble farming roots that had no place in private school. Doing your job, making good, big-for-*some*thing. The go-out-of-your-way-for-anybody aloha spirit of Big Happiness. And above all, respect. The very idea of Hawai'i's collective "local" identity had taken root in Percy's valley around the time he was born, when the Waiāhole-Waikāne Community Association banded together ostensibly to preserve the kinds of values his grandfather Manuel Roberts had instilled in his own seven children. In resisting the outsiders who wanted to pave the valleys over for mainland retirement housing, and later, Japanese golf courses, they prevailed because they defined their fight as one of "them" against the unique and admirable "us-guys" group based on the Hawaiian culture of *'ohana*-aloha-respect to which everyone in Hawai'i likes to think they belong—even (perhaps most especially) local haoles. Kim hadn't outright said it (in fact, to say much of anything "outright" would not have been "local"—it would have been patronizing and insulting), but the implication could not have been clearer: Percy was a walking embodiment of these values, and when people like Percy die then part of what makes Hawai'i a unique place, a local place, also dies.

When the jury reached a verdict at just after 2:00, the hallway outside of Judge Sakamoto's courtroom became swelteringly hot, packed with Meheulas jostling against Kipapas. The defendant's sister and mother now crowded in front of the door, the Kipapas having agreed to waive the witness exclusion rule now that the case was over so Venda Meheula could see the fate of her son. Inside the benches quickly filled, and the jury filed in. When he saw that it was the haole woman carrying the folder, Mr. Kipapa gave me a look. She was asked to stand, and then to hand over the folder to the bailiff. The bailiff in turn handed it to the clerk, who read it out: "We, the jury . . . after a unanimous vote. . . . find the defendant guilty as charged."

A wave of relief swept over the back of the courtroom—one that fell short of the opposite front-row bench where Meheula's sister began to sob. I turned to see tears of relief streaming down Tyler's big round face. Kurt had the slightest of smiles on his face. Mr. Kipapa turned to shake my hand. And Meheula did not react at all. "You are ordered to report for sentencing on September the sixth," Judge Sakamoto was saying.

Glenn Kim immediately stood, his job not over: "Your honor, given the severity of the crime and the vicious nature in which it was committed, the state wishes to submit a motion that the defendant's bail be revoked. This is murder two, your honor, the most serious crime a person can commit other than murder one." Though Domingo stood to argue that his client was not a flight risk since he had been free on bail since September without incident, Judge Sakamoto granted the state's request and Meheula was led out the side door of the courtroom by two beefy sheriffs.

LATER THAT NIGHT I squeezed my way around the living room to make a plate from the big foil trays covering the table where Percy and I had first sat and talked story so long ago. The Waimānalo homestead house was now stuffed with Kipapas—Kurt and Jolyn, their sons Joe and Kurty-boy and their wives and kids, Mike and Taylor and Malakai and the rest of Kurt's army of adopted children. Selisa and Kirk showed up with Brando, Bronson, and Brandee—Percy's favorite, his niece. Mr. and Mrs. Kipapa were there, and Tyler, his giant black "In Loving Memory" shirt stretched over his big body, Percy's smiling face beaming out. Cousins and friends and more kids showed up as the night drifted by with big hugs all around and congratulations.

Then everyone started shushing, and someone turned up the volume on one of the two TVs tuned into two different channels for the lead story on the ten o'clock news. First they showed Domingo talking about an appeal. And when Glenn Kim's now-familiar face filled the screen, the room erupted in cheers, finally quieting down in time to hear him point to his observation that Meheula had "accounted for every single wound, no more, no less" as his "most convincing argument." Leaning down slightly to reach the reporter's microphone, he said of Percy's 'ohana, "The immediate family are all really, really *good* people."

The story over, the TVs turned off, I looked around the room to see the same collection of folks who'd loudly seen Percy off to Japan or welcomed him home at gathering after gathering over the years. But the cheers had died quickly, and now the crowded room felt, if anything, quiet. And maybe someone else picked up on it, too—maybe Tyler, maybe everyone there— that right about now, at just this kind of collective lull, was when you would expect to hear that big Daiki laugh shout out across the room and rescue the party from silence.

CHAPTER 13

HONEYBOY

CONCLUSION: Based on these autopsy findings and investiga-
tive and historical information available to me, in my opinion,
this 55-year-old man died as a result of sequela of an accidental fall
due to documented cardiac arrhythmia, namely drowning and a
broken neck. The sand in his upper esophagus and larynx indicates
he aspirated at the time of his fall into the water. Differential blood
chloride levels, while not diagnostic, are with other data consistent
with salt water drowning. There was no injury which could not
have been due to the decedent's striking rocks at the time he was
already unresponsive. He could have sustained the neck fracture
at the time he collapsed onto rocks in the shallow surf at the onset
of his irreversible arrhythmia. Toxicological studies performed on
autopsy blood were negative for alcohol and negative for drugs . . .
The manner of death is, in my opinion, accidental.

—William W. Goodhue Jr., first deputy medical examiner, City and
County of Honolulu, July 13, 2004

KEALI'I MEHEULA'S CONVICTION hadn't brought Percy back to his family, of course, but it also hadn't uncovered what had really happened, and why, on May 16. Glenn Kim's strategy to expose the defendant as a liar had been enough to win. But it hadn't even tried to explore why Meheula would plunge a knife into Percy's heart at a time and in a place where he knew absolutely that he would get caught, then rush to the top of the Rodrigues driveway so he could tell everyone in sight what he'd just done. As Meheula's lawyer had put it, however ineffectively, it didn't make logical sense.

In an effort to find out why Meheula might have done such a thing, I'd finally gathered the nerve to drive up that long and winding driveway on ʻOkana Road a few weeks after the trial knowing that the house had been raided and labeled a "frightening" working meth lab stocked with dangerous chemicals and firearms. The many "Beware of Dog" signs nailed to the trees didn't help any, either. But when Lori Rodrigues came to the door with two adorable kids at her side, everyone dressed nicely for a funeral they were headed for that day, it was impossible to picture her as some kind of chronic, let alone a drug kingpin. After I apologized for just driving right up—try finding the one "Rodrigues" you're looking for in the Oʻahu phone book—and explained what I was up to, she gladly gave me her number and invited me to call the next time I was over from Hilo. Our schedules never worked, but we did speak for over two hours on the phone a few weeks later.

When the bloody, knife-wielding Kealiʻi had shown up in her house that night, Lori told me, she quickly turned to Donna and Venda and sent them to check on Percy. "When I said, 'Go check on Percy,'" she went on, "Venda said, 'Don't say nothing, don't say nothing!' I was like, 'You know what, I have to say something. How do you think *that* family's gonna feel?' The next morning I called someone, because when it showed on the news, 'One died, one wounded,' I was like, 'One *wounded*? What are they talking about?'" Lori called her brother, Keith Ryder, who put her in touch with his good friend James Anderson, an HPD homicide detective. Anderson advised her to cooperate fully with the investigation, which she was more than happy to do.

"It was shocking to me when Kealiʻi came up to my doorway and started saying all this about Percy," she said, "and then the mom just sits there. I mean if it was my son I would be jumping out of my seat. I was like, 'Why?' and you know, 'What was going through her head?' At the moment you don't think nothing, but after a while just thinking about what her reactions were at the time, she wasn't really excited. You know for me, I was like 'What? What?' Venda was just sitting there disgusted and just looking at me. It was no big deal. I don't know, I just keep on thinking, 'What part did she play in it?' I'm thinking like, 'She took long down there' [when she went to check on Percy]. I think of Venda: 'I just don't get it. I mean I hear people saying they seen you guys all day cruising around up in the valley where Percy lives, you guys riding all over and then out of the blues your son comes here and drops you off,' not even at my driveway—it was in the middle of my hill, I mean that wasn't right—usually they just drive up, or she'd call me. She never did call—she just walked up my hill. I didn't hear any car. And the son comes later, half an hour, forty-five minutes and just kind of looks around my house, and goes. What's up with that? I can't help but feel, 'What's that about? Were you giving your mother a warning?' I don't get it."

Since she'd been excluded from the courtroom as a witness, I explained to Lori that Venda and Keali'i's story had been that they'd come to her house to buy drugs.

"That's a lie," she said, without being defensive—she would later speak freely of her own addiction, and her ongoing recovery after graduating from Hina Mauka. "Percy hardly had money! That's what makes me think *more*. Because you know I would just come out straight: 'Yeah, they came for drugs.' But it *wasn't*. And that's what gets me all thinking." She'd even told the detective, "You know, Coons, I have nothing to hide, you know what I mean, and why would I lie? They *didn't*—not once ask or talk about drugs. Why wouldn't Percy come up my house? Why would they drop Venda off in the middle of my driveway?" And then Keali'i appears, knife in hand, spouting out the two lines that, to Lori, sounded almost rehearsed. "'He was stealing my shit,'" she repeated. "'He was fooling around with my girlfriend.' And then he turned to go 'Ma, Ma,' because he knew I knew he was lying."

☾ ☾ ☾

"HIM AND THE MADDA told Percy about Honeyboy," Percy's mother told me, referring to Meheula, "and Percy said he was mad that they did that to him, so now they paranoid. And Honeyboy, they say he don't go in the water. They found him in the water. Hau'ula. And this gal came up to my brother, he's an ex-policeman, and she said, 'You know the sumo wrestler, the one that died? I heard that he knew something about Honeyboy, and they think he going tell the policeman.' So Stanley said, being a cop, you say, 'I heard,' they not going take that. You gotta say 'I *saw*' or 'I *know*.' She said, 'That's the word that's going around, that they wen' kill Honeyboy.'

Short Hawaiian, he used to feed all the birds down Hau'ula, he don't bodda nobody. So they was mad at Percy already. They was aiming for him. But see, my nephew had a girlfriend. One night Percy told her, 'I'm going tell you something, but please take it to the grave.' He told her about Honeyboy. But he neva tell us—he told her."

When Mrs. Kipapa had first brought up Honeyboy a year earlier, I'd considered it so peripheral to my main interest that I hadn't even transcribed what she'd said. It came from an angry place, as though she were just continuing to vent about the terrible man who had taken her son. But Honeyboy kept coming up in other interviews. And now Percy's mother was bringing him up again. At first it had rung with about as much truth as Tyler's Samoan mafia fantasy, where Meheula was "taking the fall for somebody." After Glenn Kim had thoroughly disproved our musta-been-five-guys-wen'-mob-him theory, it began sounding like one of those if-enough-people-say-it-enough-times-then-it's-gotta-be-true stories. But when Percy's mother brought it up again, this time I listened.

So back in Hilo I dug into the state newspaper index's computer search engine and typed in the keywords "Honeyboy" and "Honey Boy." When the words "Body of Hau'ula Man Found Floating at Beach" appeared on the list I knew I was moving from gossip into reality, with half of me not wanting to read on. The article, from a June 2004 issue of the *Honolulu Advertiser*, said that Honeyboy had been found floating face down with a head wound. It quoted Officer John Lambert as saying, "Apparently he slipped on the rocks and hit his head." The article explained that "the case has been classified as an unattended death, pending autopsy. But," it went on, "friends and family members gathered at the scene" pointed out that Honeyboy's change purse and shirt were missing, with his brother saying Honeyboy had not been in the water "since we were small kids."

On my next trip to O'ahu, I drove straight to the Kāne'ohe police station across the street from the fire station where Keali'i Meheula had gone for help after stabbing himself in the leg. I went in, took a deep breath, and asked for Officer Lambert. The officers on duty kindly took turns explaining to me that he worked at the Kahuku station. They handed me a Post-it with the number written on it, offered to call Lambert for me, and when I declined, gave me directions to Kahuku.

In Kahuku I had to be buzzed into the building. After shouting through the thick glass separating the lobby area from the office that I was looking for Officer Lambert, I waited for a couple of minutes listening to somebody's mother sobbing into her cell phone as she sat on the hard wooden bench behind me. When Lambert appeared, he neither invited me in nor stepped out to speak with me, so I shouted through the glass again, explaining my project and how it had led me to Honeyboy, and did he remember the case—all in as condensed a version as possible since he was making it absolutely clear that I was wasting his time. He gave me the identical line he'd given the *Advertiser* reporter three years earlier about Honeyboy falling off the wall, this time adding the word "seizure." Pleading ignorance into his line of work, I gave him every chance to come away with the benefit of the doubt when I asked if the death was ever investigated further, but he shook his head, told me it was an "unattended death," and that I could call HPD's Criminal Investigation Division if I had any other questions, indicating that the conversation was over.

The brief article in the *Advertiser* had also painted Honeyboy as one of those well-liked small-town fixtures whom everyone knows—a lot like Percy—so when I saw a big local guy patrolling the beach park with a leaf blower as I drove back through Hauʻula, I stopped. Of course he knew Honeyboy, and he referred me to Sam—the guy from the City and County Parks who was then walking towards us. Sam told me that Honeyboy had always had candy and cookies for the kids, and that when he walked home in the afternoon a whole flock of them would follow along. I asked why the death had never been investigated, and he offered that maybe the family just wanted to let it go, to finish with the peaceful narrative that God had taken him, that it was his time. Still, he pointed out where Honeyboy's sister lived in Hauʻula, and where his brother—the one quoted in the newspaper—lived in Kahana Valley.

When I pulled up to the little house up in the valley, a solid-looking Hawaiian man dressed in farmer's overalls walked out to greet me, his eyes narrowed into a warm smile, gray sideburns reaching down from under the bandana covering his head. He shook my hand warmly as I introduced myself and apologized for just showing up. I explained that I was writing about Percy. He listened respectfully as I went on about how gossip and rumors surround such things as a guy getting stabbed to death in Kahaluʻu, and that I was trying to eliminate a rumor that involved his brother. "I know it's been three years," I said, "and if you'd rather let it rest and not bring any of it up again, I'm happy to drive away right now. I don't even know if it will wind up being that important."

"Come," he said, and then turned to lead me down a steep grassy incline to two folding metal chairs set up under the back of the house, which was supported by head-high posts. He lit a cigarette, the homemade "Primo" tattoo on his softball-sized fist revealing a clear difference between himself and his Pied Piper brother. And for the next two hours I listened as he talked about Honeyboy, growing up in Hauʻula in the 1960s, and how certain he was that his brother had been murdered.

First it was the plastic money case that Honeyboy kept around his neck, the T-shirt, the fact that they'd found him in the water. And then there was a Samoan guy, Pisaga—"They call 'im 'Saga'"—who had been driving by Hauʻula Beach Park around the time of "my brother's murder," he said. "He saw, it looked like somebody pushing one log, yeah? Like hour later, then he finds out that Honeyboy, that's who they found in the water. And I ask him: 'What kind guy was? Pushing the log.' 'Ho, he looked like one Portagee guy.' And to him, he thought, 'Ho, what's this guy doing pushing one log in the water, and at high tide too, ah?' But neva dawned on him. And then he see the guy running down on the beach, he neva know where the guy went, yeah? So he come back off the beach, go home. And an hour later he find out they find Honeyboy in the water. 'Ho shit, I was right there, I seen one guy pushing . . . I thought it was one log!'"

Honeyboy's brother went into the "unattended death" narrative, speaking slowly to make his point: "Was high tide. And how can be high tide, Honeyboy no swim, falls off the wall, supposedly, breaks his neck, and drowns. And sand bottom. The next morning I wen' there and look. There's no rocks. Get sand, and you know the drop is kind of high. It's over three feet, and even though you going fall, at high tide you just going fall in the water, and you neva hit notting on the bottom 'cause there's only sand." He recalled that the detective investigating the area fronting the wall was up to her waist in water. "When I went down there, my brother was already on the gurney. The police officer wen' lift up the sheet—Dr. Shlachter gotta pronounce him dead, yeah? Then I seen his forehead is like a massive, like somebody wen' hit'im with *some*thing. Swollen, a big bash, and get blood, like he was hit with one object. How the hell the sheet get blood on the sheet? And don't tell me the water was banging him up against the wall—he'd be *damaged*, his face, not only that one area on his forehead. And my bradda, he's not a fighter. I tell you somet'ing, you go every island, even the mainland, yeah?" and off he went into a Honeyboy story like the one Sam had told me at the beach park, this one about Honeyboy disappearing at the airport. "You go to the place where we supposed to go? He's already there. Somebody knew him" and gave him a ride.

As the cigarette butts accumulated in the can by his chair, his monologue drifted back into other Honeyboy memories; a 1960s memory of a Hauʻula neighbor's hedge, square-cut like a hibiscus hedge but made of budding pakalolo; the recent history of Kahana Valley. And then almost as an afterthought, he hit me with this: "And you know one nodda t'ing too, yeah? Last year, when Meheula wen' get sentenced. I was down there in the coconut grove" at the entrance to Kahana Valley. "And this wahine, she's a prison guard at Hālawa. This white Nissan SUV comin' in, and this person was waving at me." He said the woman, a former Hauʻula neighbor named Luka Kahele, had been looking for him after overhearing Venda Meheula say she had killed Honeyboy. "Luka told me, 'Eh, if you need da kine, we can back that story up because I was right there in my friend's house, and she put on the speaker phone and Venda was telling her friend everything why Percy died,'" he told me. "And Luka was saying that Percy died because he was going say something about Honeyboy's murder. Not 'Honeyboy's death' now. It was like, 'murder.'"

I asked about an investigation, and he said he'd repeatedly called a detective named Frank Camero, leaving messages advising the detectives to go after Meheula rather than rely on the medical examiner's report, which had concluded that Honeyboy had drowned. "And no return calls. Nothing. And you know what? We didn't even get back my brother's personal stuffs. You know supposedly they find that stuff, that one that hang on his neck? We neva get nothing back—his ID, you know all the stuff that was on him. Especially that container that was always on his neck, that's where he hold his money, his medication. I'm calling his office and leaving all these messages to tell him, 'You guys, you gotta go and check up on this guy Meheula, because he had somet'ing to do with my brother's murder.' That's why Percy died. It's because, gotta be wen' bodda him, and he was going say something."

I drove up to Hau'ula again the next day—passing the road signs for Ka'a'awa, Kahana, Punalu'u, Hau'ula, Lā'ie, and Kahuku, which weren't just signs anymore but rather the towns Percy and Charles and Shane would check out when they cruised to the beach back in high school, and where Bob Nakata had learned about the pervasive ice problem in 2002. And they were places where, I was learning, it was remarkably easy to find whomever you were looking for. Right now I was looking for Saga.

But when I pulled over just past the bus stop in Hau'ula, I saw a weathered board with the painted word "Honeyboy" nailed to a pine tree, and a tattered white sandwich-board sign still standing, its black hardware-store stick-on capital letters reading "ALOHA" and "LEIS AND COOKIES FOR SALE." Shaded with pines, coconut trees, and a big monkeypod tree, this would have been the perfect spot to wait for the tourists to pass, cooled by the stiff breeze coming off the emerald ocean. I later learned that, because of the trees, everyone called the place "Jungles." The area was ringed with the rounded rock wall remains of some colonial house—a full square foundation on the opposite side of the bus stop, and the odd ruined wall on Honeyboy's side. The ocean frothed with strong rips and eddies criss-crossing over a shallow reef at low tide—hardly a place for anyone to be swimming, let alone a big man who had not set foot in the water for some forty years. Not fifty feet from the road, I found a place behind a head-high section of the wall remains next to a thick *hau* bush where I was completely hidden from the road. Honeyboy could easily have been lured there—especially by someone he knew—and then mugged for the plastic case around his neck without anyone knowing. And then they throw him in the water?

This detective work might have been fun in some sort of Magnum P.I. way, except that now I had a much better sense of Honeyboy as a real person with a loving family of his own. This was no cop show—someone had likely violently killed a universally loved human being right here, where a hand-scrawled *Honeyboy, in loving memory* sign still weathered away in the salt air more than three years later. I took a long look at the homemade memorial, got a few pictures, and drove off, having lost the nerve to start asking around for Saga.

TWO WEEKS LATER I was back on Oʻahu at the bedside of Willidean Makepa. A couple of years older than Percy, Dean had grown up in Waiāhole and lived for a few years just up Waikāne Valley Road from Percy. A self-described tough-girl "tita," Dean drove a Comanche, handled herself well on dirt bikes, chopped wood, and was a pretty good mechanic before she was run off the road one day near Waiāhole Beach Park, where she wound up flipping her bike in a ditch and breaking her neck. Now a quadriplegic with limited use of her hands, she had a miraculously positive outlook on life.

"It was a blessing in disguise," she told me of her accident.

We spent nearly two hours talking about her life in Waiāhole and Waikāne, and about how close she'd gotten to Percy the last couple of years of his life, and even how well she'd known Meheula. "Kealiʻi used to go with my cousin," she told me. "But I neva knew he would be like that, to, you know, kill anybody. I used to hang out with the mom all the time. We always used to cruise together. My cousin knew her from in the eighties. We was good friends. I don't know what happened. I neva would dream in a million years that this would happen. We all was shocked." Clearly, she had no reason to make anything up or say anything negative about Meheula or his mother. "I neva thought that would happen because him and Percy, they was close friends," she went on. "He was always the hunter kind type. Couple times we would be driving in the mountain, we would see Percy and Kealiʻi kicking back, listening to the radio. And I guess Percy knew something about Kealiʻi, and knowing the type that Kealiʻi is, so paranoid, I think that's the reason why he did that to Percy, because Percy knew. It was so sad, because you know," she went on, "two weeks before it wen' happen, he confided in me, and this other friend of his, Joshua Wilson. It was like he knew he was going die. There was couple times we was having some beers together while we was waiting for his cousin, and he loves to sing! We was trying to harmonize. And then he said, 'You know Dean,' like he would confide in me in some stuff about Kealiʻi."

Before we finished, I asked her if she'd be willing to talk to a detective about all that she'd told me.

"I did," she said. "I wen' talk to one detective—I think it was Randall something. It was over the phone. I seen Joshua Wilson at the beach park, and he told me 'Dean, I wen' talk to one detective and they like talk to you for, you know, what Percy was telling you.' I told him, 'Why? You wen' talk to them already?' He go, 'Yeah. Wait, I go call 'em up for you.' And the detective told me, 'I like meet with you,' and stuff li'dat, and then I waited. I told him over the phone briefly, but not really get into it. He said, 'Let's talk about it more over lunch or something, I'll meet with you and Joshua.' But I never did meet up with him."

These four-day trips to Oʻahu were giving me a sense of urgency to find out as much as I could before going back to Hilo, where I would try to piece together what was turning into a stack of rumors, gossip, and the half-remembered stories of two- and three-year-old events told by people who had been trying to forget them, some of whom had been using ice for more than twenty years. So two mornings later I was back in front of the rock wall up in Hauʻula, when a round old uncle walking the beach met me with a smile, happy to tell me where Saga lived back down near Crouching Lion. He added that Saga often stopped by his sister's house just down the street from the Hauʻula bus stop after his morning swim. The house was easy enough to find, and when I explained to Saga's gray-haired sister why I wanted to talk with him, she called him up and handed me her cell phone. I tried to be vague, hoping to set up a meeting where I could make him more comfortable, but he wanted details. "Well, it's about Honeyboy," I said. "I was talking with his brother the other day, and he said you might have seen something."

"No, I neva see notting," he said.

"Nah nah nah," I said. "It's not like that—he meant before it happened, that you saw some guy hanging around."

"No, sorry, bradda. I neva see notting."

The call got cut off, so I handed the phone back to Saga's sister and thanked her.

"Did you get the information you were looking for?" she asked.

"Not really," I told her. "But that just means that what I was looking for was just another rumor, so in a way it was a big help."

She gave me Saga's number anyway.

I felt kind of bad that our call had been cut off before I could explain everything, and I imagined him getting angry at Honeyboy's brother for maybe implicating him as a witness, or even an accessory: "What, you said I wen' see somet'ing!" So I called him again just to clear it up.

"Eh, I'm glad you wen' call me back!" Saga said immediately. "See, I been t'inking: I *did* see somet'ing that morning. Looked like one Portagee guy sitting on top the wall, on the right side of the bus stop."

I pulled over to get the whole thing, and wound up directly facing the bus stop and the ocean behind it. On the right was the nearly intact square foundation of the old rock wall, and to the left of the bus stop were the thicker trees and Honeyboy's sign. Saga went on animatedly about a guy wearing a hooded sweatshirt sitting on the rock wall looking up towards the 7-Eleven side, where Honeyboy would be. "Was one young guy," he said, "maybe twenty-six, twenty-seven, and he kept *looking*. Real early in the morning, was." Saga went swimming every morning, he told me, and he'd never seen this guy before or since.

"Didn't you see him pushing a log in the water?"

"No, that was the firemen," he said. He'd later gone for his usual long swim, and by the time he'd gotten out, the cops and firefighters were on the scene, pulling the now-stiffened shirtless corpse from the water. From a distance it had looked at first like a log.

I told him how Honeyboy's brother remembered it, with the Portagee-looking guy pushing the log through the water.

"He get 'um wrong," Saga said. We laughed about how the brain works at recalling certain things, and speculated how a brother's memories would have been simmering in anger, leading to a much different story. "But I seen da guy," he said. He invited me to call him any time, and seemed happy to do all he could to help catch the guy who killed Honeyboy.

☾   ☾   ☾

AFTER WEEKS OF CALLING Luka Kahele's unit at Hālawa, all the while trying to figure out the protocol for calling someone out of nowhere and asking them to talk in detail about a murder, I finally got in touch with her and somehow managed to persuade her to meet me the following Saturday at Hauʻula Beach Park. (She joked, half-seriously, that she'd worried the repeated phone calls had been coming from an obsessed inmate.) I got to Hauʻula early enough that day to drive around Homestead Road, and I saw Saga's gunmetal-gray Explorer parked in front of his sister's house. Saga, gray-haired like his sister but with the long, wiry body of a guy who swims a lot, greeted me like a long-lost friend—a big hug and a how-you-my-bradda. He went through the whole story again, wide-eyed now and pointing this way and that—except when he was animatedly acting out the shifty Portagee-guy's part. He explained that when the guy saw that he was being watched, he started walking, making like he was on his way somewhere rather than just sitting there stalking. "I seen the guy twice," Saga said this time. "I rememba now. I seen him couple days before. And then I seen him that day. And then I neva seen him again." Again he insisted that I call him if I needed any more help.

Luka was easy to pick out at the beach park pavilion. She had the size to not be messed with, and the warm face that explained why she might be concerned that some inmate would want to find her upon his release. As it turned out, she was a good friend of Percy's sister-in-law Jolyn. "Actually Jolyn gave me a call" not long after Meheula had been convicted, she said, explaining that one of Percy's friends had told her the Honeyboy story. "The girl that was on the phone—and I was on the phone with Jolyn, we had a three-way call—she was saying that that's why he did it to Percy: because he was telling people what had happened." So now the story went that the same Percy Kipapa who had been ready to give up his sumo career before ratting out Troy, who had held the Honeyboy story inside for nearly a year before spilling his guts one night to two trusted friends as he feared for his life, was now "telling people." "When the actual call came," Luka went on, "Jolyn wanted me to know this because she knew that I knew Honeyboy's family. Honeyboy's family had stuck with the examiner's report saying that it was natural causes. It was a tough decision for me to tell them, because I knew that their family wanted to let it rest. I don't know. I told him because I had to."

I asked her to tell me exactly what she'd heard on the phone, and from whom.

"Basically what I heard on the phone was, they know the reason why Keali'i had killed Percy was because Percy knew about Keali'i murdering Honeyboy, and Percy was going out and telling people."

"You want to hear what you told Honeyboy's brother?" I asked her, and she laughed. I explained his version of how Luka had told him she'd heard Venda on speakerphone.

"Oh, no, that's not how it worked," she said. "Trust me, if I'd have heard Venda, I would have called HPD! I would have recorded it or something. But at that time it was mind-boggling trying to remember all these things because Jolyn just called me out of the blues and goes, 'Listen, you gotta listen to this girl.' Out of the blues, and it started getting interesting, and I was like, 'Wow, this girl does have a lot of information.'"

I told her what Saga had told me, about having seen the Portagee guy twice.

"According to the girl," she said, "it was planned. They planned to hit him. They knew Honeyboy had money—he had cash on him all the time from selling leis. All of us knew Honeyboy always had money on him. But Honeyboy wasn't smart—he didn't know how to count, he didn't know how to read and write—so a lot of people would pick on him. He would always give the kids money to go buy stuff, but if you're from the community, you know Honeyboy and that was just Honeyboy. We knew it had to be someone who wasn't really from around here that killed him. He was the nicest person."

"So why wasn't it investigated?"

"I remember because he died on my birthday," she said. "Honeyboy never took his shirt off. *Never* took his shirt off. He always had a rope with a plastic container on it with all his goodies inside—he never took it off of him. He never goes into the water. And when they found him he was in the water with no T-shirt on, his thing wasn't around his neck. And that wasn't Honeyboy. He had a big bump on his head, and when the doctor came to pronounce him, he said foul play was involved. Dr. Shlachter, from Lāʻie. He did say it was foul play, and they wanted it investigated, and it wasn't investigated."

"The cop in Kahuku told me he had a seizure."

"No, he had a pacemaker," she said. "So then the Honolulu medical examiners came to pick up his body, and they left it there for a while to do their investigation, and everybody knew. His whole family was there, and we all told the cops: 'There's *no way* he took his shirt off. There's *no way* he took his money thing off of his neck. There's *no way* he would be in the water, and there was no reason for that,' and they still classified it as an unattended death."

LUKA ALSO HAPPENED TO KNOW Joshua Wilson, so before we parted she directed me to his parents' house and told me what his truck looked like. I found the truck first, out in front of one of the houses in Ka'a'awa that look across the highway and right onto the ocean. It was parked on the thin strip of grass by the fence: a black lifted four-by-four with tinted windows and chrome rims. Inside the gate a screaming rottweiler was chained to a post by the front door. Beyond that I could see a sullen-looking young guy with a goatee working with an older man on a length of hollow-tile wall, a trough of wet cement between them, a woman looking on. I waved and smiled as I approached—an apology for just walking right into their yard—and introduced myself over the fierce barking of the dog.

"I'm looking for Joshua Wilson," I said, trying not to sound like a cop. "I'm a friend of Percy Kipapa's."

The guy with the goatee lifted his hand as if to identify himself, while his father looked on suspiciously. I reached out to shake his hand as I introduced myself, but he looked down, almost embarrassed that his own hand was filthy with the cement. I shook it anyway and explained that I was writing a book, and I had been looking for him to talk story about it. "Not now, I mean—I can see you're busy."

"Yeah, yeah," he said.

"It doesn't have to be now, or even today. I'm sorry to just walk up here like this." I looked at his father, and then back to Joshua. "It's just that I saw your truck outside. I just talked to Luka Kahele and she told me what you drive, so."

"How about tomorrow?"

He gave me his number and we set up a time for the next morning.

When I got to his house the next day, the rottweiler screamed as before. Josh greeted me with a handshake and led me around the back of the house, which they had stripped and sanded as part of what was looking like a major renovation. We sat at a picnic table in the backyard, which opened out onto a valley greener and deeper than even Percy's beloved Waikāne, and for over an hour we talked. Josh had known Percy since the fifth grade, and he had seen him daily in the months before his murder. He told me that Percy had given him a *yukata*—the robe that young *sumōtori* wear. When I brought up Percy's encounter with the Red Rags at King Zoo, his thin lips curled up in the hint of a smile. "That's how Percy was, though," he said, speaking slowly, full of humility. "He was a gentle giant. I mean, plenty times me and him got into it, but he would always back down kine, when he could probably just manhandle you."

I wasn't sure how to bring up Honeyboy, but then Josh did it for me.

"Percy already knew that something was going to happen," he said, "'cause he told us that the guy was gonna kill him. He told me and Willidean that."

"Do you remember him telling you that?" I asked him. "Do you remember the situation when he told you? Dean said he told you folks separately."

"He told her before, and then it just so happened that I was down Waiāhole Beach Park, and the guy's mother—she told me she wanted to kill him. Venda told me she wanted to kill Percy for, Percy was trying for go there with her or something. I just was listening, you know what I mean, 'Yeah, yeah, yeah.' So I went driving up Percy's road, I seen Percy there with Willidean, I wen' stop right there, I told him, 'Eh, Percy. How come? Venda, she like kill you, ah?'" And then Percy, having just unburdened himself to Dean, repeated the story for Josh. "He said they wen' go beat up that one guy in Hau'ula," Josh went on, "Honeyboy, and t'rew him in the water not knowing he didn't know how for swim. And they went straight up to Percy's house, and they was bragging to him about what they took from the guy."

"That plastic thing he kept around his neck," I said.

"His little container. He always sold dope, ah? Weed, ice, or whatever."

This bit of information came out as matter-of-factly as the story about meeting Percy in fifth grade. Josh said it as though it was something everyone already knew about Honeyboy.

"He sold ice?" I finally asked.

"Occasionally. From what I understand. He sold weed for years. That was his thing, yeah? That and leis."

"So the guy was a good target," I said, trying to move on, but still thinking, *Honeyboy? Ice?* How had Luka put it? *That plastic container with all his goodies inside—he never took that off.* Goodies.

"Yeah, because he was pretty much helpless, Honeyboy," Josh went on. "Honeyboy is a nodda one just like Percy. He got along with everybody.

He was a real humble, humble, man. I knew Honeyboy pretty long, too. 'Cause when I was young, we used to go up to Kahana and Honeyboy was always around. And he was in Hauʻula for a long time. He always sat over there at that bus stop, by that wall. He was there for years. He was harmless. And they was bragging how they did it," he went on. "They told Percy how they threw him in the water, not knowing that they killed the guy. They didn't know."

"And then they find out that they killed the guy and it's time to shut up."

"Yep. And I mean, word travels fast that the guy is dead. And the thing was, Percy knew, ah? That's why Percy said he had the feeling that . . . Kealiʻi was in jail at that time, and what he told me and Willidean was, that when Kealiʻi came out, Kealiʻi going kill him."

"People are remembering this as 'Percy was there when it happened,'" I told him, "or 'They wanted him to come, but he said no, I'm not li'dat.' But you're remembering it as they came and told him about it *after* because they didn't know Honeyboy was dead."

"That's what Percy told me."

"You really clearly remember it that way. It's not, 'He must have said. . . . ' You really clearly remember him saying it that way."

"That's what he said," Josh said again. "He said that Kealiʻi was going to come back to kill him because he knew what they had done."

"But he explained to you how he came about knowing it."

"That's how he found out, because after they did it, they went straight to his house. They was bragging to him about what they just did, and what they took."

"I don't mean to be grilling you but . . ."

"Oh, no no no," he said, indicating that he didn't mind.

I explained how I'd come to find how anger had shaped the memories of Honeyboy's brother. "But you clearly remember Percy saying that he found out about Honeyboy because they had done it already, and then they told him about it, they were bragging about it."

"They went up there to turn him on," he said, "and they was bragging to him about what they did."

"Because they suddenly had stuff."

"What he told me was, they said 'Guess where we got this stuff? Guess where we got 'um from?'"

We sat and let this sink in, and then I told him that another version of the story involved Percy getting killed because he was "telling people."

"I don't think Percy told really anybody," Josh reasoned, "because he had a hard time telling me, and we was brought up from small time. And he only told me because I was confronting him about Venda—that's the only reason he told me." What had Kaleo said? *Percy, him, he probably kept a lot of things to himself. If something's wrong, he just going back up in his own corner and just wait it out.* Or as Fats had put it, Percy not going squeal.

"And Venda had wanted to kill him before he'd even told you," I said.

"She told me straight she wanted to kill him," he said. "She told me anodda t'ing: 'He's lucky my son ain't out. 'Cause I'll make him killim.' She's parked inside there by the beach."

Josh was ready to go on for much longer if I'd wanted to. I thanked him for putting up with my questions, my having just shown up out of nowhere, and I assured him that if I included any of the sensitive stuff he'd just told me about, I'd show him a draft and make sure he was okay with it. "You can put whateva down, it don't bodda me," he said, lifting his palms off the table. "The truth is—you know what I mean?"

As I drove off, the small grove of pines between the highway and the windswept ocean reminded me immediately of Jungles, and the now-weathered "Honeyboy" sign still hammered to a tree up there in Hauʻula. I pictured Honeyboy handing out cookies to all of the little Hauʻula kids, or waiting beside the road for a ride to Wahiawā to buy his pies. There he sat in his spot taking pictures with busloads of happy tourists, everyone buying a lei and a couple of gardenias. "He's just Mr. Aloha," someone else from Hauʻula had told me. "Happy-go-lucky." The terms everyone used were "He knew everybody" and "He was the sweetest guy"—the same terms everyone always used to describe Percy. I could see Honeyboy walking home, followed by a flock of neighborhood kids.

Josh's story, Dean's story, Luka's story all brought me back to the trial, to the Kealiʻi Meheula *story* that Glenn Kim had been able to dismiss as so much fantasy. *Unless he can convince you that Percy was acting like a monster that night, self-defense goes out the window.* A monster. We all know Percy was no monster, just as we know it is physically impossible for a 430-pound man stuck behind the steering wheel to reach up with his right hand and choke the man in the passenger seat. But everyone's lie is built upon some foundation of truth. Percy and Keali'i going up into the valley smoking ice day after day—I didn't want to believe it when I heard it at the trial, but I'd come to admit that it was probably true. And then I later learned enough about addiction to point out its truth without making excuses for Percy or judging him. Percy's sullen mood that night—Maydell Pakele's testimony that he looked like he had something on his mind, even Mr. Kipapa's memory of his behavior earlier that day corroborated the description. But the part of Meheula's story that came to ring truest of all was the moment when he and Percy were sitting in the dark on Waikāne Valley Road and, as Meheula told it, "He started snapping at me, telling me why was I talking shit about him ratting on me." I hadn't believed any of this at the trial because I hadn't heard about Percy taking the fall up in Nagoya after banging the police car. I didn't know enough about the kind of local-boy loyalties that would get Troy to say, "He took 'um by himself, brah. He took 'um like a *man*." Back then I didn't know much about addiction either, and how frightening it might be for an addict to be labeled a "rat" and then watch his supply get cut off. And I didn't know anything about Honeyboy yet. Snapping? Of course Percy was snapping. Percy *wasn't himself?* Well, no. He wasn't.

Now listen to the abrupt change in Meheula's language when William Domingo prompts him about what Percy might have had on him to rat him out: "About my drug sales in the past." Compared to what comes directly before, he says it with precision, a well-rehearsed line someone else could have written. As Domingo might have put it himself, this didn't make logical sense. Why would an addict rat out a friend who was a dealer? Or any dealer? Sure, Percy and Keali'i were talking about "ratting" as they sat there in the dark. But was it really about "drug sales in the past"? Hadn't Percy driven past the tattered remnants of Honeyboy's lei stand often enough to feel guilty about "eating it" for so long? Was he trying to convince his friend to admit it had been a big mistake? That he'd only intended to rob Honeyboy? That he had no idea the guy couldn't swim? *Wasn't himself.* The image of Percy "snapping," combined with Venda's recent threats to unleash her pit-bull son, with Keali'i's recent threats from jail, and with

Keali'i's own testimony, all further suggest it wasn't the first time they'd had the discussion. And maybe just bringing it up again had been enough to set Keali'i off on the kind of paranoid "rampage" he was known to fall into, accentuated by the ice that they had both just smoked.

And maybe it wasn't even true—a possibility that might also explain such a rampage. The "Frank Camero" that Honeyboy's brother had told me about turned out to be HPD homicide detective Phil Camaro, who set up a meeting for me with detectives Roland Takasato (undoubtedly Dean's "Randall something") and James Anderson, the ex-father-in-law of Keali'i's sister. The two detectives imagined how the "seizure" theory would have gained traction, particularly since someone had called Honeyboy's personal doctor. A body already in the stages of rigor mortis ("like one log") could have been pronounced dead over the phone, they said. And the "pacemaker" theory could just as easily have confirmed the seizure, as it did in the autopsy. Nevertheless, they assured me an investigation was indeed underway—though they refused to go into any detail, citing the privacy rights of people they'd interviewed. They went on to promise me they would follow up with Honeyboy's brother and with Saga. They also advised me not to show Saga a picture of Keali'i, as I had planned, because now that I had spoken to the police I had what they called "agency," meaning that it could be argued in court that the police had sent me to push Saga towards identifying a particular person. Two years later, I found that they hadn't bothered to call either Honeyboy's brother or Saga, and their investigation has apparently gone nowhere. I have also since received a short but rambling typewritten answer to my request for an interview from Keali'i Meheula, who began serving a fifty-five-year minimum sentence in Arizona after losing his appeal in 2007. He declined to speak with me, and he asked that I leave his name out of any book about Percy. So we may never know.

But what we absolutely do know is that whether or not Keali'i killed Honeyboy, *Percy believed he did*, and that even if he had come to believe it in some other way than how he'd told Josh and Dean—and Percy was nothing if not perceptive—it was because he, too, knew that Honeyboy was selling ice. Keith Ryder's cousin out on the barge, Venda Meheula with her 1998 drug conviction, my own dealer friend who put his "fuckin' *ass* into it" enough to get right up next to "the load"—they had all gone out and found ice. But Honeyboy *was* "the sweetest guy." Josh Wilson hadn't just revealed to me some secret "dark" side to him. In fact, Keith Ryder would later tell me that everyone knew Honeyboy was dealing. But you couldn't just dismiss Honeyboy as some evil drug pusher any more than you could lump Percy in with the gun-toting, child-neglecting chronics in Edgy Lee's movie. What had Luka told me? *Honeyboy wasn't smart—he didn't know how to count, he didn't know how to read or write—so a lot of people would pick on him.* If you're the dealer who fed Honeyboy, the setup couldn't have been any more perfect, because by all accounts he would hardly have known the difference between your crystals and the leis Mrs. Beppo gave him to sell. Mr. Aloha would have thought he was *helping* you. No, Honeyboy hadn't gone out and found ice. Ice had marched out of Kāneʻohe to zap Kahaluʻu, and then zap Waiāhole and Waikāne, and then zap every Windward community all the way to Hauʻula, and it had found him.

CHAPTER 14

THE FALL

State and City public planning agencies have expressed concern for maintaining the element of choice in the selection of homes and lifestyles. It would appear, however, with projected development in the Study Area, choice would merely become limited to a rather narrow range of price alternatives. The spacial imperatives of traditional lifestyles and subsistence patterns of communing with nature could not survive in such an environment. . . . Further, with encroaching residential development and related higher housing costs and land and tax values, a portion of the Study Area residents would either be tempted or forced to abandon their traditional ways of life and employment and accept the historical and tragic trend of welfare or menial city jobs and the high density urban squalor of public housing.

—Eckbo, Dean, Austin, and Williams, *H-3 Socio-Economic Study: The Effects of Change on a Windward Oahu Rural Community*, 1973

WHEN THE BOMBS STARTED RAINING DOWN on her family's Waikāne land just after Pearl Harbor, Percy's great-aunty Ellen Roberts heard more than just the earth-shaking explosions. The blasts announced yet another offensive in the invasion her own father had begun fighting off just after the Great Mahele, when the 1,756.8-acre "Ahupua'a of Waikāne" kuleana was purchased from the government by former missionary E. O. Hall, whom historian Jon Osorio quotes as having argued publicly that the "so recently barbarous" Hawaiians were not ready for "all of the liberties that can properly be bestowed upon them." The valley's thirty-five original resident families—all Hawaiian—spent the next twelve years scraping up enough money to buy the land back from Hall. They formed the Hui Kuai ʻAina o Waikāne, complete with a constitution and by-laws to preserve their traditional common land use practices. But then Lincoln McCandless began picking off the thirty-five *hui* shares one by one. By 1929, he claimed to have grabbed thirty-one and a half shares, thus forcing Aunty Ellen to sue him in Land Court to quiet title on her family's two original shares—a suit yet to be settled in 1942. McCandless had long since begun leasing common valley land out to Japanese tenant farmers, less for profit than to stake a more tangible claim for himself. And then when Aunty Ellen saw hundreds of American soldiers literally invading her ancestral land ostensibly for the same reason, McCandless's daughter having leased out the rest of the valley for the Waikāne Training Facility, she knew that a dragged-out lawsuit would not be enough to save the Roberts legacy.

So she ordered Percy's grandfather Manuel and his seven children to move into the valley. "That was his favorite aunty," Percy's uncle Henry Roberts told me. "I rememba going down to the Kamaka residence with her—and those days they neva had truck, four-wheel drive, or whateva, so she told the boys to go saddle four horses. I was ten at the time, and I was always on my fadda's side. So we went up in the valley, and she said ʻManauela, this is our kuleana. Fence ʻum up, and work the land.'" The thirty-one-year-old Manuel may have thought to move elsewhere or to do something other than farming—his options back then not limited to being a "ten-dolla whore" greeting affluent tourists—but he knew that when Aunty tells you to do something, you don't ask questions. You do what she says, even if it means changing your last name from that of your stepfather to Roberts. "The next day—*the next day*—we was up there with sickles cutting the California grass, the *honohono* grass," Uncle Henry went on. "By the end of the week we was planting taro."

"Percy knew all this, but he could not do notting," his mother told me. "Day in, day out, he sat on that hill looking down on that land." That was why a couple of months after the funeral, on Percy's birthday, his family made the trek up to Grandpa's Hill. There they waited for a good stiff breeze to spread his ashes out far over the rugged jungle that had once been the Roberts farm that Mrs. Kipapa described in the ten pages of memoir she'd written the night before I came to talk about her father. In neatly written script, her pages begin:

Dad: Manuel Roberts, Born 10/25/1909 to Cecilia Roberts out of wedlock.

Dad said what he knows is his father was a merchant seaman. An accident caused his father to die at sea. His mother was pregnant with Dad when she met this man named Kahikina. She married him and had two sons and one daughter. Dad was half-Hawaiian and spoke beautiful Hawaiian. I used to love to hear him pray in Hawaiian before we went to sleep.

We were farmers. We ate off the land. We had taro. When we needed meat, Dad would slaughter a cow or a pig. We got milk from the cows, all fifteen grandchildren. My job was to milk three cows twice a day. One cow would give 14 quarts in the morning and the evening. Then we would pasteurize it before the children drank it. We had healthy children. The chickens laid eggs, so we had eggs also. Lunch and dinner we always had tomato and cucumber. If there was no cold cuts we would make sandwich with onion, tomato, cucumbers, and mayonnaise. As far as your eyes could see, we had long rows of Chinese peas and string beans. Sometimes I wanted to cry because it seemed like there was no end to these rows. We had to water the plants with a fireman's hose. Dad would go to the Fire Station and ask for an old throw-away hose. Then he would generate water from our spring water well. He called it *hana wai*—work the water. He would say, "*Hele hele huki* the *lepo*"—hurry up and push the dirt so the water don't run away. It was a hard job.

We had pigs, ducks, turkeys, chickens. We had maybe fifteen cows Dad would let go in pastures. We had sweet potatoes growing in the mountains, lush green onions. When we harvest, we would go to the river nearby to wash the green onion. The land was so rich we could grow anything. We belonged to the land. We had 3 acres of taro we had to harvest every Thursday and Friday. We made poi every Friday night. Dad and my brothers would *kālua* a pig. Mom would make 'ahi—Hawaiians' favorite fish. Dad would deliver it all every Saturday. We had a stall at Ala Moana. By 11:00 a.m., always sold out.

"By 1950 we had one of the biggest sweet potato farms in Hawai'i." Uncle Henry went on. By the time George Kipapa began coming to the valley in 1959, the Roberts' farm was thriving. "You been up there, ah?" Mr. Kipapa asked me. "Okay. If you take the road going up, that road going up to the left is the flats. You take the road going down, you come by the big mango trees over there? That's the portion of land over there that we were farming. And you go further up, all the *mauka* side on the left side, we used to farm on that land. And you drive further, there's another property that we were farming." Though Manuel Roberts could have easily fed his family on just one of these parcels, more important was that he push back against the relentless creep of McCandless's Japanese tenant farmers and the soldiers at the training facility. The tractor he used to plow his farm even had the kind of caterpillar treads found on a tank. It's easy to picture him driving it like one as he marked off what he figured amounted to two thirty-fifths of the *ahupua'a*, one man against the entire Marine Corps.

And just as another star was being added to the flag he sometimes saw those marines carry into his valley, the family's tenuous hold on the land strengthened further—just the way Aunty Ellen had hoped: Manuel's daughter Priscilla was pregnant. Kurt Kipapa came into the world weighing nearly ten pounds, bringing the joy a baby brings to any Hawaiian family. But the birth had been difficult, and the joy came with news that, in its full cultural context, was tragic. "The doctor called me out the room," Mr. Kipapa told me, "and he suggested to me not to have any more kids. I look at him, I tell him, 'You know I come from a big family.' When I had the break of the news like that, I was sad. I felt I was being punished. 'What happened? Why was I put in this situation?'" When the three Kipapas arrived back in the valley, Manuel Roberts listened to the story of what the doctor had said, took one look at his big new grandson, and gave Kurt his Hawaiian name, Kamua, which means "the first."

None of this went unnoticed by McCandless daughter and heir Elizabeth McCandless Marks. The anecdote about "greedy man" Lester Marks being called out by a defiant Manuel Roberts from high up on the seat of his tractor suggests that it wasn't the first interaction between the two men. Then Marks raised the stakes in 1962 with Circuit Court Case No. 8966, his suit to quiet title on what he claimed as the McCandless Estate's thirty-one and a half shares of the Hui o Waikāne, which included the Roberts shares still in dispute. After receiving his summons, Manuel consulted Wilford Goldbold, the lawyer who brought the family's 1929 suit to quiet title on its shares. Goldbold laid out the merits of the 1929 case, and then suggested another option: adverse possession. If Manuel Roberts could prove that he had been working the land for more than ten years, "adverse" and "openly hostile" to the McCandless Estate, it would be his. Roberts asked Goldbold to delay their answer to the court, and he hired a surveyor who measured up his four Waikāne plots totaling fifty-nine acres. As Mrs. Kipapa's memoir continues:

> Dad fought with the McCandless Estate for twenty-eight years, from 1942 to 1970. He went to many trials. I would drive him to court every week for a while when they did his deposition. Dad needed money to help him pay for the deposition. Four of us could help—the other three had divorce problems. Dad always used to say, "You guys just remember: I'm doing this for the family to keep our land, so I will fight this greedy man to the end." And he did.
>
> Once, Dad got all of us kids together. There were seven of us, so he put seven sticks together. I think the sticks were the long cowboy matches—the kind you can light on your boots or even on a rock. Anyway, he put the sticks in a bundle and told the older boys—Sonny, Henry, and Jerry—to broke it in half. No one could. So Dad said, "You see: just like family. No one can break us apart because we're family. We stick together." I can never forget that.

"Her and I, we needed to find a companion for Kurt," Mr. Kipapa told me, going on about the shocking news that he and his "Love," as he called Priscilla, would have no more children. "My sister-in-law had twins, and we used to raise the two of them together with my son. And there were a lot of boys around, my nephews and that. So whenever we went on a trip, we would always bring my nieces and nephews. And like Christmas time, we would share, and buy gifts for everybody, and we didn't expect anything back—we just wanted the kids around."

As Kurt grew, so did the reams of paper in the various motions and requests and memoranda that made up Case No. 8966. Wilford Goldbold eventually retired, and Robert Fukuda took his place. At issue were the validity of the Roberts family's claim to the *hui* shares Aunty Ellen began fighting for in 1929, and how much land Manuel Roberts was working.

Kurt is a fifth grader at Waiāhole School when Mrs. Kipapa's memoir continues:

> In September of 1970 Dad went to many hours of questions. He had one lawyer; McCandless had many lawyers questioning him. He once told us the questions they asked him made him cry a lot. I wished I could have been there but he would tell me, "I don't think you can come in. Just wait for me here."

After two grueling months of depositions, there was nothing left for the Roberts/Kipapa family to do but wait. They went ahead with plans to build an addition on the house the Kipapas had built on the *hui* allotment down by the highway. And then Mr. Kipapa and his father-in-law began one of the more thankless do-it-yourself construction tasks imaginable, digging a hole deep into the muddy soil and installing a new cesspool. The willingness to sink so much money, time, and sweat into a property that could just as easily be taken from them at the judge's whim was spurred on by what the family could only see as a good omen, if not a miracle itself: after nearly eleven years, Priscilla Kipapa was pregnant again. The fifty-nine acres that Manuel Roberts was about to be officially awarded may have been a lot for one man, but here was another sign that it would fill up after only a couple of generations. Once that happened, who could challenge the Roberts family's claim? In the noisy image of the schoolyard full of grandchildren that his seven children had given him, Manuel could see what Aunty Ellen had envisioned: both of the family's legacies—its land and its sons and daughters—intertwined.

"You see, everybody over here," Mr. Kipapa later recalled, "they knew the Roberts family live up here, so when they mention the Roberts farm, they meant the *whole area* over here is the Roberts'. They even call the road—they don't mention like Waikāne Road—it's 'Roberts Road,' ah? You ask any-kine guys like in their forties and fifties li'dat, 'You guys used to ride motorcycle up Waikāne Valley?' They'll say, 'What, you mean the Roberts' place?'"

Selisa was born without incident, and although she would go on to grow up in the house that her father and grandfather had just finished enlarging, the joyful news stopped there. The Honorable Samuel P. King's judgment indeed provided Manuel Roberts with an adverse possession "award." But of the fifty-nine acres Percy's grandfather had been cultivating for nearly thirty years, he was given the three-acre taro patch up in the valley along with the house lots now already filled by his children and their families—a total of just over nine acres. Just as one part of the family's legacy was strengthened, the other was taken away, leaving no place for Selisa or Kurt to settle when the time came for them to start families of their own. "He got us seven together and asked if we wanted to go to Supreme Court to fight it further," Mrs. Kipapa's memoir concludes. "The saddest part was that we had two divorces going on, and only three of us could afford, but we had small children, beginning a family. It was hard. We always look back and wonder if we made the right choice."

Days later, George Kipapa went up the valley to visit his father-in-law. "About ten o'clock, ten-thirty, we always go up and see him, sit down, talk story. This time he was sitting down in his chair, where he sit down normally. In the front of him was a plate of salmon, with poi, onion, and salt. So he look at me: 'George, come eat.' So I look at him, and it's only a small portion, and he was not a small person—he was a *big guy*. And I know already he can take care of it himself—he don't need my help! But he was willing to share that with me. So we started to eat, and he told me, 'George you know if I die tonight, at least I die with a full stomach.' I put my stuff down and I tell him, 'Why are you telling me this?' I had *never* heard him talk like that. *Then* he turn around and he tell me, 'George, are you afraid to die?' I look at him—you know, I loved that man so much. So I told him, 'Look Pa, five days ago tonight, God gave us a daughter.' I really was thankful. I told him, 'You know Pa, I wish one day that I can watch her kids grow up, and hopefully someday see them get married. I'm really happy to have her. I really don't know what kind of woman she'll turn out to be, but nevertheless . . . ' "

Records for Case No. 8966 depict McCandless Estate lawyer Alan Kay's two-pronged strategy to grind Manuel Roberts out of his family farm. The first was to prove that McCandless had legally obtained the original Roberts *hui* shares. Kay found his evidence at the Bureau of Conveyances, where book no. 291, page 193, provides a deed, dated in 1907, transferring the shares to McCandless. Although Judge King notes that "the official record of the deed in the Bureau of Conveyances is a typewritten copy, even the signatures being typed," he concludes that "the Roberts

Heirs have no interest in the *hui* lands of Waikāne." Next, Kay set about doing what Glenn Kim referred to in Percy's murder trial as "dirtying the victim." As Mr. Kipapa recalled, "When we saw how he was cross-examined by McCandless' lawyers—about six, seven lawyers cross-examining him—there was sadness in my heart. I don't think I could go through that." The questioning, both in depositions and before the court, comes off as a coordinated effort to catch Manuel Roberts contradicting himself on minor details, or to outright paint him as a liar. The I'll-slit-you-from-ear-to-ear confrontation is just one example. Kay's Memorandum of Points and Authorities in Opposition to Manuel Robert's Claim of Adverse Possession recalls the incident young Priscilla witnessed with this: "It is noteworthy that [Manuel's] daughters failed to corroborate their alleged presence, and instead testified that there were no problems with McCandless, with Priscilla even saying she had never heard of Lester Marks."

"What! I neva talked to anybody," Mrs. Kipapa told me when I brought up what I'd found down at the Circuit Court. "That's all bullshit!" Interestingly, reaching back some sixty-five years into her memory in first telling me the story, she had referred to Lester Marks as "McCandless," her lingering anger having caused her to conflate everyone involved with McCandless himself.

Kay then uses the contradictory nature of Manuel's claims to the land—claiming an "adverse" relationship to the *hui* to which he also says he belongs—to paint him as an opportunist. Although paying land taxes was not a requirement for an adverse possession claim, Kay questions the timing of Manuel's attempts to begin paying taxes on his land "after he engaged counsel." (The record also notes that Manuel's reason for previously declining to pay taxes into the *hui* account controlled by the McCandless Estate was simple: prominently displayed on the tax receipt was the word "Rental.") In calling the size of Manuel's adverse possession claim into question by citing a 1955 Farm Loan for which he claimed only fifteen acres, Kay uses Manuel's own deposition ("he did not want his cattle placed as security under the chattel mortgage") to call him a criminal who lied on the loan application. Kay uses the testimony of other valley residents—even while admitting that many of them are "tenants of the Plaintiffs under short-term leases"—to further discredit Manuel's claims to having worked particular parcels of land, concluding with this:

"As unpleasant as the subject may be, it is submitted that the innumerable untruths, hedging, and changes in Manuel Roberts' testimony necessitate that his entire testimony claiming adverse possession be given no weight."

"You know what," Uncle Henry recalled, "these guys, they went and testify against my dad that there was no farm up there. But they did not send anybody up there to see. The only guy testify for my dad was the Water Works, because they went up and down and they saw us, and they said, 'This man was farming all the time.' But the tenants—one guy was Motorake, he said, 'No no, he neva farm, he neva had nothing up there.'"

Mrs. Kipapa can still name another former valley neighbor who frequently passed one of the Roberts' parcels. "So my father said, 'You know, I'm going court, so you know, you see I get cows, so if they ask you, can you tell?'" She recalled. "He said, 'Oh, no worry.' When he went, you know what he said? 'No, I neva see cows.'"

"The witnesses that they had that was going help him out," Mr. Kipapa said, "they all kind of turned against him, 'cause they all had leases on the property of McCandless, so McCandless had 'em in a bind, yeah?"

And so Judge King's "Findings of Fact" wound up being peppered with such phrases as "There is an issue of credibility," and "I am unable to find any evidence," and "The evidence as to his use of the northern portion is very skimpy and unsatisfactory." The muddy taro patch next to Waikāne Stream, and the house lots next to the highway—in light of how effectively Case No. 8966 dirties its victim, one cannot help but wonder why King hadn't just given those plots to the McCandless Estate, too.

It's difficult to imagine what it would take to get the proud Manuel Roberts to come to tears in front of a roomful of lawyers, and I don't think it's even possible to imagine the devastation he would have felt upon learning of Sam King's final judgment any more than someone could ever really know what it feels like to lose a son. Even after my four years of trips into the valley and through the pages of research, and my painstaking revision upon revision in order to try to feel what it might have been like to be Percy Kipapa—to really *feel 'um*, as Charles Kekahu had put it—I cannot really know the emptiness, the anger, the physical pain that Manuel Roberts must have felt when the links his Aunty Ellen had asked him to forge wound up not being enough. By all accounts, the sunup-to-sundown farm routine had turned him into a bull of a man who should have lived long past the age of sixty. But within weeks of receiving his nine-acre award, Manuel Roberts was dead.

"It's like he knew he was going to die," Mrs. Kipapa said. "And you know when they put him on the ambulance, there was a whirlwind of leaves went up. It was really something."

How the family could move on after such a loss is another thing that's hard to imagine, but it certainly had something to do with their continued strong faith, as well as the legacy that no judge could ever take from them: their sons and daughters. On July 16, 1973, George and Priscilla welcomed the baby of the Roberts clan—their youngest son, Percy Pōmaikaʻi Kipapa. "I had myself blessed a couple times to protect the baby," Mrs. Kipapa told me, "so we called him ʻPōmaikaʻi,' which means ʻblessing.' And he liked that name."

❨ ❨ ❨

THE YEAR PERCY KIPAPA WAS BORN, a consulting firm named Eckbo, Dean, Austin, and Williams (EDAW) completed a socioeconomic study for the Hawaiʻi Department of Transportation to predict the impacts of a proposed federally funded trans-Koʻolau highway that would link Kāneʻohe's Marine Corps Base with Pearl Harbor. The firm had worked for the state before on such projects as the Kauaʻi General Plan and the 1969 State Land Use Commission's districts and regulations review, in which they recommended filling in Heʻeia fish pond for urban development. This time, EDAW interviewed a long list of community groups in their Study Area, including Native Hawaiian groups, land developers, the Honolulu Planning Department, and the Kahaluʻu Coalition, among many others. The Study Area stretched from Kualoa—a few bends in the road north of where the Kipapas turned into Waikāne Valley with their newborn blessing—to roughly the place just outside of Kahaluʻu where Percy's body was found slumped over the wheel of a GMC pickup thirty-one years later.

Bob Nakata was the one who pointed me to the EDAW study, which examines the H-3 freeway in the larger context of the Honolulu City and County General Plan. "Temple Valley's suburbanization happened in the mid-sixties, but the plans were laid in the fifties," Bob said of the General

Plan. "What you see in 'Ewa, Kapolei, Ko Olina, was being planned right here. Campbell Estate on that side, and the Dillinghams on this side, were competing for who would get Second City. Deep draft harbor, right out here." He pointed out the window of his second-floor office, just up the hill from the Kahalu'u boat ramp's dusty parking lot. "They were going to dredge it all out, I don't know how far out. So this strip of low-lying land was going to be the wharfs and heavy industry. At the edge of the lagoon that was created for flood control there would be a twenty-acre sewage treatment plant. Hotel resort in this valley, hotel resort over the fishpond in that area over there. He'eia Kea Boat Harbor was going to be four times bigger than the Ala Wai. Hawaiian Electric was going to put a power plant there, and oil barges I guess would have come into the boat harbor. The He'eia meadowlands were to be a golf course. The He'eia fishpond was to be a fancy marina. I think the point where He'eia State Park is, somebody wanted to put a fancy restaurant and I don't know what else up there. They were going to create an artificial island in front of King School. Oh yeah, the piece that I'm forgetting: Temple Valley? That's where the oil refineries were going to be. It was wild!"

Walled in by its steep curtain of mist-shrouded green mountains, Temple Valley provides the serene backdrop for scores of slick magazine ads, television scenes, and tropical movie shots. Though it's difficult to imagine someone at a City and County planning meeting saying, "I know! Let's build an oil refinery in Temple Valley," the 1957 General Plan map depicts everything as Bob explained. It was later amended (after Campbell Estate won the battle for a Leeward oil refinery) to make way for "the most desirable density of population throughout the City and County of Honolulu." A flip of the page from the then-existing O'ahu map to the 1964 General Plan map changes the Study Area's colors from "diversified agriculture" light green and "open space" white to the same "residential" yellow that covers Kaimukī. When I mentioned the plan to Mr. Kipapa, he said: "In the early sixties, I seen that plan. Joe Pao—he came up here to meet the family, we met at the church. He turn around and he say, 'You know, there's possibly twenty-five years or more of jobs if they build up here, and here's some of the things they're going to have: a cemetery, high school, intermediate school, a big shopping center, all up here.' There was supposed to be a six-lane highway coming all the way up from Kāne'ohe" to send Honolulu commuters into a sea of same-looking houses crammed onto five-thousand-square-foot lots serviced by a paved Waikāne Valley Road. "Now the thing is, because of the tide, they had to take that highway and move it inland."

"In front of the church," Mrs. Kipapa added, referring to the little country chapel less than fifty yards from the Kipapa's carport. "Right where my brother's house is."

"Now the question you gotta ask is, 'Where you gonna get the material from to fill all this in?'" Mr. Kipapa pointed to his backyard, where they used to grow taro. "Because this is all swamp." He paused for a moment and then said, "I was working construction—I seen the plan. The only problem was that I wasn't educated enough to know about these things."

The EDAW study concluded that the General Plan, which by 1973 had already resulted in an "invasion" of "newcomers," increased traffic, spoiled scenery, depleted natural resources, and overtaxed government services such as schools, fire protection, waste disposal, hospitals, and police, had completely ignored local people like the Kipapas. Seventy pages detail how development in the Study Area was already impacting the "wellbeing, health, standard of living, and lifestyle of existing area residents, especially longtime residents of the community." The H-3 freeway would "perpetuate a *de facto* 'growth policy,'" accelerating such already-visible impacts as the disappearance of existing employment opportunities on family farms, "family breakdown including separation, divorce, and runaway children," "more persons [in need of] welfare payments," and an increase in the "rates of juvenile delinquency and adult crime." Instead of the rugged terrain between Kahaluʻu and Waikāne, EDAW suggested developing the vast "Central and West Oʻahu" sugar plains, where construction would be much cheaper, no deep-rooted communities would be affected, and a broader range of earners could afford housing. The Windward Coast was better off designated as a "greenbelt" to protect the "positive contribution that this scenic area makes to Oʻahu's tourist industry."

Though city planners responded by eventually moving the "Second City" to Kapolei as EDAW suggested—no doubt at least partly in response to the Waiāhole-Waikāne Community Association's tremendous 1970s anti-development victories—the Department of Transportation went ahead with H-3 anyway, and just *said* it was designed to support "planned development in the central and western parts of O'ahu." The Study Area disappeared from the conversation, and no one at the DOT bothered to concretely relate Leeward Kapolei with a highway serving an entirely different, distant section of the island. A host of local and national environmental groups, Native Hawaiian activists, and concerned citizens like Bob Nakata fought the project for the next twenty-four years, in the process winning a major reroute (through Hālawa Valley instead of Moanalua Valley), a less-dramatic reroute around a Hawaiian archeological site, and a battle to halt completely until an Environmental Impact Statement and further archeological studies were completed. George Cooper, the author of *Land and Power in Hawai'i*, and archeologist C. Kahaunani Abad would even go on to prove H-3 in violation of the National Historic Preservation Act, asserting in a 1992 *Honolulu Star-Bulletin* op-ed piece that the state DOT, the federal DOT, the archeological consultant Bishop Museum, and the State Historic Preservation Office had been lying "for over a decade" about the number of culturally significant sites that the highway would destroy.

But in the end, the H-3 opponents were out of their league. The push for the new highway had become the latest version of a familiar narrative—one that would later play itself out with the Hawai'i Super-ferry, and then again with plans to hide a stadium-sized telescope atop Mauna Kea by painting it white. Community opposition to such proposals is greeted by a sophisticated public relations machine aided by a general lack of comprehensive local news reporting, which results in such official descriptions of events as the DOT's eventual version of Native Hawaiian involvement in H-3. "For the opening of H-3," the DOT's Web site reads, "a cleansing *Oli* was performed by members of The Nation of Kū. This group of native Hawaiians had fought the project for years, but they believed that it was time to make peace with the freeway." Opposition is then overwhelmed by outside money—for instance, in the form of the telescope's offering a few token scholarships for Native Hawaiians (thus forcing opposition groups to "choose" between their beliefs and their children's education), or in the form of the kind of high-cost assault on public opinion that had some 70 percent of O'ahu residents believing, despite what the map in front of them clearly said, that H-3 would lead Windward commuters into downtown. The public relations machine's overwhelming success leaves the rest up to elected public officials, such as Senator Daniel Inouye, who in 1986 authored a bill to exempt H-3 from all environmental laws. The rest of the Hawai'i delegation followed along, including Neil Abercrombie, who boarded a plane in Honolulu vowing to kill the project, had a single meeting upon arrival in Washington (with the DOT), and then cast the deciding vote to pass it. Two construction-related fatalities, several injuries, eleven years, and $1.3 billion later, the four-lane super-highway linking Percy Kipapa's valley to the rest of the world opened, just in time for him to take it home from the airport after returning from Japan for good.

It all calls to mind an incredible story Mr. Kipapa once told me about how he was run over by a nine-ton bulldozer while working construction in Kāne'ohe. His immediate reaction was to look around for his hard hat, because one of his coworkers had been fired for failing to wear his hard hat. Then he was taken to the hospital in critical condition with various internal injuries and blurred vision. Mr. Kipapa pledged to God that if his strength and his eyesight returned, he would never take another sip of alcohol and never utter another swear word—two promises he has kept to this day. "It was a miracle that I pulled through," he said. The symbolism is obvious: while struggling to maintain one way of life, he is literally run over—as the EDAW study predicted in its figurative way—by another.

THOUGH THE DEVELOPMENT that EDAW warned against has yet to hit the Study Area on the scale imagined by the 1964 General Plan, the impacts they were already able to identify back in 1973 clearly have hit hard. "After Waiāhole/Waikāne, we became very sophisticated and good at blocking stuff," Bob Nakata told me. "And in the meantime, sugar went out," leaving the Leeward plains ripe for development. Although it ultimately failed, Bob calls the H-3 fight a "sequel" to the 1970s battle for the valleys—part of a seemingly endless string of such sequels, including the fights against the golf courses, for the return of Windward water, and so on. And ice? "We couldn't get rid of it," Bob said. "And you know, the two go hand in hand: beating all those guys, and the rise of the drug problem. Our energy went into the external fight, not the internal. My blunt assessment is that we had tremendous victories on the land use side, and we failed on the social side."

Considering that every one of Bob's struggles were battles in the same war, and considering what he was really up against, his assessment is not surprising. Nearly forty years later, it is not difficult to consider all of Hawai'i the Study Area, look at the obvious impacts of so much development that prices out local residents, and then read the EDAW report as an indictment of the kind of "New Hawai'i" addiction that got H-3 built despite its incredible financial, environmental, cultural, and social costs, its dubious utility, and even the fact that anyone on the take could still have been paid off had the 1.3 billion federal dollars been shifted to the more useful alternatives that Bob and others spent much of the 1980s fighting for. Briefly, "New Hawai'i" refers both to the shift from agriculture to tourism and to the construction of housing for people other than existing local residents that began with the late-1950s advent of commercial-jet air travel. Such development required capital, which came in the form of partnerships with foreign and mainland investors, including the military—an economic model based on the decades-long practices of a man once known in Washington as "Mr. Hawai'i" and known to Honolulu planners as the author of the idea for an oil refinery in picturesque Temple Valley.

His name was Walter Dillingham. A descendant of an original missionary family, Dillingham was eulogized a few years after statehood by Senator Hiram Fong, who proclaimed that he had "lived a life that spanned the full spectrum of Hawaiian history: he was born and raised under a monarchy; he saw the transition of his beloved islands to a Republic, to an incorporated Territory under the American flag, and finally to the full stature of a state in the Union. He left his imprint on every period." Fong could have been speaking literally with regard to O'ahu's shoreline, which Dillingham's Hawaiian Dredging Company forever altered all the way from Pearl Harbor, to the 1,875-acre Honolulu airport, to the Ala Wai Canal and beyond. Dillingham brought back from Washington millions in military construction projects, such as the one that blasted six miles of coral from Kāne'ohe Bay so the marshy Mōkapu Peninsula could become a vast U.S. Marine base where the fourteenth fairway of a "morale" golf course now covers what was once one of O'ahu's most sacred heiau. And all the while, he was grabbing up cheap, swampy land, including over 1,200 acres in the EDAW Study Area. As Mr. Kipapa might have said of such acquisitions, "The question you gotta ask is, 'Where you gonna get the material from to fill all this in?'" Dillingham would have had a ready answer with the make-work deep-draft harbor he'd planned to dredge just offshore from the Kahalu'u canoe boat ramp.

By the time Percy returned from Japan, New Hawai'i had long since become an ocean liner that couldn't be turned. All of the Big Five *kama'āina* corporations had stopped growing sugar on O'ahu and started growing houses and golf courses (with Castle and Cooke Sugar becoming Castle and Cooke Homes, etc.), and all of them had either partnered with mainland interests or sold out altogether. (Such partnerships and eventual sellouts constitute the thesis reflected in the title of Noel Kent's decades-old book, *Hawai'i: Islands under the Influence*, which details how Hawai'i came to surrender complete control of its own destiny, with the whole state becoming, in effect, as castrated as Kevin Chang's tattooed pit-bull owner.) One of the Dillingham Corporation's initial partnerships, born not long after Walter Dillingham's death in 1963, followed the model he had begun himself by looking to the military to build Hawaiian Dredging. In the 1960s, Dilco teamed with American Airlines to erect one of the more powerful symbols of New Hawai'i to grace the growing Honolulu skyline. Upon land filled with the coral that Hawaiian Dredging had blasted from Honolulu Harbor, and rising to a height of thirty-six stories right next to what was then the world's largest shopping center—itself a $25 million project carried out by Dillingham's son—stood the shining white tower of the Ala Moana Hotel.

Upon opening its doors in 1970, the Dillingham Corporation's hotel cast the longest shadow among those of the many resorts that were quickly becoming work alternatives to O'ahu's blazing-hot cane fields, providing nearly six hundred frontline jobs for former plantation workers, waves of Filipino immigrants, and local Hawaiians from as far as Wai'anae, way out on the Leeward Coast. The twelve-hundred-room tower seemed a kind of plantation all by itself, from its largely imported upper-management staff on down to the housekeepers and food and beverage staff kept in line by the overseers provided by the new University of Hawai'i School of Travel Industry Management. Long after Dillingham had passed away, there stood the symbol of his way of doing business, welcoming guests from afar and offering menial jobs for local people, such as the ones who serviced the Snack Bar out on the pool deck overlooking the sun-drenched Pacific. That was where a twenty-four-year-old mother of three began waiting on tourists as Hawai'i ushered in the 1980s, faithfully punching the clock and then greeting them with "aloha" until a wrong bend for some heavy object sent her out on disability with a herniated lumbar disc. Her name was Venda Meheula.

Court records of the civil suit that Venda Meheula brought against the hotel show that the Snack Bar closed while she was out on disability leave. Its workers were reassigned to other outlets, including Mango and Miso, the Asian cuisine restaurant where Venda used to help out as a hostess when the manager found himself short-staffed. When Venda returned to work, she learned that she had been terminated. She was invited to apply for one of the two open hostess positions at Mango and Miso, but when manager Gary Ward gave the positions to two brand-new hires over the Hawaiian from Wai'anae, she went to the union. The Department of Labor Relations hearing officer concluded that it didn't matter that the new hires—the sisters Mary Lau and Nancy Lau—"knew some Japanese," or that one had graduated from the School of Travel Industry Management, and the other had "a pleasant and sweet personality." Venda Meheula should simply have been reassigned. When the hotel appealed to the DLR director, and won, the young mother initiated her civil suit. As the suit dragged into the 1990s, she was fired from another food services job after reinjuring her back (she had failed to disclose her prior injury in order to get the job in the first place), and then was fired by Hertz for damaging a car with the courtesy van she was assigned to drive for affluent tourists.

Criminal court records involving Venda Meheula that stretch through the 1990s suggest the familiar path towards the kind of pit-bull rebellion that Kevin Chang and I discussed. A terroristic-threatening and firearm-possession case from 2004 helps explain why she had looked so comfortable on Judge Karl K. Sakamoto's witness stand—she *had* been there before. Her arrest in 1998 for dealing evokes the fact that ice's initial rise in Hawai'i coincided with her heroic efforts to *gaman* through back pain at minimum-wage service jobs to help support her family. And though we learn that she was paroled a year after her five-year sentence was handed down in 2001, leaving her free to "render aid" to a dying Percy Kipapa when she should have been locked up, more telling than anything in the criminal files is what appears between the lines of the civil suit, and that is the energy the Ala Moana Hotel's lawyers seem to have brought to the task. They went up against the union. They fought the Department of Labor Relations. They appealed the court decisions again and again, all so that the $17,932 back-pay tab for which Venda Meheula was suing would not have to be picked up by Azabu USA's Kitaro Watanabe, who had just bought the hotel for $70 million and was planning a $31 million facelift.

Eckbo, Dean, Austin, and Williams could never have imagined that the "newcomers" set on developing the Study Area would be financed by such obscene amounts of money, or connected as they were either directly or peripherally to the lucrative drug trade linking Korean ice factories, *yakuza* couriers, and the growing number of Hawai'i dealers and addicts. When former Legal Aid Hawai'i director Tony Locricchio wonders aloud why someone would plunk down so much money on a hotel that a constant 100 percent occupancy wouldn't even meet the debt service, what he is really saying is that the purchase must have been made for the purpose of laundering money, even after Japanese banks began to provide such obviously *yakuza*-connected investors as Kitaro Watanabe with multimillion dollar lines of credit. According to *Yakuza* authors David E. Kaplan and Alec Dubro, the new owner of Dillingham's hotel, who would be arrested for hiding millions of dollars in assets the same year that Venda Meheula was first arrested for dealing ice, routinely turned to the Sumiyoshi-kai crime group to "hide" his buildings from bank investigators through threats and other strong-arm tactics, even holding an investigator hostage. Watanabe would come to own six major Hawai'i resorts, plus the Waikāne land for his planned golf course.

"By the end of the 1980s," Kaplan and Dubro wrote, "golf development had become one of the most mobbed-up industries in all of Japan." In Hawai'i, it had become glaringly obvious that if the words "Japanese investment" and "golf course" appeared in the same sentence, then full-body tattoos and severed pinkies had to be involved. It hadn't taken any incredible investigative reporting to uncover the *yakuza* ties of golf course investors such as Ken Mizuno (Olomana), Yasuo Yasuda (Maunawili), and Kizo Matsumoto (Turtle Bay), which suggests that the powers that be had known of the criminal associations all along. "That was the joke in Japan," Locricchio told me one afternoon at his Maunawili home, whose front door still boasts a bullet hole as a reminder of his fight against the golf course now visible from his lanai. "You could buy a Hawai'i politician for the price of a good dinner in Japan. And it was true." He explained how, prior to Yasuo Yasuda's purchase of the valley for $7 million, state law had required a two-thirds majority legislative approval to use agricultural land for anything other than farming. "But how did that constitutional protection thing get swept aside? What had happened was a massive campaign contribution to more than two hundred Hawai'i politicians, coordinated through Yasuo Yasuda, who was alleged to be a *yakuza* member. He was a Korean pachinko-parlor owner, and the allegations have been made— which I never comment on," he said with a smile, "that he was *yakuza*." Locricchio, together with Maunawili Community Association President Viki Creed and head of Hawai'i's Thousand Friends Donna Wong, filed a complaint with the Federal Election Campaign Commission. "They came down with what is still today the largest penalty—$2 million in fines, and it involved the most politicians ever," he said. But Yasuda's land had already become worth upwards of $40 million, and that's when things, as we have seen, got ugly. "The city and the professional agents who directed the police that day," Locricchio said, "because they coordinated this totally unnecessary attack on defenseless old people like Mr. Delay, who died from the brutal trauma of being carried out of his home of forty-plus years—each and every one of them have the kind of blood on their hands that does not wash away after all these years. They brought in helicopters, SWAT teams. The number of guns was just . . ." All he could do, nearly twenty years later, was shake his head. "This is a wonderful place to live," he finally went on, "if you don't know too much." Of Hawai'i's 1980s golf invasion, Kaplan and Dubro conclude, "The locals proved themselves more than willing to take money from suspect investors, knowing that when the *yakuza* made money, they too would profit. The only people who lose are ordinary Hawaiians, who see property values pushed out of reach, drugs and vice increase, and corruption spread across their fair land."

❆　❆　❆

MISSOURI-BORN, CALIFORNIA-RAISED Linda Lingle's political career roughly parallels Venda Meheula's descent from hard-working mother to convicted drug dealer. Meheula's start at the Ala Moana Hotel Snack Bar and her 2002 prison release are neatly bookended by the first of Lingle's two Maui County Council terms, in 1980, and her first inauguration as governor. With Lingle as the mayor of Maui from 1990 to 1998, a sleepy island sustained by agriculture, and by the concentrated resort community in Lahaina, exploded into a direct-flight-served mainland retirement community. Timeshares spread across acres of former pineapple and sugar fields and all the way up the once-empty Kīhei Coast. Cars jammed the backcountry two-lane highways. Finite water sources were sucked nearly dry enough for the Maui Water Board's Johnathan Starr to tell *Honolulu Weekly* that "We're already using more than a million gallons a day more than we're responsibly supposed to take out of the ground." The same article informed 2002 voters that Lingle had blocked proposed Board of Water Supply restrictions because they discouraged investment, had "supported rampant development" at the expense of Maui's aquifers, and planned to do away with the State Water Commission. In addition to being sued successfully by the Environmental Protection Agency over "repeated sewage spill violations" during Lingle's term, Maui County had been found guilty by the Hawai'i Supreme Court for the illegal permits it granted one developer, and then found in violation of the Coastal Zone Management Act when it skipped the permit process altogether and started construction in Kaunakakai. The list goes on, including Lingle's use of county attorneys to fight for Kahului Airport's expansion.

Running under the slogan "A New Beginning," Lingle narrowly defeated two-term Governor Ben Cayetano's lieutenant governor, Mazie Hirono. Upon the advice of the University of Hawai'i Professional Assembly, with whom I'd marched in the 2001 strike aimed mainly at the Cayetano/Hirono administration, and disenchanted as I was with the cozy relationship between the now-ousted Bishop Estate trustees Lokelani Lindsay, Dickie Wong, Gerard Jervis, and Henry Peters and nearly every identifiable name in the Hawai'i political establishment as revealed by the authors of the 1990s "Broken Trust" op-ed pieces, I voted for Lingle myself. The new governor was greeted with the ice crisis, and she was given the last word in Edgy Lee's sensational 2003 wake-up call. Seated in front of the State Seal, the California-raised governor looked into the camera and pronounced to a riveted audience across eleven television stations, "Together we *will* win this war on ice."

No one sits closer to that war's front lines than Hina Mauka's Andy Anderson, who told me, "At the lieutenant governor's summit, a number of us that were involved in the flip-chart deal pushed for treatment on demand, and he said, 'We're not even going to try that. That's an impossible goal to reach.' And that's what we heard. That, and the outcries from families and the mothers and the fathers not being able to get into treatment, and the anger, and the disappointment." Of Lingle's subsequent veto of Act 40 (the legislation related to the Joint Task Force's Final Report), her refusal to release the funding after her veto was soundly overridden, and her pronouncement that "treatment doesn't work," Andy said, "We were upset about that, but the administration was new, and we didn't want to have any retaliation against us either. We had to apply through the Department of Health—they could have sabotaged us that way. And that's why we didn't want to raise a big ruckus, because if we did, they might not release the money for the programs where we can help people. What Aiona's office kept saying was that, 'we have to do an evaluation of all the agencies to make sure they meet the criteria and standards for contracts.' They wanted to show who was in control."

Andy Anderson was mystified that Hina Mauka's tremendous treatment successes were repeatedly ignored by the administration. "We're in twenty-one schools," he told me. "We have a counselor in each public high school in the state—not just Hina Mauka, but all the nonprofit agencies that do this. Every public high school, middle school, and intermediate school in the state has or will have an outpatient program to assess every kid who has any kind of problem with ice or with alcohol or marijuana, or any kind of drug. This is *treatment*. We have a sixteen-week structured regimen of individual counseling and sixteen weeks of at least one group therapy a week, with a lot of education about addiction and ice, and alcohol and cocaine and marijuana, and what recovery is, and how families are affected. We're the only state that's doing anything like this. I mean, I would think, if I were a smart politician, I'd be blowing that horn all over the place."

"Did Duke Aiona have anything to do with this program?" I asked.

"They released the money," he said evenly. Andy had finally triggered the release in late 2004 by bravely citing the unambiguously laudable results of the Department of Health's Adolescent and Adult Substance Abuse Treatment Performance Outcomes to refute the governor's claim that "treatment doesn't work." The document proved conclusively that treatment is worth every penny in the returns it generates from diminished ER visits, law enforcement budgets, prison costs, and a host of other social services expenditures. But the Department of Health's document he'd handed me was now three years old. "This was the last time we got any data from them," Andy said.

And there is Lieutenant Governor Duke Aiona's 2005 Hawai'i Drug Control Plan. It is difficult to look at that seven-page collection of platitudes to "move forward" against "underage drinking" merely as a product of incompetence. The plan looks more like the administration's attempt to get us to stop thinking about ice altogether—a strategy the governor continued by failing to mention the word "ice" in her 2005 State of the State address or any State of the State address since, and by omitting "ice" or even "illicit drug problem" from among the nine bulleted "Initiatives of the Lingle-Aiona Administration" on her Web site. Worse: the plan clearly tried to make it appear as though Lingle and Aiona were *doing something*— a side show designed to draw political support away from continuing to fund Act 40, the only major attempt ever made to free thousands of local families from ice's deadly grip. Worse still is the thought that the lieutenant governor may have purposely put together a program he knew the legislature would not support. That way, legislators could be cast as impediments, and he could cast himself as a "fighter" in the drug war.

Four months after Percy Kipapa was killed, some hundred-or-so people gathered at Key Project—far less than half of the initial town hall meeting's turnout in 2003. The meeting, covered by the *Honolulu Advertiser*, took on the kind of talk-story format that Keith Ryder had steered the crowd towards back in 2003, with a few people offering inspiring testimonies of their sons or cousins having gone through treatment, gotten jobs, gotten their marriages back together. But the overall tone of the meeting was one of frustration. Those who bothered to attend were incensed that cops were letting known dealers set up shop again under the banyan tree. Cops shot back with the argument that the number of beats hadn't been increased since the appearance of ice, despite a doubling of the Windward population. But when they boasted that ice-related arrests were up by 10 percent since the campaign had started, Kahaluʻu resident George Marantz had had enough. He stood and brought up Percy's murder, pointing out that the ʻOkana Road house had since been raided twice, leading to the arrests of five people—all of whom, including Percy's admitted killer, were out on bail. "Why are they still on the street?" he asked. "Why not lock them up where they belong?"

By the end of the year, the *Honolulu Star-Bulletin* was quoting Duane "Dog" Chapman's wife as saying, "We can't find a house big enough for us and the kids. We're struggling being so cramped. The housing market is nuts and we need help." The Bounty Hunter's help came in the form of a new $2.6 million contract for the 2006 television season. A lucrative line of "Dog" logo gear would follow, along with two best-selling books. And two years later, the State House would devote two hours of its packed schedule to unanimously pass a resolution against Mexico's call to extradite Chapman on kidnapping charges related to the bounty hunt he'd filmed for his A&E pilot show in 2004. After swarming around the celebrity couple for pictures and handshakes, the house members then awarded the Chapmans, according to the *Star-Bulletin*, "a state of Hawaiʻi Certificate of Commendation for their service to the Hawaiʻi community for the cause of justice and public safety."

"Me, I'm not happy with the way things are," Keith Ryder told me more than four years after he'd mobilized an entire state against ice. "Right after we did our sign-waving, we started a neighborhood watch. We were recognized by HPD. We got the walkie-talkies, the signs. And it was working. We were trying to get more people to sign up, but people were saying, 'I don't have time to do it.' Eventually after three years, it's all the same people and everybody's tired. We looked like we were beating the problem, so we say, 'Let's try to take a break for six months.' Six months came and went, a year came and went. Everything is back to the way it was. And then you try to revive something that's already gone dead . . ."

As Andy Anderson told me, "I don't think we could regenerate that same kind of energy. I don't think that could happen here again on any issue. And that's sad. Because the community was galvanized." When I asked Bob Nakata how things were so long after the great ice-awareness storm, he said, "Somewhat better, but not a whole hell of a lot better. The only substantial result I would say is that people are far more willing to talk about it when they have a problem."

"With all we now know about treatment," I said, "and with the way it's become okay to admit that you have a drug problem and need help, and with what we now know about the demographics of ice users, you'd almost think the whole ice problem is fixable, but that there are people who don't want it fixed."

"Yep," he said. "There are so many people benefiting from it. That is exactly true."

"Nobody has really done the story on the climate for ice," Tony Locricchio said. "It should never have been able to grow at the rate that it did. Especially because not only was the handwriting on the wall—it was written in flashing neon. The impetus to do something about it finally came not from government, where it should have—it came from elsewhere. One of the inconsistencies is that it was successful in getting the passage [of Act 40 through the Legislature]. And then she sat on it," he said, referring to Governor Linda Lingle, who went on to out-raise her 2006 reelection campaign opponent $6.5 million to $330,000 and win in a landslide, with much of her war chest coming from mainland real estate and construction donors.

❨   ❨   ❨

"Tom enomoto, don't develop our valley." "Buyers Beware! Don't Buy Enomoto's Problems—You'll Be Sorry! Bachi!" "We'll Fight You Beyond the Limit!" Protest signs lined Waiāhole Valley Road like back in the day, one of them even connecting Enomoto to that era's villain: "Tom Enomoto Is a Repeat History of Joe Pao." According to documents at the City and County Office of Planning and Permitting, Enomoto's company, Royal Fountains LLC, had been trying since 2004 to subdivide the land into three three-acre lots on the property's southern edge on Waiāhole Valley Road and one 315-acre lot behind it, which, it appeared, would also eventually be subdivided. When I asked Bob Nakata about it, he could only give me a word-on-the-street answer: "It sounded like he's talking about five-acre fake farms," he said. The petition to subdivide was turned down twice because of an inadequate water supply. But then Enomoto installed an eight-inch water pipe—enough to supply Hawai'i Kai—and it looked like the politically connected developer, now out of Leeward subdivision space, had turned to Waiāhole/Waikāne to finish the job Joe Pao had begun, his path cleared by twenty years of ice-induced hopelessness among the decimated sons and daughters of the Waiāhole-Waikāne Community Association. By 2007, the association had dug in for battle: "Open Your Eyes and See the Crooked Guys!"

"I hate being focused on for anything, because I'm a very, very private guy," Enomoto told me a year later. We were sitting in his fifth-floor office, which overlooks an old Ke'eamoku condo's parking lot and the back of the Don Quixote discount store. The building's creaky elevator had let me out into the kind of hallway you might follow to a discount travel agent. Tom had answered the door himself, and with a warm smile invited me into a room whose only hints of money were a big koa desk and the mural-sized original Herb Kane painting covering the wall behind it—the one depicting King Kamehameha's armies pushing a human waterfall of resisting Hawaiians over the Pali. "And I don't know why I thought this [interview] would be a good situation." He pointed to the shelves behind me, which contained things like ornamental samurai swords and pictures of Enomoto with people like Bill Clinton and John Waihe'e. A photo of Percy dressed in his *keshō mawashi* stared out from its place next to a *tegata* handprint embossed with the kanji characters for "Big" and "Happiness." Kevin Chang had sent them with a letter requesting access for the Kipapas to the site of Percy's ash scattering. "I had Percy's stuff on my shelf," Enomoto said. "You know, propped against those samurai swords? Right *there*, for maybe a year. And I don't know why. I just put it there and left it there all this time, so maybe it was an omen that I was going to be involved with him in some way." He'd been sitting at his desk when he read my letter requesting what would be his first-ever formal interview. "When you mentioned Percy, I had his picture there all this time," so he'd e-mailed to set up an appointment. I wanted to talk with Enomoto, among other reasons, because he owned Grandpa's Hill.

"It's not me," he said, to clarify the ownership issue. "It's an entity that I have a stake in. It's maybe seven years? I don't know. Or maybe more like ten years now. It's kind of embarrassing—I haven't really done anything with it. I ended up being involved because the Japanese company failed. It's not something I looked at, shopped around for, and purchased. If I was going to do a development, I wouldn't end up with that project."

"You would never have bought in Waikāne."

"No!" He said this with a laugh that indicated a deep understanding of the history of the community's fight to preserve its local roots. In fact, Tom struck me as quintessentially "local" in the way most of the jurors at the murder trial had—a plate-lunch-eating guy from Kalihi more likely to be teeing it up at the Ala Wai than at any country club (although he doesn't even play golf himself). I'd come expecting to meet some shady mafia-connected "fixer" impatiently indulging me with a couple of one-word answers before ushering me to the elevator, but Tom turned out to be as open, humble, and hospitable as Glenn Kim had been to me over the phone. He even e-mailed an apology the next day for having gone on for more than two hours. "It sort of fell into our hands," he said, of the land, "and I think if you—well, you've been out there. You go up there a few times, and you kind of fall in love with the place. And going up Waiāhole Valley Road, everything about it, even the overhead power is nice—the telephone poles, the homes with the big banyan trees in front of them—everything is part of a picture that, it's just something that's really, really nice. The roads are trying to flow with the existing gradient, and it flows very well. It's almost like soft music." As for the water pipe, he told me, someone living on one of his lots had wanted to restore an old taro patch. "I think we had a puny little inch, inch-and-a-half pipe," he said, "which was okay for two or three houses, but if you're gonna do any kind of agriculture, you're gonna need more. And the engineer asked me, 'What size do you wanna tap off?' I said, 'What size should I?' He said, 'You can go with the eight inch, or you can go with the six, or four.' So I said, 'What's the cost difference?' He said not much, because you've gotta dig the trench anyway. So I said, 'Put in the eight-inch.' And guys went crazy!" He shook his head with a smile, and then went on. "At one point I studied carving out a few lots if we could find people from the valley. You know, 'Don't get mad at me, I'm selling it to your neighbor!' But if it was something open, general, I don't think so. I think the most important thing [with any development] is that you bring a project that that community is okay with.

I've never had controversies with our projects. We just don't do it that way. Life is too short."

These were hardly the words of a "stealth bomber." Over the course of these two hours, and the three hours we spent together the following year when he invited me to lunch at the Likelike Drive Inn, I could see that the image of Enomoto as some corrupt political insider had come about partly because no one knew anything about him beyond the brief snippets I'd been able to find in my extensive trip through the newspaper archives. His strong wish to be a "private guy" had only increased the suspicion that he had to be up to no good, when in fact he just loathed attention. This aversion even reached the point where he refused to comment on such misunderstandings as the Waiāhole Valley Road signs when they appeared on the nightly news because he thought a response would just prolong the story. Tom just seemed like the guy who would be furthest from the lightbulb at the family party, totally uncomfortable in a large gathering. But get him alone? If he'd had much to hide, he would not have gone on as long, and certainly not as candidly, as he did with me, a person he had never met and whom he knew was writing a very public story. What became clearer as the hours passed was that I was not talking to some updated version of Joe Pao.

Bob Nakata later agreed, telling me how Tom could not simply be lumped in with the kind of heartless developer that would butcher a prize bull in front of its owner. He just had a different way of looking at the world—a view Tom summed up himself in rationalizing away such cultural realities as Percy's attachment to his grandfather's land. ("Capitalist society is by nature fluid," was how he'd put it; "you move in and out of assets, and people who hang onto those old values of being in the same location for four hundred years end up losing out.") As Bob explained, "I was telling him once how Hawai'i was a place that should have an inter-religious center for peace. You know, because of the Hawaiian influence, and how we tend to be more tolerant of each other's differences. And he was fascinated. At that point he was involved with the Ward Estate, so he said, 'You know we can set it up here, and put all this commercial stuff around it.'" Bob chuckled at his story's odd-couple image. Tom later explained that the center would have been able to finance itself by leasing out surrounding land to for-profit "commercial stuff" in the same way the Oceanic Institute leases fifty acres to Sea Life Park. As with the Oceanic Institute, the nonprofit peace center would have controlled the commercial enterprise and thus would have been able to limit growth—an idea that suggested that maybe Tom Enomoto and Bob Nakata, of all people, were not such an odd couple after all. "In his own way," Bob said, "Tom has tried to move the human enterprise in a positive direction."

I began to see that dismissing Tom as a "facilitator" would be to miss the bigger point—a bit like blaming Keali'i Meheula for killing Percy and leaving it at that. Tom was *local*, in the same us-guys cultural sense with which the word had hung over Glenn Kim's successful prosecution. His 1991 move to downzone the Hoyu land to conservation district, for instance, may well have been done because his friendship with then-Department of Land and Natural Resources chair Bill Paty assured a subzone classification that permitted golf courses. But had the golf course been built, the zoning change would also have prevented any possible Hoyu plans to push further with suburban housing—something Tom may also have anticipated with Minami's Ko'olau Country Club, also built on conservation land, which remains surrounded by hundreds of acres of green rainforest nearly twenty years later. And then there is the Minami Foundation, created long after any need to "buy off" opposition had passed, all because Tom was able to use a minor procedural hurdle—having Paty approve an extension to finish the 90-percent-completed golf course—to extract a million-dollar donation from a Japanese billionaire. More than just a charitable enterprise, the Minami Foundation has allowed Tom to maintain some say in what happens to that thousand-acre property, even years later, even after it has passed through the hands of several owners. Recently he persuaded the Hong Kong company selling the property to donate a million dollars. "If I know in the back of my mind that they would easily give another million," he told me, "then I'm gonna try for it, because the foundation does good stuff. I told the guy he should feel *really* proud because we're gonna give him a *lot* of credit, he's a wonderful man, the community loves him. And for guys like that—he's reported to be a billionaire." You could almost picture Tom saying this from behind the wheel of an F-150, his pit bull chained in the back. "I never thought about it before," Bob Nakata told me after citing other examples of Tom's control over outside investors, "but Robin Hood is probably the model."

If Tom has succeeded it's been because he's been able to manipulate the last point of any real *local* control in the New Hawai'i model—an elusive "point" existing somewhere in Hawai'i's unusually complex web of state agencies. The state's actual environmental laws may have been written weaker than those of other states, but its multilayered building codes and permitting and zoning requirements and the like provide the longest possible chain of desks upon which an application can be stalled—desks generally staffed by "us-guys" *local* people. Until very recently, no matter how much money a developer had, he could do nothing without dealing with a *local* facilitator. True, one needn't look hard to find examples where this setup has failed as a "check" of any kind; real examples of corruption dating back to the 1960s are also easily found. But even if the "facilitators" were corrupt, or had plenty of ambition to steal from the rich but cared not of giving to the poor—even if they were the Lums, just for one example— they had the chance to *stand in the way* of development, even when they did so unwittingly, as the Lums did with Greek investor Charles Chidiac, whose $800 million Big Island resort remains unbuilt thanks to their incompetence at navigating through all the desks.

Now most of the desks are empty. In the years immediately following California-raised Governor Lingle's historic 2004 appointment of fellow journalism major Melanie Chinen as the first-ever State Historic Preservation Division director with no expertise in archaeology, architectural history, or history (the U.S. Department of the Interior's recommended qualifications for the position), a wave of twenty-one resignations washed over the division, destroying what had been a key *local* check against outside development. Both in reconfirmation hearings for then-DLNR chair Peter Young, and in a lawsuit brought by an archeologist whose contract Chinen failed to renew allegedly because of his concern over Lingle's chief of staff's orders to "fast-track" SHPD approval for Superferry-related harbor improvements, it emerged that a foul-mouthed tyrannical Chinen's management incompetence could not have more clearly matched her historic preservation incompetence. And if a decimated SHPD had been the goal all along, it worked. Six-figure federal preservation grants were put at risk. Nearly two hundred archaeological reports for Oʻahu alone have gone missing. Many of the positions in the division remain unfilled. A week before Chinen resigned "for family matters" at the end of 2007, Society for Hawaiian Archaeology president Thomas Dye told *West Hawaiʻi Today* that "For 25 years, the administrations in the state have been able to fill those positions with fully qualified individuals who did a good job. It's only the Lingle administration that can't seem to do that." As Dye had earlier told the *Honolulu Advertiser*, realistically speaking, "we're back to the era before historic preservation laws were enacted back in the '70s, when it was OK to just go out and bulldoze." And then the financial crisis hit, allowing Lingle to begin "fundamentally restructuring government"—a phrase that has largely meant identifying similar desks in other key *local* agencies (the Agricultural Department, the Division of Conservation and Resources Management, the Division of Forestry and Wildlife, the Bureau of Conveyances, etc.), targeting them for layoffs, and blaming the budget crisis.

ALL OF THIS PUT TOM ENOMOTO in the unfamiliar position of *steward* for Waikāne Valley trying to figure out some more productive use for it than an illegal weekend four-by-four park and a dumping ground for stripped stolen cars. So far, whatever he has done has accomplished the same thing that Bob Nakata has spent a lifetime trying to do—even during the time when the 1980s tsunami of Japanese bubble money was washing over New Hawaiʻi, and certainly in 2010 as he steered the land through foreclosure towards a buyer other than someone who might in fact be a "repeat history of Joe Pao." Not long after our conversation, the property was bought at auction by Hilo-born Dominic Henriques, whose wife graduated from Castle High around the same time as Percy's sister did. The local couple have no desire to develop the land, wishing only, as Henriques told me, to build a single home and enjoy the valley's spectacular beauty. When I first asked Tom what he planned to do with the land, he went down a list of ideas he'd considered over the years. "We were really gung-ho on a plan to create a pick-your-own organic farm" at one point, he said. "One of the guys associated with the project is on the board with the College of Tropical Agriculture at the university. So we came up with this rationale: everywhere they do fruits on a commercial basis, it ends up being a monoculture. We said, 'Why don't we do something that's a little more natural? Let's plant guava, and if it doesn't grow, pull it up, throw it away.' And plant some mountain apples, and oranges, and pineapples, everything. Even vegetables. Just plant a whole bunch of anything you could think of—seeds are cheap—and it just grows naturally." What Tom was describing, of course, and pretty accurately other than the "pick-your-own" part, was the farm of Manuel Roberts.

❨   ❨   ❨

ONE CAN IMAGINE THE AUTHORS of the General Plan expecting the EDAW report to come out as a bulleted and vague rubber stamp of H-3, listing such things as "availability of housing," or "positive economic impact." The firm, after all, had been hired to compose sixteen such reports for the state over the preceding ten years, often arguing in favor of development. But this time EDAW looked to the people who would be impacted most severely. "We have done extensive research into existing social, economic, and physical systems pertinent to the area," they explain, "and we have analyzed these systems in the context of historic and present conditions." Such analysis would certainly have taken them to the court case affecting nearly two thousand acres in the Study Area—Case No. 8966, which was decided only a year before their study began. Deep within the stack of pages on file at the courthouse downtown, EDAW would have found McCandless Estate attorney Alan Kay's memorandum urging the court to move quickly. "It is patently apparent that the Legislature of the State of Hawai'i is extremely concerned with the shortage of land," Kay wrote in 1970, "which has been further compounded by the recent rapid growth in population in the State of Hawai'i, as evidenced by substantially all of its legislation involving land. The Legislature is particularly anxious that all available land be put to its potentially highest and best use." Kay then cites Samuel King, the case's presiding judge, as having stated earlier that "the interests of the general public . . . [are] deeply involved due to the shortage of land in Hawai'i." In an affidavit filed around the same time, Kay points out "that a general development plan for areas in Waikāne and Waiāhole has been completed . . . and that said development cannot be practically commenced until after the various interests of the parties in Case No. 8966 are determined." Such words go a long way towards explaining why someone with over thirty-five thousand acres would expend so much energy and cause so much pain to try for the final fifty-nine, or why a judge would award a family six highway-front acres he knew would have to be condemned to accommodate the General Plan's "high standard" freeway. Let someone else evict them.

Eckbo, Dean, Austin, and Williams may not have imagined *yakuza* kingpins going on to flood the area with ice or carpet it with fairways, and they may not have predicted the tenacity of the area residents who fought off so much of the development. But because they made the effort to attach real faces to the abstractions offered by the New Hawai'i model, they wound up coming to far different conclusions than what the State Department of Transportation likely expected. "These are the things they talked about," Bob Nakata told me when he first brought up the study. "Increase in substance abuse, destruction of subsistence livelihoods—just a *devastating* future." John A. Burns, George Ariyoshi, John Waihe'e, Daniel Inouye, Spark Matsunaga, Daniel Akaka, and Neil Abercrombie all had it in their job descriptions to read the EDAW study, which could not have told them more clearly that Hawaiians like Percy Kipapa had a good chance of being killed from the trauma of such upheaval—if not by a "newcomer" then, all the more tragically, by a man with a Hawaiian last name, someone implicated in the study's warning: "As younger people are exposed to non-traditional life styles in the schools, through the mass media, and by exposure to life in Honolulu and to the newcomers in the Kahalu'u area, there is a growing generation/culture gap that will have a social impact in the years ahead." And if EDAW did look at Case No. 8966 in the course of their research—and they certainly must have—they were warning what would likely happen directly to the descendents of Manuel Roberts. That is, they weren't talking about people "like" Percy. They were talking about Percy. "The study was aimed at H-3," Bob went on. "But the guys who did the study were *really good*. When I came home from the mainland in '72 they were doing it. I didn't realize how good they were." Then he leaned forward and said, "*They never got another contract from the state.*"

I immediately thought back to the day of the funeral, when we were all gathered at the foot of the driveway on 'Okana Road wondering how Keali'i Meheula could have killed Percy all by himself. That was when I rode off with Tyler Hopkins, Percy's big sumo brother, who turned to me and said it: "Dat fucka taking the fall for somebody."

EPILOGUE

Every time I wrestle small guys and try to push them, they run around me. Pisses me off more, so when I grab 'em, that's when I really hurt them. Like that guy Chiyotaikai: I popped his shoulder out the first time I wen' wrestle him. I grabbed him, I wrapped my arm inside him like this, I dragged him to the rope. All my strength I lifted him up like this. I heard "pop," so I threw him on the ground. I heard like what I thought was one knuckle popping. The next tournament he was walking sideways, and he get tape all over his shoulder. And when he wrestled me he just tried to slap me down, so I just grabbed him and dragged him out.

—Percy Kipapa, November 18, 1998

Covered in sweat and sand all alone in the clay-floored training area, his thick chest heaving up and down as he gulped for air, the *sekitori* grabbed a towel. Five days into the May 2006 tournament, all of the underlings had either gone off to their matches in the Kokugikan or to the kitchen to prepare his lunch.

When he wiped the sweat from his chest and turned towards the door across from where I sat on the viewing platform, the jumpy Japanese beat reporter who was waiting there with me panicked, shuffling forward across the hard wood on his knees, and then piercing the room's churchlike aura with this: "*Sumimasen!* Ozeki! If I could just ask you a few questions!"

Ozeki Chiyotaikai turned and walked straight for the little man, neatly folding his towel and barking, "I'm not through yet!" He laid out the towel on the edge of the stagelike platform and said, "Get back!"

The guy scurried all the way back to the wall, and we waited as the *ozeki*—Chiyotaikai had long ago been promoted to sumo's second-highest rank, a mere step away from *yokozuna*—went through a long set of push-ups, his thick fingers digging into the towel, narrow bulbs of muscle bulging out on the backs of his thick arms. When he was through with the set, he stood, breathing hard again, looking up with a wince, the sweat now stinging his eyes. He grabbed the fingers on one hand with the other and pulled out, the stubs cracking and his face wincing again.

Chiyotaikai was a good six inches shorter than Percy, a compact, round rock muscled with thick legs and pythonlike arms—the ones that flew like pistons during a match—growing out from the kind of bulbous shoulders you'd find on a fullback, not an ounce of fat on him.

And he was far from finished. He turned his back to us and filled the room with the sounds of his bricklike feet slapping the hard clay as he lifted each leg high, leaning to the left as far as he could to get his right foot as high as possible, his left quad rippling, swelling, throbbing under the effort, his right leg pausing for just a moment at the top of the arc before coming down, down, down to the clay with a *slap!*, answered by the sound of his exhaling breath: *shhhhhh!* And then he did the same with his left leg, and then again, and again. You could see his face wince as he fought to keep his balance, and then when he began to lean just a little bit too far, causing him to shift his weight abruptly so as not to fall over, you could tell that this was not just another mid-tournament morning workout. Chiyotaikai was exhausting himself.

Next he walked over to what looked like the smoothed telephone pole in the corner across the room, stood to face it, and sent his thick hands into a slow slap-thudding rhythm against the wood, off-beat with a loud, exhaling *shhhhhh!*, his muscled back a map of mountains and valleys. As I watched the lone figure of a man safely anchored in the top echelons of sumo training with the focus of some lower-division kid gunning for the top, it finally hit me that Yokozuna Asashoryu, who had recently dominated sumo to the point where he almost never lost a tournament, was injured, leaving the Emperor's Cup up for grabs for the first time in four years.

Chiyotaikai did another set of the leg lifts, and three more sets of pounding his hands into the pole, and then called from the back for a beefy low-ranker—bigger than himself, but covered in a layer of fat—for *butsukari-geiko*, that human-blocking-sled exercise where one man charges into the other and pushes him across the sand-covered clay. Seven, eight, nine trips across the ring and Chiyotaikai was again gulping for air, his chest heaving, the sweat pouring.

"*Mashita!*" he heaved out. He took a sip from the bamboo ladle handed to him, spit it onto the clay, and squeezed in one more set of leg-lifts before squatting, rising to his toes, and then holding the position for a minute, two minutes, three, his eyes wincing again, and just by watching him you could feel the burn in his now-tired legs.

At last he stood, brought his hands together in front of his face, bowed towards the miniature Shinto shrine over in the corner, clapped once, and headed out the door.

The beat reporter jumped and went outside, around to the backdoor, where I found him standing in the drizzling rain scribbling in his notebook and talking with Chiyotaikai, who stood two steps up in the doorway, the towel now draped around his shoulders.

"What about your knee?"

"I'd rather not talk about that."

"Does it hurt?"

"Well, it's raining today. It always hurts when it rains. A lot of places hurt when it rains." And then he waited while the reporter scribbled everything down.

"You've won four straight this tournament. How are you feeling?"

"I'm feeling good." Again he waited.

"The *yokozuna* is absent. How does that affect the tournament?"

"I've got more of a chance now."

It was pretty much the standard interview, as routine as practice had been, and straying from the routine as much as practice had with the point about Asashoryu's absence. In any case, by the time it was my turn, Chiyotaikai could not have more clearly wanted to go inside and head for the bath.

I introduced myself, apologizing for bothering him after such a hard practice, and for my near-complete inability to speak in the proper honorific

Japanese he was due, while he respectfully listened. And when I said the word "Daiki," his face lit up with a smile that stretched back into years of recognition. I told him the sad news, which he remembered hearing the year before, and I told him what I'd promised his mother about writing a book, apologizing again for bothering him after such a hard practice, and asking if he could just answer a couple of questions.

All signs of wanting to go inside and soak in the bath were gone.

"You two came up together," I said.

"In *jūryō*," he said.

"And *makushita* and *sandanme*," I said, and he nodded. "Didn't you practice together a lot?"

"All the time," he said. "Back then, he was *huge*." He was getting animated now, a different man from the one who'd spoken to the reporter. When he mentioned Percy's size, I tried to imagine them in a match. Though he stood in the doorway two steps above me, our eyes were nearly level. "He was almost two hundred kilos then," he went on, his eyes widening. "It was like charging into a wall." He slapped the doorframe next to him, his hand imitating one *sumōtori* bouncing right off of another.

He thought for a moment and then said, "After, we used to go out and drink. He loved music." The *ozeki* bobbed his shoulders in the same imitation of Percy's dancing style everyone had been doing at his funeral.

"And this, too," I said, stealing Bumbo's spot-on take on Percy resetting his glasses with the pointed index finger.

"So, so, so, so!" he said with a smile.

"Do you remember your matches with him?"

"I remember," he said. "I could beat him, you know."

"Did you ever do *butsukari-geiko* with him?" I asked, referring to the blocking-sled exercise he'd just completed.

"Bwaa!" he said, imitating a guy getting thrown back. "It was like getting run over by a truck. You know, I used to beat him," he said again. "Our record together was 5–2. I was the winner."

I wanted to keep going, and probably should have, but I already felt like I'd kept him away from his bath and his lunch long enough. So I thanked him deeply, wishing him well in the tournament all the way to the Emperor's Cup.

He turned to one of his boys and had him bring a souvenir ceramic cup for me—one of the ones emblazoned with the old-fashioned woodblock prints, this one with the kanji for "Daiki" glazed onto it in large black lines. "The 'dai' means 'big,'" he said, putting his stubby finger on the character, "and the 'ki' means 'happiness.' That name suited him. You can give this to his mother for me." He gave me the cup and smiled, holding out his hand for me to shake.

I walked away, going over in my head all I'd just heard from Ozeki Chiyotaikai, in the lead a third of the way through the tournament. "Our record was 5–2," was what he'd said. "I was the overall winner." He'd said it without a trace of arrogance. The smile that appeared on his face when he recounted his career record against Percy, whom he hadn't faced in nearly a decade—that tone, "I was the overall winner"—it was almost as though he'd surprised himself, like the numbers should have read the opposite way, like of course Percy should have been the one who'd come out on top. The words had come out like this: I *did* it. Ozeki Chiyotaikai, ten years later with what he considered a great chance to win his fourth major tournament, was proud of himself because he had been able to come away with a winning record against Percy. And he sounded a lot like all those blue-coated retired *sumōtori* had that day when Percy and I sat in the sumo arena, when they all took turns coming to pay their respects with a "*mottai nai*," spoken in pure admiration, because they *knew* Percy. Because they missed him. And what they all knew, better than any of us, was that when you held up your hands to indicate that you carried no weapons, when it was a game that hadn't been rigged since sometime long before he was born, Percy Kipapa could *fight*.

GLOSSARY

LOCAL AND HAWAIIAN WORDS AND TERMS

ahupuaʻa Traditional Hawaiian land division/community, usually occupying a fertile valley

ʻāina Land; literally, "that which provides"

ainokea Local slang for "I no care"

bachi Mystical payback resulting from bad behavior

haʻaheo Pride

hale House

hana wai Work the water

hau A tropical shrub/tree that forms a dense thicket where it flourishes in coastal areas

he inoa no Traditional ending to a Native Hawaiian chant that roughly translates into "in honor of"

hui Group

imu Oven

imua Move forward; advance

kālua To cook

kamaʻāina "Of the land," referring to permanent residents not necessarily born in Hawaiʻi

kanikapila Informal gathering of musicians and singers

kuleana Responsibility; land parcel granted during the Great Mahele of the mid-nineteenth century (see *mahele*)

loʻi Taro patch

lomi Traditional Hawaiian form of massage

luna Overseer

mahele Division, often referring to Hawaiʻi's Great Mahele of the mid-nineteenth century, when common and royal land was divided and parceled out to a handful of Hawaiʻi residents

makai Towards the sea

mālama To care for

mana Spirit

mauka Towards the mountains

'ohana Family; depending on context, could refer to either immediate family or extended family

paniolos Cowboys

solé Local slang referring to Samoans; literally "brother" in Samoan

tita Local slang for a tough and outspoken woman

JAPANESE TERMS AND WORDS

baka yarō Extremely strong expletive, though the literal translation is only "You stupid idiot!"

banzuke The ranking sheet listing professional sumo's eight hundred or so competitors

beya Compounded form of *heya*, meaning "room," but in this case referring to a *sumo beya*. Sumo's professional league, the Japan Sumo Association (Nihon Sumo Kyokai), is composed of groups of sumo competitors who live and train together in one of fifty-odd *sumo beya* throughout Tokyo.

butsukari-geiko A sumo training exercise in which one *rikishi* charges into the chest of another, who willingly accepts the charge and provides resistance as the first *rikishi* pushes him across the sand-covered ring

dame A negative response along the lines of "no" or "it is forbidden"

dohyō The raised platform, composed of clay with sunken straw boundaries, on which the sumo ring is situated

gaijin Literally "outside person," but used by Japanese to refer to any foreigner (notably, rather than "American" or "Australian," and even in contexts when the speaker is outside of Japan)

gaman To endure in the face of pain, adversity, and long odds without complaint

ganbare The encouraging command form of *gaman*

geta Traditional Japanese wooden slippers

hayaku Quickly

jonidan The second (and nonsalaried) division towards the bottom of sumo's six-division ranking sheet

jonokuchi The initial (and nonsalaried) division at the bottom of sumo's six-division ranking sheet

jūryō The fifth division on sumo's six-division ranking sheet, also the first salaried division

kachi-koshi A term indicating that a *rikishi* has won a majority of his bouts in a major tournament

kanji   The pictographic characters, borrowed from written Chinese, that constitute much of the written Japanese language

kawaigari   Literally "tender loving care," but referring to, at best, overwhelmingly physically demanding training, and at worst, the cruelest form of hazing

keshō mawashi   An elaborately stitched and brightly colored apronlike garment worn by *sekitori* during sumo's ring-entering ceremony

kōenkai   A group of sponsors dedicated to supporting a *rikishi* according to sumo's ancient patronage system, sometimes translated as "fan club"

kōhai   "Junior" in sumo's all-important relationship-defining *senpai-kōhai* seniority system

Kokugikan   Hall of national sport. The ten-thousand-seat Tokyo arena, built exclusively for sumo, is where half of the Japan Sumo Association's six annual major tournaments are held.

makunouchi   The top division on sumo's six-division ranking sheet

makushita   The fourth (and nonsalaried) division on sumo's six-division ranking sheet

mashita   A mumbled abbreviation of the phrase *arigato gozaimashita*, or, "Thank you very much"

mawashi   The beltlike clothing worn by *rikishi* during practice or competition

mottai nai   "What a waste." Can be spoken in a more positive tone suggesting a misplacement of superior abilities.

nagaizumō   A sumo match that takes a long time—usually up to and beyond a minute or so

nani   "What"

osssh   The mumbled sumo greeting, an abbreviation of the phrase, *ohaiyo gozaimasu,* or, "Good morning!"

oyakata   One of the fifty-odd "elder" positions in the Japan Sumo Association, all of which are held by *rikishi* who retired after careers of some distinction. The Japan Sumo Association is run entirely by its *oyakata.*

rikishi   The most common reference to those who actively do sumo (the others being *o-sumo-san* and *sumōtori*)

saigo   Last, the end

sandanme   The third (and nonsalaried) division on sumo's six-division ranking sheet

seishō   A facilitator able to reconcile the interests of the worlds of business and politics

sekitori   A *rikishi* who has attained a position in one of the top two divisions on sumo's six-division ranking sheet; literally, "takers of the barrier"

senpai   "Senior" in sumo's all-important relationship-defining *senpai-kōhai* seniority system *shiko*   The high single-leg-lift stomp performed for leg strengthening during training, and for symbolic purposes preceding a bout

sumōtori   One who actively competes in sumo

tachiai   The initial charge that begins a sumo bout

tegata   Ink handprint; sumo's equivalent of an autograph

tsukebito   Those of lower rank assigned to attend to the needs of a *sekitori*

yakuza   Japanese mafia

yokozuna   The top-ranked *rikishi* in all of sumo

yukata   Robelike garment worn by those of lower rank when not competing or practicing

-zeki   The suffix used with the name of a *sekitori* as a point of honor

SOURCES

Adams, Al. "Business beyond the Reef." Hawai'i Public Radio broadcast, September 22, 2006.

Agard, Keoni. "A Report on Adverse Possession: How It Affects Native Lands of Hawaiian Kuleana Owners." Unpublished manuscript, Hamilton Library, University of Hawai'i, 1977.

Aguiar, Eloise. "Anti-Ice Campaign Stalling, Some Fear." *Honolulu Advertiser,* July 14, 2003.

———. "Anti-Drug Effort Opens Doors." *Honolulu Advertiser,* May 20, 2003.

———. "Hawaiian Man Fights to Reclaim Family's Land." *Honolulu Advertiser,* September 7, 2004.

———. "Ice Film Got Discussions Going." *Honolulu Advertiser,* September 26, 2003.

———. "Kahalu'u Keeps Battling 'Ice.'" *Honolulu Advertiser,* September 27, 2005.

———. "Kahalu'u Seeks 'Ice' Clampdown." *Honolulu Advertiser,* April 2, 2003.

———. "Waiāhole Cleanup to Flush Out Drugs." *Honolulu Advertiser,* August 8, 2003.

———. "Waikāne Valley Cleanup Sought." *Honolulu Advertiser,* November 14, 2003.

Aiona, James R. *Hawai'i Drug Control Plan: A New Beginning.* Office of the Lieutenant Governor, State of Hawai'i, January 2005.

Alper, Chris. "Town 'n Country: Development Looms for the North Shore." *Honolulu Weekly,* January 8, 1992.

Alton, Helen. "Waikāne Project Killed by Council." *Honolulu Star-Bulletin,* October 16, 1979.

Anderson, Andy. Personal interview, July 12, 2007.

————. "Being Open about Addiction Recovery Gives Others Hope." *Honolulu Advertiser*, September 16, 2007.

Anderson, James. Personal interview, December 20, 2007.

Antone, Rod. "Police Arrest 3 in Raid on 'Ice' Lab." *Honolulu Star-Bulletin*, July 22, 2005.

Apgar, Sally. "Ice Storm: Hawai'i Tries to Kick a Deadly Addiction." *Honolulu Star-Bulletin*, September 7, 2003.

————. "Politics Keep Program Treating Meth on Ice." *Honolulu Star-Bulletin*, January 17, 2005.

Arakawa, Lynda. "Lingle Urged to OK Drug Money." *Honolulu Advertiser*, May 5, 2004.

Arakawa, Lynda, and Kelly Yamanouchi. "Lingle Disappointed by Ice Proposal." *Honolulu Advertiser*, January 14, 2004.

Austin, A. Aukahi. "Alcohol, Tobacco, Other Drug Use, and Violent Behavior among Native Hawaiians: Ethnic Pride and Resilience." *Substance Abuse and Misuse* 39, no. 5 (2004): 721–746.

Blakeman, Karen. "Group Accuses Lingle of Hurting Drug Fight." *Honolulu Advertiser*, August 25, 2004.

Borreca, Richard. "Lingle Calls Wide Win 'a Vote of Confidence.'" *Honolulu Star-Bulletin*, November 10, 2006.

Boyer, Peter J. "American Guanxi." *New Yorker*, April 14, 1997.

————. "Ron Brown's Secrets." *New Yorker*, June 9, 1997.

Boylan, Dan, and T. Michael Holmes. *John A. Burns: The Man and His Times.* Honolulu: University of Hawai'i Press, 2000.

Boylan, Peter. "Isles Making Gains in Battle Against Ice." *Honolulu Advertiser*, September 10, 2006.

————. "Officer Admits to Selling 'Ice' to Woman." *Honolulu Advertiser*, December 28, 2005.

————. "Veteran Police Officer Arrested in Meth Case." *Honolulu Advertiser*, March 30, 2005.

Boylan, Peter, and Derrick DePledge. "Hawai'i War on Ice on Right Track." *Honolulu Advertiser*, August 21, 2005.

Brannon, Johnny. "Tax Hike Not Ruled Out in War on Ice." *Honolulu Advertiser*, January 13, 2004.

Braswell, Barbara J. "Pride and Partnership: Completing the Interstate H-3 Project." *Public Roads*, May 1998. U.S. Department of Transportation Federal Highway Administration, http://www.tfhrc.gov/pubrds/may98/h3.htm.

Brown, Joyce M. *Adverse Possession in Hawai'i: Who Were the Players.* Unpublished manuscript, Leeward Community College Library, William S. Richardson School of Law, 1991.

Carlisle, Peter. "Hawai'i's Ice Age: A Message from Honolulu Prosecutor Peter Carlisle." May 31, 2006. City and County of Honolulu, http://www.co.honolulu.gov/prosecuting/meth.htm.

Carlson, Ragnar. "Peter Young under the Gun." *Honolulu Weekly*, March 23, 2005.

Catterall, Lee. "Popularity, Precedent Could Keep 'Dog' Free." *Honolulu Star-Bulletin*, March 24, 2007.

Chang, Kevin. Personal interview, January 2, 2009.

Chiem, Linda. "Hina Mauka Known as Safe Harbor for Recovery." *Pacific Business News*, November 13, 2006.

"Chinen Out at State Historic Preservation." *West Hawai'i Today*, November 29, 2007.

Ching, Carrie. "Body of Hau'ula Man, 53, Found Floating at Beach." *Honolulu Advertiser*, June 19, 2004.

Choo, David K. "Dog Inc.: Inside the Business of Bail Bonds and Bounty Hunting." *Hawai'i Business*, June 2006, 31–36.

City and County of Honolulu. "Waikāne Valley Nature Park Master Plan." June 30, 2007. http://www.honolulu.gov/parks/facility/waikane/info.htm.

City and County of Honolulu, Department of Planning and Permitting. File No. 2005/SUB-283. Proposal for Subdivision of Lands of Waikāne and Waiāhole. November 3, 2005.

City and County of Honolulu, Planning Commission. "Oahu General Plan." City and County of Honolulu, 1961.

"City Collects Back Taxes on Waikāne Property." *Pacific Business News.* June 8, 2005.

Coffman, Tom. *The Island Edge of America: A Political History of Hawai'i.* Honolulu: University of Hawai'i Press, 2003.

Conrow, Joan. "Marijuana's Scarcity and Rising Price May Be Keys to 'Ice' Boom." *Honolulu Star-Bulletin*, July 23, 1996.

Cooper, George, and C. Kahaunani Abad. "Early Signs of Halawa Cultural Value Were Ignored." *Honolulu Advertiser*, September 4, 1992.

Cooper, George, and Gavan Daws. *Land and Power in Hawai'i: The Democratic Years.* Honolulu: University of Hawai'i Press, 1985.

"Costly, Long Delayed—but Done." *Honolulu Advertiser*, December 11, 1997.

Covey, Herbert C., ed. *The Methamphetamine Crisis: Strategies to Save Addicts, Families, and Communities.* Westport, CT: Praeger, 2007.

Creighton, Thomas H. *The Lands of Hawai'i: Their Use and Misuse*. Honolulu: University of Hawai'i Press, 1978.

Daranciang, Nelson. "Former State Archaeologist Files Suit." *Honolulu Star-Bulletin*, November 8, 2007.

———. "Gov Urged to Release 'Ice' Funds." *Honolulu Star-Bulletin*, August 28, 2004.

Dawson, Theresa. "Senate Committee Holds Marathon Hearing on Reappointment of DLNR Administrator." *Environment Hawai'i* 17, no. 11 (May 2007): 17.

Dayton, Kevin. "Arizona Prison Will House Hawai'i Inmates." *Honolulu Advertiser*, June 26, 2007.

———. "Children of Ice." *Honolulu Advertiser*, September 14, 2003.

———. "Seoul Admits Major Role as 'Ice' Supplier." *Honolulu Advertiser*, April 24, 1986.

———. "State in Need of Archaeologists." *Honolulu Advertiser*, May 26, 2007.

———. "Survey: Hawai'i War on Pot Pushed Users to 'Ice.'" *Honolulu Advertiser*, April 1, 1994.

DePledge, Derrick. "Aiona to Push His Plan Again." *Honolulu Advertiser*, August 21, 2005.

DePledge, Derrick, and Peter Boylan. "Hawai'i War on Ice 'on the Right Track.'" *Honolulu Advertiser*, August 21, 2005.

Dooley, James. "Golf Developer Yasuda Agrees to Leave Isles." *Honolulu Advertiser*, February 1, 1989.

———. "Japanese Pay Record Prices for Isle, Mainland Golf Courses." *Honolulu Advertiser*, August 21, 1988.

———. "The Japan-Hawai'i-Vegas Connection." *Honolulu Advertiser*, August 25, 1988.

———. "Lewis Accuses Kawasaki of Waikāne Valley Conflict." *Honolulu Advertiser*, January 29, 1990.

———. "Powerful Japanese Politician May Be Trying to Buy Waikāne Valley." *Honolulu Advertiser*, June 26, 1987.

———. "Real Estate Business an Easy Crime Target." *Honolulu Advertiser*, August 23, 1988.

———. "Resort Official Former Yakuza Member." *Honolulu Advertiser*, August 23, 1988.

———. "Tom Enomoto: Quiet but Powerful." *Honolulu Advertiser*, June 23, 1991.

———. "Waihe'e Tie Costs Enomoto a Job." *Honolulu Advertiser*, October 18, 1990.

———. "Yakuza Linked to Golf Course Buyer." *Honolulu Advertiser*, August 22, 1988.

Eagar, Harry. "Aiona: Focus Shifted from Gateway Drugs." *Maui News*, March 24, 2006.

Eckbo, Dean, Austin, and Williams, with Morris D. Fox. *H-3 Socio-Economic Study: The Effects of Change on a Windward Rural Community*. December 14, 1973.

"Eloy Prison Says Aloha to Hawaiian Inmates." *Arizona Republic*, June 6, 2007.

Engle, Murray. "Valley Kids Say: Move?—No Way!" *Honolulu Star-Bulletin*, August 31, 1978.

Enomoto, Tom. Personal interviews, June 24, 2008; September 11, 2009.

"Final Report of the Joint House-Senate Task Force on Ice and Drug Abatement." Hawai'i State Legislature, January 2004.

"47 Arrested Here in U.S. Drug Sweep." *Honolulu Star-Bulletin*, August 31, 2005.

Frankel, David Kimo. "Hawai'i in the Balance: Who's Better for the Environment, Linda or Mazie?" *Honolulu Weekly*, October 23, 2002.

"Frontline: The Fixers: An Interview with Anthony P. Locricchio." 1995. PBS Online. http://www.pbs.org/wgbh/pages/frontline/shows/fixers/interviews/locricchio.html.

"Frontline: The Fixers: An Interview with Charles Chidiac." 1995. PBS Online. http://www.pbs.org/wgbh/pages/frontline/shows/fixers/interviews/locricchio.html.

Fujikane, Candace. "Between Nationalisms: Hawai'i's Local Nation and Its Troubled Racial Paradise." *Critical Mass* 1, no. 2 (1994): 23–57.

Fujimori, Leila. "Man with Leg Wound Arrested in Stabbing of Friend." *Honolulu Star-Bulletin*, May 18, 2005.

———. "Slain Man Ex-Sumo Wrestler." *Honolulu Star-Bulletin*, May 19, 2005.

Fujiwara, Vicki, and Jerry Rochford. *Kahalu'u*. Video recording. Honolulu: Windward Video, 1977.

———. *Kailua and Kāne'ohe*. Video recording. Honolulu: Windward Video, 1977.

———. *Two Green Valleys*. Video recording. Honolulu: Windward Video, 1977.

———. *Water: Man's Greatest Need*. Video recording. Honolulu: Windward Video, 1978.

———. *Windward Passages*. Video recording. Honolulu: Windward Video, 1977.

"Gangster Admits Helping Hide Assets." July 27, 2001. *Japan Times Online*, http://www.japantimes.co.jp.

Gaspar, Eric "Fats." Personal interviews, July 21, 23; September 22, 2006.

Glauberman, Stu. "Long, Winding Road of Controversy Over H-3." *Honolulu Advertiser*, April 13, 1992.

Goldsberry, Steve. "H-3 Freeway Deserves a Prize for Killing the Earth." *Honolulu Star-Bulletin*, May 17, 1990.

Gomes, Andrew. "Hawai'i's Rural Fight Rekindled in Valley on O'ahu." *Honolulu Advertiser*, February, 28, 2010.

———. "Ko'olau's Title as Nation's Toughest Course Is a Costly One to Maintain." *Pacific Business News*, October 17, 1997.

Goodhue, William Jr. "Autopsy Report for 'Honeyboy.'" Department of the Medical Examiner, City and County of Honolulu, July 13, 2004.

Goodwin, Charles L. "Statement before the House Government Reform Subcommittee on Criminal Justice, Drug Policy, and Human Resources." August 2, 2004. Federal Bureau of Investigation Congressional Testimony, http://www.fbi.gov/congress/congress04/goodwin080204.htm.

Gordon, Mike. "85 Deaths from 'Ice' Set Another Ominous Record." *Honolulu Advertiser*, January 16, 2006.

———. "Taking Out the Trash." *Honolulu Advertiser*, July 2, 1995.

"Governor Linda Lingle: Biography." September 20, 2007. State of Hawai'i, http://www.hawaii.gov/gov/biography.html.

Grey, Briane M. "Statement before the House Government Reform Subcommittee on Criminal Justice, Drug Policy, and Human Resources." August 2, 2004. U.S. Drug Enforcement Association, http://www.dea.gov/pubs/cngrtest/cto80204.html.

Griffin, P. Bion, and Dorothy Pyle. "The Archaeology of Ko'olau-Poko, O'ahu, from the Ahupua'a of Waiāhole to the Ahupua'a of Waikāne." Lāwai: Environmental Communications Inc., 1974.

Halualani, Rona Tamiko. *In the Name of Hawaiians: Native Identities and Cultural Politics*. Minneapolis: University of Minnesota Press, 2002.

Haning, William. "ICE and the Search for a Political Solution." *Honolulu Advertiser*, February 12, 2006.

Hastings, Barbara. "Scarcity of Marijuana Here Now Has Users Just Saying 'Yes' to 'Ice.'" *Honolulu Advertiser*, October 12, 1989.

"Hawai'i Losing Drug War." *Honolulu Advertiser*, March 5, 1989.

"Hawai'i Water Commission Splits over Waiāhole Water Case." July 14, 2006. Earthjustice, http://www.earthjustice.org/news/press/2006/hawaii-water-commission-splits-over-waiahole-water-case.html.

Henriques, Dominic. Telephone interview, July 7, 2010.

Hill, Peter B. E. *The Japanese Mafia: Yakuza, Law, and the State*. New York: Oxford University Press, 2003.

"Hina Mauka Success a Win for Community." *Honolulu Advertiser*, October 28, 2007.

Honeyboy's Brother. Personal interview, June 10, 2007.

Hopkins, Tyler. Personal interviews, July 20, 21, 22, 2006; June 12, 2007; December 21, 2008.

"House Panel Stands with 'Dog.'" *Honolulu Advertiser*, March 8, 2007.

Hurley, Timothy. "War on Ice Intensifies." *Honolulu Advertiser*, October 10, 2004.

"'Ice' Claiming More Lives in Honolulu." January 16, 2006. LexisNexis Academic, http:www.lexisnexis.com.

Joerger, Pauline King. "The Great Mahele." Unpublished manuscript, Hamilton Library, University of Hawai'i, 2001.

Kakesako, Gregg K. "Marines Are Urged to Clean Up Waikāne." *Honolulu Star-Bulletin*, November 14, 2003.

———. "Waikāne Plans Dropped." *Honolulu Star-Bulletin*, November 13, 2003.

Kalima, Bumbo. Personal interview, July 20, 2006.

Kalima, George. Personal interviews, July 20, 21, 22, 23, 2006; September 7, 2007.

Kamita, Keith. "Written Testimony." *The Poisoning of Paradise: Crystal Methamphetamine in Hawai'i*. House Congressional Hearing, 108th Congress. August 2, 2004.

Kanahele, George. "The New Hawaiians." *Social Process Hawai'i* 25 (1982): 21–31.

Kaplan, David E., and Alec Dubro. *Yakuza: Japan's Criminal Underworld*. Berkeley: University of California Press, 2003.

Karasuda, RaeDeen Keahiolalo, and Katherine Irwin. "Dog's 'Tough Love' on Crime Isn't Helping." *Honolulu Advertiser*, September 5, 2005.

Kekahu, Charles. Personal interview, June 16, 2007.

Kelly, Jim. "Japanese Sell $430M Worth of Hotels." *Pacific Business News*, February 10, 2006.

Kent, Noel J. *Hawai'i: Islands under the Influence*. Honolulu: University of Hawai'i Press, 1983, 1993.

King, Samuel P., and Randall W. Roth. *Broken Trust: Greed, Mismanagement, and Political Manipulation at America's Largest Charitable Trust*. Honolulu: University of Hawai'i Press, 2006.

Kipapa, George. Personal interviews, 2005–2008.

Kipapa, Kurt. Personal interview, June 9, 2006.

Kipapa, Percy. Personal interview, November 18, 1998.

Kipapa, Priscilla. Personal interviews, 2005–2008.

Kipapa-Cockett, Selisa. Personal interviews, July 23, 2006; June 7, 2007.

Klee, Hilary, ed. *Amphetamine Misuse: International Perspectives on Current Trends*. Amsterdam: Harwood Academic Publishers, 1997.

Knowles, Gordon James. "Gambling, Drugs, and Sex: New Drug Trends and Addictions in Honolulu, Hawai'i, 1998." *Sociological Practice: A Journal of Clinical and Applied Sociology* 1, no. 1 (1999): 45–69.

Kobayashi, Ken. "Ex-Drug Official Gets Jail for 'Ice.'" *Honolulu Advertiser*, December 22, 1998.

Kobayashi, Ken, and Peter Boylan. "Secretary with FBI Linked to Drug Ring." *Honolulu Advertiser*, April 8, 2006.

Lee, Edgy. *"Ice": Hawai'i's Crystal Meth Epidemic*. Video recording. Honolulu: Pacific Arts Foundation, 2003.

Lee, Stacy. "Kipapa Celebrates Large Joy." *Honolulu Advertiser*, July 15, 1995.

———. "Percy Kipapa (Daiki) Now Has His Own Banner." *Honolulu Advertiser*, July 6, 1997.

———. "Percy Kipapa: Hawai'i-born Juryo Finds a Place for Himself in Japan." *Hawai'i Herald*, May 3, 1996.

Leidemann, Mike. "The Heart and Soul of Waikāne Is Found at One Store." *Honolulu Advertiser*, February 9, 1997.

Leone, Diana. "Water Official Quits in Protest." *Honolulu Star-Bulletin*, February 12, 2005.

Lewis, Ferd. "Kipapa's Learning That Getting Ahead Can Be Dirty Work." *Honolulu Advertiser*, June 26, 1995.

Lind, Ian. "Developer Flouts Limits on Donations." *Honolulu Star-Bulletin*, May 6, 1993.

———. *Down and Dirty: The Lousy Facts about Politics in Hawai'i*. Honolulu: Monitor Books, 1993.

———. "Profits or the People?" *Honolulu Star-Bulletin*, November 10, 1997.

———. "Suit Claims Deal Helped Waihe'e Pal." *Honolulu Star-Bulletin*, May 13, 1995.

———. "Waihe'e Aide: Lease Story Irresponsible." *Honolulu Star-Bulletin*, June 11, 1993.

———. "Weinberg's Legacy: The Unassailable $2 Billion Weinberg Foundation Now Wants $75 Million of Taxpayer Money." *Honolulu Weekly*, May 22, 2002.

"Local 'Ice' Documentary Pre-Empts Season Premiers." *Honolulu Star-Bulletin*, September 25, 2003.

"Local Town Plans." Kāneʻohe: Windward Regional Council, 1975.

Locricchio, Anthony P. Personal interview, June 23, 2008.

Lum, Curtis. "City Buys Waikāne Valley Land." *Honolulu Advertiser*, June 21, 1998.

——. "Ex-Wrestler Fatally Stabbed; Friend Held." *Honolulu Advertiser*, May 18, 2005.

——. "4 Arrested at Address Where Body Was Found." *Honolulu Advertiser*, May 26, 2005.

——. "Officer Charged in Drug Heist." *Honolulu Advertiser*, December 14, 2004.

——. "Suspect Allegedly Admitted to Killing." *Honolulu Advertiser*, May 19, 2005.

Lynch, Kay. "Humble Lifestyle Still an Endangered Windward Species." *Honolulu Advertiser*, April 13, 1992.

Lynch, Russ, and Ken Andrade. "Impact of Japanese Buying Argued." *Honolulu Star-Bulletin*, April 26, 1988.

Maiaba, Pisaga. Personal interview, August 11, 2007.

Makepa, Willidean. Personal interview, July 13, 2007.

"Man Accused of Murder Out on Bail." *Honolulu Advertiser*, August 17, 2005.

McGregor, Catherine et al. "The Nature, Time Course and Severity of Methamphetamine Withdrawal." *Addiction* 100, no. 9 (September 2005): 1320–1329.

McLaughlin, Sean, and Jo Scheder. "The H-3 Controversy." *Honolulu Peace Talks*. Video recording. Honolulu: UH Peace Crew, December 6, 1985.

Melendy, H. Brett. *Walter Francis Dillingham, 1875–1963: Hawaiian Entrepreneur and Statesman*. Lewiston, NY: Edwin Mellen Press, 1996.

"Metal Bat Used in Death of Sumo Wrestler." September 28, 2007. *Daily Yomiuri Online*, http://www.yomiuri.co.jp/dy/.

Miike, Lawrence H. *Water and the Law in Hawaiʻi*. Honolulu: University of Hawaiʻi Press, 2004.

Morgan, Patricia et al. *Ice and Other Methamphetamine Use: An Exploratory Study*. San Francisco: Institute for Scientific Analysis, 1994.

Moyers, William Cope. *Broken: My Story of Addiction and Redemption*. New York: Viking, 2006.

Nakaso, Dan. "Experiences in, on Court Benefit Aiona." *Honolulu Advertiser*, October 24, 2002.

——. "TV Blitz, Forums Put Harsh Glare on Ice." *Honolulu Advertiser*, September 25, 2003.

——. "War on Marijuana Bitter, Costly, Endless." *Honolulu Advertiser*, April 2, 3, 4, 2000.

Nakata, Bob. "Fund Drug Programs Now." *Honolulu Advertiser,* September 21, 2004.

———. Personal interviews, July 2, 2007; December 22, 2007; August 1, 2008; March 15, 2009.

"Neglect Alleged in Sumo Death." October 1, 2007. *Japan Times Online,* http://www.japantimes.co.jp.

Newport, Tuck. "Whither Waiāhole-Waikāne?" *Hawaiʻi Observer,* July 1976.

Noborikawa, Kaylee. "Preservation Unit under Probe." *Honolulu Star-Bulletin,* August 6, 2009.

———. "State Preservation Division Admits Criticisms Are Correct." *Honolulu Star-Bulletin,* August 9, 2009.

Ohira, Rod. "Residents Want Waiāhole-Waikāne Master Plan." *Honolulu Star-Bulletin,* June 21, 1990.

Ohnuma, Keiko. "Local *Haole:* A Contradiction in Terms?" *Cultural Values* 6, no. 3 (2002): 273–285.

Okamura, Jonathan. "Local Culture and Society in Hawaiʻi." *Amerasia* 7, no. 2 (1980): 119–137.

———. "Social Stratification." In *Multicultural Hawaiʻi: The Fabric of a Multiethnic Society,* edited by Michael Haas, 185–204. New York: Garland Publishing, 1998.

———. "Why There Are No Asian Americans in Hawaiʻi: The Continuing Significance of Local Identity." *Social Process Hawaiʻi* 35 (1994): 161–177.

"1.6 Billion in Isle Marijuana Wiped Out in '89, Officials Say." *Honolulu Advertiser,* December 14, 1989.

Osorio, Jonathan Kay Kamakawiwoʻole. *Dismembering Lāhui: A History of the Hawaiian Nation to 1877.* Honolulu: University of Hawaiʻi Press, 2002.

Paiva, Derek. "A&E Pulls 'Dog the Bounty Hunter' from TV Schedule." *Honolulu Advertiser,* November 2, 2007.

Panek, Mark. *Gaijin Yokozuna: A Biography of Chad Rowan.* Honolulu: University of Hawaiʻi Press, 2006.

Pang, Gordon Y. K. "Lingle Budget Focus Criticized." *Honolulu Advertiser,* December 24, 2003.

"Police Find 'Ice' Drug Lab At Kahaluʻu Home." July 22, 2005. *The Hawaiʻi Channel,* http://www.KITV.com.news/4760503/detail.htm.

"Pot Plants Seized." *Honolulu Advertiser,* October 3, 1992.

Pratt, Mary Louise. *Imperial Eyes: Travel Writing and Transculturation.* New York: Routledge, 1992.

"Project Censored: Right Here at Home." *Honolulu Weekly,* February 5, 1992.

Rees, Bob. "History of the Construction of the H3 Freeway." *Island Issues.* Video recording. Honolulu: KFVE, June 28, 1998.

——. "A Unified Theory of Hawai'i's Universe of Power." *Honolulu Weekly*, October 13, 1993.

——. "Working in Hawai'i, Living in Fear." *Honolulu Weekly*, November 10, 1993.

Roberts, Henry. Personal interview, March 16, 2009.

Rosa, John P. "Local Story: The Massie Case Narrative and the Cultural Production of Local Identity in Hawai'i." *Amerasia* 26, no. 2 (2000): 93–115.

Rowan, Chad. Personal interview, May 28, 2009.

Ryan, Tim. "'Dog' Signs New $2.6M Contract for Series." *Honolulu Star-Bulletin*, December 16, 2005.

——. "'Dog' Takes a Bite Out of Reality TV." *Honolulu Star-Bulletin*, September 24, 2003.

——. "'Dog' Will Have His Day on Television." *Honolulu Star-Bulletin*, January 8, 2004.

——. "'Epidemic' Shows 'Ice' Is Everyone's Problem." *Honolulu Star-Bulletin*, September 23, 2003.

——. "Series Catches 'Dog' on the Hunt." *Honolulu Star-Bulletin*, April 12, 2004.

——. "Worth the Fight, Worth the Wait." *Honolulu Star-Bulletin*, July 13, 1998.

Ryan, Tracy. "Let's Not Get 'Edgy' Over Ice." *Hawai'i Reporter*, September 29, 2003.

Ryder, Keith. Personal interview, July 2, 2007.

Sample, Herbert A. "Lingle Says Government Needs to Be Reworked." *Maui News*, September 4, 2009.

Sanburn, Curt. "Farms into Fairways: Gen Morita Fights 'Resortification' in Japan and Abroad." *Honolulu Weekly*, December 11, 1991.

San Nicholas, Claudine. "Agricultural Inspector Layoffs Slammed." *Maui News*, September 5, 2009.

Schaefers, Allison. "Law Targets 'Ice Houses.'" *Honolulu Advertiser*, May 20, 2003.

Shinn, Alan. Personal interview, July 16, 2007.

Sing, Terrance. "Ice Epidemic Poses a Broad Economic Threat for Hawai'i." *Pacific Business News*, September 26, 2003.

Song, Jaymes. "Dog Chapman's Son Sold Tape to Enquirer, Lawyer Says." *Honolulu Advertiser*, November 1, 2007.

Souder, Mark. "Opening Statement." *The Poisoning of Paradise: Crystal Methamphetamine in Hawaiʻi.* House Congressional Hearing, 108th Congress. August 2, 2004.

"Stable Master Faces Ax over Wrestler's Hazing Death." October 3, 2007. *Japan Times Online,* http://www.japantimes.co.jp.

State of Hawaiʻi, Department of Health, Alcohol and Drug Abuse Division. "Report to the Twentieth Legislature, State of Hawaiʻi, 2005." December 2004.

State of Hawaiʻi, First Circuit Court Civil Case No. 8966: *Elizabeth Loy Marks et al., vs. Emily Ah Nee et al.*

State of Hawaiʻi, First Circuit Court Civil Case No. 1CC88-0-000577: *Venda Meheula vs. Mario Remil et al.* Agency Appeal. April 11, 1990.

State of Hawaiʻi, First Circuit Court Criminal Case No. 98–1096: *State of Hawaiʻi vs. Venda Meheula.* Possession of Illegal Narcotics; Promotion of a Dangerous Drug in the Second Degree; Unlawful Use of Drug Paraphernalia. July 7, 1997.

State of Hawaiʻi, First Circuit Court Criminal Case No. 05–1–0749: *State of Hawaiʻi vs. Venda Meheula.* Terroristic Threatening in the First Degree; Possession of a Firearm by a Person Convicted of Certain Crimes. April 15, 2005.

State of Hawaiʻi, First Circuit Court Criminal Case No. 05–1–0917: *State of Hawaiʻi vs. Kealiʻiokalani Meheula.* Terroristic Threatening in the First Degree. May 1, 2005.

State of Hawaiʻi, First Circuit Court Criminal Case No. 05–1–1067: *State of Hawaiʻi vs. Kealiʻiokalani Meheula.* Murder in the Second Degree. May 17, 2005.

State of Hawaiʻi, Intermediate Court of Appeals Criminal Case No. 05–1–1067: *State of Hawaiʻi vs. Kealiʻiokalani Meheula.* Appeal from the judgment of conviction and sentencing filed October 6, 2006.

State of Hawaiʻi, Land Use Commission Docket No. A91–667 Decision and Order: SMF Enterprises Inc. Petition to Amend the Agricultural Boundaries into Conservation Land Use District for Approximately 326.76 Acres at Waikāne. January 27, 1992.

State of Hawaiʻi, Planning Office and the Department of Transportation. *General Plan of the State of Hawaiʻi: Hawaiʻi's Next Twenty Years.* Honolulu: State of Hawaiʻi, 1961.

Stauffer, Robert H. *Kahana: How the Land Was Lost.* Honolulu: University of Hawaiʻi Press, 2004.

Steele, Julia. "Fields to Fairways: The Saga of a New Lanai." *Honolulu Weekly,* July 15, 1992.

Sullam, Brian. "The Education of a Local Community." *Hawai'i Observer*, November 1974.

———. "Joe Pao Rips Off the Bishop Estate." *Hawai'i Observer*, October 1975.

———. "The Mobilization of a Local Community." *Hawai'i Observer*, December 1974.

Suzuki, Miwa. "Japan's Ancient Sport in Crisis." October 3, 2007. *Yahoo! News*, http://news.yahoo.com.

Suzuki, Shinobu. "Daiki: Hawaiian's Star on the Rise." *Sumo World*, March 1996, 11–12.

Takasato, Roland. Personal interview, December 20, 2007.

Talaimatai, Troy. Personal interview, July 23, 2006.

"The Truth about H-3: The Destructive Billion-Dollar Highway That Does Nothing to Solve Oahu's Contemporary Transportation Problems." Honolulu: Stop H-3 Association, 1986.

Thompson, Jack, Derek Ferrar, and Julia Steele. "Up in Smoke." *Honolulu Weekly*, April 22, 1992.

Thompson, Pete et al. "Kahalu'u and the Development of Windward O'ahu." *Hawai'i Observer*, October 1973.

"Top Azabu Executives Arrested in Japan." *Honolulu Star-Bulletin*, June 25, 1997.

Topping, Donald M. "Drugs and Crime in Hawai'i." Drug Policy Forum of Hawai'i, Honolulu, 1995.

———. "Has Marijuana Eradication Led to Ice Epidemic?" *Honolulu Star-Bulletin*, February 9, 1996.

———. "Minimizing Drug Damage." *Honolulu Weekly*, March 2, 1994.

Toth, Catherine. "Leadership Corner: M.P. 'Andy' Anderson." *Honolulu Advertiser*, April 17, 2006.

Trask, Haunani-Kay. "Settlers of Color and 'Immigrant' Hegemony: 'Locals' in Hawai'i." *Amerasia* 26, no. 2 (2000): 1–24.

———. "Stealing Hawai'i: The War Machine at Work." *Honolulu Weekly*, July 17, 2002.

"Troubled Waters." *Honolulu Weekly*, February 10, 1993.

Tsai, Michael. "'Dog' Director Keeps Up with Action." *Honolulu Advertiser*, April 18, 2005.

———. "The Law According to 'Dog.'" *Honolulu Advertiser*, April 12, 2005.

Tuggle, David E. et al. *Strategic Integrated Resources Management Planning for Selected Properties of Marine Corps Base Hawai'i: Camp H. M. Smith, Pu'uloa*

Training Facility, and a Portion of Waikāne Valley. Honolulu: International Archaeological Research Institute, 1998.

Tummons, Patricia. "Blazing Trails in Waikāne Valley." *Honolulu Weekly*, July 24, 1991.

———. "Core Natural Resource Programs Face Crippling Curbs in New DLNR Budget." *Environment Hawai'i* 19, no. 8 (2009).

———. "Positions Unfilled, Funds Unspent at DLNR." *Environment Hawai'i* 18, no. 10 (2008).

"2 Big Island Men Held after Drug Raids." *Honolulu Star-Bulletin*, June 23, 2007.

Valdez, Ric. "Ice Age." *Honolulu Weekly*, May 21, 2003.

Viotti, Vicki. "DLNR Loses Another Deputy." *Honolulu Advertiser*, February 12, 2005.

Vorsino, Mary. "Hawai'i Star Apologizes for Racist Remarks." *Honolulu Advertiser*, November 7, 2007.

Waite, David. "Hoyu Drops Beachfront Acquisition." *Honolulu Advertiser*, June 23, 1990.

———. "'Ice' Profit at $580K a Week." *Honolulu Advertiser*, August 9, 1999.

———. "Man Accused of Murder Out on Bail." *Honolulu Advertiser*, August 17, 2005.

———. "Pot Growers Are Feeling the Law's Heat, Paty Says." *Honolulu Advertiser*, March 19, 1990.

Waitzfelder, Beth E. et al. "Substance Abuse in Hawai'i: Perspectives of Key Local Human Services Organizations." *Substance Abuse* 19, no. 1 (1998): 7–22.

"Warrant Issued for Sumiyoshi-Kai Chairman." May 19, 2001. *Japan Times Online*, http://www.japantimes.co.jp.

Whitefield, Debbie. "Who's Who in Windward Hui." *Honolulu Star-Bulletin*, July 6, 1978.

Whittaker, Elvi. *The Mainland Haole: The White Experience in Hawai'i*. New York: Columbia University Press, 1986.

Wiles, Greg. "Japan Company with Isle Links in Bankruptcy." *Honolulu Advertiser*, October 1, 1992.

Wilson, Christie. "More Whites, Fewer Asians in Hawai'i." *Honolulu Advertiser*, August 9, 2007.

———. "Vegas Seeing More Hawaiian Transplants." *Honolulu Advertiser*, August 9, 2007.

Wright, Walter. "Hawai'i Losing Drug War." *Honolulu Advertiser/Star-Bulletin*, March 5, 1989.

Yamaguchi, Andy. "Appeal Loss May End Challenges To H-3." *Honolulu Advertiser*, March 21, 1989.

Yamamoto, Eric. "The Significance of Local." *Social Process Hawai'i* 27 (1979): 101–115.

Yamane, Marisa. "Kahalu'u Stabbing Turns Fatal for Former Sumo Wrestler." May 17, 2005. KHON2 Online, http://www.khon2.com/.

Yudko, Errol, Harold V. Hall, and Sandra B. McPherson. *Methamphetamine Use: Clinical and Forensic Aspects*. New York: CRC Press, 2003.

Ziegler, Rick. "Hawai'i's Road to Ruin: A Personal Account." Unpublished manuscript, Hamilton Library, University of Hawai'i, 1980.

———. "Highway Wars: The Stop H-3 Trilogy." Unpublished manuscript, Hamilton Library, University of Hawai'i, 2003.

INDEX

Abercrombie, Neil, 270, 288

Act 40, 172–173, 176, 178, 184, 277–278, 280

Aguiar, Eloise, 160

Aiona, James "Duke," 158, 160, 170, 173, 184–187, 277–278

Akaka, Daniel, 288

Akebono, 4, 6–7, 10, 13–22, 26–27, 43, 48, 64, 68–79, 87–89, 92, 110, 115, 117, 122–124, 134, 137, 140

Ala Moana Hotel, 272–274, 276

American Airlines, 272

Amfac, 36

Anderson, Andy, 102–103, 153, 157–159, 162–163, 171–172, 176–179, 186, 277–279

Anderson, James, 238, 255

Ariyoshi, George, 39, 288

Aweau, Larry, 7–8, 64–65, 126

Azabu USA, 56, 61–62, 105, 142, 167, 274

Azumazeki Oyakata. See Kuhaulua, Jesse

Baker, Rosalyn, 184

Baker, William, 109

Baptiste, Bryan, 157

Benitez, Darren, 91

Bettencourt, David, 172

Bishop Estate, 36, 57, 106, 276

Bishop Museum, 269

Blaisdell, Neal, 36

Blakeman, Karen, 177

Bradda Waltah, 9, 26

Breathless, 133, 137, 142, 145

Burns, John A., 36, 288

Cabhab, Harold Jr., 183

Campbell Estate, 105, 267

Carlisle, Peter, 161, 170–171, 183

Carlton, Barry S., 170

Castle and Cooke Homes, 272

Castle High School, 5, 51, 55, 59, 62, 64, 101, 167, 286

Castle Medical Center, 80, 215

Cayetano, Benjamin, 135, 276

Chang, Carol, 156

Chang, Kevin, 93, 110, 145–146, 164, 170, 174, 191, 272–273, 281

Chapman, Duane "Dog," 180–182, 194–196, 279

Chinen, Melanie, 285

Chiyonofuji, 64

Chiyotaikai, 116, 289–293

Clay, Bryan, 185

Conrow, Joan, 108

Coons, Theodore, 206, 208–210, 217, 231, 239

Corn, James Jr., 184
Creed, Viki, 275
Cruz, John, 44

Da Kine Bail Bonds, 180–182
Department of Health, 103, 170, 172,
 176–177, 277–278
Department of Land and Natural
 Resources, 58, 104, 156, 284–285
Department of Transportation, 266,
 268–270, 288
Dillingham, Walter, 271–272
Dillingham Corporation, 267, 272,
 274
Domingo, William C., 194, 197–198,
 200–203, 206–217, 219–224,
 229–230, 232–236, 237, 254
Dooley, Jim, 57, 106
Dubro, Alec, 108–109, 142, 274–275
Dye, Thomas, 286

Eckbo, Dean, Austin, and Williams,
 257, 266, 268, 270–271, 274,
 287–288
Enomoto, Tom, 57–58, 60, 100, 105,
 280–286
Environment Hawai'i, 104
Ewelika, 35

Feleunga, John, 7, 10, 18, 20–21, 71–72,
 87, 138
Fernandez, Bobby, 38
Freitas, Donna, 202–208, 212, 216–
 218, 223, 228, 232, 238
Fong, Hiram, 271
Fukuda, Robert, 261
Fung, Walter, 210

Gaspar, Eric "Fats," 46–47, 66, 70, 74,
 80, 111–115, 137, 139, 253
Gentry, Tom, 57

Goldbold, Wilford, 260–261
Goodhue, William Jr., 237
Grayline, 174
Great *Mahele,* 25, 34–35, 200–201,
 234, 257

H-3 Freeway, 36, 57–58, 106, 143, 257,
 266, 268–271, 287–288
Ha, Cho Sam, 109
Hall, E. O., 257–258
Hamilton, Bethany, 185
Hanabusa, Colleen, 173
Hastings, Barbara, 60–61
Hawaiian Dredging Company,
 271–272
Hawaiian Memorial Park, 89, 97
Hawai'i Business, 181–182
Hawai'i Drug Control Plan, 185
Hawai'i Herald, 67
Hawai'i Observer, 36
Hawai'i Raceway Park, 105
Hawai'i's Thousand Friends, 275
Hawai'i Substance Abuse Coalition,
 184
Hawai'i Superferry, 269, 285
Hertz Car Rental, 273
Hina Mauka, 102–103, 153, 157, 163,
 277
Hirono, Mazie, 276
Honeyboy, 174–176, 178, 183, 191,
 237–256
Honolulu Advertiser, 57, 60–61, 77, 80,
 105–109, 160, 177, 181, 240–241,
 278, 286
Honolulu Star-Bulletin, 58, 103, 105,
 108, 173, 181–182, 184, 269, 279
Honolulu Weekly, 103–104, 161, 276
Hopkins, Tyler, 19, 40, 46, 69, 75,
 85–88, 91–98, 111–115, 124, 129, 131,
 135–140, 142, 146, 163, 166, 192,
 194, 209, 212–214, 235–236, 288

Horita, Herbert, 57
Hoschuh, Fred, 171
Hoyu Kensetsu, 63, 104–105, 142,
    284
Hui Kuai ʻAina o Waikāne, 258
Hyatt Regency Hotel, 142

Inouye, Daniel, 57–58, 270, 288
ʻIolani School, 58, 105
Irwin, Katherine, 181

Japan Sumo Association, 8, 17, 26, 42,
    122, 134, 140, 144
Jervis, Gerard, 276
Johnson, Alan, 177

Kaeo, Desiree, 188, 220
Kahaluʻu Coalition, 266
Kahana Valley, 241, 243
Kahekili Highway, 25, 93, 128, 143
Kahele, Luka, 243, 247–250, 253,
    256
Kalima, Abbi, 84
Kalima, Bumbo, 8–10, 40, 66,
    79–81, 84–94, 111, 137, 173,
    187–188, 292
Kalima, George, 8–12, 23, 40, 66,
    69–73, 84–95, 111–114, 121, 135,
    137–138, 142, 164–165, 187–188
Kalima, Haywood, 81–83, 89
Kalima, Ipo, 84
Kalima, Kalani, 84
Kalima, Kari, 84
Kamaka, Ray, 57, 126, 166, 258
Kamehameha Highway, 38, 128,
    160
Kane, Herb, 281
Kanehailua, Marshall, 107
Kaplan, David E., 108–109, 142,
    274–275

Karasuda, RaeDeen Keahiolalo, 181
Kay, Alan, 263, 287
Keever, Beverly, 103
Kehaku, Charles, 5–9, 12, 25, 30–32,
    39, 47, 49, 51–53, 101, 126, 131,
    143–144, 147, 265
Kekauoha, Kaleo, 46, 111, 138–139, 141,
    192, 253
Kent, Noel J., 272
Kim, Glenn, 193–220, 224–237, 240,
    253, 264, 282, 284
Kim, Harry, 162
King, Samuel P., 262–263, 265, 287
King Intermediate School, 5, 9, 46,
    49–51, 53–54, 128, 145, 190, 250,
    267
Kipapa, George, 28–29, 54, 61–62, 65,
    79, 90–91, 124–127, 131, 133, 138,
    140, 145, 193, 234–235, 259–263,
    265, 267, 270
Kipapa, Jolyn, 90, 118, 165, 197–198,
    206–207, 236, 248–249
Kipapa, Kurt, 1, 7–8, 14, 21, 29–30,
    43, 53–55, 59, 63–65, 89–92, 113,
    120–121, 137, 142, 165, 173, 197, 207,
    234–236, 260
Kipapa, Pricilla, 28, 30–31, 51, 61–62,
    65, 90, 125, 136, 164, 188, 191–192,
    194–195, 197, 200–201, 206, 236,
    240, 258–266, 268
Kipapa-Cockett, Selisa, 29–30, 51–52,
    90, 96, 120, 124, 126, 127, 148, 165,
    200, 236, 262–263
Konishiki, 7, 43, 44, 47, 64, 66, 85,
    114, 136, 192
Ko Olina, 57, 267
Kreins, Bill, 181–182
Kualoa-Heʻeia Ecumenical Youth
    (KEY) Project, 37, 145, 153–154,
    157–158, 160, 190, 278
Kubo, Ed, 158, 160–161, 170, 183

Kuhaulua, Jesse, 5–6, 11, 16–17, 27–28, 44–45, 47–48, 64–66, 69–71, 77–78, 87, 114–115, 122–123, 126, 136, 140–141, 199
Kyo-ya, 142

Lambert, John, 175, 178, 240–241
Lau, Mary, 273
Lau, Nancy, 273
Lee, Cal, 53
Lee, Edgy, 63, 161–163, 216, 256, 276
Legal Aid Hawai'i, 39, 58, 274
Levi, Matt, 161
Lewis, Ferd, 77–78, 84, 125
Lind, Ian, 58, 105
Lindsay, Lokelani, 276
Lingle, Linda, 135, 172–173, 176–178, 183–184, 275–278, 280, 285–286
Locricchio, Anthony P., 58–60, 274–275, 280
Luana Hills Country Club, 60, 144
Luke, Sylvia, 185
Lum, Gene, 59–60, 285
Lum, Nora, 59–60, 285

Magaki Beya, 8–10, 13, 73
Maiaba, Pisaga, 242, 244, 246–249, 255
Makepa, Willidean, 165, 188–191, 194, 245, 251–253, 255
Marantz, George, 279
Marks, Elizabeth McCandless, 34, 38–39, 260
Marks, Lester, 34, 260, 264
Matayoshi, Mrs., 9
Matooka, Francis, 109
Matsui, Hideki, 113
Matsumoto, Kizo, 57, 167, 274
Maunawili Community Association, 275

McCandless, Lincoln, 34–37, 38, 63, 106–107, 166, 258, 260–265, 287
McCartney, Mike, 157
McKinney, Chris, 37, 207
Mehau, Larry, 57
Meheula, Keali'i, 168, 173, 188–190, 194–196, 198–199, 201–240, 243, 245, 248, 253–255, 284, 288
Meheula, Venda, 190–191, 201–202, 204–206, 208–210, 215–218, 224, 231–232, 235, 328–239, 243, 248–249, 251, 253–255, 273–275
Minami Foundation, 58, 284
Minami USA, 58, 105, 284
Mizuno, Ken, 57, 167, 274
Modafferi, Gary, 102
Morgan, Patricia, 103–104, 108
Musashimaru, 43

Nakata, Bob, 36–39, 49–50, 55, 57–58, 106–107, 153–155, 157–161, 177, 187, 207, 244, 266–267, 269–271, 279–280, 283–284, 286, 288
Nangaku, Masao, 57–58, 105
National Institute of Drug Abuse, 61, 103–104, 171

Olomana Golf Links, 57, 144, 167, 274
Operation "Green Harvest," 56, 59–60, 63, 101–103, 107–108, 171
Operation "Wipeout," 56, 101–102, 104
Osano, Kenji, 142
Osorio, Jon, 257

Pacific Business News, 161
Pakele, Maydell, 219–220, 231, 254
Panek, Noriko, 23–24, 79, 81, 139, 147–152, 173, 187
Pang, Russell, 177, 184

Pan-Pacific, 60–62
Pao, Joseph R., 36, 38–39, 57, 60, 106, 267, 280–281, 283, 286
Paty, William, 58, 105, 107, 284
Peters, Henry, 276
Picanco, Shane, 5–9, 20, 25, 30–32, 39, 47, 49–53, 55–56, 65–66, 70, 117, 134, 143, 164, 244
Pickard, Tom, 62
Price, Warren, 103
Punuciel, Bernie, 99–100

Rees, Robert, 57
Reppun, Charlie, 106
Reppun, John, 58, 153, 157
Reppun, Paul, 106
Roberts, Arnold, 36, 38, 62, 70
Roberts, Ellen, 257–258, 260–262, 265
Roberts, Henry, 33–38, 62, 90–91, 258–259, 261, 265
Roberts, Manuel, 33–35, 38, 62–63, 166, 234, 258–266, 287–288
Roberts, Stanley, 189, 239
Rodrigues, Lori, 99, 194, 201–205, 211, 216–217, 221, 229, 232, 238–239
Rowan, Chad. *See* Akebono
Rowan, Ola, 47
Royal Fountains LLC, 280
Ryder, Keith, 153–155, 157–160, 182–183, 194, 207, 238, 255–256, 278–279
Ryder, Roy, 154

Sakamoto, Karl K., 193, 206, 229–230, 235, 273
Sea Life Park, 284
Shinn, Alan, 158
Shlachter, Marc, 175, 242, 249
Sierra Club, 106
SMF Enterprises, 104
Smith, Linda, 176

Starr, Johnathan, 276
State Historic Preservation Division, 269, 285–286
St. Louis High School, 53–56, 59, 136, 199, 201
Sullivan, Mary, 211
Sumiyoshi-kai crime group, 274
Suzuki, Gail, 212–214
Sylva, Robert, 183

Takamiyama. *See* Kuhaulua, Jesse
Takasago Beya, 41, 46, 85, 87, 89, 139–140
Takasato, Roland, 255
Talaimatai, Troy, 3–4, 6–7, 10–12, 18, 20–22, 40, 43, 46–49, 66, 69, 71–75, 78, 87, 111, 122, 129, 132, 137, 140, 248, 254
Tamura, Masayuki, 108
Thompson, Pete, 35–36
Topping, Donald, 60, 63, 103–104, 108
Tosanoumi, 116
Trias, Jasmine, 185
Tsutsui, Haruko, 51
Tummons, Pat, 104
Turtle Bay Hilton, 57, 167, 274

University of Hawai'i Professional Assembly, 276

Waiāhole School, 7, 9, 31, 36, 38, 49–50, 54, 132, 262
Waiāhole-Waikāne Community Association, 38, 50, 99–100, 104–105, 143, 158, 234, 268, 281
Waiāhole Water Ditch, 34, 106
Waihe'e, John, 57–58, 105, 281, 288
Waikāne Invistments, 105
Waikāne Training Facility, 34, 166, 258, 260

Waikīkī, 24, 118, 121, 132, 136, 142, 145, 150, 187
Waite, David, 107–109
Waldorf, Marcia, 194
Ward, Gary, 273
Watanabe, Kitaro, 56–57, 61–63, 104–105, 142, 167, 274
Weinberg, Harry, 57
West Hawai'i Today, 286
Wilson, Elaine, 178
Wilson, Joshua, 190–191, 194, 245–246, 250–253, 255–256
Windward Parties, 106

Windward Partners, 36
Wong, Dickie, 276
Wong, Donna, 275
Woods, Claire, 184

Yakuza, 47, 108–109, 130, 142, 167, 274–275, 288
Yamaguchi-gumi, 109, 167
Yasuda, Yasuo, 57, 59–60, 167, 274–275
Young, Peter, 285

Zoller, Duke, 208, 210, 212, 217

ABOUT THE AUTHOR

MARK PANEK received his Ph.D. from the University of Hawaiʻi at
Mānoa in 2004. He is presently an associate professor of English at the
University of Hawaiʻi at Hilo. This is his second book.

Production Notes for Panek | *Big Happiness*
Cover design by Julie Matsuo-Chun
Text design and composition by Publishers' Design and Production
    Services, Inc., with display type in Charlemagne and text type in
    Adobe Caslon Pro
Printing and binding by Sheridan Books, Inc.
Printed on 60 lb. House Opaque, 500 ppi